JAVA BEANS

DEVELOPER'S REFERENCE

Dan Brookshier

New Riders

New Riders Publishing, Indianapolis, Indiana

Java Beans Developer's Reference

By Dan Brookshier

Published by:
New Riders Publishing
201 West 103rd Street
Indianapolis, IN 46290 USA

Copyright©1997 by New Riders Publishing

Printed in the United States of America 1 2 3 4 5 6 7 8 9 0

Library of Congress Cataloging-in-Publication Data

CIP data available upon request

Warning and Disclaimer

This book is designed to provide information about **Java Beans**. Every effort has been made to make this book as complete and as accurate as possible, but no warranty or fitness is implied.

The information is provided on an "as is" basis. The author(s) and New Riders Publishing shall have neither liability nor responsibility to any person or entity with respect to any loss or damages arising from the information contained in this book or from the use of the disks or programs that may accompany it.

Publisher	*Don Fowley*
Associate Publisher	*David Dwyer*
Marketing Manager	*Mary Foote*
Managing Editor	*Carla Hall*

Product Development Specialist
Brad Jones

Senior Editors
Sarah Kearns
Suzanne Snyder

Development Editor
Chris Cleveland

Project Editor
Brad Herriman

Copy Editor
Keith Kline

Technical Editor
Nataraj Nagaratnam

Software Specialist
Steve Flatt

Software Acquisitions
Pete Bitar

Acquisitions Coordinators
Stacey Beheler
Alan Evans

Administrative Coordinator
Karen Opal

Cover Designer
Karen Ruggles

Cover Production
Aren Howell

Book Designer
Anne Jones

Production Manager
Kelly Dobbs

Production Team Supervisors
Laurie Casey
Joe Millay

Graphics Image Specialists
Casey Price
Clint Lahnen

Production Analyst
Erich J. Richter

Production Team
Kim Cofer
Janelle Herber
Linda Knose
Malinda Kuhn

Indexers
Tim Taylor
Nick Schroeder

About the Author

Dan Brookshier has been programming since 1976. He has written software for many industries including communications, aerospace, oil & gas, insurance, baseball, chess, transportation, and many others. Dan is a globetrotting programmer and has worked in Norway, England, China, and currently lives and works in north Texas. He is the lead instigator for the Talk-Java/Drink-Java user groups that meet in North Dallas and Las Colinas. He has a Bachelor of Science degree in Engineering from California State Polytechnic University in Pomona (Cal Poly). In his spare time Dan kayaks and juggles.

Dedications

To my Mom and Dad who have always wanted to see their son's work at the bookstore.

Acknowledgments

I would like to thank my all of my editors for all their input and for the vast improvement of my writing skills. I would also like to thank all the participants of the Java Beans list group who have helped me understand what issues needed to be covered by this book. I am also very grateful to all the members of the Talk-Java/Drink-Java and the JavaMUG user groups who have sat through many of my Java and Java Beans presentations.

Trademark Acknowledgments

All terms mentioned in this book that are known to be trademarks or service marks have been appropriately capitalized. New Riders Publishing cannot attest to the accuracy of this information. Use of a term in this book should not be regarded as affecting the validity of any trademark or service mark.

Contents at a Glance

Table of Contents

Part II: Working with Beans

Part III: Beans and Related APIs

Core Java Beans API   415

Internationalization API   617

INTRODUCTION

Software should be developed like builders construct buildings, from manageable pieces that can be easily configured and stuck together with bolts, nails, and mortar. The act of design should be similar too. There should be a paradigm for building certain types of things. Architects, when designing a barn or a skyscraper, have a design pattern built from common practice, experience, and standard procedures.

Software development is not anywhere near the maturity of building construction. Unfortunately programs are nothing like buildings. A wall in a building is a very stable thing; once put up, a wall can only be painted or a few pictures added. With software, our walls are automata that interact with their environments. Software needs to be robust and easily modified to meet the new conditions of the environment that they work in. Unfortunately, software is relatively static, only able to deal with a few set tasks. To create robust software, programmers need a way of adding new functions to existing programs or to quickly write new programs to solve new problems. The simplest way to help developers is to give them libraries of easily configurable software components. These components act like the bricks of the program, easily put in place to add new functionality.

The holy grail of software development has long been the reusable software component. Software that is debugged and working is a valuable commodity. Software developers would prefer to reuse, rather than re-create each time a similar task is required. Traditionally there have been two problems with reusable software. The first is that reusable components are harder to write because they must apply to many situations and configurations for slightly different tasks. The second problem is that to be reused, the software component needs to be in an environment in which designers know that a software piece exists and they understand how to connect each reusable piece into a new application.

Java Beans solves the first problem by creating a model that lets developers create reusable components called Java Beans, which can be connected to existing code. The configuration of components is augmented with editors that follow a specific behavior so that the IDE can easily present and enable the user to modify the component.

The second problem is finding and understanding how to use reusable software. Java Beans aid in understanding the standards that are used to define each Bean. These standards are simple templates or signatures that specify naming and base class or interface inheritance. Because these signatures are human-readable, a Bean developer, the application builder tool, and end users can all recognize and understand the meaning of the Bean's methods. In addition, another object called a BeanInfo holds specific naming and documentation that is associated with the Bean. Information from the BeanInfo is available in the application builder tool where it can be viewed in a context sensitive manner. In combination with the JavaDoc tool, the Bean user is supplied with a wealth of information.

Because of the overall design of Java Beans, there is a possibility that component libraries can be built. These libraries can be queried, not just as a search of documentation; in fact, such a tool could query the compiled classes to discover data types, subclassing and even the class types of parameters in methods. Even more important, because tools can be written to examine code for the interface, class, events, methods, and parameters, there is less need for component developers to document the API (Application Programming Interface) for their code. In fact, simple components that follow the JavaBeans specification can be dropped into a component library and used immediately.

In the world of GUI (graphical user interface) components, the focus is on generic visual components like spreadsheets, graphics, text viewers, and so on. Each of these components should be generic enough to use in most programs. Unfortunately, most GUI component systems burden the developer with a lot of extra work to create components. Also, because of the complexity of creating a complex component, few programmers understand how. Many programmers resort to custom software rather than going through the trouble of creating a reusable component. Many component technologies also are not cross platform and are usually incompatible between developer tools. Because of the many problems with current component technologies, there is little incentive to create components for in-house use by developers.

Java Beans seem to solve many of these problems. There is still a lot of information that the developers need to understand to write a good Bean. Java Beans are easy to create.

Some existing classes can be converted to a Bean with little effort. However, a commercial Bean is a slightly bigger beast. Commercial Java Beans need to be capable of running in different countries and different languages. Beans need to be well documented and easily understandable by other developers.

To create complex or commercially viable Java Beans, the developer needs to understand the basic concepts of the enhanced JDK (Java Developer's Kit) 1.1. There were several major additions to the language capabilities and to the core packages. Some of the new classes and APIs added to the 1.1 release of the JDK, such as serialization, introspection, and the new event model, are pivotal to making Java Beans work. Others, like the classes that make up the new Internationalization API, are important for enhancing the robustness of Java Beans. There is also a new way of packaging Java applications through JAR files, which is used as the primary method to deliver Java Beans. In short, most of the JDK additions will be used to create Java Beans. As many of these subjects will be covered as possible. The primary aim is to have the examples give you a basis for using these APIs, though entire books could be written on each subject. The documentation for many of the new features has been included in the last section of this book, to provide a quick reference.

Java Beans and Events

The whole structure of event handling is different from the original 1.02 implementation. The event model is now much more intuitive and more efficient. The event model also lends itself more to using completed components without the need to subclass components to access their events or to create complex event handlers in main programs. The JDK documentation calls the new event system the Delegation Event Model. Developers will find that this model is similar to Motif's callback model, the Source and Listener Model, and the Publisher Subscriber Model found in other languages.

Java Bean Persistence

Persistence is the storing of the current state of objects and subsequent retrieval. In effect, persistence is a snapshot of an object that can be retrieved later so that the object can be re-created at another time and run from the point that the object was saved. Persistence is also known as serialization, because it converts an object to a serialized stream. Persistence has a wide range of uses from data storage to interprocess network communication. The JavaBeans API uses persistence to save the state of Beans in an application design tool. The application designed with such a tool, instead of executing code to create and configure a Bean at run time, will simply restore the state saved by the application editor.

The ability to use persistence enables the application design tool to work with live components rather than representations. Also, persistence elevates most of the code generation tasks normally associated with connecting components and main programs. Using persistence is very easy, but can be controlled for specific purposes. This book covers both the simple and more advanced uses in Chapter 7, "Java Bean Persistence."

Java Bean Introspection and Core Reflection

Introspection is the act of inward examination. For Java Beans, introspection is an inward examination of the API (Application Programming Interface) for a Bean. This API can be read by toolkits or programs in which the Bean resides. This API information can be used to generate code to manipulate the Bean or to directly create objects and control them programmatically. Of all the enhancements made to the 1.02 JDK, the Core Reflection API, and the Introspection class of the Bean API are the most powerful and useful. The introspection and reflection capabilities of Java are the cornerstone of application development tools that will use Java Beans. Introspection and reflection make writing an IDE to manipulate Java a much simpler task, while increasing overall functionality and capability.

Building Custom Component Editors for Java Beans

One of the larger problems normally associated with building software components is controlling the editing of component properties. First, there is the problem of validation of data. Some properties may only accept ranges of data or specific formats. Custom editors add this capability without modifying the original Bean. Another problem with traditional component architectures is editing data that is not easily done in a property editor. For instance, instead of typing the name of a state, the state could be selected from a map. Custom editors can be used to present data in a customized visual representation that is more appropriate for how people think rather than how programs do. All of this is possible without modifying the actual Bean component; rather, an external set of classes is used to handle these tasks. The added benefit of keeping editors and Java Beans separate is that the code in the final application, using Java Beans, does not need to have the editors included, thus reducing the final memory size of applications.

Packaging Java Beans

The packaging of Java Beans, covered in this book, encompasses two primary subjects. The first is checking to see if your component is ready. Quite a few items should be checked to ensure that a Bean is functional and easy to use. These items include designing for use in the application development tool, documenting your Bean, and designing for use in multithreaded environments. The other topic is how to create and use JAR (Java Archive) files and manifests to deliver Beans. This includes the packing and unpacking of Beans and the creation of manifest templates, which are used by design tools to recognize Java Beans.

Java Bean Internationalization

The new Internationalization API is of extreme importance to developers of both Java Beans and Java programs. The Internationalization API adds several new date, time, number, and text formatting utility classes that were lacking in the 1.02 version. In addition, many of these classes can be used so that a different representation can be created in separate countries and languages. In Chapter 11, "Java Bean Internationalization," we will cover the basics, and in particular, show how easy it is to add internationalization capabilities to Java Beans.

Part I

Beans Foundations

CHAPTER I

Java Beans Overview

Java Beans were first introduced to the world in 1996 during the first Java One conference. The Bean API goal was narrowly defined:

> A Bean is a reusable software component that can be manipulated visually in a builder tool. (from JavaBeans™ 1.0 API specification)

The goal, however, was met and then some. Java Beans are reusable and can be used from within application builders, but they can do much more. To start, here is a more accurate definition of Java Beans than the original goal implies:

> A Bean is a component that can be manipulated as a live object from within an application builder. The Bean is associated with a BeanInfo object that defines the Bean, its customizer, properties, property editors, events, and methods.

This is a very accurate definition of a Bean. The first statement, that the Bean is manipulated as a live object, is probably the most profound and revolutionary when compared to older technologies. Most programmers have used GUI builders. Many GUI builders are advertised as WYSIWYG (What You See Is What You Get). Such a statement was usually only true of components that came with the GUI editor. The extent to which a GUI editor was WYSIWYG stopped, as the title implied, at what you see. In other words, the visual layout was accurate, but the components that were only representations, not the actual objects being created. Some inherent problems exist with the component representation model, the foremost because it is only a representation and not the true component. Since the GUI editor only has a representation of the component, the representation and the actual component may differ slightly. Worse still, such a model prevents complex components from being displayed because a representation also needs to be designed.

Serialization

The underlying reason that Java Beans are so easy to manipulate as live objects is that code does not need to be generated to duplicate the setting that a programmer using an application builder might change. The reason that no code needs to be generated is that the state of the Bean object can be saved at any time. By saving the persistent state of the Bean, developers and IDE manufacturers can avoid much of the drudgery involved in the creation and configuration of components. A Bean can be recreated at will by deserializing its saved state. Parts of the Bean specification do provide a mechanism for Bean configuration through the generation of code, but such code generation is not as flexible and dynamic as the very simple serialization techniques that can be employed.

Core Reflection and Introspection

One of the key features of the JavaBeans API is the capability to manipulate a Bean in its running state. The technology that allows this to happen lies in the Core Reflection API. A Bean can be examined through the Introspector class, which uses the Core Reflection API to discover classes, interfaces, methods, and their parameters. Also, after a method has been found, the method can be called. This includes constructors and static class methods. The power gained by the Core Reflection API and the Introspector class is enormous. Using just a Bean's class text name, the class can be loaded, examined, and categorized programmatically. After the class has been examined, it can then be instantiated by calling its constructor (using the Constructor class) or loading a saved instance of the class through deserialization. The Bean, an object now, can then have its methods called through the Method class.

For example, a Bean that is used as a button can have its class loaded and the Introspector class is used to read the class's design including the classes extended, the interfaces implemented, and methods. The data gathered by the Introspector class is returned in a BeanInfo object. The BeanInfo can be used by an application builder tool to connect the button to other components and change the button's attribute properties, such as color.

The dynamic discovery and capability to call constructors and methods is very powerful. With such programmatic capabilities combined with method signatures and programming patterns, it becomes possible to connect Beans to programs without ever requiring code to be written.

The BeanInfo Interface and Design Signatures

Design signatures are simple conventions for representing parts of a program in consistent ways. For example, if a method name begins with the word "set" and the method has one parameter, the method can be assumed to be used for setting a value in a class. The patterns are designed so that they can be recognized by using the Core Reflection API. The Introspector class uses the Core Reflection API to discover and then categorize the methods in a Bean into the categories of property access, event generation, and miscellaneous methods. The Introspector class places this information into a BeanInfo object. The BeanInfo object is the implementation of the BeanInfo interface. The BeanInfo interface defines methods that are used to retrieve the Bean descriptor, properties, methods, and events that describe a Bean. The BeanInfo class is used as a standard view of a Bean that can be used by an application builder to manipulate a Bean and presents its methods, properties, and events. The BeanInfo can either be built from scratch by the developer or created using the Introspector class. It is also possible to create only parts of a BeanInfo object and use the Introspector class to fill in the blank sections by using Core Reflection. This combination makes it easier for a developer to modify part of a Bean's programmatic and IDE representation without implementing all the information presented by the BeanInfo class.

Bean Related APIs

Beans can be used with all the other packages and classes in the base JDK and with any other class that a Bean requires to perform its function; there are primary classes, however, that should be considered core to the Bean API. These APIs include the following:

◆ Serialization

◆ Internationalization

◆ Core Reflection

◆ The delegation event model

These APIs are so important to the proper development and understanding of Beans that they have been covered in this book. In addition, several other parts of the Java core packages can be used to create specialized Beans. These APIs include RMI, IDL, 2D JDBC, and others. Each of these APIs can be used to create Java Beans that fulfill a variety of useful components.

The BeanBox

The BeanBox, the application provided with the Beans Developer Kit (BDK), is a demonstration of how to build application design tools that are Java Beans-compliant. The problems solved by enabling a Java Beans component to be used as a true object are countless. A quick example of how much better it is to edit with live components is best described in relation to Java layout managers. When you use a FlowLayout manager from within a Bean-aware design tool, for example, the components added to it are arranged exactly as they would be in the final application. The reason is that the IDE saves the panel, its settings (including the FlowLayout), and all the Beans added to it. This is far different from a traditional IDE where the key difference is that Beans are serializable. The new Java Serialization API saves the persistent state of objects. Instead of an IDE generating code to set up the GUI, Java Beans, after being configured, are saved as objects. When the application is run, the Beans are deserialized back to their saved state. This is not WYSIWYG programming, this is "What You See Is Final," or WYSIF, programming.

Such a live environment holds many more possibilities than solving the layout problem. Because objects are live, they are also capable of being connected, configured, and tested all from within the IDE. For a simple example of this type of programming, the BeanBox application that comes with the BDK will be used to connect a few of the sample BDK Java Beans. The BeanBox is used to create an application that has an animation Bean and two button Beans that start and stop the animation. Start the BeanBox application according to the instructions that come with the BDK for your computer and follow the steps below.

1. You first select and position the Juggler Bean onto the BeanBox canvas.

2. Then select and place a button Bean called OurButton. This button Bean has several properties. The one you are interested in for this example is Label. Change this button's label to Start Juggling.

3. From the Edit menu, select Events, Mouse, mouseClicked. The BeanBox will now show a line from the button to wherever the mouse is moved. Move the mouse pointer over the Juggler Bean that you previously placed on the BeanBox canvas.

4. As soon as you click on the Juggler Bean, a dialog box appears with the Juggler's class methods. Scroll down the list until the *startJuggling()* method is visible. *startJuggling()* is selected. Press the OK button in the dialog box.

5. Select the OurButton Bean on the palette again, but place the button in another area of the BeanBox canvas. For this button, the label is set to Stop Juggling.

6. Select the edit, Events, Mouse, mouseClicked menu item again. Move the mouse to the Juggler Bean again and click it. When the dialog box appears with the Juggler Bean's methods, the stopJuggling method is selected.

Figure 1.1 shows the resulting BeanBox after the previous steps have been performed.

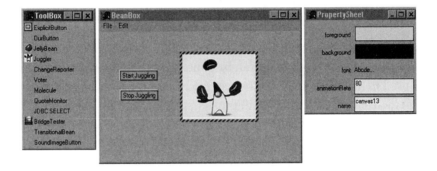

Figure 1.1

The BeanBox application.

Now that everything is hooked up, use the mouse to click on the Start Juggling button. The Juggling Bean will start juggling and will not stop until you use the mouse to click the Stop Juggling button.

If the Juggler Bean is selected while it is juggling, its property sheet can be edited. In particular, changes to the animationRate property will be immediately noticeable if changed.

The BeanBox is the prototype for a Bean GUI editor, which is quite powerful (as you can see). The BeanBox can also be used as a basis for developing applications and even Beans that can act as containers for Beans. Bean containers open new horizons for plugable components that require little or no human intervention. This type of container technology is similar to OLE and ActiveX containers except there is much more control provided by the Bean Architecture.

In Chapter 3, "Exploiting the BDK Examples," each of the Java Beans examples that come with the BDK will be explored. These examples and those in the rest of this book can be used as a basis to understand how Java Beans can be written and used in applications.

Application Development without Coding

Another feature that sets Java Beans apart from other technologies is that there is little or no code required to connect Beans. This is possible because Java Beans are connected while a program is running. This is different from other technologies. Most other technologies are connected in several phases. For example, in Visual C++, if a button component is added to an application the IDE generates a code fragment that the developer must complete to interface the button's press and release actions to other parts of the program. Once completed, the developer can compile, link, and test the program.

With Java Beans, the model is quite different. First, a component, like a button, is added to a live workspace. The workspace can be either the actual application or a simple panel (like that used in the BeanBox). To connect the Button the developer selects a source event from the Button, such as clicked, pressed, or released, and then selects the target Bean that is to accept the event. At this point one of two things can happen depending on the application builder. The first method for connecting events is that the target for button events is added directly to the Button. Directly connecting Beans means that the listener must implement the event listener that matches the event source. In the case of the previous example, this is not possible. The Juggler Bean is a mouse event listener, but mouse events are not associated with starting or stopping animation. Instead, there needs to be a way of adapting the events from other objects, like buttons to the requested actions, such as the *startJuggling()* method.

The most likely hookup method between a Button and other parts of a developer's program is that a small class is created and dynamically compiled. This new hookup class implements the Listener interface for the Button events and calls a specific method in the target Bean. This scenario is much more useful than the first because the event adapter class is capable of connecting the event to another class that may not be an event listener. For example, in the previous explanation on how to create and connect the Juggler Bean to button type Java Beans, the *stopJuggling()* and *startJuggling()* methods were connected to the button Bean's clicked events. What the BeanBox application did to perform this operation was to create an adaptor class. Here is the adaptor class that connected the clicked event to the *startJuggling()* method:

Listing 1.1: Event adaptor class to connect mouse clicked events to a Juggler.startJuggling() method

```
01. // Automatically generated event hookup file.
02.
03. package sun.beanbox;
04.
05. public class ___Hookup_33187480 implements java.awt.event.MouseListener,
➥java.io.Serializable {
06.
07. public void setTarget(sun.demo.juggler.Juggler t) {
08.        target = t;
09. }
10.
11.     public void mouseClicked(java.awt.event.MouseEvent arg0) {
12.         target.startJuggling();
13.     }
14.
15.     public void mousePressed(java.awt.event.MouseEvent arg0) {
16.     }
17.
18.     public void mouseReleased(java.awt.event.MouseEvent arg0) {
19.     }
20.
21.     public void mouseEntered(java.awt.event.MouseEvent arg0) {
22.     }
23.
24.     public void mouseExited(java.awt.event.MouseEvent arg0) {
25.     }
26.
27.     private sun.demo.juggler.Juggler target;
}
```

The event hookup adapter is a very simplified class and as stated before is generated by the BeanBox application. On line 5, the class name is partially serialized to make the generated name unique. Line 5 also shows that the MouseListener interface is implemented by this class and that the class is serializable. On line 7, the class constructor for this Bean accepts the target class object. In this particular adapter we are calling a method in the Juggler Bean object so its object is the parameter passed. The target is assigned to a field that is to be used later. The *target* field is serializable. This means that the *target* object, referencing the Juggler Bean object, will be serialized when the current state of the application is saved. The serialization also means that the connection to the target is still in place when the application is restored through deserialization.

On line 11, the method that is to be called for mouseClicked events is populated with the call to the *startJuggling()* method (line 12). The other methods that are part of the MouseListener interface are implemented with no code because they are ignored by this adapter.

So far, the explanation of what is going on has not explained why this is different from Visual C++. The primary difference is that the objects are live. The moment that the hookup is complete between the *startJuggling()* method and the start juggling button's clicked event the button can be clicked with the mouse and the Juggler Bean will commence with the juggling.

The primary reason that the application builder can operate in a live environment is because of the dynamic class loading capability of Java. The event adapter is first compiled and then it is loaded by name to create a class that can then be used to create an object. The BeanBox constructs the new event adapter with the Juggler object as the target. The new adapter object can then be added as a mouse listener to the start juggling button Bean.

Beans also have the advantage of serialization and introspection through the BeanInfo class. The introspection enables methods to be found and called without prior knowledge. The Serialization API makes it possible to save the state of the running application. Once saved, the application can be restored exactly as it was saved.

 Note

Sound familiar?

Some readers may have seen something similar to Java Beans before. A few live GUI builders have been created. In fact, some languages such as Forth, Smalltalk, and Lisp have had GUI editors that worked in a similar fashion. No one denies that Java might be following in the footsteps of others. The difference here is that Java, with its cross-platform capability, C syntax-like charm, plus all the other advantages such as built-in exceptions, garbage collection, serialization, and Core Reflection creates an environment that could be the winning combination that could make this technology really work. With such advantages and industry acceptance from IBM, Symantec, Borland, Texas Instruments, and many others, the Bean concept has leapt into being far faster than other component technologies.

Bean Component Details

This section describes the main parts of the Bean's architecture. The basic rule, as has been mentioned, is that Java Beans are components. This usually means that the Bean is treated as a single entity used in a larger program.

Cases do arise, however, where the strict component definition may not be entirely accurate. The Juggler Bean that is part of the BDK, for example, could be used as a single component added to an applet or application that makes it a complete application. The same could be true for a spreadsheet, editor, or other Bean that could be used as a single component.

The only requirement for a Bean component is that it be accessible through a primary class. The primary or Bean class locates a BeanInfo class if one exists.

Types of Beans

The following four types of Beans are possible:

- ◆ Component
- ◆ Container
- ◆ Invisible
- ◆ Applet

These categories are not enforced by the Bean API, but are treated as such by their base classes. In other words, the only thing that makes a component Bean a component is that it inherits from the java.awt.Component class. The same is true for container Beans, except that the Container class is in the inheritance hierarchy.

Visible Java Beans

Beans that are child classes of Component and Container classes are also called visual Beans because they are used to build GUI applications. Visual Beans are primarily added to Container objects, including objects of type Frame, Applet, and Panel. Remember that a class inheriting from a container has other classes extended from Component.

Invisible Java Beans

Invisible Java Beans are invisible because they do not inherit from any class based on Component class. Invisible Beans can, however, generate Frame-based components such as windows and dialogs, but are not associated with or added to a java.awt.Container-based object. Invisible Beans can be anything from a database connection to a filter or algorithm. Any class that has either properties or follows the delegation event model can be an invisible Bean. In Chapter 6, you will create a Bean that simulates a nuclear reactor. The NuclearReactor Bean has no visible aspect, but does have parameters and does follow the delegation event model so that it can be treated as a Java Beans class.

Applet Java Beans

Applet Java Beans are a relatively new type of Java Beans component. Because an Applet is an extension of the Container class, an applet can be treated as a container or as a component. The use of applets as Java Beans opens the use of small Applets that have primarily been used for spicing up web pages, and using them as-is, to spice up applications or other Applets.

Applet Java Beans are treated differently than normal Java Beans because applets require a context to operate within. To create the context, the application builder tool, like the BeanBox, creates a class that extends the AppletContext interface. The implementation of AppletContext is used by the Applet to access resources and associations to other Applet-based Java Beans in the application. There is also a container class created that implements the AppletStub interface. The AppletStub interface is used to hold the Applet object and to store the Applet's parameters (parameters that would have normally been defined with parameter tags in the Applet HTML tag).

Bean Minimum Requirements

There are just a few rules to create a Bean. Here is a list of the primary attributes that Beans should have to be considered:

- ♦ **Bean can be instantiated** (not abstract or an Interface).

- ♦ **Bean has a class constructor method that takes zero parameters.** This is the absolute minimum requirement for a Bean. The Introspector class will, as a minimum, create a list of public methods that the Bean supports. Other Beans in response to events can call these methods. The primary reason for a constructor with no parameters is that most Beans are created automatically if they are not otherwise loaded with a default-serialized state. If the Bean is created from its class only, it is impractical to call a Bean's specialized constructor because the IDE has no pre-defined concept of the Bean. Beans are created with class defaults (for example, the defaults set at parameter initialization and in the default constructor), any other change of parameters is done through the IDE's Property interface or through a Bean customizer. Additionally, a Bean can have constructors that do accept parameters, but these constructors should only be considered as optional and primarily used by developers that do not have a Bean-aware application development tool.

◆ **Bean implements Serializable or io.Externalizable.** These interface classes need to be implemented so that a Bean can be serialized. The Bean does not need to have serializable data, but it does need to be at least serialized so that the Bean's object can be recreated through the deserialization process. Normally, Beans are not created in programs by using the constructor. Beans are primarily instantiated from an object stream. If the Bean cannot be serialized, there is no way to use the Bean unless code is generated to call the Bean's constructor. Although this type of creation is possible, it is unlikely because it does not fit with the way that most Beans will be used.

◆ **Bean follows method signature rules.** This is so that the Introspector class can properly categorize the methods. Method signatures are rules of naming methods, specifying return types, parameters, and exceptions that can be used to categorize methods. Without proper adherence to method signatures, a Bean cannot be properly understood by the Introspector class.

◆ **Bean is an instantiable class and has a default constructor.**

Extending a Bean with a BeanInfo Object

As discussed previously, Beans should follow the delegation event model, have property accessor methods, and be serializable. It is also possible to add a definition that extends the Bean's IDE representation and to define an interpretation and presentation of properties, events, and methods that will override the defaults found through the Introspector class. Because the capabilities of the BeanInfo are quite extensive, this chapter covers each category of information in the BeanInfo interface. This is, however, just an overview. Chapter 8, "Bean Introspection," covers the BeanInfo in much more detail.

A Bean is Separate from its BeanInfo

The first rule of using BeanInfo is that, although BeanInfo is an interface, it should not be implemented by a Bean. Part of the requirements for the Java Beans component architecture is that the description of a Bean component is not required to be a part of the application containing the Bean. In other words, the application does not carry with it any of the information or tools required for integrating the Bean with the rest of the application. This is similar to saying that a house is built with a team of workers who, when the work is finished, are not a part of the resulting house.

The separation of Bean from builder information reduces the amount of memory that is required by the application. Imagine the absurdity of building a house that has extra rooms to house the workers that build it. For the same reason, there is no need to keep information about a Bean with the final application.

In addition, the BeanInfo is found by name. For example, to find the Juggler Bean's Bean info, the string "BeanInfo" is appended to the name of the Juggler Bean class name. The result, JugglerBeanInfo is the name of the class that implements the BeanInfo for the Juggler Bean. This class is instantiated by name to create a class and the resulting object that is used to access information about the Bean. If the Bean implemented the BeanInfo interface, the application builder tool would be unable to locate the class.

BeanInfo Objects are Never Accessed Directly

Another essential concept is that a BeanInfo object is not accessed directly. The primary way that information about a Bean is gathered is through the Introspector class. The Introspector is the class that is in charge of locating a BeanInfo object. Any information that the BeanInfo object does not supply is added by the Introspector through Core reflection and comparing results to Java Beans design signatures.

The Introspector creates a new BeanInfo object that is the union of the information from a Bean developer BeanInfo object and the information gathered through Core Reflection.

Information in a BeanInfo Object

The following is a breakdown of the information returned by the BeanInfo interface. If any of these methods is implemented to return a null, the Introspector class uses the Core Refection API to attempt to discover the same class of information. The information returned via most of these methods is based on the FeatureDescriptor class. FeatureDescriptor holds information that will primarily be used by an IDE to better display that part of a Bean's API. The following table documents the methods in the FeatureDescriptor class:

Table 1.1: Methods in the FeatureDescriptor Class

Method	Description
attributeNames()	Returns a list of attribute name strings. Attributes are used as a way to associate a list of names and objects with a particular attribute of the feature. This list can be used by the IDE as a set of possible values that can be used to configure a property.
getDisplayName()	Returns the display name of the feature. The display name is the title for the feature displayed to the user. This name should be set to the localized name.
getName()	Returns the programmatic name of the feature. This is the true name of the feature. This is the programmatic name, not the localized name.
getShortDescription()	Returns the description used to explain or describe the feature. This string should be localized (that is, returns a string that is language and country specific).
getValue(String)	Retrieves the value of a named attribute.
isExpert()	Returns a Boolean that designated this feature as being used by experts (true) or not (false). The expert flag can be used to control access to features that may not be understood and may confuse novice users.
isHidden()	Returns the hidden flag setting. The "hidden" flag identifies the Bean as a component intended only for tool use or a Bean not based from the component class.
setDisplayName(String)	Sets the display name that is the title for the feature displayed to the user. This name should be set to the localized name.
setExpert(boolean)	Sets the expert flag value. The expert flag designates a particular feature as one that should or should not be accessed by novice users.
setHidden(boolean)	Sets the value of the hidden flag. The "hidden" flag identifies the Bean as a component intended only for tool use or a Bean not based from the component class.
setName(String)	Sets the true name of the feature. This is the programmatic name, not the localized name.
setShortDescription(String)	Sets the value to be displayed to explain this feature. This string should be localized.
setValue(String, Object)	Sets an attribute object that matches the given name with the specified value.

The only information in the FeatureDescriptor class that will be set by the Introspector class is the name of the feature. The name is used as the value returned by getName() and getDisplayName() methods.

The BeanInfo Interface Methods

The following sections describe each of the BeanInfo interface methods. These are simple overviews; a more detailed explanation of the BeanInfo is covered in Chapter 8.

getIcon() Method

This method returns the icon used to represent the Bean in an IDE.

getBeanDescriptor() Method

The Bean descriptor is used to describe the Bean as a whole. The descriptor is also used to associate a Bean customizer object.

getPropertyDescriptors() Method

The *getPropertyDescriptors()* method returns an array of PropertyDescriptor classes that the Bean implements. The property descriptor describes methods that meet the set/get signature. In addition to the base FeatureDescriptor methods, the PropertyDescriptor has Method objects for the get and set methods. A PropertyEditor object can be used to modify the edit process of this type of property. Also included are methods to get the type of the property.

getDefaultPropertyIndex() Method

The *getDefaultPropertyIndex()* method returns the index into the array returned by the *getPropertyDescriptors()* method. The default property is the property most likely changed by a user. The label property of a button, for example, is the primary attribute that will be changed by developers.

getEventSetDescriptors() Method

The *getEventSetDescriptors()* method returns an array of EventSet objects. Event sets are used to define the "add" and "remove" listener methods and the type of event.

getDefaultEventIndex() Method

The *getDefaultEventIndex()* method returns the default event index into the array returned by the *getEventSetDescriptors()* method. The default event is the most likely event that a developer will want to connect to. The mouse-button-clicked event of a button, for example, is the primary event set that will be used by developers.

getMethodDescriptors() Method

The *getMethodDescriptors()* method returns an array of MethodDescriptor classes that the Bean implements. These methods include the set/get property methods and the add/remove methods. The Method descriptor describes methods, their return types, and parameters.

getAdditionalBeanInfo() Method

The *getAdditionalBeanInfo()* method is used to retrieve another layer of the BeanInfo. This is useful if a Bean inherits from another Bean. The new Bean would describe its event sets, methods, and properties in its BeanInfo and return the Base Bean's BeanInfo object to describe the remaining part of the Bean's API that was inherited.

Beans Should Not Implement BeanInfo

Remember that BeanInfo is an interface. In general, however, there is little reason for the BeanInfo to be part of another base class. The BeanInfo could be implemented by a Bean, but this is not recommended. In fact, the introspection process locates BeanInfo classes by the name of the Bean appended to the string BeanInfo. A Bean called MyButton, therefore, would have a BeanInfo called MyButtonBeanInfo. The Introspector class will be searching for this name. There is no reason to ever call a BeanInfo class a name other than <bean name>BeanInfo, so a Bean cannot implement the BeanInfo class and have it properly recognized by the Introspector.

Now that you know why a Bean should not implement the BeanInfo object, it's important to review situations where this is reasonable, and how to make the Introspector work properly. Atomicity is one reason why a Bean might want an internal representation of its BeanInfo. *Atomicity* means that the Bean is treated as a single object. In other words, the Bean and its BeanInfo are integrated as one object. Sometimes software agents or servlets are transported to different servers where a single, self-contained class could be a preferable entity than a collection of classes. Having the BeanInfo available, by just casting the Bean as a BeanInfo, could make it simple for a Bean-aware application to access the Bean's API. This does require that the target application understand that the Bean carries the BeanInfo as an implemented interface. The only time that this makes sense, however, is when the Bean does not follow the standardized method signatures (an unlikely event for such a class—this is, after all, a hypothetical situation that has not yet been designed).

Enabling a Bean to implement its own BeanInfo and to make this BeanInfo available to the Introspector class is quite simple, as described in the following step-by-step procedure:

1. A Bean implements the BeanInfo interface.

2. Another public class is created called <bean name>BeanInfo, and inherits the Bean class as a base. This new class does not need to implement any other interfaces. A Bean called Foo that implements a BeanInfo class, for example, is created.

3. A class called FooBeanInfo is created that extends the Foo class.

Again, this is not recommended. Even possible scenarios are contrived and unlikely. The whole concept of Beans is also oriented at the complete separation of a Bean from its API description. Such a separation helps to keep IDE or application builder-oriented code out of the final application. If a Bean is to be used in a Bean-aware application other than an IDE or application builder, the Bean should be 100 percent compatible with the Bean method signatures.

Enhancing IDEs with a Custom Property Editor (PropertyEditor Interface)

A primary way to enhance an IDE's capability to edit a Bean property is to provide a PropertyEditor for a particular category of properties. Examples of these are Bean properties that set and get parameters of the Color class (such as foreground and background colors). The PropertyEditor interface defines an interface that changes the property sheet's presentation and/or displays a custom component editor (such as a color palette for Color properties). The Custom property editor is found either by the name of the class it edits or by associating a PropertyEditor in the PropertyDescriptor class. The PropertyEditor has the following capabilities:

- Acts as a property change handler

- Holds and changes a copy of the parameter

- Is associated with property type (not the Bean)

- Can present a drop-down selection used to set the property

- Can display a small image or icon in the property sheet

- Acts as a custom component editor built by the property editor

- Returns a Subclass of component to be displayed in a dialog that is used to graphically edit the component

- Interacts with the custom property editor

Editing the Bean as a Whole

The Customizer interface associates a customized editor with a Bean. The Customizer interface can be invisible or subclass the Frame class. Customizers display and edit related Bean properties or properties that need a better interface than the IDE property sheet and property editors can provide. Bean customizers are different from PropertyEditor classes mainly because customizers manipulate Bean objects directly.

Delivering Beans

The thoroughness of JavaSoft, as regarding Java Beans, includes the packaging and cataloging of class and support files. In addition, the method of packaging and extracting is covered by Java software. Because of the Java-based tools and libraries, the solution is 100 percent portable between Java platforms. There are two parts to the package mechanism, JAR files and JAR Manifests. Each of these is described in the sections that follow.

JAR Files

Traditionally, software has been delivered in some type of compressed archive file. This is also true of Java Beans that use a file format and compression system called JAR files. A Java Archive, rather than relying on second-party tools like pkzip or other existing archiving formats, JavaSoft has decided to use public domain formats combined with public domain compression algorithms. Because the compression and file format are in the public domain, JavaSoft was able to add the combined system to the Java core API. JAR files are used for Beans as well as for compressing legacy Java applets and applications. There is a package, java.util.zip, which was added in the JDK 1.1 to provide the capability for Java programs to create and read the contents of Java files. A stand-alone tool named jar (or jar.exe on 95/NT/DOS operation systems) is used to archive and extract files from a JAR file. The jar tool is used as a command line executable to manage JAR files in a fashion similar to other archive tools, such as WinZip and StuffIt.

The layout of the JAR file is based on the standardized layout for ZIP files. The JAR tool automatically preserves the directory tree of the files archived. The directory tree is very important to Java code because the directory tree is used to specify the package name of class files.

JavaSoft provides JAR compression through the public domain ZLIB compression algorithm. This compression algorithm was originally part of the PNG graphics specification. Readers may question the compression efficiency of such a system, but ZLIB is efficient enough to perform its given function of general compression. Also, being in the public domain, ZLIB does not add to the cost of the Java system, which is still delivered as a public domain programming environment.

The primary reason for adding an archiving system is to supply a standardize format that is cross-platform and supported by the java.utl.zip package included in the Java Core API. Since the Core API is a required part of all Java installations, there is no reason for additional software to read or create JAR files.

 Note

> A JAR file is not a ZIP file. Both file types do follow the same file layout, but do not use the same compression algorithm. JAR files are not readable by tools from PKWare and others. A tool, such as WinZip or PKUnzip, can read the directory structure of a JAR file, but it will not be able to properly extract the contents.

The JAR Manifest

The JAR Manifest is a simple description of each file in a JAR file. The manifest includes the name of each file, checksum, and other information used to identify particular classes as Beans. In addition, the user can add extra information that can be used to help manage data in the JAR file.

The Manifest file is also discussed in detail in Chapter 10, "Packaging Java Beans." The most important part that should be understood is that a class file that is the main class for a Bean must be marked with a line Java-Bean: True. By adding this tag line IDE tools and other Bean-aware applications like the BeanBox application, can identify the correct Bean class. Remember that a Bean is indistinguishable from non-Bean classes. Without this Bean marker, there would be no way to tell the main Bean apart from support files that may or may not be usable as Bean classes.

Listing 1.2 shows a typical entry in a JAR Manifest for a Bean. Note that there are two checksums—also known as a file hash—and a line to denote the types of hash algorithms used.

> **Listing 1.2 : Section of a JAR Manifest file showing an entry for a JavaBean class**
>
> ```
> Name: RoundButtonBean.class
> Java-Bean: True
> Hash-Algorithms: MD5 SHA
> MD5-Hash: S2+dpTzNIk/xn7Q5TqzPxw==
> SHA-Hash: E+XYVoHTwz5YR71KK8FKjljWB6k=
> ```

File Hash Checksums

The JAR tool also generates unique file hash checksums. These checksums validate the data integrity of the files in a JAR file. Two types of checksums are provided: CRC 32 and Adler 32. The CRC 32 checksum is specifically used as part of the GZIP compression and decompression format. Adler 32 is similar to CRC 32 except that it can be computed slightly more quickly. The only other reason for having these two types of checksums is to avoid the possibility that a file could be modified, yet still have the same checksum number calculated by both hash algorithms. In most cases, unless you are developing your own JAR tool from the java.util.zip package, you will not be concerned with the file hash.

Uses and Types of Beans

It is important to understand how wide the range of Java Beans usage can be. If you can imagine the need, a Bean can be developed that fits it. The following sections provide just a few of the different uses and configurations of possible Bean applications.

The Malleable Bean

Beans are extremely versatile. There are so many possibilities for useful components that there will be no end to the types of Beans that can be created. Just creating different types of button Beans could occupy the rest of your life (any large hardware store should convince you of this). Besides the different types of Beans, there is also the possibility of creating single Beans that can be configured into several different views or modes of operation. There can be Beans made of groups of Beans to create complex Beans. The goal is to design the Bean to be easily configurable to the desired set of tasks.

Beans and Scripting Languages

The structure of the Bean API makes Beans ideal for use in scripted languages and applications. Because of the reflection tools and the BeanInfo interface, it is a simple manner to interpret scripted instructions to build, configure, and connect Beans. Netscape already has plans to extend its JavaScript language to enable it to use Java Beans. The benefit to be gained by such a mix is that custom components and functionality of the Java language environment can be used to extend the scripted language without sacrificing the simplicity afforded by a simple interpreted language.

Bean Bridges: Interfacing Beans with Programming Languages

Other base languages such as C++ or Visual Basic can use Java Beans. By using wrappers called bridges, the interface between these other languages and Beans running in a JVM can be accomplished. The similarity to at least a part of the older technologies such as OLE, OpenDoc, and ActiveX make it a simple matter to enable Beans to run in the same type of application to component interfaces.

The reverse situation is also true. Java applications can use other component technologies such as OLE, OpenDoc, and ActiveX by encapsulating the foreign component in a Bean wrapper and an accompanying BeanInfo object. Although native code has been usable by Java since its introduction, it will be much simpler to interface these other standard technologies with the Bean API.

Bridging from other technologies to Java should be done sparingly, skeptically, and if possible: Never! Just by adding a small amount of non-Java code, applications increase vulnerability to security attacks or susceptibility to native code bugs that could affect the Java environment. Remember that it is almost impossible to trace problems between software language boundaries. Also, native components will need to be tested thoroughly before being integrated with Java. Whenever possible, stick to 100 percent Java applications for portability, debugging, error control, and security.

Beans in Applets or Applications, BeanBox, and IDEs

Applications or applets can use Beans in very similar manners. The only difference is the security level between applets and applications. For signed applets, security can be reduced so much that in such a situation the only difference between applications and applets is that applets run from within web browsers. The key point to remember is that Beans are, in the end, simply Java. There is no reason to think about them differently. There are additional attributes and a certain amount of standardization, but nothing that is associated primarily with applets or with applications.

When Beans are run within Bean-aware applications such as the BeanBox or application development IDEs, there is a slight difference because of the underlying program and the fact that IDEs and the BeanBox rely heavily on the BeanInfo object associated with each Bean class. If the Bean or a collection of Beans is serialized, it can be used in an application or applet just as it normally would have been.

A myth crops up from time to time that Beans require a BeanBox application to run. This myth is false. In fact, the BeanBox is only a tool for connecting Beans, similar to using a GUI builder in an IDE. The BeanBox is supplied in the BDK as both an environment to test Java Beans and to serve as an example of a Bean-aware application.

In fact, Beans can be used in normal applications as normal classes and without the need to serialize a predefined state. To repeat the point, Beans are just Java classes. Using the BeanBox and Bean-aware IDEs just makes them easier to use.

Bean-Aware Software

Bean-aware software falls into two categories. The first is the type of application used by developers to connect Beans to create applications. Such Bean-aware programs are called application builders, IDEs, or GUI editors. These are the original targets of the Bean API. A whole range of software can also benefit from the Bean API. Software capable of adding Beans dynamically with little or no user intervention is a powerful paradigm. Applications, web browsers, applets, and servlets can be written to accept Beans dynamically. The range of Beans that can be accepted by such software is more limited, mainly because such applications would be more oriented to specific applications or models of specific behavior. To add the Beans, it may also be necessary to include the BeanInfo and related classes along with the Bean to aid in the connection process. The following list shows some simple examples of such Bean-aware software:

◆ **Java Beans that are containers for specialized Java Beans.** This type of Bean-aware software is like a specialized layout container. The component connects to the Beans added and/or connects the Beans in the container to each other. An excellent example of this type is a Spreadsheet container that holds spreadsheet cell Beans or other spreadsheets.

◆ **Applets that accept either pointers to URLs that contain lists of Beans to load or that are designated as parameters in the HTML applet tag.** This type of Bean-aware applet could load specialized Beans without the need for the web developer to use an applet builder to create an application. This works by just plugging the appropriate Bean component's name into a list. This type of applet could be used in applications where pages are built dynamically based on user input or other information held on the server.

◆ **Servlets that discover Beans on different servers.** Servlets are Java classes similar to Beans that can be sent to servlet servers, such as Jeeves, to perform tasks at the server and possibly relay information back to the sender. Servlets can also move between cooperating systems to perform tasks at different nodes of a network. Another name for servlets is Software Agent. Servlets could be used as agents to find Java Beans that handle specific data or have certain functionality. A more complex servlet could attach to the Bean to use it to process data or serialize the Bean and send it back to the originator of the servlet. This paradigm holds the most promise for servlet or software agent computing.

Selling Your Java Beans

The software component market is a growing concern. Many companies are dedicated to either manufacturing, selling components, or adding value to their products by supplying useful components. A large freeware and shareware supply of software components also exists. Several aspects to delivering Beans are covered later in Chapter 10.

Summary

Java Beans were first introduced to the world in 1996 during the first Java One conference. Again, we quote from the JavaBeans™ 1.0 API specification:

> A Bean is a reusable software component that can be manipulated visually in a builder tool.

What has resulted from a simple statement is a component architecture that, combined with the rest of the JDK 1.1 API, is a very important leap in how components are developed and used. In addition, the Core Reflection API can be used to support application builders, as well as for creating other applications that are Bean-aware. Bean-aware containers hold much promise for building dynamic, long-lived applications. With the capability to dynamically add Java Beans to applications, products can be extended long after their first release without redistributing the whole program. The application builder tools are then able to understand and manipulate Bean components, and so likewise can applications or Beans themselves.

This chapter has covered Java Beans in general and the related Java APIs that are involved. The rest of the book covers in detail much of the information covered in this chapter.

CHAPTER 2

Software Component Architectures

by James L. Weaver

As mentioned in Chapter 1, "Java Beans Overview," JavaSoft defines a Java Bean as a reusable software component that can be manipulated visually in a builder tool.

A *software component* in this definition is a reusable software building block. A *builder tool* in this definition is typically an IDE (integrated application development environment). There are other possibilities, however. One such possibility is a web page authoring tool, where Beans could be dragged and dropped onto a page. Another possibility is the BeanBox test container that is included in the BDK (Beans Development Kit) that JavaSoft has made available for developers to test their Java Beans.

This chapter focuses on the concept of software components and their underlying architectures. Software components and architectures are first covered in a generic sense, and then specific examples are explored, including Java Beans. This chapter also discusses security issues surrounding web-enabled component architectures.

Understanding Software Component Architectures

A software component is a reusable software building block. A software component architecture enables the building of applications by assembling pre-existing software components. A *container* groups one or more components together, so that they can communicate with each other as well as with the container. Software component architectures are also referred to as:

- ◆ Software component models

- ◆ Component models

- ◆ Component object models

- ◆ Component architectures

- ◆ Component frameworks

Each of these terms are synonymous with software component architectures.

A Brief History of Software Reuse

The software industry has always embraced the concept of reuse. Over the years, the scope, or granularity, of reuse has increased, which has produced a subsequent increase in productivity. Four levels of granularity exist as detailed in the following list:

- ◆ **Source code:** since programming began, sections of source code were made available to, and reused by other developers.

- ◆ **Function libraries:** when structured programming came in vogue in the 1970s, function libraries were shared.

- ◆ **Objects:** as object-oriented programming matured in the 1980s, class libraries were shared by developers and sold by third parties.

- ◆ **Software components:** the 1990s have given rise to GUI development, where third-party software components have become instrumental in enabling developers to build reliable applications quickly. ActiveX components, for example, have become popular tools for building Visual Basic applications.

Java Beans belong to the "software components" level of reuse granularity. An increasing number of Java Beans are becoming available from software component developers. Integrated Java development environments typically come with several Beans that developers can use.

Some of the more popular software components are those that function as higher-level GUI widgets, such as multicolumn list boxes and toolbar managers. Components also can be small applications, such as a drawing program, that can be embedded in a compound document. Components also can be non-visual: a timer component, for example, emits a tick event at a predetermined interval.

Typical Behavior of Software Components in an IDE

Visual Basic was one of the IDEs that popularized the concept of using software components to build applications. Using Visual Basic, a developer can create an application by dragging software components such as buttons and progress bars from a toolbar onto a window. This is typical of IDEs that use component architectures. In these IDEs, software components have three major attributes:

♦ Properties

♦ Events

♦ Methods

The sections that follow examine each of these attributes in greater detail.

Component Properties

Properties are the attributes of a component. For example, a button component has several properties including height, width, and label. Properties can generally be manipulated in an IDE through the use of a *property editor.* A property editor enables the developer to see and change the properties of a component. This requires the component architecture to have a mechanism to expose a component's properties to the IDE.

When the developer saves the application, the state of the components' properties are saved as well. This is known as *persistence.* When the application is run, the components' properties start out with the saved value.

The application can examine and change a component's properties as well. For example, an application could change the a property of a progress bar to make it reflect that a process is 60 percent complete.

Component Events

Most components can have *events* happen to them. For example, when a component such as a button is clicked with a mouse, a click event is generated. The developer typically specifies what should be performed as a result of the event by associating code with the event for a particular component. Many IDEs have a code window that appears when the developer specifies a component/event pair to associate code with.

Component Methods

The *methods* of a component are functions that can be called from the application or the IDE. Methods are often used to set and get the state of a component's properties.

Some Major Component Architectures

There are several component architectures in use today other than Java Beans, but some of the more well-known architectures include the following:

- ◆ Live Connect from Netscape
- ◆ OpenDoc from CI Labs
- ◆ ActiveX from Microsoft

Bridges are being created by JavaSoft and these vendors to enable Java Beans to function as native components and containers in each of these architectures. The following sections look at these architectures in more detail.

LiveConnect from Netscape

LiveConnect is an architecture used in Netscape's web browsers that enables communication between components. There are three main types of components that run in Netscape's browsers:

- ◆ **Java applets:** applets are Java programs designed to run within a web browser.
- ◆ **JavaScript code and associated objects:** JavaScript is a scripting language developed by Netscape that provides executable content to static HTML (HyperText Markup Language) pages. JavaScript is an interpreted language, and the code resides in the same document as the HTML for a given web page. Associated objects are:
    - ◆ objects created by JavaScript
    - ◆ objects that represent browser components such as frames or buttons
- ◆ **Netscape plug-ins:** plug-ins extend the functionality of Netscape browsers within the context of a web page. For example, a Shockwave for Director plug-in enables a web page that has an embedded Director movie to display the movie in a given rectangular area of the page.

LiveConnect enables these three types of components to communicate with each other. Some examples of this communication between components include the following:

♦ A JavaScript program running on a web page can call a method of a Java applet that exists on that same page.

♦ A JavaScript program can also affect the behavior of a plug-in by calling the plug-in's API.

♦ A Java applet can change the state of a JavaScript object that represents an HTML component such as a text field.

With LiveConnect, the web page becomes a container, which contains components that can communicate with each other and with the container. This architecture enables the idea that a web-based application can live within a browser window and can consist of frames, Java applets, plug-ins, and HTML, which are controlled by JavaScript code.

OpenDoc from CI Labs

OpenDoc is a cross-platform software component architecture. It was started by CI Labs in 1993, which is an association of vendors including Apple, IBM, and Novell. OpenDoc supports software components such as GUI widgets through its OpenDoc Component Architecture, and supports software components such as embedded documents through its OpenDoc Document Architecture. Components developed with these standards are interoperable, and are referred to as "parts."

One of OpenDoc's underlying technologies is IBM's SOM (System Object Model.) SOM is a framework that runs on multiple platforms and enables OpenDoc components to dynamically communicate with each other. These components can be written in a number of different languages, and SOM enables components to communicate with each other even when on different platforms. In this way, SOM competes with CORBA (which is a distributed object mechanism), and also competes with DCOM (which is mentioned in the next section.)

OpenDoc also has an API called the Open Scripting Architecture that supports controlling OpenDoc components through a scripting language.

ActiveX from Microsoft

ActiveX is a component architecture from Microsoft that is based upon an earlier technology known as OLE (Object Linking and Embedding.) ActiveX has been optimized for use on the web, and presumably was named for its capability to provide executable (active) content to web pages.

ActiveX components are known as *controls*, and there are a large number of them available from Microsoft and third-party ActiveX control vendors. Visual Basic, Visual C++, and Visual J++ support ActiveX controls which can be developed in several languages, including Visual Basic, C++, and Java.

The main technology that enables ActiveX is DCOM (Distributed Component Object Model) from Microsoft. DCOM provides the underlying infrastructure by which ActiveX components can communicate.

This section has discussed some of the major component architectures. The next section compares these component architectures to Java Beans.

Comparing other Component Architectures to Java Beans

Before examining the specifics of Java Beans, you should be aware of a common misconception. What is being described here is nothing like what is seen with other high-end visual tools such as Visual Basic, Visual C++, and Delphi. These technologies depend on a very static and limited view of their components. The results of using these tools is software written in part by the IDE and possibly definition files generated by the GUI (Graphical User Interface) builder.

The Core Reflection API and the Java Beans API, as described in the opening section of this chapter, provide a programmatic view of software. Components are configured directly in running software as opposed to a GUI editor that is only a representation of how the program should look. Figure 2.1 depicts the underlying difference between the ways that a component can be shown in a traditional component tool and a Java Beans development tool.

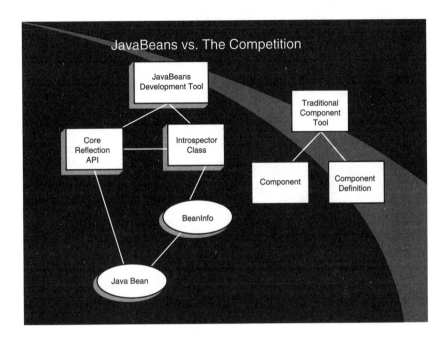

Figure 2.1

Java Beans development tool versus traditional component tools.

In Microsoft Visual C++, for example, the GUI builder is only a model of the program. The programmer develops a GUI that is stored as a set of instructions used to build the final GUI when the program is run. With Java, the components are changed as they are running.

To further clarify the differences, when a button in Visual C++ is connected to code to be run, the IDE lays out a code fragment for which the user must add specific code to perform an action on the other component. With Java and the Beans API, it is not always necessary to write code to do this. The programmer connects the button press event with the event listener in the target component. All of this can happen while the target program is running. The result of the new configuration in a Java component is either stored as a persistent state or the IDE can generate code to accomplish the same task.

Figure 2.2 shows an example of a tool that enables the developer to build an applet by hooking Beans together without writing code. The name of this particular tool is AppletAuthor from IBM.

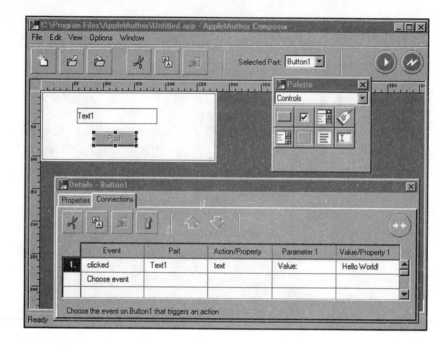

Figure 2.2

The Hello World applet being built in IBM's AppletAuthor.

The applet being built in this figure is the classic "Hello World!" applet. The user interface of this tool contains the following elements:

◆ **A tool palette:** in the upper right window is the tool palette, which holds Beans grouped in several categories.

◆ **The applet drawing area:** in the upper left window is the applet drawing area. Components are selected from the tool palette and drawn on the applet drawing area.

◆ **The details window:** the window across the bottom contains two different tabs. The Properties tab shows the properties of the selected component, and the Connections tab enables the developer to wire the Beans together. In this very simple example, the first row of this window specifies that when the clicked event occurs in the button, the Text1 part (AppletAuthor calls components, parts) will be affected. The manner in which it is affected is specified in the Action/Property, Parameter, and Value columns. In this case, the text property of the Text1 part will be set to "Hello World!" when the button is clicked. Figure 2.3 depicts the running applet.

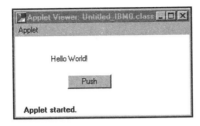

Figure 2.3

The Hello World applet.

 Note

> The current version of IBM's AppletAuthor at this writing is beta 0.7,
> which uses JDK (Java Development Kit) 1.0.2. The capability to view a
> running Bean in a builder tool as described previously is supplied by the
> features in JDK 1.1. Presumably, IBM will adopt these features in future
> versions of AppletAuthor.

To sum up the differences, Java Beans and Core Reflection enable an IDE to do most of
the work, while other technologies such as Visual C++ and Visual Basic require that the
programmer do the final work of specifying tasks in response to actions. Also, unlike
other systems, a Java Beans-enabled IDE works with running software and not a model of
what the program might look like. Instead of WYSIWIG (What You See Is What You
Get) development, the Java programmer is working in the WYSII (What You See Is It)
environment. Core Reflection is able to eliminate several steps in the development
process, with the added benefit that it is also done in a secure and type safe manner
because it is 100 percent Java.

Components the Old Way: Component Definition Files and Class API Interfaces

Exposure of a Bean's API to the IDE is very different from other component technologies. Most other component integration to an IDE was done through a file that defined the
API of the component. The problem with a file-based definition is that the API must be
defined separately from the code. These files are usually vendor-specific in contrast to
being standardized as part of the language.

This creates problems because the definition file is not a part of the language and therefore cannot be compiled. Without compilation, there is no way to validate types and
names of components and methods, which could cause surprises at runtime. The files are

also disconnected from the code that they define and are prone to errors caused when a component is updated and the definition is not.

API definition files are not easy to create. This is mainly because they must be understood by the programmer almost as a second programming language. Many things that were required by the definition files, including code templates to be pasted into user programs and special purpose wizards, are necessary to edit special properties like colors or graphics.

Definition of the component description files is also often proprietary to the manufacturer's IDE, making it difficult or impossible for users to create and add new components to the IDE. Proprietary component definition files also make it impossible to share components between different manufacturers. Some companies have standardized on the Microsoft component models, but there are still many inconsistencies between different vendors.

Newer component technologies such as ActiveX have improved on older file-based components. ActiveX components implement special interfaces expected by an IDE. With an expected API query by the IDE for functionality, a component's functionality can be determined.

The ActiveX solution is not as complex as previous methods, but still requires effort on the programmer's part to add the ActiveX API to the base component.

Another problem with the older component technologies is their need to insert code into a user's program. The problem can be seen in tools such as Visual C++ or Java GUI builders such as Symantec Café. Both of these development tools have code blocks that the user must not change. This forces the programmer to do all editing of the GUI from within the GUI designer tool and not in code where it may be easier and more efficient to perform such tasks as ordering or adding custom components that are not a part of the tool's component palette. Worse still, if changes are made within the GUI code blocks, the GUI Editor usually erases changes without warning.

Components the New Way: The Core Reflection API and BeanInfo

The nature of Java Beans is that their API is visible programmatically. In other words, a program can read the Bean's interface by reading the Bean's class file. This means the methods of a Bean can be queried by IDE tools, which enables the developer to see the behavior of the Bean as it occurs at runtime.

The key to the visibility and manipulation of Beans is made possible by the Java Core Reflection API. Core Reflection enables developers to write software that can analyze and interpret other programs. Because of the programmatic analysis, Beans do not need extra definition files or added classes that expose standard interfaces for IDEs. By using a new extension to the Java language called Core Reflection, the Bean can be examined directly at the code level.

Core Reflection is the examination of classes and interfaces and their corresponding methods and fields. In the Beans environment, the Introspector class uses the Core Reflection API to ask a Bean about its properties, events, and its methods. The end result is a BeanInfo object, which is the Bean's component API. The IDE can then use the BeanInfo object to display information to the user and to manipulate the Bean and integrate it with the main program that the IDE user is developing.

This section has compared some of the component architectures from a functionality perspective. The next section compares two of these architectures from a security perspective.

Understanding Component Security Issues

Component-related security wasn't as big of an issue before components could be automatically downloaded as a result of viewing a web page. Now, security is a huge issue. With the power of executable content comes the associated responsibility of protecting the user's machine from accidental or intentional harm. The two component architectures that are most prevalent in the area of automatically downloading components from a web page are Java Beans and ActiveX. These two technologies take drastically different approaches to security. Java Beans run in the Java Virtual Machine, *sandbox*, and ActiveX controls that aren't written in Java do not run in the Java Virtual Machine.

Living in the Sandbox

The creators of Java have created an environment that protects the machine hosting a Java program from having its security compromised. This environment has been referred to as the *sandbox*, and is made up of several elements as described in the following list:

◆ **Java Virtual Machine (VM):** the Java VM interprets and executes the byte-code that the Java classes consist of.

◆ **Byte-code verifier:** the byte-code verifier verifies that the byte-codes perform legal operations and will not corrupt the Java VM.

- ◆ **Class loader:** a class loader is responsible for loading Java classes. It also ensures that the Java system classes are loaded from the correct location and not replaced with bogus system classes that are potentially damaging to the end user.

- ◆ **Security Managers:** a Java security manager controls a Java class' access to system resources. By default, Java classes, including applets and Beans, are considered untrustworthy when loaded from a web page. This mistrust gives these Java classes very little access to the hosting machine. For example, an untrusted applet cannot read or write to a file, print to a printer, or communicate with a host machine other than the machine from which the applet was retrieved.

Java classes can earn the trust of the hosting machine by being digitally signed by a trusted signer. This authenticates the source of the class, and ensures that the class has not been tampered with. Classes that can be trusted may be granted access to system resources outside of the *sandbox*, such as the file system and printers.

With all of these security precautions, the hosting machine can be assured of protection against Java Beans loaded over the network.

Life without the Sandbox

ActiveX components not written in Java do not run in the *sandbox*, so there are more potential security holes. There is nothing in the ActiveX world that is analogous to the protection that the byte-code verifier provides. Like Java classes, ActiveX components can be digitally signed, but there are no security managers that protect system resources if the component is not as safe as assumed.

Also, because the *sandbox* (via the Java VM) provides a consistent execution environment, Java Beans will run virtually anywhere without any modification. ActiveX controls are not completely cross-platform, because they are written to the API of the target platform.

Summary

This chapter has discussed the concept of component architectures, and has described and compared some of the major component architectures. This chapter also covered some security issues surrounding the two leading web-enabled component architectures— ActiveX and Java Beans.

Chapter 3, "Applying the BDK Examples Globally" discusses how to apply the examples shown in the BDK (Beans Development Kit) to Beans that you develop for real applications.

Applying the BDK Examples Globally

By Bill la Forge

Senior Research Engineer
The Open Group
http://www.opengroup.org/~laforge

When learning a new programming paradigm, examples are indispensable. Fortunately, JavaSoft has included 12 example Beans, including the BeanBox, in its BDK (Beans Development Kit).

This chapter takes a close look at all the example Beans except for the BeanBox. Each Bean demonstrates something vital that you need to understand. Each of these Beans is independent of the others; that is in large part the intent of Beans. The fact that they can indeed be used together speaks well for the reusability of Beans.

The following list highlights the Beans of the BDK that are discussed in greater detail in this chapter. Note that all of these examples are visible Beans, as each is derived from an AWT component.

- ◆ TransitionalBean (extends Canvas)
- ◆ JellyBean (extends Canvas)
- ◆ ChangeReporter (extends TextField)
- ◆ Voter (extends Label)
- ◆ OurButton (extends Canvas)
- ◆ ExplicitButton (extends OurButton)
- ◆ Juggler (extends Canvas)

- ◆ BridgeTester (extends Panel)

- ◆ Molecule (extends Panel)

- ◆ Select (extends Panel)

- ◆ QuoteMonitor (extends Panel)

As you look at each Bean, you need to refer to the Java source files for that Bean. These are included in the BDK in directory demo\sun\demo (per beta 3 of the BDK). The intent of this chapter is to point out the significance of the code and the purpose of various classes defined in the various Java packages.

The BDK and JDK 1.1 are both available for download from:

`http://splash.javasoft.com/beans/bdk_download.html`

You will need Solaris 2.4, Solaris 2.5, Windows 95, Windows NT 3.5.1, or Windows NT 4.0.

The Bean TransitionalBean (extends Canvas)

Transitional Beans are designed to run under JDK 1.0.2. This was a way of getting a head start on Beans before JDK 1.1 was available.

The class TransitionalBean is 20 lines of code, it has a simple Color property, and it is serializable.

The package sun.demo.transitional is a little different from the other demo packages. It contains a very simple Bean, TransitionalBean. It also contains a class that could be a Bean, OurButton, which demonstrates how to convert old AWT events to the new event model. And it contains an applet: Flipper.

The transitional package is a complete, stand-alone example that is short and to the point—all in all, a great example of how to program with Beans.

The following list provides a brief description of the files that comprise the transitional package:

- ◆ **TransitionalBean.java:** a very simple Bean

- ◆ **OurButton.java:** a wrapper for Button that uses the new event model

- **ButtonPushEvent.java:** a custom event

- **ButtonPushListener.java:** a listener interface for ButtonPushEvent

- **Flipper.java:** an Applet Bean container

Figure 3.1 shows the TransitionalBean and the Flipper applet.

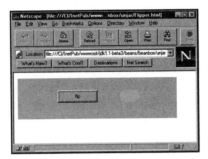

Figure 3.1

TransitionalBean Flipper applet.

Validating TransitionalBean as a Bean

What makes this class a Bean? Well, it has a constructor that takes no parameters, a null constructor. Something else that helps is that it extends Canvas. It, therefore, indirectly extends java.awt.Component. That helps because many Bean development systems may at first only work with classes that extend Component.

One other thing is not in the code. Beans are typically packaged into JAR files similar to ZIP files. A JAR file usually has a text file called a manifest, which describes the contents of the JAR file. One of the things in the manifest is an indication that a class or serialized object file is a Bean. The JAR file for the transitional package has a manifest that indicates that file TransitionalBean.class is, in fact, a Bean.

If you look in directory Beanbox\unJAR in the BDK, you will find the file transitional.mf. This is the manifest file for the transitional package. It is just a text file with a block of text for each file that was in the transitional JAR file. In the first block—a description of file sun/demo/transitional/TransitionalBean.class—you will see that the second line of that block indicates that the file is a Bean.

Defining Properties on a Bean

In the simplest case, a property can be no more than a data member of a Bean that can be read or written by using a method. At the end of TransitionalBean, the variable *ourColor* is indeed a property. It has been given an initial value of orange. This initial value is important. Otherwise, an error that *ourColor* was not initialized would appear when the property is read. Properties are usually read before they are written to. Therefore, don't forget to initialize your properties.

The *getColor()* method is a read accessor method. This means that it identifies a property—color—and that it returns the value of that property; it obviously returns the value of *ourColor*. But what makes it a read accessor method? It is such because the method signature conforms to a particular pattern as shown in the following line of code:

```
public Type getProperty();
```

In this case, "Type" is Color and "Property" is Color. Thus, you have a property "Color" that is of type awt.Color. By conforming to this pattern, a bean container (like the Beanbox) can recognize the method as providing read access to a particular property of the bean. The bean container will then provide the GUI code for displaying that property.

Similarly, the *setColor()* method is a write accessor method – it identifies a property, Color, and enables you to set the value of that property. The method signature for write accessor methods must have the following pattern: public void setProperty(Type);

Again, "Type" is Color and "Property" is Color.

As it turns out, Bean containers can use the new Reflection API to find all the read and write accessor methods just by searching for methods that meet these patterns. This is why it can be said that TransitionalBean has the property "Color." (Note that a property needs only to have a read or a write accessor method to be considered a property.)

The Serializable Nature of TransitionalBean

TransitionalBean is serializable—it can be written to a file that will save the current value of *ourColor*. Later, you can deserialize that same file and you will have a new TransitionalBean object. This results because *ourColor* has been set to the value that was saved and not necessarily to orange.

Note

> The interface sunw.io.Serializable was intended for use with JDK 1.0.2. With JDK 1.1, java.io.Serializable should be used instead.
>
> An exception to the above is when a bean might be used in a Applet. Until the various browsers start supporting JFK 1.1, none of the new classes will work.

Serializing an object does not really have anything to do with properties, except that properties are almost always serialized. Generally, everything (all data members) gets serialized unless it is marked as transient.

 Note

> The keyword, transient, has been part of the java language, but has had no meaning until JDK 1.1. It provides a simple way of tagging those data members that are not to be serialized.

JAR files—the preferred way to organize Beans—have two different kinds of Beans: class files and serialized objects. Class files can be Beans, when the manifest file indicates that they are, and so can serialized objects. The convention here is that class files must have a file extension of .class, while files that contain serialized Beans must have a file extension of .ser.

Method java.Beans.Beans.instantiate loads Beans. Given the name of a Bean, *instantiate()* first looks for a file by that name that ends in .ser. If it finds that file, it deserializes it. If it doesn't find that file, it then tries to load a class with the same name as the Bean. If it finds that class, it then creates an instance of that class.

The nice thing about the *instantiate()* method is that you don't care whether the returned Bean is a new object with default data members, or whether it was created from an old Bean that was serialized and saved as a .ser file.

The *instantiate()* method proves quite helpful when you have a complex Bean with a lot of obscure properties. After you have those properties set the way you want them, you can save the Bean. In fact, you can have more than one .ser file based on the same class, with the parameters set differently for each file—and all this with very little application code. Figure 3.2 shows the TransitionalBean and its corresponding PropertySheet.

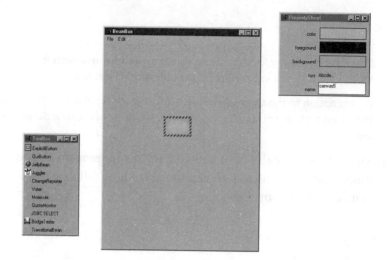

Figure 3.2

TransitionalBean and its corresponding properties.

The Custom Events of TransitionalBean

Class ButtonPushEvent defines a custom event derived from sunw.util.EventObject. This event will work with the new event model that is a part of JDK 1.1 and that is used almost exclusively by Beans. It was, however, intended for use under JDK 1.0.2.

With the advent of JDK 1.1, custom events should be derived from java.util.EventObject.

Another difficulty arises here with regard to some Bean containers because a custom event cannot be passed between Beans that come from different JAR files, even when that event is defined in both JAR files. The pass is impossible because for each JAR file there may be a different class loader. This is significant because even though the event classes have the same name, they are effectively different classes if they are from different class loaders.

Whenever possible, therefore, use standard events. In this case, java.awt.event. ActionEvent would serve just as well as ButtonPushEvent and would significantly increase the reusability of the code.

Note

> Class loaders are classes that derive from java.lang.ClassLoader. The primary role of a class loader is to define new classes that were not defined on the CLASSPATH. Each class loader effectively defines a name space of class definitions, so it is entirely possible to have different classes with the same name defined by different class loaders.

The TransitionalBean Listener Interface

Whenever you have a custom event, you need a listener interface. Listener interfaces are needed so that Bean containers can determine that Beans are able to register listeners. The section "The Bean OurButton" covers this in greater detail.

This listener interface extends sunw.util.EventListener. Again, this was done to allow Bean development under JDK 1.0.2. With JDK 1.1, listener interfaces should extend java.util.EventListener.

ButtonPushListener has a method, push, that takes a ButtonPushEvent parameter. In general, you need one method for each event that the listener is expected to handle.

A Wrapper for java.awt.Button

The class OurButton shows how to wrap a component that uses the old event model into a Bean. It also supports listener registration, required of any Bean that needs to be able to send events to other Beans.

For all practical intents, OurButton is a Bean. It does, however, fail in one important respect. If you look back at the manifest file for the TransientBean package, you will see that it is not listed as a Bean on the manifest. Not being listed as a Bean, a Bean container will handle it as an ordinary class, and it can not be accessed by the user.

Serializing OurButton

OurButton has the property Debug, whose state is kept in data member dbg. Serialization preserves the state of this property. (Note that this property is not used for anything. It simply shows how to define such a property.)

In the code for OurButton, the Vector listeners save pointers to event listeners. Because listeners are not transient, the event listeners added to listeners will be preserved when OurButton is serialized. (This appears to conflict section 5.3 of the Java Beans 1.0 API specification, but is consistent with all the other Beans examples.)

Note

> Class java.util.Vector is repeatedly used in the Beans examples for
> Listener registration. Vectors are little more than variable length arrays
> of objects.

A *boolean* Property

OurButton has two accessor methods for the Debug property: *isDebug()* and *setDebug()*.
isDebug() is a special form of the read accessor for boolean properties. The following
pattern is the alternate form of a read accessor:

```
public boolean isProperty();
```

In this case, "Property" is Debug. Conforming to this pattern would allow a bean container for OurButton to display the Debug property of OurButton.

Listener Registration for OurButton

Under the new event model, an object that sends events must register event listeners. For
this discussion, *listeners* are objects that have implemented the listener interface appropriate for the event that will be sent. When an event is generated, it is sent to all the
registered listeners.

Bean containers must be able to determine which event listeners each Bean can register.
This is accomplished with the Reflection API. For this to work, however, a Bean must
have both an *add()* and a *remove()* method for listener registration. These methods must
conform to the following patterns, respectively:

```
public void addTypeListener(TypeListener);
public void removeTypeListener(TypeListener);
```

The "Type" would be the type of event. In the case of OurButton, it registers
ButtonPushListeners. It, therefore, indicates this to the Bean container with the following
two methods:

```
public void addButtonPushListener(ButtonPushListener) {...}
public void removeButtonPushListener(ButtonPushListener) {...}
```

These methods add a ButtonPushListener to or remove a ButtonPushListener from the
Vector object, listeners.

The OurButton.handleEvent method is where an AWT event is processed. This is where the contents of listeners calls the *push()* method on each registered ButtonPushListener. One important consideration, however, is that the listeners object is not used directly.

Instead, a clone of listeners is created and then the elements of the clone are processed. This is done to reduce the likelihood of a deadlock, where one thread has locked OurButton and is attempting to call a synchronized method on another object locked by a second thread attempting to call a synchronized method on OurButton.

The Applet Bean Container for TransitionalBean

Flipper is a Bean container—or at least, it holds two Beans and connects them with an adapter. It does this programmatically instead of using reflection. It is not, therefore, capable of holding just any Bean. But from the perspective of the Beans, it is their container.

Flipper creates two beans. The first, jb, is an instance of TransitionalBean. The second bean is btn, which is an instance of OurButton.

Flipper is itself an adapter for jb; it implements ButtonPushListener. The Flipper.push method handles the ButtonPushEvent, changing the Color property of jb every time an event is received.

Flipper registers itself with btn as a listener with the following call to addButtonPushListener:

```
btn.addButtonPushListener(this);
```

When btn generates an event, it passes the event to Flipper. Flipper then changes the color of jb.

The important thing to note here is that, except for registering a listener, the jb and btn Beans have no knowledge of their Bean container or of each other. Everything outside of a Bean is the responsibility of that Bean's container.

The Bean JellyBean

JellyBean does not look like much. It changes color and the source files are quite short—in a word, marvelous! It is an easy to understand, working example of a Bean with a number of important features such as:

- ◆ event listeners

- ◆ bound properties

- ◆ constrained properties

- ◆ BeanInfo

Class JellyBean can be found in package sun.demo.jelly. It has a single source file: JellyBean.java. It also has a BeanInfo class: JellyBeanBeanInfo.

Validating JellyBean as a Bean

A manifest file is divided into a series of sections, each section dealing with a different file. The sections are each a series of tags, the first tag naming the file associated with that section. Beans must have a Java-Bean tag, and the manifest for the jelly package, jelly.mf, includes the Java-Bean tag for JellyBean.class. You can find it in the BDK directory Beanbox\unJAR.

Right now the BeanBox imposes a further restriction: BeanBox can only handle Beans derived from java.awt.Component. JavaSoft has indicated, however, that it will be removing this restriction in a subsequent release.

JellyBean Properties

JellyBean has two properties: Color and PriceInCents. These properties are defined by having either a *get()* or *set()* method that conforms to the following patterns, respectively:

```
Type getProperty() {...}
void setProperty(Type) {...}
```

If you have only a *get()* method, the property is read-only. Conversely, if you have only a *set()* method, the property is write-only.

The big deal about properties is that you do not need any code for the user interface. You really only need to have a variable to hold the value, a *get()* method to return the value, and a *set()* method to change the value.

The catch is that only a few basic types are supported by the JDK. You may, therefore, have to write your own editor class to support the types used by your application. The editor classes provided by the JDK are in the package sun.Beans.editors. The types supported are as follows:

boolean	Font
byte	int
Color	long
double	short
float	String

Figure 3.3 shows JellyBean and its corresponding PropertySheet.

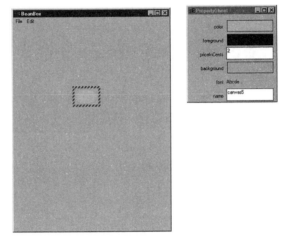

Figure 3.3

JellyBean and corresponding properties.

Listener Registration for JellyBean

The new JDK 1.1 event model provides a means of passing information from one object to another. This information is passed as an instance of a class that extends java.util.EventObject. The objects that receive the events must implement a listener interface for the events they receive. Listener interfaces must extend java.util.EventListener.

One complicating factor is that Beans may have no persistent knowledge about other objects. For an object to receive events, it must be registered with the Bean that generates the event.

JellyBean provides for the registration of two different kinds of listeners: PropertyChangeListener and VetoableChangeListener. Registration is defined by having both an *add()* and a *remove()* method that conform to the following patterns, respectively:

```
void addEventListener(ListenerType) {...}
void removeEventListener(ListenerType) {...}
```

To be capable of registering a PropertyChangeListener, JellyBean has the following methods:

```
void addPropertyChangeListener(PropertyChangeListener) {...}
void removePropertyChangeListener(PropertyChangeListener) {...}
```

Bound Properties for JellyBean

Occasionally, you may need to notify other Beans when a property has been changed. This is called a bound property. The Beans that need to receive notice of property changes must implement the interface java.Beans.PropertyChangeListener.

The *changes* variable in JellyBean references an instance of class java.Beans.PropertyChangeSupport to maintain the list of all registered property change listeners and to construct the java.Beans.PropertyChangeEvent object passed to these listeners. This involves only a few lines of code:

1. At the end of JellyBean.java, *changes* are initialized with an instance of PropertyChangesSupport as shown in the following lines of code:

   ```
   private PropertyChangesSupport chages = new
           PropertyChangeSupport(this);
   ```

2. In the *setColor() method*, the changes.*firePropertyChange()* method is called after the Color and PriceInCents properties have been changed. This makes Color a bound property as shown in the following lines of code:

   ```
   public void setColor(Color newColor) {
           Color oldColor = ourColor;
           ourColor = newColor;
           changes.firePropertyChange
                   ("color",oldColor,newColor);
           repaint();
   }
   ```

3. The *addPropertyChangeListener()* method calls the
changes.*addPropertyChangeListener()* method as shown in the following lines of
code:

```
public void addPropertyChangeListener
        (PropertyChangeListener l) {
    changes.addPropertyChangeListener(l);
}
```

4. The *removePropertyChangeListener()* method calls the
changes.*removePropertyChangeListener()* method as shown in the following lines of
code:

```
public void removePropertyChangeListener
        (PropertyChangeListener l) {
    changes.removePropertyChangeListener(l);
}
```

After a Bean has one bound property, it is only one more line of code in the *set()* method
for every additional bound property, keeping the overhead for bound properties at a
minimum.

Constrained Properties for JellyBean

Beans are designed to maximize code reuse; reuse, however, is a complication for
properties because the legal values for a property may depend on what the Bean is being
used for. When this happens, you have a constrained property.

Constrained properties let other objects veto changes before a property is changed.
Objects that need to receive notice of potential changes must implement interface
java.Beans.VetoableChangeListener. When a change is not legal, a
java.Beans.PropertyVetoException is thrown.

JellyBean has one vetoable property, PriceInCents. The code needed for vetoable properties is very similar to the code for bound properties as documented in the following set of
procedures:

1. The variable *vetos* is initialized with an instance of
java.beans.VetoableChangeSupport as shown in the following lines of code:

```
private VetoableChangeSupport vetos = new
    VetoableChangeSupport(this);
```

2. The *setPriceInCents()* method is declared as throwing PropertyVetoException. The vetos.fireVetoableChange method is then called before the change is made, as shown in the following lines of code:

```
public void setPriceInCents(int newPriceInCents)
        throws PropertyVetoException {
    int oldPriceInCents = ourPriceInCents;
    vetos.fireVetoableChange("priceInCents",
        new Integer(oldPriceInCents),
        new Integer(newPriceInCents));
    ourPriceInCents = newPriceInCents;
    changes.firePropertyChange("priceInCents",
        new Integer(oldPriceInCents),
        new Integer(newPriceInCents));
}
```

3. The *addVetoableChangeListener()* method calls the changes.*addVetoableChangeListener()* method as shown in the following lines of code:

```
public void addVetoableChangeListener
        (PropertyChangeListener l) {
    changes.addVetoableChangeListener(l);
}
```

4. The *removeVetoableChangeListener()* method calls the *changes.removeVetoableChangeListener()* method as shown in the following lines of code:

```
public void removeVetoableChangeListener
        (PropertyChangeListener l) {
    changes.removeVetoableChangeListener(l);
}
```

Giving JellyBean an Icon

The real power of Beans is in the code that you don't write. Beans are powerful and lightweight because of the use of reflection to second guess the intentions of the Bean programmer.

Several problems can arise from depending on reflection, as shown in the following list:

◆ The programmer needs consistency in how the reflection data is analyzed. Bean users may have different systems of analysis that might draw different conclusions about the programmer's intentions.

◆ The intentions of the programmer may differ from what is apparent from analyzing the code.

◆ Additional information may be needed that cannot be determined by reflecting on the code.

The answer to these problems is the class java.Beans.Introspector. This class provides the standard analysis of the reflection data. It also provides a simple hook (in the guise of the BeanInfo class) that enables the Bean programmer to override any part of that analysis and to provide supplemental information as well.

For every Bean, the programmer has the option of providing a BeanInfo class. The BeanInfo class need only meet two requirements:

◆ It must extend SimpleBeanInfo

◆ The class name must be the same as the class name of the bean, but with the addition of "BeanInfo"—in this case, JellyBeanBeanInfo

The file JellyBeanBeanInfo.java defines a BeanInfo class for JellyBean. It overrides the *getIcon()* method to provide four different icons. To do this, it uses the *SimpleBeanInfo.loadImage()* method to load the icons as shown in listing 3.1.

Listing 3.1: Loading icons for JellyBean

```
01.public class JellyBeanBeanInfo extends SimpleBeanInfo {
02.    public java.awt.Image getIcon(int iconKind) {
03.        if (iconKind == BeanInfo.ICON_COLOR_16x16) {
04.            java.awt.Image img =
05.                loadImage("JellyBeanIconColor16.gif");
06.            return img;
07.        }
08.        if (iconKind == BeanInfo.ICON_COLOR_32x32) {
09.            java.awt.Image img =
10.
11.            return img;
12.        }
13.        if (iconKind == BeanInfo.ICON_MONO_16x16) {
14.            java.awt.Image img =
15.                loadImage("JellyBeanIconMono16.gif");
16.            return img;
17.        }
18.        if (iconKind == BeanInfo.ICON_MONO_32x32) {
19.            java.awt.Image img =
```

continues

```
continued
20.
21.        return img;
22.    }
23.    return null;
24.  }
25.}
```

The resources named in the *loadImage()* method are typically loaded with a java.lang.ClassLoader. Because the class loader is responsible for locating the resource, you can have several Beans in an application that has been loaded with different class loaders, each with its own set of resources.

 Warning

> When creating a JAR file for a Bean, it must include all the resources used by that Bean and by its BeanInfo class. JAR files are covered in greater detail in Chapter 10, "Packaging Java Beans."

The Bean ChangeReporter

ChangeReporter is a subclass of TextField. It displays the property name and the new property value on the last PropertyChangeEvent that it was given. These events are produced when the bound property of a Bean is changed.

After you get past the initial comment, you are left with less than 20 lines of code. ChangeReporter is a good example of a Bean that works with the bound properties of other Beans.

 Note

> Class ChangeReporter can be found in the package sun.demo.misc. Note that there is only the one source file: ChangeReporter.java.

Serialization for ChangeReporter

ChangeReporter implements Serializable. This means that its current state—effectively, the state of TextField that it extends—can be saved and restored. And no, you will not find any code that supports this. It is all handled by the Java Virtual Machine!

Why then, do you even need to specify that ChangeReporter implements Serializable? It is how you tell the Java Virtual Machine that you have carefully reviewed your code and have specified transient on data members that are not to be serialized.

Accepting PropertyChangeEvents with ChangeReporter

Notice that ChangeReporter does not implement the PropertyChangeListener interface.

This means that ChangeReporter cannot be registered as a listener on an object that generates PropertyChangeEvents. Even so, the BeanBox enables you to connect JellyBean and ChangeReporter.

The BeanBox is a code generator. When JellyBean and ChangeReporter are connected, the BeanBox generates an adapter class. This adapter class implements PropertyChangeListener. Now, when the *propertyChange()* method is called on the adapter class, the adapter then calls *reportChange()* on the ChangeReporter Bean.

Having BeanBox generate adapter classes is pretty heavy, but there is an advantage. It means that any Bean with a method that accepts an event can be used as a listener for that event. Even more important, it means that you can have several different methods that accept the same event. Each of these methods can be wired to different Beans. For example, the Juggler Bean has two methods, start and stop, which are each wired to a different button.

 Tip

Personally, I don't like forcing Bean containers to generate code. It adds considerable overhead to the act of adding a Bean to such a container. There is, however, no real alternative—at least until *java.Beans .getInstanceOf()* is fully implemented.

Well okay, there is an alternative to having a Bean container generate code. Method *java.lang.reflect.Method.invoke()* can be used by a generic adapter to call the appropriate method, but you would still need a different generic adapter for each type of event. This is just too much complication for too little gain.

A simpler alternative is to require each Bean that does not implement the Listener interfaces to provide its own adapters. (Seems like a reasonable trade-off between the Bean programmer and the Bean container

continues

programmer). Remember that Beans, like BeanBox, can be containers. You might just be able to get around the need to have the container generate code when a Bean is added—albeit with some, hopefully small, loss of reuse.

Figure 3.4 shows the ChangeReports Bean in the BeanBox application and its corresponding PropertySheet.

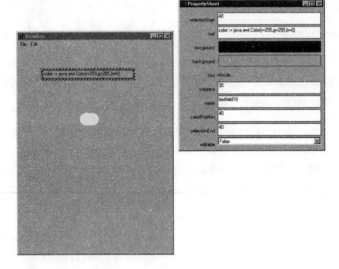

Figure 3.4

ChangeReports Bean and corresponding properties.

Using ChangeReporter Programmatically

Now it is time to review that header comment in ChangeReporter's source code. In that comment, you will find class DemoChangeReporter.

DemoChangeReporter is a standalone program for demonstrating ChangeReporter. In addition to having data members and methods, this class defines another class, PropertyChangeAdapter.

Nested classes, at least the ones that are not static, have a second *this* member to reference the enclosing object. This second *this* member is used implicitly in the propertyChange method to refer to reporter—a data member of the enclosing object. When making an explicit reference, the new *this* is qualified by the name of the enclosing object. So for PropertyChangeAdapter, the fully qualified name is DemoChangeReporter.this.

If it looks like nested classes were made for adapters, you are pretty close to the truth. Using nested classes, the code for adapters is so clean that it is sometimes difficult to see how the code works. This is one area where Java and C++ diverge. Nested classes are a very effective language extension.

For a stand-alone example of nested classes, look at DemoNestedClasses.java in package sun.demo.misc. This is a program that uses the Juggler Bean. It has two ActionListener adapters and is a good example of why adapters are necessary.

The Bean Voter

Another delightfully brief Bean, Voter, sports a simple Boolean property and shows how to reject proposed changes to constrained properties defined on other Beans.

 Note

> Class Voter can be found in the package sun.demo.misc. There is only one source file, Voter.java.

VetoAll Property of the Voter Bean

Voter property *VetoAll* sets a bit that governs how it treats constrained property changes. The value of this bit is displayed as "Yes" or "No." Almost no code is needed to do this as shown in the following set of procedures:

1. The boolean variable vetoAll is declared with an initial value of true. Initialization of property variables to default variables is required, because a property will likely be displayed before it is set to a different value as shown in the following line of code:

   ```
   private boolean vetoAll = true;
   ```

2. The presence of the *void setVetoAll(boolean) {...}* method indicates to the Bean's container that *VetoAll* is a writable property. This method sets the vetoAll flag as well as the text of the label that this class extends as shown in the following lines of code:

   ```
   public void setVetoAll(boolean x)
   {
       vetoAll = x;
       setText((vetoAll) ? "No" : :"Yes");
   }
   ```

3. The presence of the *boolean getVetoAll() {...}* method indicates to the Beans container that *VetoAll* is a readable property. This method returns the value of the boolean variable vetoAll as shown in the following lines of code:

```
public boolean getVetoAll()
{
    return vetoAll;
}
```

Vetos Property Changes

Voter identifies itself as a candidate for a VetoableChange adapter by having a method—in this case, *vetoableChange()*—that takes a *PropertyChangeEvent* parameter and that is declared as throwing a *PropertyVetoException,* as shown in the following lines of code:

```
public void vetoableChange(PropertyChangeEvent x)
    throws PropertyVetoException
{
    if (vetoAll)
        throw new PropertyVetoException("NO!", x);
}
```

The *vetoableChange()* method either throws the *PropertyVetoException* or it doesn't, depending on the value of vetoAll. Note, however, the constructor of PropertyVetoException. This exception is unusual in that it takes a second parameter—the *PropertyChangeEvent* being vetoed.

Figure 3.5 shows the Voter Bean in the BeanBox application and its corresponding PropertySheet.

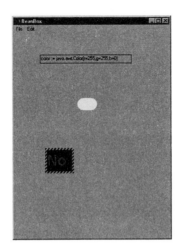

Figure 3.5

Voter Bean and corresponding properties.

The Bean OurButton

The sun.demo.buttons.OurButton Bean is derived from the java.awt.Canvas class. This makes OurButton a "from-scratch" AWT component. It is quite different from the sun.demo.transitional.OurButton Bean previously discussed, which was derived from java.awt.Button.

This new OurButton is a little longer than any of the Beans you have looked at so far, but it includes some interesting code (particularly the ActionListener registration). This is important because it shows how to register listeners when there is no support class that is the equivalent of PropertyChangeSupport or VetoableChangeSupport that you saw in JellyBean. However, the support class java.awt.AWTEventMulticaster can be used with Component, Container, Focus, Key, Mouse, MouseMotion, Window, Action, Item, Adjustment, and Text Listeners.

Unfortunately, OurButton uses the JDK 1.0.2 style of event handling for mouse and keyboard events.

Note

Class OurButton is found in the sun.demo.buttons package. It has a single source file of OurButton.java.

Registering ActionListeners for OurButton

Without a support class to handle ActionListener registration, a Vector, *pushListeners*, is used.

The Bean's container is notified that this class handles ActionListener registration by the presence of the *add()* and *remove()* methods shown in the following lines of code, respectively:

```
void addActionListener(ActionListener) {...}
void removeActionListener(ActionListener) {...}.
```

These methods add or remove the listener to pushListeners.

The *fireAction()* method shown in listing 3.2 is where the ActionListeners are sent an ActionEvent, but it starts with a debug statement. Debug is a boolean property that turns the debug output on or off.

Listing 3.2: Sending ActionEvents to ActionListeners with fireAction()

```
01.public void fireAction() {
02.    if (debug) {
03.        System.out.println("Button " + getLabel() + " [ccc]pressed.");
04.    }
05.    Vector targets;
06.    synchronized (this) {
07.        targets = (Vector) pushListeners.clone();
08.    }
09.    ActionEvent actionEvt = new ActionEvent(this, 0, null);
10.
11.        ActionListener target = (ActionListener)targets.elementAt(i);
12.        target.actionPerformed(actionEvt);
13.    }
14.    Component parent = getParent();
15.    if (parent != null) {
16.        parent.postEvent(new Event(this, Event.MOUSE_DOWN, null));
17.}
```

After the debug statement, *pushListeners* is cloned. This is important for the following reasons:

♦ It keeps the time that OurButton is locked to a minimum.

♦ It prevents deadlocks caused by a listener attempting to call a method on OurButton while OurButton is locked.

An ActionEvent is created with a reference to the OurButton object. Then, the *actionPerformed()* method is called on each registered listener, passing the same ActionEvent to each ActionListener in turn.

Finally, a MOUSE_DOWN event is posted to the parent of OurButton. This last process uses the old event model.

OurButton Bound Properties with Interaction

The properties of OurButton are detailed in the following list:

♦ **Debug:** turns the debug statement in fireAction

♦ **LargeFont:** selects between font sizes 12 and 18

♦ **FontSize:** sets the size of the font

♦ **Font:** a write-only property that sets the font

♦ **Label:** changes the text displayed

♦ **Forground:** a write-only property for changing the foreground color

♦ **Background:** a write-only property for changing the background color

All of these are bound properties that call *firePropertyChange()* on the PropertyChangeSupport object, *changes*. The code for the FontSize property is shown in listing 3.3.

Listing 3.3: FontSize property

```
01.public void setFontSize(int x) {
02.    Font old = getFont();
03.    setFont(new Font(old.getName(), old.getStyle(), x));
04.    changes.firePropertyChange("fontSize", new Integer(old.getSize()),
```

continues

```
continued
05.        new Integer(x));
06.}
07.
08.public int getFontSize() {
09.    return getFont().getSize();
10.}
```

The required *addPropertyChangeListener()* and *removePropertyChangeListener()* methods are present and call the same method on changes as shown in the following lines of code, respectively:

```
public void addPropertyChangeListener(PropertyChangeListener l) {
    changes.addPropertyChangeListener(l);
}

public void removePropertyChangeListener(PropertyChangeListener l) {
    changes.removePropertyChangeListener(l);
}
```

Of particular note is the *setLargeFont()* method, which demonstrates property interaction on bound properties. This method calls *setFont()* before calling changes.firePropertyChange. Because *setFont()* also calls *changes.firePropertyChange*, each listener is effectively called twice when the LargeFont property is called.

Figure 3.6 shows the OurButton Bean in the BeanBox application and its corresponding PropertySheet.

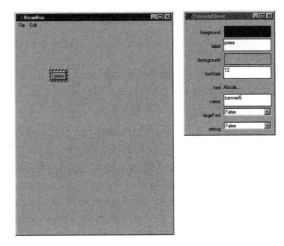

Figure 3.6

OurButton Bean and corresponding properties.

The ExplicitButton Bean

The ExplicitButton Bean has no data and no methods. It extends OurButton and that's it—well, almost. It does have a BeanInfo class, and that class in turn specifies a Customizer class. It turns out that this Bean has some interesting code after all, as shown in the following line:

```
public class ExplicitButton extends OurButton {
}
```

 Note

> Class ExplicitButton can be found in package sun.demo.buttons. The three source files for this class are as follows: ExplicitButton.java, ExplicitButtonBeanInfo.java, and OurButtonCustomizer.java.

A BeanInfo class must have the same name as a Bean class, extended with "BeanInfo." It should also extend java.Beans.SimpleBeanInfo as shown in the following lines of code. It really only needs to implement interface BeanInfo, but it is usually easier to just extend SimpleBeanInfo.

```
public class ExplicitButtonBeanInfo extends SimpleBeanInfo {
    .
    .
    .
}
```

BeanInfo.getPropertyDescriptors for ExplicitButtonBean

Class java.Beans.PropertyDescriptor enables you to specify the name of a property. You must also specify whether the property is bound or constrained. You can also specify the access methods for the property and even a custom editor for that property.

Remember that the Beans container will provide a GUI for a Bean based on what it had inferred from the information it has gathered about the Bean using the Reflection API. It is only thru a BeanInfo class for the Bean that explicit information can be given. For example, the OurButton class has inherited from java.awt.Canvas many methods that conform to Beans method patterns. This results in a confusing list of options being presented by the Beans container. The ExplicitButtonBeanInfo class restricts the Beans container to only a few appropriate methods, making the bean far easier to configure. Listing 3.4 defines property descriptors for ExplicitButtonBean.

Listing 3.4: Defining property descriptors for ExplicitButtonBean

```
01.public PropertyDescriptor[] getPropertyDescriptors() {
02.    try {
03.        PropertyDescriptor background =
04.                new PropertyDescriptor("background", beanClass);
05.        PropertyDescriptor foreground =
06.                new PropertyDescriptor("foreground", beanClass);
07.        PropertyDescriptor font =
08.                new PropertyDescriptor("font", beanClass);
09.        PropertyDescriptor label =
10.                new PropertyDescriptor("label", beanClass);
11.
12.        background.setBound(true);
13.        foreground.setBound(true);
14.        font.setBound(true);
15.        label.setBound(true);
16.
17.        PropertyDescriptor rv[] = {background, foreground, font, label};
```

```
18.        return rv;
19.    } catch (IntrospectionException e) {
20.        throw new Error(e.toString());
21.    }
22.}
```

For ExplicitButton, limit the properties to background, foreground, font, and label. All four are specified as being bound properties.

As a point of interest, look at the new syntax used to initialize beanClass and customizerClass at the end of ExplicitButtonBeanInfo. Classes now have a static data member, class, which can be used in place of the old static method Class.forName(String className).

```
private final static Class beanClass = ExplicitButton.class;
private final static Class customizerClass = OurButtonCustomizer.class;
```

BeanInfo.getDefaultPropertyIndex for ExplicitButtonBean

The getDefaultPropertyIndex() method specifies that property 3, label, is the default property as shown in the following lines of code:

```
public int getDefaultPropertyIndex() {
    return 3;
}
```

BeanInfo.getEventSetDescriptors for ExplicitButtonBean

Class java.Beans.EventSetDescriptor enables you to specify the events generated by a Bean, how those events are to be processed, and the display name.

For ExplicitButton, the event names are set to "button push" and "bound property change" as defined in listing 3.5.

Listing 3.5: Setting events for ExplicitButtonBean

```
01.public EventSetDescriptor[] getEventSetDescriptors() {
02.    try {
03.        EventSetDescriptor push = new [ccc]EventSetDescriptor(beanClass,
04.                "actionPerformed",
05.                java.awt.event.ActionListener.class,
06.                "actionPerformed");
07.
08.        EventSetDescriptor changed = new EventSetDescriptor(beanClass,
09.                "propertyChange",
10.                java.beans.PropertyChangeListener.class,
11.                "propertyChange");
12.
13.        push.setDisplayName("button push");
14.        changed.setDisplayName("bound property change");
15.
16.        EventSetDescriptor[] rv = { push, changed};
17.        return rv;
18.    } catch (IntrospectionException e) {
19.        throw new Error(e.toString());
20.    }
21.}
```

BeanInfo.getIcon for ExplicitButtonBean

Two icons are given for ExplicitBean. These resources are located by the Bean's class loader as defined in listing 3.6.

Listing 3.6: Defining icons for ExplicitButtonBean

```
01.public java.awt.Image getIcon(int iconKind) {
02.    if (iconKind == BeanInfo.ICON_MONO_16x16 ||
03.        iconKind == BeanInfo.ICON_COLOR_16x16 ) {
04.        java.awt.Image img = [ccc]loadImage("ExplicitButtonIcon16.gif");
05.        return img;
06.    }
07.    if (iconKind == BeanInfo.ICON_MONO_32x32 ||
08.        iconKind == BeanInfo.ICON_COLOR_32x32 ) {
09.        java.awt.Image img = [ccc]loadImage("ExplicitButtonIcon32.gif");
10.        return img;
11.    }
12.    return null;
13.}
```

BeanInfo.getBeanDescriptor for ExplicitButtonBean

This method identifies the customizer to be used with a Bean. In this case, the class OurButtonCustomizer is given as the customizer for ExplicitButton as shown in the following lines of code.

```
public BeanDescriptor getBeanDescriptor() {
    return new BeanDescriptor(beanClass, customizerClass);
}
```

Customizers for ExplicitButtonBean

Customizers are intended for use with complex Beans that require something more than a property sheet to configure. OurBeansCustomizer serves strictly as an example of how to program a customizer. Using a customizer to set a single text field is overkill! An edit Bean, for example, might need a customizer if the options and preferences were extensive. And having the configuration capability in a customizer that is separate from the Bean itself keeps the Bean code to a minimum.

Customizers must extend (directly or indirectly) java.awt.Component. In the case of OurBeanCustomizer, it extends Panel. Customizers must also implement interface java.Beans.Customizer. Although there is no SimpleCustomizer class like there is for BeanInfo, you can just return null for Customizer methods where you want the default behavior.

The customizer class of a Bean must be specified in that Bean's BeanInfo. Note that this allows more than one Bean to use the same customizer class, allowing a rather complex GUI to be shared by a family of Beans that are configured the same way. Since a customizer may be more complex than the Beans it configures, this could mean significant code reuse.

The key method here is *setObject()*, where the target Bean of the customizer is identified.

As with all customizers, OurButtonCustomizer must send a PropertyChangeEvent object to all PropertyChangeEventListeners each time there is a change to a property as described in the following set of procedures:

1. The PropertyChangeSupport object, support, is defined with a reference to the customizer as shown in the following lines of code:

```
Private PropertyChangeSupport support = new
    PropertyChangeSupport(this);
```

2. The required *add()* and *remove()* methods are present. These methods call the *add()* and *remove()* methods on support as shown in the following lines of code, respectively:

```
public void addPropertyChangeListener(PropertyChangeListener l) {
    support.addPropertyChangeListener(l);
}

public void removePropertyChangeListener(PropertyChangeListener l) {
    support.removePropertyChangeListener(l);
}
```

3. With each change to labelField, support.firePropertyChange is called after the target's label field is updated as shown in the following lines of code:

```
public boolean handleEvent(Event evt) {
    if (evt.id == Event.KEY_RELEASE && evt.target == labelField) {
        String txt = labelField.getText();
        target.setLabel(txt);
        support.firePropertyChange("", null, null);
    }
    return (super.handleEvent(evt));
}
```

Figure 3.7 shows the ExplicitButton Bean in the BeanBox application and its corresponding PropertySheet.

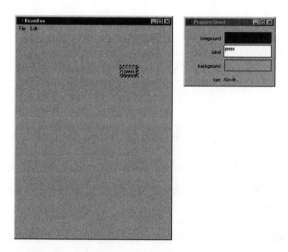

Figure 3.7

ExplicitButton Bean and corresponding properties.

The Bean Juggler

Juggler is a simple animation class. It demonstrates the restoration of transient data when the Bean is deserialized.

 Note

> Class Juggler can be found in the sun.demo.juggler package. It has a single source file, Juggler.java. It also has a BeanInfo class, JugglerBeanInfo.

Juggler Properties

Juggler has only one property, *AnimationRate()* for the Juggler Bean. The accessor methods *getAnimationRate()* and *setAnimationRate()* consist of a single line of code to return or set the rate of animation. Note that the rate is not transient, meaning that it is serializable.

Accepting ActionEvents with Juggler

Juggler has two methods that accept ActionEvents: *start()* and *stop()*. Note that in both cases, the event parameter serves only to identify the method to the reflection analysis of the Bean container. The event itself is not used.

Serialization with Special Handling

There are two transient data members, images and animationThread, that must be restored when the Bean is deserialized. This is accomplished by providing both *writeObject()* and *readObject()* methods.

Care must be taken to have the signatures of these methods exactly correct so that the serialization process will recognize that they are present. In both cases, a default method on the stream parameter is called to handle the serialization. In the case of *readObject()*, however, there is a subsequent call to *initAnimation()* to restore images and animationThread.

BeanInfo.getIcon for Juggler

Juggler also has a BeanInfo class, identified as such by the name Juggler with BeanInfo appended to it. The JugglerBeanInfo class extends SimpleBeanInfo to enable everything to default except for the one overridden method, *getIcon()*.

The method *getIcon()* specifies the name of a resource holding an icon. This resource is loaded by *loadImage()*, which in turn uses the Beans ClassLoader to retrieve the resource.

Figure 3.8 shows the Juggler Bean in the BeanBox application and its corresponding PropertySheet.

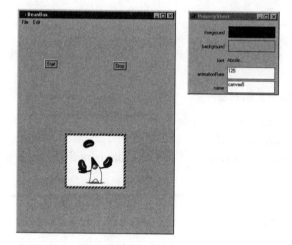

Figure 3.8

Juggler Bean and corresponding properties.

The Bean BridgeTester

BridgeTester is definitely the odd one of the lot—a little bit of everything, with a few dead ends thrown in for good measure. Note, however, that this customizer may well be worth a closer look. Even the custom event may clarify a few things. BridgeTester may also serve as a good reference for properties because it has int, double, short, float, char, byte, string, and Boolean properties—effectively, every kind of supported property except for the properties that can be found in OurButton, font and color.

 Note

Class BridgeTester can be found in package sun.demo.test. It has three source files: BridgeTester.java, BridgeTesterEvent.java, and BridgeTesterListener. It also has a BeanInfo class, BridgeTesterBeanInfo, and a Customizer called BridgeTesterCustomizer.

The panel for BridgeTester has four buttons and eight Labels. The first button fires the custom event; the other three do not do anything. (Just one of those dead ends mentioned previously.) The labels display the various properties. Figure 3.9 shows the BridgeTester Bean in the BeanBox application and its corresponding PropertySheet.

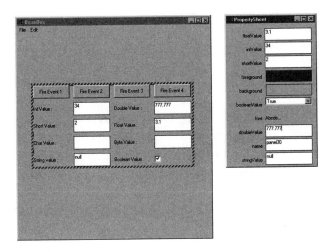

Figure 3.9

BridgeTester Bean and corresponding properties.

Bound Properties for BridgeTester

The properties of BridgeTester can all be read and written to. The Bean container can easily determine this by using the Reflection API because each property has accessor methods with the following signatures:

```
public Type getProperty();
public void setProperty(Type);
```

The one exception to the get/set property pattern is the Boolean property, *BooleanValue*, that has the method *isBooleanValue()* in place of the method *getBooleanValue()*. This conforms to the alter pattern for getProperty, which is only valid for boolean properties as shown in the following lines of code:

```
public boolean isBooleanValue() {
    return booleanValue;
}
```

The eight properties of this Bean are all bound properties. Bound properties notify PropertyChangeListeners when a property is changed. This allows other beans to be notified when a property changes. This notification of changes is detailed in the following lines of code:

```
public void setBooleanValue(boolean newValue) {
    boolean oldValue = booleanValue;
    booleanValue = newValue;
    changes.firePropertyChange("booleanValue", new Boolean(oldValue),
        new Boolean(newValue));
}
```

The PropertyChangeSupport object, *changes*, tracks the registered PropertyChangeListeners. This object will also generate the necessary PropertyChangeEvent object when a property change occurs, and will send the event object to each of the registered listeners.

The Bean container must recognize that this Bean has bound events. To that end, both an *add()* and a *remove()* method must be present with the following signatures, respectively:

```
public void addPropertyChangeListener(PropertyChangeListener);
public void removePropertyChangeListener(PropertyChangeListener);
```

Each of these methods are present on the BridgeTester Bean. They call the same method on the *changes* object as shown in the following lines of code, respectively:

```
public void addPropertyChangeListener(PropertyChangeListener l) {
    changes.addPropertyChangeListener(l);
}
```

```
public void removePropertyChangeListener(PropertyChangeListener l) {
    changes.removePropertyChangeListener(l);
}
```

The final requirement is that each of the bound properties call *changes.firePropertyChange*, passing the property name, the old value, and the new value to the object *changes* after the property has been updated.

Constrained Properties for BridgeTester

BridgeTester has one constrained property: *IntValue*. This means that other Beans will have the opportunity to object to a new value before the property is changed.

The code for constrained properties is very similar to bound properties. Also note that *IntValue* is both a bound and a constrained property. The VetoableChangeSupport object, *vetos*, is used in place of the object *changes*. The only difference between *changes* and *vetos* is that the *vetos.fireVetoableChange()* method may throw a *PropertyVetoException*. The code for the IntValue constrained property is illustrated in listing 3.7.

Listing 3.7: IntValue constrained property

```
01.public int getIntValue() {
02.    return intValue;
03.}
04.
05.public void setIntValue(int newValue) throws PropertyVetoException
06.{
07.    int oldValue = intValue;
08.    vetos.fireVetoableChange("intValue", new Integer(oldValue),
09.        new Integer(newValue));
10.
11.    intField.setText(String.valueOf(intValue));
12.    changes.firePropertyChange("intValue", newInteger(oldValue),
13.        new Integer(newValue));
14.}
```

The *addVetoableChangeListener()* and *removeVetoableChangeListener()* methods shown in the following code are virtually identical to the *add()* and *remove()* methods for PropertyChangeListeners:

```
public void addVetoableChangeListener(VetoableChangeListener l) {
    vetos.addVetoableChangeListener(l);
}

public void removeVetoableChangeListener(VetoableChangeListener l) {
    vetos.removeVetoableChangeListener(l);
}
```

The two real differences between a bound and a constrained property can be found in the *BridgeTester.setIntValue()* method. This method throws *PropertyVetoException*, which indicates the new property value was rejected. vetos.fireVetoableChange, which is the source of the PropertyVetoException, is called before the change is made to the property rather than after the change is made.

Custom Events for BridgeTester

Custom events are vital because they enable you to expand on the data being passed between Beans, while retaining all the flexibility inherent in having the Bean container manage the relationships between the Beans. There is, however, a limit to the use of custom events.

 Note

> The JAR file is the appropriate package for shipping Beans. JAR files hold the class files, the serialized objects, and the resources needed by the Beans held in the JAR (for example, gif files for icons). The JAR also has a manifest file that identifies that classes or serialized files are Beans. But a Bean container may choose to use a different ClassLoader for each JAR file, potentially impacting on the use of custom events.
>
> So long as a custom event is being passed between Beans from the same JAR, no problem arises. If the Bean container uses multiple ClassLoaders, however, events that pass between Beans from different JARs need to be defined as system classes (in the class path). With that said, take a look at that custom event.

The custom event is defined in the BridgeTesterEvent.java class file shown in listing 3.8. It extends class java.util.EventObject (required) and has two read/write parameters: stringValue and intValue. A key requirement here is the source parameter on the constructor. It is passed to the constructor for EventObject.

Listing 3.8: BridgeTesterEvent class

```
01.public class BridgeTesterEvent extends java.util.EventObject {
02.
03.   BridgeTesterEvent(Object source, String stringValue, int
➥intValue) {
04.      super(source);
05.      this.stringValue = stringValue;
06.      this.intValue = intValue;
07.   }
08.
09.   public void setStringValue(String stringValue) {
10.
11.   }
12.
13.   public void setIntValue(int intValue) {
```

```
14.     this.intValue = intValue;
15.  }
16.
17.  public String getString() {return stringValue;}
18.  public int getIntValue() { return intValue; }
19.
20.
21.  protected String stringValue;
22.  protected int    intValue;
23.}
```

When you define a custom event, you need to define a listener interface for that event as well (this is essential for the add and remove listener methods needed for listener registration). The BridgeTesterListener.java file defines this listener interface. It extends the java.util.EventListener class (required) and has a method, eventNumber1, that is to be called when an event is fired as shown in the following code. This is needed by the Bean container to be able to construct the adapter classes that may be needed when Beans are wired together.

```
public interface BridgeTesterListener extends java.util.EventListener {

    void eventNumber1(BridgeTesterEvent ble);

}
```

Returning to BridgeTester.java, a java.util.Vector, *listeners*, tracks the registered listeners for BridgeTesterEvents. You also have the usual required methods for listener registration as shown in the following lines of code:

```
// Event Listeners handling
    public synchronized void addBridgeTesterListener(BridgeTester
⮡Listener1) {
    listeners.addElement(1);
    }

    public synchronized void removeBridgeTesterListener(BridgeTester
⮡Listener 1) {
    listeners.removeElement(1);
    }
```

The *add()* and *remove()* methods call addElement and removeElement on *listeners* to maintain the list of listeners registered for BridgeTesterEvents.

The *BridgeTester.fireEvent* method in listing 3.9 is called when a MOUSE_UP is detected over event1Button. This method is carefully written to minimize deadlocks. A clone of listeners is made. And BridgeTester is only locked while the clone is made. The clone is then used to call method *eventNumber1()* on each of the registered listeners.

Listing 3.9: BridgeTester.fireEvent method

```
01.private void fireEvent() {
02.      BridgeTesterEvent evt = new BridgeTesterEvent(this,
➥stringValue, intValue);
03.      java.util.Vector listenerObjects;
04.      synchronized(this) {
05.          listenerObjects = (java.util.Vector) listeners.clone();
06.      }
07.
08.      for (int i=0; i<listenerObjects.size();i++) {
09.          BridgeTesterListener l = (BridgeTesterListener)
➥listenerObjects.elementAt(i);
10.
11.      }
12.  }
13.
14.   public boolean handleEvent(Event evt) {
15.    if (evt.id == Event.MOUSE_UP && evt.target == event1Button) {
16.        fireEvent();
17.    }
18.    return (super.handleEvent(evt));
19.  }
```

BeanInfo.getIcon for BridgeTester

By virtue of its name, BridgeTesterBeanInfo will be identified by a Bean container as the BeanInfo class for BridgeTester. This class extends java.Beans.SimpleBeanInfo (the usual way of doing things) and overrides the *getIcon()* method to provide four alternative icons as shown in listing 3.10.

Listing 3.10: Providing alternative icons for the BridgeTester Bean

```
01.public java.awt.Image getIcon(int iconKind) {
02.     if (iconKind == BeanInfo.ICON_COLOR_16x16) {
03.         java.awt.Image img = loadImage("BridgeTesterIconColor16.gif");
04.         return img;
```

```
05.       }
06.       if (iconKind == BeanInfo.ICON_COLOR_32x32) {
07.           java.awt.Image img = loadImage("BridgeTesterIconColor32.gif");
08.           return img;
09.       }
10.
11.           java.awt.Image img = loadImage("BridgeTesterIconMono16.gif");
12.           return img;
13.       }
14.       if (iconKind == BeanInfo.ICON_MONO_32x32) {
15.           java.awt.Image img = loadImage("BridgeTesterIconMono32.gif");
16.           return img;
17.       }
18.       return null;
19.}
```

Method *SimpleBeanInfo.loadImage* is used to load the needed GIF files. These are considered to be resources, and the ClassLoader that was used to load BridgeTesterBeanInfo is given the responsibility of locating these resources.

BeanInfo.getBeanDescriptor for BridgeTester

BridgeTesterBeanInfo also overrides method *getBeanDescriptor()*. This method returns a new java.Beans.BeanDescriptor object constructed to define class BridgeTesterCustomizer as the customizer for BridgeTester, as shown in the following lines of code:

```
public BeanDescriptor getBeanDescriptor() {
    return new BeanDescriptor(BridgeTester.class,
                        BridgeTesterCustomizer.class);
}
```

Customizer for BridgeTester

As shown in the previous section, the BeanInfo for BridgeTester specifies that BridgeTesterCustomizer is the customizer for objects of class BridgeTester.

A customizer is a design-time object used to configure a complex Bean, especially when the default property sheet is inadequate. In this case, you are looking at sample code, because BridgeTester is not anywhere near complicated enough to justify having a customizer.

BridgeTesterCustomizer extends java.awt.Panel. (It is required to extend java.awt.Component.) It also implements Customizer (required). There is also a null constructor (also a requirement) as shown in the following lines of code.

```
public class BridgeTesterCustomizer extends Panel implements Customizer {

    public BridgeTesterCustomizer() {
     setLayout(null);
    }

     .
     .
     .

}
```

The *setObject()* method in listing 3.11 identifies the target object that this customizer is responsible for configuring. For every instance of a customizer object, there will always be one target object to configure. This is also a great place to define the display. In this case, two labels and two text fields are used to update two of the target's properties.

```
Listing 3.11: setObject() method for the BridgeTester Bean

01.public void setObject(Object obj) {
02.      target = (BridgeTester) obj;
03.
04.      Label t1 = new Label("String :", Label.RIGHT);
05.      add (t1);
06.      t1.reshape(10, 5, 60, 30);
07.
08.      labelField = new TextField(target.getStringValue(), 20);
09.      add(labelField);
10.
11.
12.      Label t2 = new Label("Double :", Label.RIGHT);
13.      add(t2);
14.      t2.reshape(10,40,60,70);
15.
16.      doubleField = new TextField(String.valueOf(target
➥.getDoubleValue()), 20);
17.      add(doubleField);
18.      doubleField.reshape(80,40,100,70);
19.
20.}
```

A customizer is also required to register PropertyChangeListeners and to notify them when a change to the target object has occurred. This is managed by the PropertyChangeSupport object, *support*, shown in the following line of code.

```
private PropertyChangeSupport support = new PropertyChangeSupport(this);
```

The methods *addPropertyChangeListener()* and *removePropertyChangeListener()* are defined in the Customizer interface that BridgeTesterCustomizer implements. These methods call the *add()* and *remove()* methods on support as shown in the following lines of code, respectively.

```
public void addPropertyChangeListener(PropertyChangeListener l) {
    support.addPropertyChangeListener(l);
}

public void removePropertyChangeListener(PropertyChangeListener l) {
    support.removePropertyChangeListener(l);
}
```

The BridgeTesterCustomizer.handleEvent in listing 3.12 looks for KEY_RELEASEs over its two TextFields: lableField and doubleField. When detected, it updates the corresponding property on the target object and then calls *support.firePropertyChange*. Note that the try/catch for NumberFormatException will catch any conversion errors and reset doubleValue to the last valid value passed to the target object.

Listing 3.12: BridgeTesterCustomizer.handleEvent

```
01.public boolean handleEvent(Event evt) {
02.     if (evt.id == Event.KEY_RELEASE && evt.target == labelField) {
03.         String txt = labelField.getText();
04.         target.setStringValue(txt);
05.         support.firePropertyChange("", null, null);
06.     }
07.     if (evt.id == Event.KEY_RELEASE && evt.target == doubleField) {
08.         String txt = doubleField.getText();
09.         try {
10.
11.         } catch (java.lang.NumberFormatException e) {
12.             doubleField.setText(String.valueOf(target.getDoubleValue()));
13.         }
14.         support.firePropertyChange("", null, null);
15.     }
16.     return (super.handleEvent(evt));
17.}
```

Note that if the property being updated was IntValue, you would have needed to catch PropertyVetoException, because IntValue is a constrained property.

The Bean Molecule (extends Panel)

The Bean Molecule displays and rotates 3D representations of molecules. Molecule is a real demonstration Bean, and the code is nicely polished. Its use of a custom property is direct and appropriate. And validation of the version number in the deserialization logic is a very nice touch indeed.

 Note

> Class Molecule can be found in the package sun.demo.molecule. It has four source files: Molecule.java, Atom.java, Matrix3D.java, and XYZChemModel. It also has a BeanInfo class, MoleculeBeanInfo, and a custom property editor: MoleculeNameEditor.

Figure 3.10 shows the Molecule Bean in the BeanBox application and its corresponding PropertySheet.

Figure 3.10

Molecule Bean and corresponding properties.

Properties for Molecule

The only property that Molecule has is MoleculeName. You will find the code for this property at the end of Molecule.java. Here you will find String moleculeName set to an initial value of "HyaluronicAcid."

The Bean container recognizes MoleculeName as a read/write property because of the pattern of the accessor methods that was used:

```
public Type getProperty() {...}
public void setProperty(Type) {...}
```

In this case "Type" is String, one of the supported property types, and "Property" is MoleculeName. But the BeanInfo class for Molecule overrides this default analysis. This is discussed in more detail in the section "BeanInfo.getPropertyDescriptors for Molecule."

Method *getMoleculeName()* just returns the current value of moleculeName. The *setMoleculeName()* method is more interesting. After updating moleculeName, all other member variables are reset and *repaint()* is called. The *repaint()* method ultimately calls Molecule.paint. At this point, *initialize()* is called to load the new molecule and then the figure is drawn.

Accepting ActionEvents with Molecule

Two methods in Molecule accept an ActionEvent: *rotateX()* and *rotateY()*. The Bean container will find these methods by using reflection and, when a Molecule Bean is connected to a source of ActionEvents, the Bean container will generate the necessary adapter class. The adapter class implements the java.awt.eventActionListener interface and calls the *rotateX()* or *rotateY()* method on the Molecule Bean.

Neither *rotateX()* nor *rotateY()* care about the ActionEvent they receive; any ActionEvent object will serve. Just receiving an event is sufficient to drive the rotation.

Serialization with Special Handling for Molecule

The normal serialization would simply not be reasonable for Molecule. First, all the data members except for ourVersion and moleculeName would need to be marked transient. The *paint()* method could determine that backBuffer was null and force the call to *initialize()*. Second, no version check would occur.

Using the special serialization methods in listing 3.13 gives the Molecule Bean much more flexibility. To use these methods, however, it is important that the exact signature for *writeObject* and *readObject* are used. If the signatures are not quite right, the normal serialization process will take place.

In *writeObject*, only ourVersion and moleculeName are serialized. When readObject is subsequently called to restore the Bean, first reset is called to clear all the data members. Then the previously serialized version number is compared to ourVersion and an IOException is thrown if the versions don't match. If they don't match, subsequent serialized data elements may not match. Worse, an invalid molecule name might be read, resulting in an unexpected result later. In general, version numbers are a great idea. Only after the version number has been checked is moleculeName read. The next time *paint( )* is called, it will see that backBuffer is null and will call initialize to read the data describing the molecule.

Listing 3.13: Molecule Bean serialization support

```
01. // Support for serialization.  KGH 6/2/96
02.
03.    private void writeObject(java.io.ObjectOutputStream s)
04.              throws java.io.IOException {
05.      s.writeInt(ourVersion);
06.      s.writeObject(moleculeName);
07.    }
08.
09.    private void readObject(java.io.ObjectInputStream s)
10.              throws java.lang.ClassNotFoundException,
11.                 java.io.IOException {
12.    // Compensate for missing constructor.
13.      reset();
14.      if (s.readInt() != ourVersion) {
15.        throw new IOException("Molecule.readObject: version mismatch");
16.      }
17.      moleculeName = (String) s.readObject();
18.    }
```

BeanInfo.getPropertyDescriptors for Molecule

By convention, a class named MoleculeBeanInfo, when present, will be used by the Bean container for a Bean of the Molecule class. When no such class is present, however, the default reflection analysis is used to create a BeanInfo object and the programmer forgoes the option of overriding that information.

Class MoleculeBeanInfo extends SimpleBeanInfo, which provides methods that return the default values. MoleculeBeanInfo does override the getPropertyDescriptor so that it can define the property descriptor for the moleculeName property. After a PropertyDescriptor object is created, its *setPropertyEditorClass()* method is called so that a custom editor can be used.

If the *MoleculeBeanInfo.getPropertyDescriptors()* method had not been provided, the String editor would have been used for entering the property. That would have resulted in an inferior user interface, to say nothing about having to constrain the input to only legal values.

By all means, use custom editors whenever appropriate. They add real value. For more information about custom component editors for Java Beans, see Chapter 9, "Building Custom Component Editors for Java Beans."

Custom Property Editors for Molecule

You must use a custom property editor when using a non-standard property type. You should, however, also write your own property editor when the legal values of a property do not match the full range of values for the property's type.

Property editors are not restricted to editing a single property for a single Bean. You could, for example, have a property editor to handle all Julian-formatted dates. For details on how a property editor is selected, refer to the API for java.Beans.PropertyEditorManager.

The MoleculeNameEditor class in listing 3.14 extends java.Beans.PropertyEditorSupport. It only overrides the *getTags()* method to return an array of valid Strings. Always use this approach when there is a list of choices.

Listing 3.14: MoleculeNameEditor class

```
01.public class MoleculeNameEditor
02.         extends java.beans.PropertyEditorSupport {
03.
04.    public String[] getTags() {
05.     String result[] = {
06.          "HyaluronicAcid",
07.          "benzene",
08.          "buckminsterfullerine",
09.          "cyclohexane",
```

continues

```
        continued
 10.           "ethane",
 11.           "water"};
 12.      return result;
 13.    }
 14.
 15.}
```

Two other methods on PropertyEditorSupport are worth mentioning, the *getAsText()* and *setAsText()* methods as shown in the following lines of code, respectively:

```
String getAsText();
void setAsText(String text) throws IllegalArgumentException;
```

The *getAsText()* method can be used to convert a non-String property (such as a URL) to text that the user can edit. Then *setAsText()* can be used to convert the input text back to the required property type, throwing IllegalArgumentException when it is not possible to do the conversion.

The *setAsText()* method can also be used with String parameters to validate the input.

The Select Bean (extends Panel)

The Select Bean makes use of both Beans and JDBC. It makes heavy use of a customizer that would normally only be used at design time when configuring a Bean. This means that no real advantage accrues from having segregated the BeanInfo and Customizer from the Bean itself.

Simple parameters are employed to pass information between the Bean and the Customizer; the old AWT event model is used. Furthermore, there is little for interaction with other Beans because the parameters are neither bound nor constrained. On the other hand, it would be easy enough to change how these properties are implemented. And there is a provision to reread the database when an action event is received, which means you can wire a button bean to Select.

In SelectBeanInfo.getBeanDescriptor, the *setDisplayName()* method—a method inherited from FeatureDescriptor—was called on the BeanDescriptor to set the localized display name as shown in the following lines of code:

```
public class SelectBeanInfo extends SimpleBeanInfo {

   public BeanDescriptor getBeanDescriptor() {
    BeanDescriptor bd = new BeanDescriptor(Select.class,
                             SelectCustomizer.class);
    bd.setDisplayName("JDBC SELECT");
    return bd;
   }

}
```

 Note

> The Select Bean can be found in the sun.demo.select package. It consists of the Populate.java, Select.java, SelectBeanInfo.java, SelectCustomizer.java, and Util.java files.

The QuoteMonitor Bean

QuoteMonitor is an RMI (Remote Method Invocation) application. It is also somewhat confusing because it uses a style often very close to the patterns used for Beans, although quite often falling just short of conforming to the actual requirements of those patterns. But there is gold here. Of all the examples you have looked at in this chapter, QuoteMonitor is the only one that uses the new event model for AWT events. It makes no use of the old AWT event model.

 Note

> QuoteMonitor uses the new AWT event model to handle a button press. It also contains code for closing a window, which is something you really need to be able to do.

> Class QuoteMonitor can be found in the sun.demo.quote package. All 15 source files in that package are a part of QuoteMonitor. For brevity, this chapter goes into detail for QuoteMonitor.java only.

When the QuoteMonitor Bean cannot connect to its QuoteServer, it calls the *QuoteMonitor.showBadServerDialog()* method shown in listing 3.15. This method opens a frame with a button. When the frame generates a *java.awt.event.WindowEvent* and calls

windowClosing() on all its registered listeners, or when the button generates a
java.awt.event.ActionEvent and calls *actionPerformed()* on all its registered listeners, the
method *QuoteMonitor.closeBadServerDialog()* needs to be called.

Listing 3.15: showBadServerDialog() method

```
01.public void showBadServerDialog(String host)
02. {
03.    String message[] = {
04.      "The QuoteMonitor Bean couldn't connect to the QuoteServer",
05.      "on host machine \"" + host + "\".  Either specify a hostname",
06.      "where the QuoteServer is already running or start/restart",
07.      "one on \"" + host + "\".",
08.      " ",
09.      "You can start the QuoteServer from the demo directory [ccc]with:",
10.
11.      "   gnumake -f quote.gmk run & (Solaris)"
12.    };
13.
14.    String title =
15.      "QuoteMonitor Warning: \"" + host + "\" Couldn't Connect to
⇒Quote Server";
16.
17.    if (dialog != null) {
18.      dialog.setTitle(title);
19.      return;
20.
21.
22.    // dialog = new Dialog(new Frame(), title, false);
23.    dialog = new Frame(title);
24.    dialog.setLayout(new BorderLayout(3, 3));
25.    dialog.addWindowListener(new DialogCloseHandler());
26.
27.    Panel messagePanel = new Panel();
28.    messagePanel.setLayout(new GridLayout(message.length, 1));
29.    for(int i = 0; i < message.length; i++)
30.
31.
32.    Button okButton = new Button(" OK ");
33.    okButton.addActionListener(new DialogOKHandler());
34.
35.    Panel buttonPanel = new Panel();
36.    buttonPanel.add(okButton);
37.
38.    dialog.add("Center", messagePanel);
39.    dialog.add("South", buttonPanel);
```

```
40.
41.    dialog.show();
42.  }
```

The code in listing 3.15 is constructed simply and directly. When constructing the frame, an instance of the nested adapter class, DialogCloseHandler is created and is registered as a listener with the frame. Similarly, when constructing the button, an instance of the nested adapter class, DialogOKHandler, is created and registered as a listener with the button.

The nested adapter class, DialogOKHandler, is pretty straightforward. It implements the java.awt.event.ActionListener interface. And the *actionPerformed()* method calls *closeBadServerDialog()* without regard for the ActionEvent. The code for the DialogOKHandler class is shown in the following lines of code:

```
class DialogOKHandler implements ActionListener
  {
    public void actionPerformed(ActionEvent e)
    {
      closeBadServerDialog();
    }
  }
```

The nested adapter class, DialogCloseHandler almost directly parallels DialogOKHandler. The main difference is that WindowListener contains a number of methods, so java.awt.event.WindowAdapter is extended instead. WindowAdapter is a helper class that provides a null implementation of all the required methods so that only the methods needed can be overridden. The code for the DialogCloseHandler class is shown in the following lines of code:

```
class DialogCloseHandler extends WindowAdapter
  {
    public void windowClosing(WindowEvent e)
    {
      closeBadServerDialog();
    }
  }
```

The *closeBadServerDialog()* method shown in the following lines of code performs the usual cleanup familiar to Java AWT programmers:

```
void closeBadServerDialog()
  {
    dialog.hide();
    dialog.dispose();
    dialog = null;
  }
```

QuoteMonitor is a good example of how to use the new AWT event model. It demonstrates the use of nested adapter classes to capture AWT events, and in particular shows how to close a java.awt.Window.

Summary

With the singular exception of Beans that are containers for other Beans, this chapter has provided a pretty good look at code that illustrates just about every aspect of the Bean paradigm!

The following list covers the topics treated in this chapter and the examples that best illustrate each topic.

What makes a class a Bean	TransitionalBean, JellyBean
Simple properties	TransitionalBean, JellyBean, Voter, Juggler, Molecule
Listener interface	TransitionalBean
Listener registration	JellyBean, OurButton
Bound properties	JellyBean, ChangeReporter, OurButton, BridgeTester
Constrained properties	JellyBean, Voter, BridgeTester
Action events	OurButton, Juggler, Molecule, QuoteMonitor
Window events	QuoteMonitor
Custom Events	TransitionalBean, BridgeTester
Nested class adapters	ChangeReporter, QuoteMonitor
Serialization	TransitionalBean, ChangeReporter, Juggler, Molecule

BeanInfo	JellyBean, ExplicitButton, Juggler, BridgeTester, Molecule, Select
Customizer	ExplicitButton, BridgeTester, Select
Custom property editor	Molecule
AWT event conversion	TransitionalBean
Use of Beans in an applet	TransitionalBean

It seems reasonable to conclude that the example Beans included in JavaSoft's BDK pretty well define how to program with Beans. The one qualification to that is the use of the new event model with AWT. It is pretty thin, and the only example is QuoteMonitor.

For more information on using the new event model with AWT, and for more information in general on AWT, check out `http://java.sun.com/awt`.

Part II

Working with Beans

CHAPTER 4

Java Bean Design Signatures

One of the primary features of JavaBeans is that they are easy to create. Just by following a few simple rules, any class can be suitable for use as a Bean. The rules, which we call Design Signatures, are simple programming patterns. By using the Java Core Reflection API, the JavaBeans Introspector class can programmatically categorize the parts of the Bean's API.

The Introspector class creates FeatureDescriptor classes for each of the different parts of the API and builds a BeanInfo object. The BeanInfo object is then accessed by Bean-aware tools and uses the BeanInfo data to access and control Java Beans.

Signature Basics

Signatures are all around us. Signatures are the characteristics that identify a class of things or a specific thing. The most familiar is your own hand written signature. Your signature is always different, yet certain attributes are the same. For instance, a letter, or two might be slanted a certain way, or you may dot the letter 'i' with a small circle, a dot, or a slash. The areas where your signature follows the same style are the characteristics that identify you as the source. Fingerprints are also signatures. We all have them and they are unique to the individual, but like a handwritten signature, vary over time, circumstance, and injury. Even with the variations, there is usually an aspect of a fingerprint that can be matched to a previous or future copy. Fingerprints in general, are also a form of signature that identifies the tips of fingers. Design signatures are similar to fingerprints and handwritten signatures in that they represent a type of thing as opposed to the exact thing. Here is the exact definition of a Design Signature that we will use throughout the book:

Note

> Design signatures are the characteristics of the names of classes and methods, the extension of classes, the implementation of interfaces, method parameter types, and exceptions thrown that can be used in whole or in part to recognize the uses of classes and methods. Design signatures are also used to imply that other classes or methods may exist.

Design signatures are useful for two reasons: first, they help programmers recognize the uses of classes and methods by following easily recognizable patterns. For instance, it is very simple to understand that the *setBackground()* and *getBackground()* methods of a Bean are used to set and get the background colors for a component. The second reason for signatures, and their primary use in the JavaBeans model, is so that specific types of classes and methods can be recognized so that they can be manipulated by JavaBeans-aware applications. To extend the *setBackground()* and *getBackground()*, the JavaBeans-aware BeanBox application is able to programmatically read a Bean containing these methods and determine that 'Background' is a property that it can display in a property sheet for a user to manipulate.

The Design Signature definition also states that a signature may also imply that another class or method exists. For example, the existence of a Bean implies that a BeanInfo object exists. Or, to use the example of the set/get property signature, the *set()* method implied that the *get()* method exists and vise-versa. There are differences in how these rules are applied. For instance, just because there is a Bean, a corresponding BeanInfo object does not need to exist. With the set/get property pattern, the existence of the *set()* method implies the existence of the *get()* method, but the lack of a corresponding method voids the whole signature. So for example, if we had a Bean with a *getColor()* method and no *setColor()* method, the Introspector class would not generate a PropertyDescriptor class for the color property.

Note

> This chapter is not about security, as the word signature implies. Signatures as they are described here are patterns that identify a class of things. Some who are familiar with the early discussions on Java Beans may remember the subject discussed here originally as Design Patterns. Unfortunately, there is a definition problem because Design Patterns are generally understood as a method for documenting certain software constructs that have a specific behavior or solve a particular problem

(As described by the *Design Patterns* book by Eric Gamma et al). Although Design Patterns could be applied here, the goal is to not describe a principal of design, rather it is a set of design rules that can be used by another program to understand a developer's original intent.

A good example of a get/set property pair is in the AWT button component. The button component contains a *setText( )* and a *getText( )* method that access the text property of the button. Another example is the *setBackground( )* and *getBackground( )* methods that access the background color of the component. In effect, any public set/get pair of methods is considered a property. What makes each of these pairs different is the text after the 'set' or 'get' prefix and the type of object or primitive that the pair manipulate. For example, *setText( )* and *getText( )* are associated with the name text and the String type while *setBackground( )* and *getBackground( )* methods are associated with the background property with the type Color.

Some of the design signatures are complex. The patterns for properties and for event sets, as you will see later, are made up of multiple methods that each follow a specific design signature. These signatures require that the Bean's class implement specific interfaces and expect (see note) that some methods perform actions like change notifications or events.

 Note

Because JavaBeans are based on the information found through Core Reflection, the only information available is method, class, and interface. Therefore there is no way to examine the code within methods. For this reason, the behavior of methods matching signatures is only expected to follow the standard for behavior. The developer should be diligent in ensuring that methods that meet the specifications for signatures should also implement the desired behavior.

Design Signature Conventions

Each of the design signatures documented in this chapter consist of the layout of the code, usually a method, with the marker symbols shown in table 4.1. Each of these markers defines a type or a name that is used to form part of the signature. Each definition is also followed by a list of rules that make the signature valid.

Table 4.1: Signature Placeholders

Signature placeholder	Characteristic
<PropertyType>	The type of the property
<propertyName>	The name of the property
<IndexType>	The type of the index
<indexName>	The name of the index
<EventListenerType>	The specific type of an event listener, usually an Interface
<EventListenerName>	Event listenter name

Capitalization Rules

One of the primary ways that programmers visually break apart multiple words in names is to use camel case. For example, a method that would start an engine would be written as *startEngine()*. The first word, "start," is begun as a lower case letter because this is a method. The second word, "engine," has its first word capitalized separating it from the first word "start."

Certain capitalization rules must be followed to locate methods, parameters, classes, and interfaces. You must be careful with the case of names for the following two reasons:

The IDE must present the names in a way that makes the most sense to the user.

The name needs to match the Java representation. Because Java is case sensitive, this makes these naming rules very important.

The first capitalization rule is that property names as they are presented in builder tools, start with lower case letters. From an IDE, for example, the method *setColor()* will be associated with a property called color. If the name is a single character, the character is capitalized in the IDE and within Java code it is lower case. If the name's first two characters are capitalized, the name is used to accommodate names that are or start with acronyms.

The following table shows several examples of converting from names starting with capital letters.

Table 4.2: Decapitalization Conversion Examples

From	To
Foo	foo
FooBar	fooBar
A_Box	a_Box
DOA	DOA
URL	URL
URLpost	URLpost
A	a
B	b

The following method, *decapitalize()*, (found in the Introspector class) converts strings that begin with upper case letters to lower case types. This method is used primarily to convert a property name so that the first letter is decapitialized for proper viewing in an IDE. The method is final, so an Introspector object need not be instantiated. This method will convert text according to the capitalization rules. In other words, this method can be used to create the conversions shown in table 4.2

```
final String Introspector.decapitalize(String name);
```

For Bean properties, the naming convention is that the name must begin with a lower case letter. This helps to distinguish properties from class names that are capitalized. This convention is important to remember when creating a localized name for properties. The name returned from the PropertyDescriptor class's *getDisplayName()* method should return a name that begins with a lower case letter. The opposite is true for the BeanDescriptor class's *getDisplayName()* method which should return a name that begins with a capital letter.

Overview of Design Signatures

Design signatures are divided into four different categories, Property access, event sources, event listeners, and JavaBeans. Property access and event sources are used by the Introspector class to create PropertyDescriptor and EventSetDescriptors. These categories, with a short description of each are shown in the following list. These descriptors are used by JavaBeans-aware software to access properties and connect events.

♦ **Property access:** external set and get access to Bean properties. Used to create PropertyDescriptor objects

♦ **Event Source signatures:** defines events that Bean generates. Used to create EventSetDescriptor objects

♦ **Event listener signature:** defines events that a class or Bean can handle. Matched against EventSetDescriptor objects to determine if a class can accept specific events

♦ **JavaBeans signatures:** associated classes that are used by JavaBeans-aware software to extend a Bean's access beyond the Bean classEach of the signature categories is further broken into several sub signatures. Each sub signature is either a set of methods or an implemented interface.

Property Access Signatures

The property access signature accesses a Bean's property values. Property values are items like foreground color, component dimensions, or any other aspect of a Java Bean class. Properties are atomic, in other words, they are objects like Color and String objects, or primitives like integers and floats.

The property access signature is broken up into two different sub signatures: set property and get property. The two signatures must exist or the Introspector class will not create a PropertyDescriptor object.

Set Property Signatures

Set property signature is part of the Property access signature. The set property signature is used to set the property values of a Bean. Care should be taken when creating set property methods because the value being set may fail because it is out of the range of allowable values. This is important because this pattern does not explicitly allow for exceptions to be thrown for bad values. For example, if a property value of a Bean is out of range, and the set property method throws an exception, the caller may not catch the exception causing the current thread to be suspended. If throwing exceptions is a possibility, the constrained property signature (discussed in the next couple of sections) should be used instead.

Here is the definition of the set property signature:

```
public void set<propertyName>(<PropertyType> <propertyName>);
```

<PropertyType>:the type of the property.

<propertyName>:the name of the property.

Rules: class must have matching 'get' property signature. The new property value should be a non-mutable object, primitive, or copied to prevent unauthorized access to Bean or the Bean's access to external objects.

Listing 4.1 is an example of a set property method that follows the set property signature. The method sets an integer property value of a Bean. The three characteristics that make this method a set signature are as follows:

◆ the method returns no values

◆ the method starts with the prefix 'set'

◆ there is only one parameter

Listing 4.1: Example set property signature method which sets an integer property

```
public void setMyInteger(int newInt){
    myInteger = newInt;
    // Other code as is necessary
}
```

Listing 4.2 shows another set signature. The *setMyColor()* method sets an object.

Listing 4.2: Example set property signature method which sets a Color object property

```
public void setMyColor(Color newColor){
    myColor = newColor;
    // Other code as is necessary
```

Get Property Signatures

The get property signature retrieves the current value of parameters in a Bean. The method is usually very simple, only requiring the property to be returned. The property in most cases should be immutable or a clone copy of the data held by the Bean. By passing an object that cannot be modified or otherwise access internal Bean fields, the developer is ensuring that objects external to a Bean can only change properties through the property access signatures.

```
public <PropertyType> get<propertyName>();
```

<PropertyType>: the type of the property.

<propertyName>: the name of the property.

Rules: class must have matching 'set' property signature. Property returned should be a non-mutable object or primitive to prevent unauthorized access to Bean.

Listing 4.3 is an example of a get property method, which follows the get property signature. The method sets an integer property value of a Bean. The three characteristics that make this method a get signature are as follows:

◆ the method returns a value

◆ the method starts with the prefix 'get'

◆ there are no method parameters

Listing 4.3: Example get property signature method which returns an integer property

```
public int getMyInteger(){
    return(myInteger);
}
```

Listing 4.4 shows another example of the get property signature that is returning an object. It is important to note that the object returned, of class Color, is an imutable type. Because of Color's immutability, there is no reason to clone the myColor object.

Listing 4.4: Example set property signature method which sets a Color object property

```
public Color getMyColor(){
    return(myColor);
}
```

Using Property Signatures in a Bean

Using a property signature in a Bean is very simple. Creating a property that will be found by the Introspector class only requires matching 'set' and 'get' signatures exist in the class. Listing 4.3 shows an example Bean which extends the Label class to create an Integer label. The *setIntLabel()* and *getIntLabel()* methods(highlighted) are the two sub-signatures that are recognized by the Introspector class. If this Bean were used in the BeanBox or other JavaBeans-aware application, the name of the property would be'integerLabel.'

The rest of the code that makes up this Bean is primarily used to resize the Bean to fit be large enough to display the numeric value.

Listing 4.5: Class IntergerLabel: Example of set/get signature

```
01.package NewRiders.beans.labels;
02.import java.io.*;
03.import java.awt.*;
04.public class IntegerLabel extends Label implements Serializable{
05.    /**
06.     * Construct a default integer label
07.     */
08.    public IntegerLabel(){
09.        super("?");
10.        // Center text
11.        setAlignment(1);
12.    }
13.    /**
14.     * Private data to be accessed with get/set
15.     * design signatures
16.     */
17.    private int myIntegerLabel = 0;
18.    /**
19.     * 'set' property signature used
20.     * to set an integer property.
```

continues

continued

```
21.     */
22.     public void setIntLabel(int newLabel){
23.         myIntegerLabel = newLabel;
24.         setText((new Integer(myIntegerLabel)).toString());
25.         // repaint and resize the label
26.         sizeToFit();
27.         repaint();
28.     }
29.     /**
30.      * 'get' property signature used
31.      * to get an integer property.
32.      */
33.     public int getIntLabel(){
34.         return myIntegerLabel;
35.     }
36.
37.     /**
38.      * Override of Component method to return the calculated size.
39.      */
40.     public Dimension getPreferredSize() {
41.         Font currentFont =     getFont();
42.         // Return a default size if there is no parent
43.         if (currentFont == null){
44.             return new Dimension(10,10);
45.         }
46.         FontMetrics metric = getFontMetrics(currentFont);
47.         int maxWidth = metric.stringWidth((new Integer(myIntegerLabel)).
    ➥toString()) ;
48.         return new Dimension(maxWidth + (metric.charWidth(' ')*3),
49.                     metric.getMaxAscent() + metric.getMaxDescent() + metric.
    ➥getHeight());
50.     }// End of getPreferredSize()
51.     /**
52.      * Override of Component method to return the minimum size.
53.      */
54.     public Dimension getMinimumSize() {
55.         return getPreferredSize();
56.     }// End of getMinimumSize()
57.
58.     /**
59.      * Causes a resize and a notification that the parent
60.      * should be redrawn.
61.      */
62.     protected void sizeToFit() {
63.         Dimension d = getPreferredSize();
64.         resize(d.width, d.height);
```

```
65.        Component p = getParent();
66.        if (p != null) {
67.            p.invalidate();
68.            p.layout();
69.        }
70.    }// End of sizeToFit()
71.
72.}// End of class IntegerLabel
```

Indexed Properties

Another type of property signature is an indexed property. Indexed properties are properties that are accessed like arrays. The index type is usually an integer. Indexed propeties are used to access arrays, vectors or list type properties.

Set Indexed Properties Signature

The set indexed property signature is characterized by a method with no return value, having two parameters. The first parameter is the index, while the second is the new value for the property at the specified index.

```
public void set<propertyName>(int <indexName>, <PropertyType> <propertyName>);
```

    <PropertyType>: the type of the property.

    <propertyName>: the name of the property.

    <IndexType>: the type of the index (usually int).

    <indexName>: the name of the index

    Rules: must be accompanied by a matching get index method.

Get Indexed Properties Signature

The get indexed property signature is characterized by a method with no return value, having one parameter. The parameter is the index of the property list to be returned.

```
public <PropertyType> get<propertyName>( <IndexType> <indexName>);
```

<IndexType>: the type of the index (usually int).

<indexName>: the name of the index

Rules: must be accompanied by a matching set index method.

Using Indexed Properties in a Bean

Listing 4.6 shows a list component that displays a list of integers. The highlighted methods, *setIntegerItem()* and *getIntegerItem()* are implementations of an indexed property.

Listing 4.6: Demonstration of the indexed property signature

```
01.package NewRiders.beans.labels;
02.import java.io.*;
03.import java.awt.*;
04.public class IntegerList extends List implements Serializable{
05.    /**
06.     * Construct a default integer label
07.     */
08.    public IntegerList(){
09.        super();
10.        setSize(20,60);
11.
12.    }
13.    /**
14.     * Indexed 'set' property signature used
15.     * to set an integer property.
16.     * Data converted to a string and set in a list.
17.     */
18.    public void setIntegerItem(int index,int newItem){
19.        replaceItem((new Integer(newItem)).toString(),index);
20.        // repaint and resize the label
21.        repaint();
22.    }
23.    /**
24.     * 'get' property signature used
25.     * to get an integer property.
26.     */
27.    public int getIntegerItem(int index){
28.        return (new Integer(getItem(index))).intValue();
29..    }
30.}// End of class IntegerList
```

Boolean Property Signature

The Boolean property signature is used to set and test a Boolean property. This pattern is identical to the standard property pattern, with the exception that the 'get' property signature has been replaced with the 'is' signature. For example the methods for a component's visibility might be *setVisible()* and *isVisible()*. The reason that 'is' has replaced 'get' when the type is Boolean is because the method enhances readability the when part of a Boolean logic statement. For example:

```
If (isVisible()){}
```

uses 'is' and implies the type of the method is Boolean, where the second statement,

```
If(getVisible()){}
```

is not as clear.

Is Boolean Property Signature

The "is Boolean property" queries the state of Boolean property of a Bean. The reason that this pattern should be used instead of the get property signature is that it can make generated code more understandable.

```
public boolean is<propertyName>(boolean <propertyName>);
```

<PropertyName>: the name of the Boolean property.

Rule: must be accompanied by a matching set Boolean property.

Set Boolean Property Signature

The "set Boolean property" queries the state of Boolean property of a Bean. The signature is exactly like the set generic property signature, but is included to be paired with the "is Boolean property" signature.

```
public void set<propertyName>(boolean <propertyName>);
```

<propertyName>: the name of the Boolean property.

Rule: must be accompanied by a matching is Boolean property.

Using Boolean Property Signatures in a Bean

The example Bean label in listing 4.7 shows a label that displays true or false depending on the setting of the Boolean property. The Boolean-specific signature has been highlighted. The remaining code is used for display control.

Listing 4.7: Class BooleanLabel—Example of is/set boolean property design signature

```
01.package NewRiders.beans.labels;
02.import java.io.*;
03.import java.awt.*;
04.public class BooleanLabel extends Label implements Serializable{
05.    /**
06.     * Construct a default integer label
07.     */
08.    public BooleanLabel(){
09.        super("false");
10.        // Center text
11.        setAlignment(1);
12.    }
13.    /**
14.     * Private data to be accessed with is/set
15.     * design signatures
16.     */
17.    private boolean myBooleanLabel = false;
18.    /**
19.     * 'set' boolean property signature used
20.     * to set a boolean property.
21.     */
22.    public void setBooleanLabel(boolean newLabel){
23.        myBooleanLabel = newLabel;
24.        setText((new Boolean(myBooleanLabel)).toString());
25.        // repaint and resize the label
26.        sizeToFit();
27.        repaint();
77.
28.    }
29.    /**
30.     * 'is' boolean property signature used
31.     * to get a boolean property.
32.     */
33.    public boolean isBooleanLabel(){
34.        return myBooleanLabel;
35.    }
36.
```

```
37.        // Other code as is necessary
38.
39.}// End of class BooleanLabel
```

Bound Properties

Bound properties are properties that broadcast their values whenever they are changed. Bound properties notify registered listeners whenever changes occur. The primary use for bound properties is to communicate state changes between classes. For example, the Ignition Bean would send property change events to notify an Engine Bean that the state of the ignition key has been changed from on or off. PropertyChangeEvent is a special case of event. Property change events pass the source of the change, the name of the property changed, the old value, and the new value.

The signature for bound properties has two more methods than a normal property signature. The additional methods are the *addPropertyChangeListener()* and the *addPropertyChangeListener()* methods. These add and remove methods are used to manage the listeners to property changes. The set/get signatures are essentially the same , except that the set method must generate a PropertyChangeEvent and all registered listeners must be notified by calling the *propertyChange()* methods. A property change listener is a class which implements the PropertyChangeListener interface.

As a part of the bound property signature, the class must have an *addPropertyChangeListener()* and a *removePropertyChangeListener()* method. If these methods exist, then all property signatures are potentially bound properties. All properties will be treated as bound properties by the Introspector if the add and remove listener methods exist in a Bean. The PropertyDescriptor object for the properties in a Bean will be configured to return 'true' when the *isBound()* method is called. The developer must override the value returned by the *isBound()* method to prevent a method from becoming bound. A good rule of thumb is to make all properties notify property change listeners. This makes the Bean possibly more useful, while avoiding the creation of a custom BeanInfo that modifies the *isBound()* return value.

Set Bound Property Signature

A 'bound' property is one that follows the normal property signature, with the addition that the 'set' method generates a PropertyChangeEvent and notifies all property registered property change listeners.

The set bound property is identical to the set property method except that the Bean should support a normal pair of multicast event listener registration methods for PropertyChangeListener objects.

```
public void set<propertyName>(<PropertyType> <propertyName>);
```

<PropertyType>: the type of the property.

<propertyName>: the name of the property.

Rules: class must have matching 'get' property signature, *addPropertyChangeListener()*, and *addPropertyChangeListener()* methods. After method has modified the property, the method must create a PropertyChangeEvent and call the *propertyChange()* method of all registered listeners with the source property name, the old, and new values.

An example of a bound set is shown in listing 4.8. This example is only a code fragment which shows how the method should change the value of the internal state and then fire a property change event. This example also uses a property change support object (changes) which does the actual listener notification.

Listing 4.8: Bound 'set' signature method and accompanying property change source signature methods

```
01.    public void setIntLabel(int newLabel){
02.
03.        // Create a copy of the old value.
04.        Integer oldValue = new Integer(myIntegerLabel);
05.
06.        // Change the value
07.        myIntegerLabel = newLabel;
08.
09.        // Notify all listeners that a change has occurred.
10.        changes.firePropertyChange("intLabel",
11.                                   oldValue,
12.                                   new Integer(myIntegerLabel));
13.
14.        // Other code as is necessary
15.
16.    }// end of set
```

In listing 4.9 the creation of a PropertyChangeSupport object is shown along with the implementation of the add and remove property change support methods.

Listing 4.9: Sample of add and remove property change event methods

```
01.    /**
02.     * Property change support object.
03.     */
04.    PropertyChangeSupport changes = new PropertyChangeSupport(this);
05.    /**
06.     * This is add property change listener half
07.     * of the property change support signature.
08.     * The method uses the PropertyChangeSupport object.
09.     */
10.    public void addPropertyChangeListener(PropertyChangeListener l) {
11.        changes.addPropertyChangeListener(l);
12.    }
13.
14.    /**
15.     * This is remove property change listener
16.     * half of the property change support signature.
17.     * The method uses the PropertyChangeSupport object.
18.     */
19.    public void removePropertyChangeListener(PropertyChangeListener l) {
20.        changes.removePropertyChangeListener(l);
21.    }
```

To make using bound properties easier to handle, use the PropertyChangeSupport class. Either inherit from the PropertyChangeSupport directly or make it a private member of the class and add *addPropertyChangeListener()* and *removePropertyChangeListener()* methods.

Get/Is Bound Property Signature

The signature for retrieving a bound property is identical to a normal 'get' signature as is the 'is' signature for Boolean properties.

Using Bound Property Signatures in a Bean

Listing 4.10 is the example of listing 4.5 rewritten as a bound property Bean. The important changes have been highlighted to show the differences. The primary change is that the set method now calls the *firePropertyChange()* method of the PropertyChangeSupport object. The example also has an *add/remove property change listener* method. The methods used the PropertyChangeSupport object to keep track of registered listeners. There is also the import of the java.beans package to give access to the PropertyChangeSupport class, which is used to manage property listeners.

Listing 4.10: Example label which notifies listeners when the integer label value changes

```
001.package NewRiders.beans.labels;
002.import java.io.*;
003.import java.awt.*;
004.import java.beans.*;
005.public class BoundIntegerLabel extends Label implements Serializable{
006.    /**
007.     * Construct a default integer label
008.     */
009.    public BoundIntegerLabel(){
010.        super("?");
011.        // Center text
012.        setAlignment(1);
013.    }
014.    /**
015.     * Private data to be accessed with get/set
016.     * design signatures
017.     */
018.    private int myIntegerLabel = 0;
019.    /**
020.     * Bound 'set' property signature used
021.     * to set an integer property. Method notifys registered
022.     * property listeners that a bound property change has occurred.
023.     */
024.    public void setIntLabel(int newLabel){
025.
026.        // Create a copy of the old value.
027.        Integer oldValue = new Integer(myIntegerLabel);
028.
029.        // Change the value
030.        myIntegerLabel = newLabel;
031.
032.        // Notify all listeners that a change has occurred.
033.        changes.firePropertyChange("intLabel",oldValue,new
➥Integer(myIntegerLabel));
034.
035.        // Redisplay the label
036.        setText((new Integer(myIntegerLabel)).toString());
037.
038.        // repaint and resize the label
```

```
039.          sizeToFit();
040.          repaint();
041.      }
042.      /**
043.       * 'get' property signature used
044.       * to get an integer property.
045.       */
046.      public int getIntLabel(){
047.          return myIntegerLabel;
048.      }
049.      /**
050.       * Property change support object.
051.       */
052.      PropertyChangeSupport changes = new PropertyChangeSupport(this);
053.      /**
054.       * This is add property change listener half of the property change
     ↪support signature.
055.       * The method uses the PropertyChangeSupport object.
056.       */
057.      public void addPropertyChangeListener(PropertyChangeListener l) {
058.          changes.addPropertyChangeListener(l);
059.      }
060.
061.      /**
062.       * This is remove property change listener half of the property
     ↪change support signature.
063.       * The method uses the PropertyChangeSupport object.
064.       */
065.      public void removePropertyChangeListener(PropertyChangeListener l) {
066.          changes.removePropertyChangeListener(l);
067.      }
068.
069.          // Other code as is necessary
070.
071.}// End of class BoundIntegerLabel
```

Property Change Listeners

In order for a class to be notified by bound property changes, the class must implement the PropertyChangeListener interface. This interface has a *propertyChange()* method which is called when a bound property triggers a change event.

Listing 4.11 shows an example property change listener. The ListenerLabel class echos property changes to a label. The highlighted sections of the class are associated with the implementation of the PropertyChangeListener interface. The bulk of the classes remaining methods are associated with maintaining the label at a size large enough to see the displayed text.

Listing 4.11: Example use of a PropertyChangeListener interface

```
01.package NewRiders.beans.labels;
02.import java.io.*;
03.import java.awt.*;
04.import java.beans.*;
05.public class ListenerLabel extends Label implements
➥PropertyChangeListener, Serializable{
06.    /**
07.     * Construct a default integer label
08.     */
09.    public ListenerLabel(){
10.        super("?");
11.        // Center text
12.        setAlignment(1);
13.    }
14.    /**
15.     * Implementation method for the Property change interface.
16.     * This method displays the old and new values
17.     */
18.    public void propertyChange(PropertyChangeEvent event){
19.        setText( "Property:"+event.getPropertyName()+
20.                " Old="+ event.getOldValue()+
21.                " New="+ event.getNewValue());
22.
23.        // repaint and resize the label
24.        sizeToFit();
25.        repaint();
26.
27.    }
33.
34.
35.    /**
36.     * Override of Component method to return the calculated size.
37.     */
38.    public Dimension getPreferredSize() {
39.        Font currentFont =     getFont();
40.        // Return a default size if there is no parent
41.        if (currentFont == null){
42.            return new Dimension(10,10);
43.        }
44.        FontMetrics metric = getFontMetrics(currentFont);
```

```
45.         int maxWidth = metric.stringWidth(getText()) ;
46.         return new Dimension(maxWidth + (metric.charWidth(' ')*3),
47.                 metric.getMaxAscent() + metric.getMaxDescent() +
↪metric.getHeight());
48.     }
49.     /**
50.      * Override of Component method to return the minimum size.
51.      */
52.     public Dimension getMinimumSize() {
53.         return getPreferredSize();
54.     }
55.
56.     /**
57.      * Causes a resize and a notification that the parent
58.      * should be redrawn.
59.      */
60.     protected void sizeToFit() {
61.         Dimension d = getPreferredSize();
62.         resize(d.width, d.height);
63.         Component p = getParent();
64.         if (p != null) {
65.             p.invalidate();
66.             p.layout();
67.         }
68.     }
69.
70.}// End of class ListenerLabel
```

Vetoable (Constrained) Property

A vetoable property is a property that is monitored for correctness by an external source. This type of property is useful for creating graphical input components that can validate changes by notifying their registered listeners. The registered listeners validate the proposed change to the property and throw an exception if the change is invalid. For example, a text-input component could be constrained to allow the input of only three characters for an airport identifier. Another example is a currency-input component that only allows a maximum dollar amount to be input.

In addition to the signature for the method, the Bean must implement the ability to add and remove VetoableChangeListener objects when they are called. Without add and remove methods, a VetoableChangeListener cannot be added via the IDE because add and remove methods are required before an event set can be created for vetoable property

events. When the set method is called, the Bean must call the
VetoableChangeListener.vetoableChange method of any registered listeners. To support
this, the Bean must implement Add Multicast Event Listener and Remove Multicast
Event Listener signatures so listeners can be registered and removed.

To make vetoable properties easier to handle, use the VetoableChangeSupport class.
Either inherit from it or make it a private member of the class and add the add and
remove property change listener patterns.

```
public void set<propertyName>(<PropertyType> <propertyName>) throws
PropertyVetoException;
```

<PropertyType>: the type of the property.

<propertyName>: the name of the property.

Rules: must have a matching bound 'set' property, *addVetoableChangeListener()*,
and *removeVetoableChangeListener()* methods. Must call *fireVetoableChange()*
method of registered listeners before changing property value.

Listing 4.12 is an example extracts from a Bean that allows an integer property called
myItem to be vetoed. The class uses the VetoableChangeSupport class to implement the
required add and remove vetoable change listener methods.

Listing 4.12: Example of a vetoable change property signature, including supporting methods to add and remove vetoable property change listeners

```
01.     public void setMyItem(int newItem)throws PropertyVetoException{
02.         // Create a copy of the old value.
03.         Integer oldValue = new Integer(myItem);
04.
05.
06.         // Notify all listeners that a change has occurred.
07.         vetoableChange.fireVetoableChange("intLabel",oldValue,new
➥Integer(myItem));
08.
09.         // None of the listeners has thrown an
10.         // exception, so it is ok to change the value
11.         myItem = newItem;
12.
13.         // Other code as is necessary
14.
15.     }
```

```
16.    /**
17.     * Property change support object.
18.     */
19.    VetoableChangeSupport vetoableChange = new VetoableChangeSupport
➥(this);
20.    /**
21.     * This is add property change listener half of the property change
➥support signature.
22.     * The method uses the PropertyChangeSupport object.
23.     */
24.    public void addVetoableChangeListener(VetoableChangeListener l) {
25.        vetoableChange.addVetoableChangeListener(l);
26.    }
27.
28.    /**
29.     * This is remove property change listener half of the property
➥change support signature.
30.     * The method uses the PropertyChangeSupport object.
31.     */
32.    public void removeVetoableChangeListener(VetoableChangeListener l) {
33.        vetoableChange.removeVetoableChangeListener(l);
34.    }
```

Vetoable Change Listener Signature

The vetoable change listener is similar to the bound property change listener except that the method in the interface can throw a PropertyVetoException exception to void the change. In listing 4.13, a Bean component called LimitMaxInt is an example of a vetoable change listener. This method has a normal property signature, used to set a maximum value. When a change occurs on a property that this class was registered with, the class checks to see if the new value is greater than the maximum set. If the maximum is exceeded, the class throws a PropertyVetoException.

The highlighted areas of the code show the parts that are directly associated with the VetoableChangeListener interface. The remaining areas of the class support the size and the maximum limit management.

Listing 4.13: Example use of a vetoable property

```
01.package NewRiders.beans.labels;
02.import java.io.*;
03.import java.awt.*;
04.import java.beans.*;
05.public class LimitMaxInt extends Label implements VetoableChangeListener,
➥Serializable{
06.     /**
07.      * Construct a default integer label
08.      */
09.     public LimitMaxInt(){
10.         super("?");
11.         // Center text
12.         setAlignment(1);
13.     }
14.     /**
15.      * Implementation method for the VetoableProperty chanage interface.
16.      * Throws PropertyVetoException if property change is greater than
➥max.
17.      * This method displays the old and new values.
18.      */
19.     public void vetoableChange(PropertyChangeEvent event) throws
➥PropertyVetoException{
20.
21.         //If the new value is greater than the max, throw an exception.
22.         if (((Integer)event.getNewValue()).intValue() > max){
23.             throw new PropertyVetoException("new value is greater than
➥"+max,event);
24.         }
25.
26.         // Display the old and new values.
27.         setText( "Property:"+event.getPropertyName()+
28.                 " Old="+ event.getOldValue()+
29.                 " New="+ event.getNewValue());
30.
31.         // repaint and resize the label
32.         sizeToFit();
33.         repaint();
34.
35.     }
36.     int max = 0;
37.     public void setMaxInt(int max){
38.         this.max = max;
39.     }
40.     public int getMaxInt(){
41.         return(max);
```

```
42.    }
43.
44.        // Other code as is necessary
45.
46.}// End of class LimitMaxInt
```

Event Source Signatures

For a Bean to be a source of events, it must have add and remove event listener methods. These methods are similar to those for the PropertyChangeEvent and VetoableChangeEvent support signatures. The main difference is that the Event is based on AWTEvent base class and that the 'add' and 'remove' methods contain the name of the event in their method name. Examples of event sources can be seen throughout the AWT, including mouse, component and window events.

There are two types of listener sources, multicast and unicast. A unicast listener is an event source that can only have one listener. A unicast source is primarily a class that can only be associated with one controller. For instance, a car Bean may only have unicast events to report events to the single driver.

Multicast events are events that can be monitored by several listeners. Multicast listeners are the usual type. Bound and constrained property events are multicast.

Add Multicast Event Listener

The multicast listener is used for one-to-many event notification. For example, a spreadsheet Bean may notify changes of its cells to multiple chart Beans. Remember that most Bean events should be multicast because a Bean should be unicast only when one listener or a limited number of listeners is allowed.

The multicast event listener pattern is used by an IDE to locate the 'add' listener pattern so that the event listener can be added. The listener class must implement the java.util.EventListener Interface.

```
public void add<EventListenerType>( <EventListenerType> <eventListenerName>);
```

<EventListenerType>: the type of the event listener. This class *must* extend the java.util.EventListener class.

<eventListenerName>: the name of the listener.

Rules: must have an associated remove<EventListenerType>() method. This method must always add to the number of listeners.

Add Unicast Event Listener

A unicast event is used for one-to-one relationships. In other words, only one source of events and only one listener can be interested in receiving events. Many times, only one listener is possible or required for security reasons. An encryption Bean, for example, allows only one listener to decode data.

The only difference between a Unicast and Multicast is the 'add' listener method's ability to throw the TooManyListenersException. The method must also necessarily throw the exception when the number of listeners is exceeded.

Note that this does not always imply that the event is unicast, only that there is an upper limit on the number of listeners. The event source could use this exception to disable the addition of events when the class is in an unknown state. Alternatively, the class could limit the total number of events. For instance, a Bean could limit the number of listeners to two. Another use of the TooManyListenersException is to stop the addition of listeners after a certain cutoff point in time. For instance a Bean that implements a meeting might stop listeners from being added after the meeting starts.

The event listener pattern is used by an IDE to locate the add listener pattern so that the interested class can be added to the Beans list of listeners. The interested class must implement the java.util.EventListener interface.

```
public void add<EventListenerType>( <EventListenerType> <eventListenerName>)
throws java.util.TooManyListenersException;
```

<EventListenerType>: the type of the event listener. This class *must* extend the java.util.EventListener class.

<eventListenerName>: the name of the listener.

Rules: must have an associated remove<EventListenerType>() method. Must throw the TooManyListenersException when the number of listeners is exceeded.

Remove Event Listener (Multicast or Unicast)

The remove event listener pattern is used by an IDE to locate the remove listener pattern so that the interested class can be removed upon request. The interested class must implement the java.util.EventListener interface.

```
public void remove<EventListenerType>( <EventListenerType> <eventListenerName>);
```

<EventListenerType>: the type of the event listener. This class *must* extend the java.util.EventListener class.

<eventListenerName>: the name of the listener.

Rules: must have an associated add<EventListenerType>() method.

Public Methods

All other public methods, including those associated with properties of event sets are also examined with core reflection. The Introspector class creates a MethodDescriptor object for each method. This enable JavaBeans-aware applications to have access to all public methods.

Such access to methods programmatically completes the public access to a Bean's API. All methods of the Bean can be called so that complete control over a Bean is possible is the Java Beans-aware application is capable of connection the methods between the Bean and other classes. The original BeanBox beta was not capable of this complete functionality.

BeanInfo Interface Signature

The BeanInfo interface is in itself a pattern that a JavaBeans-aware IDE will look for. This is also a way for the designer of JavaBeans to explicitly define the Bean interface as well as extend the behavior of how the Bean is configured via the IDE.

The BeanInfo pattern provides the only way to cause Beans to show localized language for different countries. Without BeanInfo, therefore, a Bean's method names will only be shown as their programmatic value. With BeanInfo, localized names can be supplied. The BeanInfo interface will be discussed in detail later in this book.

The Serializable Signature

The serializable signature is required for most JavaBeans so that the state of the Bean can be saved and restored. Two patterns will enable a Bean to be serialized. The first is the implement the java.io.Serializable interface. The Serializable interface is the simplest signature. There is no other change to a Bean required other than the declaration that the interface is implemented. The designer can implement added control over serialization in accordance to the Serialization API, but in most cases this may not be necessary.

In addition to the Serializable interface there is also an Externalizable interface. When a Bean implements the Externalizable interface it must explicitly control the serialization process. A class that implements the Externalizable interface is treated identically to the Serializable interface.

Designing Custom Design Signatures

The Design Signatures for JavaBeans are relatively generic, only breaking up a Bean's API into four types of information, the class, properties, event sets, and methods. These categories are sufficient to be used in an application design tool to work with components. There are more possibilities that can be gained through defining custom signatures and for either reinterpreting the data from a BeanInfo object or to create your own types of FeatureDescriptor classes.

Custom signatures are not supported by the JavaBeans API but can be supported by JavaBeans-aware containers. For example, a spreadsheet container would be have special signatures that would be introspected upon cell Beans that have specialized cell signature methods. For instance, there might be a *next()* method used to link cells.

The ability to create custom signatures and custom core that uses the Core Reflection API is limitless. As long as there is enough information in the name, types, and parameters of functions, almost any API can be recognized through properly written core reflection code.

Summary

In this chapter, we have covered the coding signatures that are required to make JavaBeans readable by the Introspector class. These signatures, when used properly, can enable a class to be used as a Bean component with very little effort. In addition to use by the Introspector, a developer, by following these signatures, is using a consistent coding style that is well defined and easily understood by other JavaBeans developers and component users. Using the signatures in this chapter thus fulfills a functionality requirement for JavaBeans and a coding standard for class development.

We have also shown that these signatures are relatively simple to implement. The ease of creating JavaBeans is one of their most important design features. Simply by following standard techniques for formatting and naming of methods and proper extension of classes through inheritance and implementation of interfaces, JavaBeans can be created as a mater of standard design and development.

We have also shown that the most JavaBeans design signatures are easily applied to component design because they depend on signature characteristics. With signature programming, a designer is free to create custom types that do not depend on interfaces or inheritance. Design signatures, when used to define class features, is much easier to implement than the more restrictive inheritance or interface implementation techniques.

We have begun to show how Beans are developed and events are used and how the basic concepts of JavaBeans might be extended to create much more complex APIs. These techniques will be explored further later in this book. However, at this point, the reader should be capable of creating simple, functional JavaBeans.

CHAPTER 5

Java Beans and Events

A big part of what makes Java Beans useful is the capability to connect a Bean to other objects through events. Events enable a Bean to broadcast information to other classes when the Bean changes its state. The opposite is also true, other objects can send events to Java Beans. Unlike procedural programming, event-based systems are asynchronous. Events happen at any time during a program's execution, causing new threads of execution, to be started in reaction to the event. Events can be used for many types of tasks including control, status, errors, input, and output.

Defining whether a Bean should use events is simple. The first and most probable reason is that many Beans are based on AWT components. Because of this, the Bean itself will be event-driven. As a component, Beans have access to all the events available from their AWT base classes. Dealing with and using AWT events can be as simple as just the extension of the AWT base class, or Beans can intercept events to change their behavior or filter and transform events.

Beans can also have internal threads that change the Bean's state, which must then be broadcast to other classes. Using events can vastly simplify the tracking of such threads by other classes. If a Bean is running a thread to perform a task and a class needs to know when the task is complete, for instance, the Bean can generate an event when done. Otherwise, the class waiting on the Bean would need to block on the thread or periodically check the status of the Bean. With events, the listening class can continue processing in its own thread without ever accessing the Bean for status. An excellent example of this is the interaction between two Beans: an animator, which shows an animation in one thread, and a file loader, which loads a file in its own thread while the animator shows animation. When the file loader completes, it fires a completion event, which stops the animator Bean.

Other Beans that use events have their data changed by other classes. Events can be generated to notify listeners that the Bean had its state changed by another class and possibly pass the new state as part of the event. For Java Beans, the PropertyChangedEvent is designed to handle this type of situation.

This chapter is oriented toward understanding events in general and how they are advantagous to Java Beans. This chapter also discusses the significant changes of the Java event model between versions 1.02 and 1.1.

Java 1.0.2 Event Model Versus Java 1.1 Event Model

Java 1.0.2	Java 1.1
Events in Java 1.0.2	Events in Java 1.1
Single thread of synchronous events	Events are asynchronous
All events propagate through *handleEvent()* method	Events can be added to the standard event queue or cause direct calls from event sources to event listeners
AWT Events are unfiltered	Events are filtered based on registered users
Events extended by ID	Events extended by class

The Delegation Event Model

Delegation is the empowerment to act for others. The easiest way to describe how the delegation event model works is to show delegation events in the real world. Selling a home is an example that uses delegation. A real-estate broker is given delegated authority to look for potential buyers. When a buyer is found, the broker calls the homeowner. The homeowner does not get called by every person interested in the home, just those ready to purchase, as filtered by the broker who uses his delegated authority. In the Java delegation event model, event sources are empowered to act for listener classes by calling a listeners' methods when events occur. On the other hand, classes that generate events are designed so that listeners are registered for classes of events. When an event occurs that matches registered listeners, the source class calls the appropriate method of the listener.

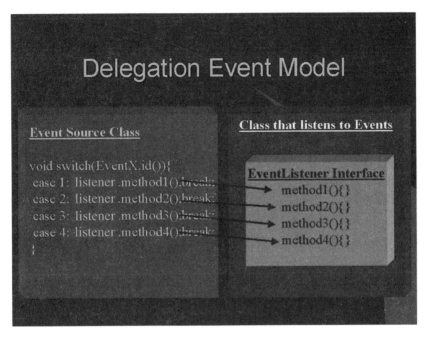

Figure 5.1

Event source and event listener classes, showing event source calling event listener methods.

Low-Level Events

Java has two types of events: low-level and semantic. Low-level events are directly associated with mouse, keyboard, component, container, and window information. Low-level events are those usually associated with hardware and default behavior of components and windows. Input events, however, are classified as mouse and keyboard. Figure 5.2 shows the low-level event hierarchy of classes defined by the AWT.

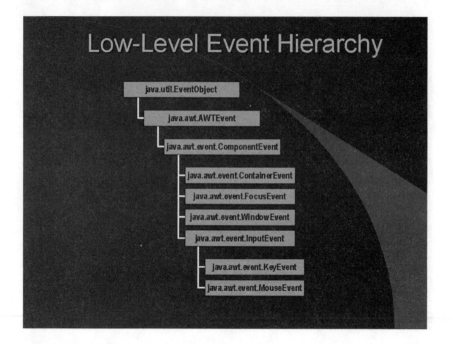

Figure 5.2

Low-level event hierarchy.

The low-level event hierarchy shows that the base of all events is the java.util.EventObject class, which contains functionality that will be used by all events. The EventObject class is used as a base for all events. EventObject also serves as a common class to use for generic event handlers such as event queues and event adapters.

The next element in the event hierarchy is the java.awt.AWTEvent class, which couches events in terms of the AWT. The ComponentEvent class is next in this tree, which groups these events into a set of events that occur to AWT components. Under the ComponentEvent class, the ContainerEvent, FocusEvent, and WindowEvent classes are used to signal state changes to components. Finally, comes the java.awt.event.InputEvent class that is the base for the KeyEvent and MouseEvent classes. Inheriting from the ComponentEvent class and the InputEvent class along with its siblings, MouseEvent and KeyEvent, the hierarchy is completed.

Semantic Events

Semantic events are the other type of events and are used to encapsulate the semantics of a user interface component's model. Figure 5.3 shows the hierarchy for semantic events.

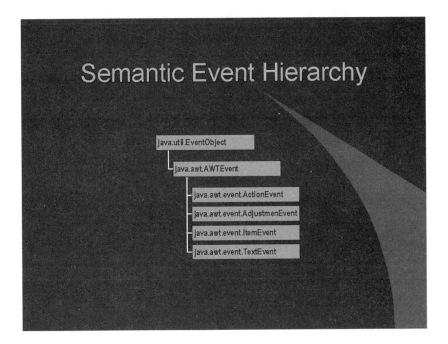

Figure 5.3

Semantic event hierarchy.

The semantic hierarchy in figure 5.3 starts the same way as the low-level events, with EventObject at the root followed by the AWTEvent. Again, the EventObject class is used for event handler classes and the AWTEvent class adds the AWT context. Unlike the final children of the low-level events, semantic events are expressed at the third level of the tree, just after AWTEvent. This is because these events are associated component actions that are the result of events. For example, the AdjustmentEvent is associated with the scrollbar object's scroll elevator button. The elevator button can be controlled by clicking on the arrow buttons, by clicking above or below the elevator or by moving the elevator button directly. However the elevator is moved, the AdjustmenEvent is fired to signal the new position.

AdjustmentEvent

The final type of event that is part of the Java core classes is the PropertyChangeEvent in the java.beans package. The PropertyChangeEvent is used to signal that a property value has changed or is about to change. The PropertyChangeEvent is inherited directly from EventObject (see fig. 5.4).

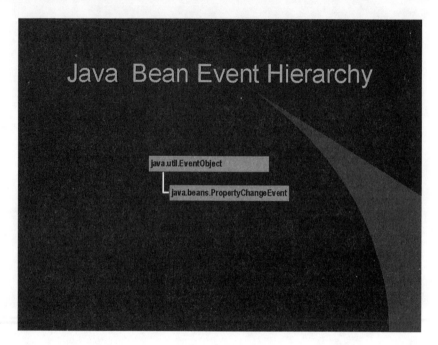

Figure 5.4

Java Bean event hierarchy.

The Base of All Events: java.util.EventObject

The EventObject class is the base class for all events. EventObject has one constructor, which takes a single parameter of type Object. The parameter is used to mark the source of the event. Usually, when constructing an event the EventObject class is the *this* reference. For example the following line of code will create a new event for the current object.

```
EventObject myEvent = new EventObject(this);
```

Much of working with the delegation model includes multiple classes and specifically named methods. In the AWT, for instance, there is a FocusEvent, FocusListener, FocusAdapter, and classes that are a source of Focus events. They have methods to add and remove Focus listeners called *addFocusEventListener()* and *removeFocusListener()*. The Java Bean Introspector class uses the names and types to locate event classes and methods. To ensure that events are properly handled for a Bean, any event that needs to be specially associated with a Bean needs to have a specific name, event support classes, and methods associated with it. Any new event that a class needs to generate should be one of those derived from the EventObject class or from other base event classes. The following class, for example, ButtonClickedEvent in listing 5.1 is used as the type of events for a user created button class.

Listing 5.1: Class ButtonClickedEvent

```
public class ButtonClickedEvent extends java.util.EventObject {
    public ButtonPushEvent(java.awt.Component source) {
        // Call the constructor for EventObject.
        super(source);
    }
}
```

Several points should be made about this implementation. First, the *source* argument for the class is an AWT Component class because this is an event for a button that is from the AWT Component class.

Event Action Context and Conditions

The next important thing to notice is that nothing is happening in the ButtonClickedEvent class other than calling the super class (EventObject) with a reference to the source object. As you can see, not much is happening in the parent EventObject class either except the assignment of the source to a member variable. The reason for this lack of activity in these classes is that the event is only the context and the type of the event. In this case, the the type ButtonClickedEvent and the context is the source component.

Another type use of the EventObject is to pass on information about about the event itself. An event for a nuclear reactor, for example, would be called NuclearReactorEvent. The object of such an event would be to convey the state of a nuclear reactor which has fuel rods, various temperatures, power output, and so on. Also, the event should represent the state of the reactor at a particular point in time. Most importantly, especially when dealing with something as dangerous as the control of a nuclear device, we need the data in the event to be immutable. If the event data is immutable there is no way for the receiver of the event to accidentally modify any of the reactors properties.

The NuclearReactorEvent event shown in listing 5.2 has the resulting event class. The event is sent for any of four types of conditions: startup, shutdown, periodic status, and error. The specific condition is set in the event ID and each ID is represented by static final class constants. Static constants are used in most events to designate the specific ID of an event. For each of these events, the reactor event has an immutable state of the reactor vessel that contains a time stamp, reactor temperature, and fuel rod status.

Listing 5.2: Class NuclearReactorEvent

```
01.import NuclearReactor;
02.import ReactorState;
03./**
04. * Custom event class to propagate events from a
05. * nuclear reactor.
06. *
07. */
08.public class NuclearReactorEvent extends java.util.EventObject{
09.    /**
10.     * Event ID for an event generated when a reactor is started.
11.i    */
12.i    public final static int REACTOR_STARTED = 1;
13.    /**
14.     * Event ID for an event generated when a reactor is stopped.
15.     */
16.    public final static int REACTOR_STOPPED = 2;
17.    /**
18.     * Event ID for an event generated for periodic status updates.
19.     */
20.    public final static int REACTOR_STATUS  = 3;
21.i    /**
22.i     * Event ID for an event generated when a reactor enters an error
➥condition.
23.     */
24.    public final static int REACTOR_ERROR   = 4;
25.
26.    public NuclearReactorEvent(NuclearReactor vessal, int
➥eventID,ReactorState status){
27.         super(vessal);
28.         eventType = eventID;
29.         vessalStatus = status;
30.    }
31.i    public int getEventID(){
32.i        return eventType;
33.    }
34.    public ReactorState getReactorState(){
35.        return vessalStatus;
36.    }
37.    private int eventType;
38.    private ReactorState vessalStatus;
39.}// end of class NuclearReactorEvent
```

Event Object Immutability

The most important feature of the NuclearReactorEvent is that access to the data is one way out. By preventing the data from being set, there is less possibility that a programmer will unwittingly change the contents of the event. Also, although it is not shown in listing 5.2, the internal objects that are returned are also immutable objects that cannot be modified after they are created. Data in an event object should always be immutable to prevent passing references that could affect behavior of the event source. In other words, the only time that internal data of an event's is set is when the object is created. This also includes the data that a status object defines. There should never be a way to modify any part of an event's state.

The nuclear reactor simulation would have problems if, for example, the temperature were linked directly to the temperature in the NuclearReactor class. When the reactor generates an error event for an out-of-range condition, the temperature being updated in a thread, the temperature may not be the same as when the event was generated. The event listener would not be able to accurately reflect what the error was, or the temperature at the time of the event. Worse still, if the event status is logged and the event referenced the real temperature and not a copy, each logged item would point back to the reactor where the temperature is periodically changing. This means that every logged message shows the current temperature and not a history of temperatures. Unfortunately, using a reference instead of a copy is an easy mistake.

 Tip

Immutability eliminates the need to synchronize any of the accessor functions. Without having to gain a lock on the data, code is generated to take up fewer instructions and operates faster. As a rule, make objects immutable to prevent synchronization problems.

Using Static Constants in Events

Another feature of the NuclearReactorEvent class, which should be copied by your event classes, is the use of static final constants to represent the valid identifiers for event IDs. This technique is preferable to just documenting the value because the developer can use these constants without fear of their values changing in future revisions of the class. Listings 5.3 and 5.4 use this type of event ID.

Listing 5.3: Class ReactorStatus

```
01.i/**
02.i * immutable state of a reactor
03. */
04.import FuelRodState;
05.import NuclearReactor;
06.import java.util.*;
07.public class ReactorState{
08.    public ReactorState(NuclearReactor reactor){
09.         this.timeStamp = new Date();
10.         this.coreTemp = reactor.getCoreTemp();
11.i       this.fuelRodState = reactor.getFuelRodState();
12.i       this.running = reactor.isRunning();
13.         this.powerOutput = getPowerOutput();
14.    }
15.    public Date getTimeStamp(){
16.        return timeStamp;
17.    }
18.    public double getCoreTemp(){
19.        return coreTemp;
20.    }
21.i   public FuelRodState[] getFuelRodState(){
22.i        return fuelRodState;
23.    }
24.    public double getPowerOutput(){
25.        return powerOutput;
26.    }
27.
28.    private Date timeStamp;
29.    private double coreTemp;
30.    private FuelRodState fuelRodState[];
31.    private double powerOutput;
32.    private boolean running;
33.}// end of class ReactorState.
```

Listing 5.4: Class FuelRodState

```
01.i/**
02.i * Immutable class to express fuel rod state
03.*/
04.public class FuelRodState{
05.    public FuelRodState(double decayLevel,
06.                        int insertionDepth,
07.                        double rodTemp){
```

```
08.         this.decayLevel = decayLevel;
09.         this.insertionDepth = insertionDepth;
10.         this.rodTemp = rodTemp;
11.i    }
12.i    public FuelRodState(FuelRod fuelRod){
13.         this.decayLevel = fuelRod.getDecayLevel();
14.         this.insertionDepth = fuelRod.getInsertionDepth();
15.         this.rodTemp = fuelRod.getRodTemp();
16.     }
17.     public double getDecayLevel(){
18.         return decayLevel;
19.     }
20.     public int   getInsertionDepth(){
21.i        return insertionDepth;
22.i    }
23.     public double getRodTemp(){
24.         return rodTemp;
25.     }
26.     private double decayLevel;
27.     private int   insertionDepth;
28.     private double rodTemp;
29.}// End of class FuelRodState
```

The Base of All AWT Events: java.awt.AWTEvent

The next event to be explored is the AWTEvent. As its name implies, this class describes AWT events. The AWTEvent inherits from the EventObject class, so all event utility functions can also be applied to the AWTEvent class and its derivatives. AWT can come from many sources such as mouse and keyboard events as well as component behaviors such as focus, resizing, and selection. In general, an AWT event is generated for each user input operation and for each component state change. Because input events originate in platform-specific code, AWT input events originate in a component's peer class (the peer class is the machine/operating-system specific code). In addition to the peer classes, additional AWT event behavior is implemented in the Component class.

The Component class (and possibly its peer in later releases of the AWT) is also where the filtering of events occurs. The type of events to be registered or unregistered is defined with event mask constants defined by the AWTEvent class. The name of each mask corresponds with the type of event being registered or unregistered. The following list documents the masks currently supported.

ACTION_EVENT_MASK

ADJUSTMENT_EVENT_MASK

COMPONENT_EVENT_MASK

CONTAINER_EVENT_MASK

FOCUS_EVENT_MASK

ITEM_EVENT_MASK

KEY_EVENT_MASK

MOUSE_EVENT_MASK

MOUSE_MOTION_EVENT_MASK

TEXT_EVENT_MASK

WINDOW_EVENT_MASK

java.awt.event.ComponentEvent

Component events are those that apply to all AWT component objects. As the following list shows, the events cover component movement and the actions of hiding, resizing, and showing.

The AWT will automatically handle component moves and resizes so that there is no reason for a component to intercept these events performing the tasks.

- ◆ COMPONENT_MOVED

- ◆ COMPONENT_RESIZED

- ◆ COMPONENT_SHOWN

- ◆ COMPONENT_HIDDEN

java.awt.event.ContainerEvent

Container events are very simple. The only actions performed are COMPONENT_ADDED and COMPONENT_REMOVED events. The main purpose of these events is to notify layout managers that the number of components has changed. The ContainerEvent static constant event identifiers consist of the following:

- ◆ COMPONENT_ADDED

- ◆ COMPONENT_REMOVED

java.awt.event.FocusEvent

The FocusEvent class is derived from the Component class. The FocusEvent class notifies listeners when a component loses or gains focus. The component that has focus is able to accept key events. Additionally, the behavior of a component can be modified depending on the focus state. A button with focus, for example, can have a rectangle drawn around it and the rectangle might be erased when focus is lost. Another possibility is that a component may run an animation or trigger a sound. The static event ID constants in the FocusEvent class consist of the following:

◆ FOCUS_GAINED

◆ FOCUS_LOST

java.awt.event.WindowEvent

Window events are very useful for knowing whether a component within a window needs to update its display. An animation Bean, for instance, might stop its animation when it receives a WINDOW_ICONIFIED or WINDOW_CLOSED event. Conversely, the animator may start its animation upon receiving WINDOW_DEICONIFIED, WINDOW_OPENED, or WINDOW_ACTIVATED events. The WindowEvent static constant event identifiers consist of the following:

WINDOW_OPENED	WINDOW_CLOSING
WINDOW_CLOSED	WINDOW_ICONIFIED
WINDOW_DEICONIFIED	WINDOW_ACTIVATED
WINDOW_DEACTIVATED	

java.awt.event.InputEvent

Input events are broken into two sub-classes: mouse events and keyboard events. Both child classes are affected by key modifiers such as Shift, Control, Alt, and other meta keys. Because of this commonality, the InputEvent class implements methods to determine the state of modifier keys when events are created. The utility methods to query specific key modifier states consist of the following:

◆ boolean *isShiftDown()*

◆ boolean *isControlDown()*

◆ boolean *isMetaDown()*

◆ boolean *isAltDown()*

In addition to the binary status of each modifier, the *getModifiers()* method can be used to retrieve the complete modifier state. The static constants defined in this class can determine mouse button status as well as check for any combination of key modifiers. The masks are directly available in the InputEvent class as final constants and consist of the following:

ALT_MASK	BUTTON1_MASK
BUTTON2_MASK	BUTTON3_MASK
CTRL_MASK	META_MASK
SHIFT_MASK	

The InputEvent class also defines the *getWhen()* method, which returns a long integer. The integer is a time stamp of when the event occurred. The time stamp can be used for event compression where only the most recent events in an event queue or event stack are used. The event time stamp can also be used to arbitrate the order of events. Arbitration is sometimes necessary when events come at different speeds or when events are queued while another process is in control. This is often caused by a complex process that happens at the same time that a mouse is moved. The mouse events are usually very high priority but the sync to the actual drawing and update of graphics may not be able to keep up. When the complex process completes the queue of mouse events, it can be discarded up to the time that the component should have been ready to accept mouse events. The time stamp can be used to ensure that stored events can be reissued in their proper order. For example, a user might move the mouse in anticipation of what is to be drawn. These anticipated events could be captured and replayed after the GUI is ready to accept events.

java.awt.event.KeyEvent

The KeyEvent class is a child of InputEvent. The class propagates the values of keys as well as their pressed, released, and clicked states. The KEY_TYPED event compresses key events so that the KEY_PRESSED and KEY_RELEASED events can be ignored for normal typing. The KeyEvent constant event identifiers consist of the following:

◆ KEY_TYPED (key press followed by a key release)

◆ KEY_PRESSED

◆ KEY_RELEASED

In addition to normal Unicode characters, the KeyEvent class can also sense the input of action keys. Action keys are all the keys on a keyboard that do not necessarily generate a textual output, such as *Home* or *Back Space*. The following list shows the types of keys recognized:

KeyEvent.VK_HOME	KeyEvent.VK_END
KeyEvent.VK_PAGE_UP	KeyEvent.VK_PAGE_DOWN
KeyEvent.VK_UP	KeyEvent.VK_DOWN
KeyEvent.VK_LEFT	KeyEvent.VK_RIGHT
KeyEvent.VK_F1	KeyEvent.VK_F2
KeyEvent.VK_F3	KeyEvent.VK_F4
KeyEvent.VK_F5	KeyEvent.VK_F6
KeyEvent.VK_F7	KeyEvent.VK_F8
KeyEvent.VK_F9	KeyEvent.VK_F10
KeyEvent.VK_F11	KeyEvent.VK_F12
KeyEvent.VK_PRINTSCREEN	KeyEvent.VK_SCROLL_LOCK
KeyEvent.VK_CAPS_LOCK	KeyEvent.VK_NUM_LOCK
KeyEvent.VK_PAUSE	KeyEvent.VK_INSERT

java.awt.event.MouseEvent

Mouse events, also derived from the InputEvent class, are used to provide both button and positional event information. Mouse events, though represented as one event class, are treated as two. This is done with separate listeners. One listener reads constant events as the mouse is moved (MouseMoveListener), and the other only gives button clicks and drag event movements (MouseListener). By separating these classes, the AWT is able to avoid the propagation of every mouse move to all AWT components. In contrast, java 1.02 with the old event system, propagated every mouse move to any component that the mouse was in. These excess mouse events, though not used, still had to propagate through the component tree from each container and component. Just this propagation of events caused a noticeable waste of processor resources. With the new model only components that specifically request the events will get them. This reduces the CPU overhead on components that are not interested in mouse events. The MouseEvent constant event identifiers consist of the following:

- ◆ MOUSE_CLICKED (mouse pressed followed by a mouse release)

- ◆ MOUSE_PRESSED

- ◆ MOUSE_RELEASED

- ◆ MOUSE_MOVED (used in MouseMovedListener)

- ◆ MOUSE_ENTERED

- ◆ MOUSE_EXITED

- ◆ MOUSE_DRAGGED (mouse movement while a button is pressed)

In addition to determining the type of mouse event, listeners can access mouse-specific positional information. This information can be used for locating the mouse within the component. An odd method that breaks the immutability rule of event objects is *translatePoint( )*. The *translatePoint( )* method causes the x/y posiition to be translated. This translation capability can be used to slightly change or warp the point to another location. This is useful when implementing a graphic system that uses handles to grab objects. The first level of event determines that the mouse is inside the bounding box of a handle and warps the point to be in the center of the box. The new, warped event is then passed to another part of the program that deals with the event as if the mouse is at the center of the graphic handle. The mouse event methods also include a duplication of the X and Y position both through separate axis and through a point object as can be seen in the following table:

Method	Action
int GetX()	Returns the x coordinate
int getY()	Returns the y coordinate
Point getPoint()	Returns a Point object representing the x,y coordinates
void translatePoint (int x, int y)	Translates the x,y coordinates (note that this permanently modifies the internal state of the objects x and y members)
int getClickCount()	Returns the number of button clicks
boolean isPopupTrigger()	Returns true if the event is associated with a pop-up menu
String paramString()	Translates the event identifier to an event name

java.awt.event.ComponentEvent

The ComponentEvent class is the base class of all component events. Component move-ment and resize events are handled automatically, so a component does not need to trap these events unless extra handling is required. The ComponentEvent static constant event identifiers consist of the following:

◆ COMPONENT_MOVED

◆ COMPONENT_RESIZED

◆ COMPONENT_SHOWN

◆ COMPONENT_HIDDEN

Event Listener Interfaces

Event listeners are used as targets for triggering actions whenever events occur. A class interested in receiving events implements the required listener and registers itself with an event source by calling the add listener function for the type of events generated. The following table lists event listeners and their respective classes:

Listener Interface	Event Source Class
ActionListener	Button, List, MenuItem
AdjustmentListener	ScrollBar
ComponentListener	Component
ContainerListener	Container
FocusListener	Component
ItemListener	Choice, CheckBox, CheckboxMenuItem, List
KeyListener	Componenet
MouseListener	Component
MouseMotionListener	Component
TextListener	TextArea, TextField
WindowListener	Dialog, Frame, Window

A class that tracks a component's key event, for example, will implement the KeyListener interface. When key events are needed, the implemented KeyListener is added to the event source by calling the *addKeyListener()* method of the event source. The source in listing 5.5 implements the previous example. For demonstration purposes, the TextEventTest class echoes the TextEvent data to the system out.

Listing 5.5: NuclearReactorListener interface

```
01.import NuclearReactorEvent;
02.i/**
03. * Listener interface for the NuclearReactor class.
04. * Note that there is a method for each type of
05. * reactor event.
06. */
07.public interface NuclearReactorListener{
08.    /**
09.      * Called when the reactor is started.
10.      * @param reactor event.
11.1.i       */
12.i    public void reactorStarted(NuclearReactorEvent nre);
13.    /**
14.      * Called when the reactor is stopped.
15.      * @param reactor event.
16.      */
17.    public void reactorStopped(NuclearReactorEvent nre);
18.    /**
19.      * Called when the reactor status thread executes.
20.      * @param reactor event.
21.i     */
22.i    public void reactorStatus(NuclearReactorEvent nre);
23.    /**
24.      * Called when the reactor has detected an error condition.
25.      * @param reactor status event at the time of the error.
26.      * @see China Syndrome
27.      */
28.    public void reactorError(NuclearReactorEvent nre);
29.
30.}// End of interface NuclearReactorListener
```

Event Adapters

Event adapters are event listener interfaces that are implemented as classes. Event adapters are used to call events of target classes that do not implement their own listener interfaces. By using adapters, older classes do not need to be rewritten to be added to event sources. Instead an adapter class is written to perform certain actions and it is the adapter that is added to an event source. Bean-aware applications like the BeanBox also generate and compile very simple adapters on-the-fly to connect Java Beans. Because classes can be compiled and loaded on-the-fly, these adapters can be added to running applications.

Event adapter base classes are also provided in the AWT. These adapter classes implement a specific event listener interface with null methods. This type of adapter is used when all or only a subset of a listener interface is required. The programmer creates a class that extends the adapter and overrides the methods that the design requires.

Event adapter helper classes are particularly useful when implemented as inner classes. As an inner class, the adapter has direct visibility of its outer class. This enables the inner class implementation to access methods and functions of the outer class directly.

Listing 5.6 is an example of an adapter for the NuclearReactorListener interface. The adapter does not implement any method. This class can be extended so that a particular event is implemented. For example, the *reactorError()* method can be used to shut down a nuclear reactor. It is important to note here that another reason for adapters is to separate the delegation of events into separate extensions of the adapter class. In other words each of the methods in the NuclearReactorAdapter class could be implemented as a separate class. This separation helps encapsulate the functionality that must exist in any particular class. If a class implemented all the methods for the event listener it could become large and unmanageable.

Listing 5.6: NuclearReactorAdapter class

```
01.import NuclearReactorEvent;
02.i/**
03. * Listener adapter class for the NuclearReactor class.
04. * Note that there is a method for each type of
05. * reactor event.
06. */
07.public class NuclearReactorAdapter implements NuclearReactorListener{
08.     /**
09.      * Called when the reactor is started.
10.      * @param reactor event.
11.i     */
12.i    public void reactorStarted(NuclearReactorEvent nre){
13.          // Null method. Override if process in this type of event.
```

continues

```
continued
14.    }
15.    /**
16.     * Called when the reactor is stopped.
17.     * @param reactor event.
18.     */
19.    public void reactorStopped(NuclearReactorEvent nre){
20.        // Null method. Override if process in this type of event.
21.i   }
22.i   /**
23.     * Called when the reactor status thread executes.
24.     * @param reactor event.
25.     */
26.    public void reactorStatus(NuclearReactorEvent nre){
27.        // Null method. Override if process in this type of event.
28.    }
29.    /**
30.     * Called when the reactor has detected an error condition.
31.i    * @param reactor status event at the time of the error.
32.i    * @see China Syndrome
33.     */
34.    public void reactorError(NuclearReactorEvent nre){
35.        // Null method. Override if process in this type of event.
36.    }
37.
38.}// End of interface NuclearReactorListener
```

External Class Adapters

External adapters are used to hook event sources to classes that do not have event listener interfaces. This process is illustrated in figure 5.5.

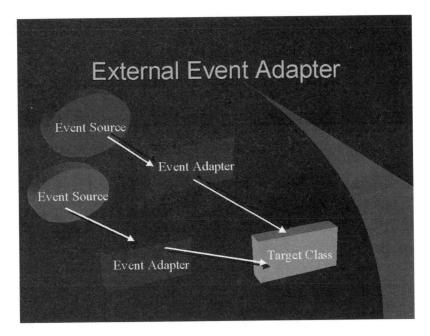

Figure 5.5

External adapters receiving and resending the event to a single class.

Inner Class Adapters

When a class needs to listen to events from multiple sources, the class can implement event adapters as an inner class. Although an external adapter could work in such a situation, the inner class requires less coding and has the added benefit of maintaining an adapter class tightly coupled to the target class. Instead, the combination of outer and inner class is more tightly coupled. The inner class is also hidden from any further reuse by other classes. Hiding the adapter in many cases is a good idea because the tight coupling of the adapter to the target class usually precludes any reuse anyway. The only possible reuse is available only by inheriting directly from the target class, which is much safer.

Figure 5.6 shows the relationships of inner class adapters, event sources, and event listeners. The figure also shows how multiple event listeners can be used to listen to multiple events—this is true even if the type of event is the same. The two event sources, for example, could be both buttons and the event listener's ActionAdapter class. The listener class is able to differentiate between the two buttons because the calls to the event listener adapters enter a separate context.

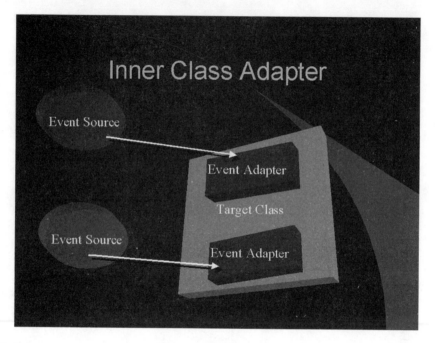

Figure 5.6

A class with two inner class adapters receiving events from two different event sources.

Using Adapters as Anonymous Inner Classes

Listing 5.7 provides an example of the utility and simplicity of using an adapter as an anonymous inner class. The class ReactorTempViewer extends java.awt.Label. The listener interface is passed to the NuclearReactor event source as an anonymous inner class extension of the NuclearReactorAdapter class. The inner class overrides the *reactorStatus()* method to retrieve the core temperature. The beauty of the inner class is that the context of the *reactorStatus()* method has full visibility of the Label class that the ReactorTemperatureViewer extends. This means that the method has access to the *isVisible()*, *setText()*, and the *repaint()* methods for the Label class. Also, in the case of this example, there would have been no reason to create an external adapter. The anonymous inner class is able to look and act as an external adapter without the need to actually create one.

Note

Inner classes may not be recognized or supported by Bean-aware applications. It is more probable that most applications will connect classes by generating specific event adapters for each connection. The use of inner classes is, however, very useful when connecting classes by hand or when rolling your own Bean-aware applications that will recognize the inner adapter logic.

Listing 5.7: Class ReactorTemperatureViewer—Demonstration of an anonymous inner class adapter

```
01.i/**
02.i * Demonstration of anonymous inner class adapter.
03. */
04.public class ReactorTemperatureViewer extends java.awt.Label{
05.    public ReactorTemperatureViewer(NuclearReactor reactor){
06.        reactor.addNuclearReactorListener(
07.            // Anonymous inner class Reactor NuclearReactorAdapter used
➥to set label value to core temp
08.            new NuclearReactorAdapter(){
09.                public void reactorStatus(NuclearReactorEvent nre){
10.                    ReactorState state = nre.getReactorState();
11.i                  setText("Core Temp: "+state.getCoreTemp());
12.i                  if( isVisible()){
13.                        repaint();
14.                    }
15.                }// end of reactorStatus() method override
16.            }// end of class
17.        );// end of addNuclearReactorListener method call
18.    } // End of ReactorTempViewer() class constructor
19.}// End of class ReactorTempViewer
```

Inner Class Adapters in Action

If the syntax of simultaneously creating and constructing a class object inside a method call makes you squeamish, the alternative is a normal inner class. The equivalent of the ReactorTemperatureViewer class has been rewritten as ReactorTemperatureViewer2 in listing 5.8. This version is slightly more complicated, but adds the capability to call the event source's *removeNuclearReactorListener()* method.

To facilitate the remove method, the event source and the adapter object need to be stored in class variables until it is time to finalize theReactorTemperatureViewer2 object. This implementation is probably preferable to the example in listing 5.7, because the event listener is removed when the component is finalized. If the previous component was used in a dialog created and destroyed several times, the NuclearReactor object would have many pointers to different instances of the ReactorTemperatureViewer class with no way to remove them. In this example, the listener is removed when finalized. Although the *finalizer()* method may not run for some time, the the visibility of the component is checked to see if repainting is required. By using the finalizer to remove the listener there is no need to specifically call the remove listener method prior to the last reference to the object going out of scope (usually an event that is difficult to predict).

Listing 5.8: Class ReactorTemperatureViewer—a normal inner class adapter

```
01.i/**
02.i * Demonstration of inner class adapter.
03. */
04.public class ReactorTemperatureViewer2  extends java.awt.Label{
05.
06.     public ReactorTemperatureViewer2 (NuclearReactor reactor){
07.          this.reactor = reactor;
08.          myAdapter = new MyAdapter();
09.          reactor.addNuclearReactorListener(myAdapter);
10.     } // End of ReactorTemperatureViewer2() class constructor
11.i
12.i    /**
13.      * Inner class
14.      */
15.     class MyAdapter extends NuclearReactorAdapter{
16.          public void reactorStatus(NuclearReactorEvent nre){
17.               ReactorState state= nre.getReactorState();
18.               setText("Core Temp: "+state.getCoreTemp());
19.               if( isVisible()){
20.                    repaint();
21.               }
22.          }// end of reactorStatus() method override
23.     }// end of class
24.     MyAdapter myAdapter;
25.     NuclearReactor reactor;
26.     protected void finalize() throws java.lang.Throwable{
27.          reactor.removeNuclearReactorListener(myAdapter);
28.          super.finalize();
29.     }
30}// End of class ReactorTemperatureViewer2
```

Note

The Argument for Inner Classes

There is a debate over the utility of inner classes and whether it violates the common precepts of object-oriented programming. Most of the debate spawns from two facts: that inner classes cannot be reused outside of their container class and that the inner class has visibility of the container's private methods and variables. The point of inner classes is not necessarily that they break these rules, rather they exist to reduce complexity when reuse and decoupling are not possible or very unlikely.

In C++, there is a close equivalent to an inner class scope possible through the friend statement. If a class declares another class as a friend, the friend class can access the target's private variables. Unfortunately, this friend class is available for reuse without necessarily being tightly associated with the target class. This inability to control inheritance and reuse could enable programmers to extend the friend or the target class without relating to either. This could possibly cause unknown effects in the target class. Java use is much more restrictive from the friend paradigm. For example, an inner class can only be created and manipulated in the context of an object of the outer class. In addition, the inner class has scope visibility only to the outer classes object that it was created in. This tight scoping and the fact that inheritance occurs in relation to the outer class makes the use of an inner class a safer approach.

Using inner classes as event adapters is one of the primary reasons that the inner class syntax was added to the Java language. Adapters fit all the reasons for inner class use: they are tightly coupled to the outer class, and they should not be inherited from in the context of being separate classes because of their tight coupling.

Hookup Adapters

For the interfacing of event sources and event listeners, IDEs and other development tools can generate code to create simple adapters between classes. Each adapter implements the listener interface of the event to be connected. The object that is to be operated on during the event is called in their respective event action methods.

A button, for example, is used to control the Juggler Bean in the BDK. When the hookup required, the button, registers a MOUSE_CLICKED event, a call to the *startJuggling()* method should be made. To accomplish this task without modifying the code of either class, a third class is created—an event hookup adapter. Fittingly, the BeanBox application has created a class to do exactly that. In the example that listing 5.9 provides, the

BeanBox creates a hookup class that implements MouseListener and calls the Juggler Bean's *startJuggling()* method from within the *mouseClicked()* method. The BeanBox can then compile the class and create with a reference to the Juggler Bean object to perform the action upon. The resulting hookup class can then be added to the button object by calling its *addMouseListener()* method with the hookup object as the listener. Once added to the button, when a clicked event occures the button calls the adapter which in turn calls the Juggler Bean's method. In listing 5.9 the hookup adapter calls the Juggler Bean's *startJuggling()* method.

Listing 5.9: Hookup adapter between BeanButton and Juggler class, generated by the BeanBox

```
01.i// Automatically generated event hookup file.
02.i
03.package sun.beanbox;
04.
05.public class ___Hookup_32eada34 implements java.awt.event.MouseListener,
java.io.Serializable {
06.
07.    public void setTarget(sun.demo.juggler.Juggler t) {
08.        target = t;
09.    }
10.
11.i   public void mouseClicked(java.awt.event.MouseEvent arg0) {
12.i        target.startJuggling();
13.    }
14.
15.    public void mousePressed(java.awt.event.MouseEvent arg0) {
16.    }
17.
18.    public void mouseReleased(java.awt.event.MouseEvent arg0) {
19.    }
20.
21.i   public void mouseEntered(java.awt.event.MouseEvent arg0) {
22.i    }
23.
24.    public void mouseExited(java.awt.event.MouseEvent arg0) {
25.
26.    }
27.    private sun.demo.juggler.Juggler target;
28.}
```

Events in Bean Components

An important part of understanding events with regard to Beans is how to extend existing components and use their events to implement new behaviors. The three most useful classes to extend are Component, Canvas, and Container. Each of these classes in turn has the *processEvent()* method that is used as the primary place to maipulate events. Other classes such as the Scrollbar have a *processAdjustmentEvent()* method, these are class specific event processing methods.

The processEvent() Method

The first method for accessing events from the Component base class is by overriding the *processEvent()* method, defined as follows:

```
protected void processEvent(AWTEvent);
```

The *processEvent()* method receives all AWT events that would normally be processed by the base class. This method is also called before many events that would normally be handled by the underlying AWT, such as movement and resize events.

By using the *processEvent()* method, all events can be handled with a single function.

Process Event Class Methods

The second method for handling events is through the process event class methods. The particular event to be processed depends on the component. The Button class, for example, has a *processActionEvent()* method that can be overridden by a child class. Also the Scrollbar class has a *processAdjustmentEvent()* method. These methods such as *processEvent()* can be used to change the behavior of components. For example, the *processAdjustmentEvent()* method could be overridden so that the scroll bar could be modified to only let the user move the elevator up and not down.

Implementing Action Listeners within Components

Remember that the event model is conservative. If a listener type is not registered on a component, those events are not proliferated to the component.

Summary

Events are a primary part of user interface programming. They can also be very useful for classes that don't have interfaces but need asynchronous communication. This chapter outlined the types of events in the Java language and demonstrated in several instances how to use events in JavaBeans and in other components.

Whenever creating JavaBeans, make certain that you understand the types of events that base classes provide. Do not attempt to reinvent the wheel. There is no reason, for instance, to add a ButtonPressedEvent to a component that already implements mouse events. Do not hesitate, however, to add events if they are extensions of existing events or otherwise represent a new semantic behavior such as the NuclearReactorEvent, which ecapsulates the events from a nuclear reactor. In addition, whenever creating new events remember to also implement event listener interfaces, event adapters, and the requisite listener notification and handler events to your Bean's class.

CHAPTER 6

Building Java Beans Step-by-Step

It is now time to really get into the grind of creating Java Beans. In this chapter, we start by discussing when and when not to create Java Beans. In addition, the various parts of Java Beans are expanded from the previous chapters and a few sample Java Beans will be created to show the steps in Bean development. Finally, you will learn how to diagnose and solve common Bean problems.

When to Create a Bean

A primary question to answer before writing a Bean is, "Should this be a Bean?" Almost any class can be considered a Bean. The minimum requirements for a class to be a Bean are as follows:

◆ Bean is a public instantiable class (no abstract class or interfaces allowed).

◆ Bean class must have a null constructor.

◆ Bean class is serializable.

Based on the preceding requirements, a class can be loaded and manipulated in a Bean-aware environment. Further functionality is added to the Bean by implementing Java Bean design signatures that the Introspector class can recognize or alternatively add a BeanInfo object that maps methods in a class to the EventSetDescriptor and PropertyDescriptor classes.

Connectable Beans

The next question to consider: "Is the Bean connectable?" The question here is associated with the Bean's methods in general and specific events or event listeners that it is a source of. This is not an absolute requirement. A Bean that was simply a rotating logo could be created that is not truly associated with the operation of other Java Beans. Nevertheless, most Java Beans are building blocks that are pieced together with events and methods. For instance, a Button Bean can be used to start an animation in another Bean when the Button receives a mouse click event. In this case, the button sends button clicked events and the animator receives a directive to start animating events (there is an event adapter used to translate the clicked events to call the start animation method of the animation Bean).

A Bean does not require a Listener interface just to receive events. In fact, any public method of a class can be thought of as an event that the class accepts. In the previous example, the animator Bean has *startAnimation()* and *stopAnimation()* methods. Each of these methods should be treated as events that the Bean listens for.

The translation between events and methods is done with event adapter objects. Event adapters implement the listener of the event source and call methods in non-listener objects. In the animation example, the event adapter implements the MouseListener interface that calls the animation Bean's *startAnimation()* method. Therefore, any class with public methods can be a listener (in BDK 1.0, only public methods with no parameters are valid, but this is not be true in most other Bean-aware editors).

The point here again is that even a simple class can be considered a Bean. Better still, there is very little work that needs to be done. A Java Beans IDE only needs to have a Java Beans-compliant class marked as a Bean so that it can add it to its palette. This makes it easy to quickly write a Bean and add it to your environment.

Multiple Use Beans

A multiple use Bean is a class that is somewhat generic or configurable for many different purposes. For example, a button is a very generic Bean. A spreadsheet Bean is a lot more complex and is configured to meet specific needs in an application. But both of these Java Beans can be used in multiple applications.

Single Use Java Beans

Even though a component might only be used once, it is still better to code it as a Bean simply so that the Bean-aware tool can more easily connect and manipulate the Bean. This could prove beneficial later because as a Bean, the component can be reconfigured over the lifetime of the main program (such as changing sizes, colors, number of entries, and so on). The flexibility of being a Bean is that they can be modified without recoding and recompilation. This could greatly reduce the amount of work that would normally be required over the life of a project.

Another reason for creating Java Beans with only one apparent use is that they can still be used in a rewrite of the same application. In such a case, for example, a button with a special animation would be used in the original as well as the rewrite. The probability that the Bean is reusable depends on how well it was initially written.

When Not to Create a Bean

Another problem is deciding when a component should not be a Bean. The most obvious is that the component is not reusable. Not making a class into a Bean simply because the class is not reusable is often a poor choice. Many Bean-aware IDEs can make programming simpler if as many classes as possible are treated as Java Beans. Because there are so many possibilities for Java Beans, the easier task is to determine what classes are unlikely to be used as Java Beans. The attributes that are good indicators of a class's ineligibility as a Bean are as follows:

◆ The class has no default constructor.

◆ The class is non-mutable.

◆ The class is not serializable.

The following sections describe these class attributes that make it impossible to convert a class into a Bean.

Class Has No Default Constructor

The primary reason that a class cannot be used as a Bean is when a class does not have a default constructor. Without a default constructor, there is no way to start a Bean in an IDE. Remember that an IDE has no idea how to start a Bean except through a default constructor.

Class Is Non-Mutable

A non-mutable class is a class that cannot be modified after it has been created. A Bean is more likely to be mutable. For example, a Button Bean is going to have various sizes that it can be set to. The Button Bean will have to be capable of adding and removing event listeners. Without the possibility for change, the button would need to be created with all of its information supplied in the class constructor. It is possible that the class could be serialized for use in a Bean-aware IDE, but there are problems with validating listeners and making the button fit properly wherever it may be placed. Therefore, a non-mutable class is a very poor candidate to be a Bean.

Class Is Not Serializable

Another very unlikely Bean, is a class that is not serializable. If the state of the class can not be saved, there is no reason to present it in a Bean-aware editor. Only serializable classes should be considered Java Beans.

Dissecting a Bean's Parts

A Bean is built from distinct sections or parts of code. Each section is associated with a part of how the Bean reacts to introspection and how it is represented in a Bean-aware application development tool. Each of the distinct parts are required if the Bean is required to represent itself in the appropriate way or if it is required to have defined Bean behaviors such as events or properties. The following sections describe each of these parts in the Bean examples to follow.

Bean Membership in a Package

To isolate this Bean from others, it is possible to create Beans that are not part of a package, but it is not recommended. Package membership isolates the Bean from other Beans. This proves very important when creating Beans that may clash with the names of components in the AWT or with names of components in other packages. Package membership also helps to group related Beans or classes required by the Bean. The package is also used as a common place to put associated classes and the Bean's custom BeanInfo class.

Class Signatures

Class signature refers to the name of the class and its base class and implemented interfaces. The class signature is important for its type and for the information that can be derived by the Introspector class.

Default Constructors

A *default constructor* is a constructor that has no parameters. The default constructor is required by a Bean-aware IDE to create the Bean. The default constructor should set all properties to a reasonable default value.

Specialized Constructors

Any additional constructors in a Bean's main class are considered specialized constructors that are used outside of a Bean-aware development environment. These constructors have parameters that change the Bean's properties to settings other than the default set in the default constructor. Specialized constructors are useful when hand coding a Bean, because they reduce the need to set up the Bean by calling set property methods after the Bean is created. In addition, the specialized constructors may be a remnant from before an existing class is transformed into a Bean. There is no reason to remove such constructors, especially because older code may still rely on these constructors.

Property Listener Interface Implementation

To register itself for property change events, the Bean must implement the PropertyChangeListener interface. This enables the class to be bound to the changing data in another class. This mechanism is like the observer/observable software pattern. The class with the property is the observable and the class with the PropertyChangeListener interface is the observer.

Add/Remove Property Listener Signatures

Add and remove property listener methods are design signatures required to add and remove property classes that implement PropertyChangeListener interfaces. Without both methods, the IDE will not recognize the Bean as a source of PropertyChangeEvent notifications. The preferred way to do this is with the SimplePropertyChange-ListenerSupport class.

The add/remove property listener methods must exist before any property can be treated as a bound property.

Vetoable Change Listener Interface Implementation

Beans that are vetoable change listeners need to implement the VetoableChangeListener interface. A vetoable change is a property change where a class can vote to accept a property change occurring in another Bean. Before a vetoable change source modifies its internal state, it first calls the *vetoableChange()* method of the listeners. If the new value is not approved by the listener, then the listener throws a PropertyVetoException, which causes the new value to be discarded. Beans that are vetoable change listeners are used primarily to control other Java Beans. A good example of a vetoable listener is a safety interlock. A safety interlock would be registered as a listener to a Bean that controlled perhaps the on/off state of a nuclear reactor. Any time that another class tries to turn on the nuclear reactor, the interlock Bean would check the state of the reactor and other safety factors to determine if the reactor could be switched on. If the interlock detects an unsafe condition, the interlock Bean throws a PropertyVetoException that causes the reactor to ignore the command to start.

Add/Remove Vetoable Change Listener Support Signatures

For a Bean to have properties seen by the Introspector class as vetoable, there must be add and remove vetoable change listener methods. The preferred way to add these methods is by using the VetoableChangeSupport class.

Any set property method that is set to a vetoable change property must be defined to throw PropertyVetoException and properly notify vetoable change listeners.

General Event Listener Interface Implementation

To enable the Bean to register itself for AWT or specialized Bean events, the Bean must implement the event listener interface of the associated event. This is not normally required because the Component class attends to most of the event handling required.

Add/Remove Event Listener Support Signatures

For a Bean to be a source of developer-defined events, there must be add and remove event listener methods. Without the add and remove signatures, the Introspector class will be unable to connect other Java Beans to specific events.

Set/Get Properties

For a property to be accessible through the property sheet, it must have a *set()* method and a *get()* method. Both methods must follow the property method signatures as described in Chapter 4, "Java Bean Design Signatures."

If the property is bound and there are add and remove property change listeners, the set property method should call the *propertyChanged()* method of subscribed PropertyChangedListeners.

If the property is vetoable, the set method must be defined to throw a PropertyVetoException and the registered property veto listeners called.

Set/Get Indexed Properties

In addition to the normal properties of a Bean that manipulate only a single value, indexed properties can manipulate arrays of properties. These indexed properties can be normal, bound, or vetoable properties. Indexed properties are used to access array-like properties of a Bean, like lists.

Set/Is Boolean Properties

Another type of property that uses a slightly different design signature is the Boolean property. Boolean properties can be expressed with set/is methods as shown in the following lines of code, respectively:

```
void setVisible(boolean);
boolean isVisible();
```

A Boolean property can also be recognized as a set/get design signature, but set/is methods in combination make code more understandable. Because Boolean properties are often used in a program's logical flow of control, the *is* method helps to clarify that the type of value returned is a Boolean. The *isOn()* method, for example, has a better connotation and implies a Boolean, where the *getOn()* method could be of any type.

Public Methods

Public methods other than those associated with events, event handling, and property control are also interpreted by the Introspector. The BeanInfo created by the Introspector will have a MethodDescriptor object defined for each method in a Bean's class. Some early versions of Bean-aware IDE application builders may have limited capability to link methods other than those that take no parameters (such as the 1.0 BDK from JavaSoft), so most interactions associated with calling a Bean can be performed with custom events. In other words, if a call to a Bean needs to pass data, create an event suited to the task. The event can be extended to include the data that would have normally been included in a vanilla method call. The method called by the event source can perform the action in the context of the object, or call the method to perform the action that would normally be called from another class.

Protected and Private Field Members

One of the tenants of good programming practice is to never expose a class member field directly. Always use an accessor method such as set/get or set/is to isolate changes to an object. This means that the member fields should never be public. Fields should be set to the default, which is package protected or private. If a field does not have accessor methods, do not make the field private unless it should only be used in the current version of the class.

If a field is private and it does not have an accessor, then it cannot be used by a child class. This can make inheritance of the Bean impossible or impractical. Use the protected modifier instead of private. Protected limits the visibility to child classes and classes in the same package.

Protected and Private Methods

Defining methods as private should be done with extreme caution when developing classes used as reusable components. The problem with private methods is that they can not be accessed by classes that inherit from these classes. This can be a huge problem when a utility method in the base component is inaccessible to child classes. If the child class needs to use the method, the users of your class will need to either directly modify your source or copy and modify it as a different class name so that private modifiers can be removed. The only time the private access modifier should be used is with methods that can only be used by the current class. The only time that this should happen is for safety or security reasons. Most methods should be protected or public instead of private.

Transient and Volatile Field Members

Transient fields are marked as such to prevent serialization. The reason for preventing serialization is to prevent data associated with the present context from being saved and restored later. It is very important that all member fields be examined to verify whether their state should be serialized. Transient fields are usually those that are part of a thread of execution as opposed to those associated with properties. A developer should err on the side of caution and mark all fields as transient unless specifically required to be serializable. Examples of non-transient fields are foreground and background colors or component sizes. Transient fields are information such as the pressed or released state of a button. A normal button should always start in its released state because the button state is transient.

Volatile fields, like transient fields, are also not serialized. Volatile fields may not be marked as such, but they may be treated as a property that holds its value in another class. A toggle button, for instance, may serialize the current state. A Bean connected to the toggle should always query the toggle's state.

Public Final Constants

Constants are another important feature of classes. Their use as part of a Bean is, however, dependent on the Bean-aware application in which it is used. There is no direct association of any type of field, final or otherwise, in the BeanInfo. Because of this, there is no reasonable expectation that a Bean-aware application can use them. Any public field can be accessed through the Core Reflection API. An advanced application could, therefore, programmatically discover the fields with the Core Reflection API, and thereby become a part of the Bean API presented by the IDE. Normally, final constants are used within a package to communicate defaults between package member classes. A primary example of their use is in defining event-specific IDs.

If a constant is needed by other applications, the best solution is to create a set/get pair of property access methods. The get method returns the constant. The set method performs no action or is defined as a vetoable property that always throws a PropertyVetoException event.

Component Size Support

Component size is one of the more important features of concern to Bean designers. There should be logic to handle any type of property change that may cause the component to need to be redisplayed. Without this logic, a possibility exists that the end user may not be able to resize a Bean appropriately. It is the designer's responsibility to design the Bean such that the minimum size of the component is always large enough to display its parts. In other words, buttons or labels should always big enough to display their contents, regardless of font size or string length. The same is true of components that are a collection of other components. If an inner component changes the minimum size, the minimum should be recalculated for the host containers. Figure 6.1 shows an example of a label component that causes truncated text and a label component that is prepared to handle adjustments in content size.

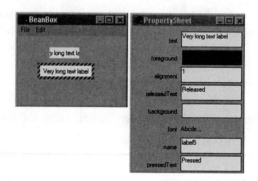

Figure 6.1

Two Bean Labels, one with correct sizing and one with autosizing.

Bean Examples

In the following sections, you will design and build several types of Java Beans. Each Bean explores the use of different method signatures and design decisions that make Java Beans work with a Bean-aware IDE. You will also learn how to use the Beans in JavaSoft's BeanBox application. The object of these examples is to provide Bean developers with a sense of the work involved and the decisions that make better Beans. The example Beans covered in the remaining part of this chapter consist of the following:

◆ **RoundButton:** a round or oval (depending on its height and width) button that has a color for the up state and a color for the down state.

◆ **OnOffButton:** a button that toggles its state between on and off. This button can be used like a light switch or toggle button.

◆ **NuclearReactor:** a collection of Beans and related classes. The example shows just the main NuclearReactor Bean. The NuclearReactor is an example of how to use invisible Beans. This Bean shows how a non-visual component can be created. The NuclearReactor Bean is controlled by other visual Bean components. Only the NuclearReactor Bean and the RodController Bean are shown in the book. Please refer to the book's accompanying CD-ROM for a complete listing of the NuclearReactor example.

◆ **RodController:** one of the Beans used to control the NuclearReactor Bean. This is a Slider component that has been modified to accept a RodControllerListener object.

Example Beans Found Elsewhere in This Book

There are other useful example Java Beans examples scattered throughout the book including the following:

◆ **InternationalButton:** a Button that forces its size to be the minimum required to make the button's label visible. This Bean can be found in Chapter 11, "Java Bean Internationalization."

◆ **SoundImageButton:** enabled with additional property editors to edit image and sounds. The SoundImageButton is found in Chapter 9, "Building Custom Component Editors for Java Beans."

In addition to the sources to the examples within the book, the accompanying CD includes the following example Beans:

◆ **StockGraph:** graphs the daily high, low, open, and close in several popular formats

◆ **StockSelect:** a list of days that can be selected to report with the StockGraph Bean

◆ **ButtonStatus:** displays the pressed or released status of a button

◆ **TwoStateButton:** similar to the OnOffButton except that the text label of the button does not change when pressed

◆ **All Beans in the BDK:** All 12 Beans for study and manipulation

◆ **Complete Nuclear Reactor Simulator:** in this book, only parts of the NuclearReactor simulator are discussed. The complete simulation including a few more Bean components and associated classes are included. The NuclearReactor example is a good place to see most of the Java Bean signatures and how they interrelate

Building the RoundButton Bean

The object of the RoundButton Bean is to create a button that is a filled circle of color. The button should have two possible colors: one for the released state, and one for the pressed state. The clients of this Bean will be MouseListener objects. As will be seen, or rather conspicuous by their absence, no code in this Bean propagates mouse events. The reason is simple, the underlying Component base class has the implementation for adding and removing mouse event listeners.

Like most of the code in this book, the class file has been broken up into several short sublistings. The code in the sublisting is discussed and then each class ends with a discussion of how it is seen by a Bean-aware IDE. The order of listing breakdown is approximately the order that would normally be taken when creating a Bean. Some, however, are results of the entire Bean—such as imported packages. The overall sequence is not as important as the compliance of each section so that the Bean is recognized properly by the Introspector class. If sections are left out or incorrectly written, the Bean may not function as designed.

The RoundButton Bean is broken up into the following Bean design issues:

- Package membership
- Class signature
- Default constructor
- Event handling
- The *paint( )* method
- Bean properties

Overall, this is a very simple Bean, containing almost the minimum required to create a useful, reusable component.

Packages Membership

Listing 6.1a begins the RoundButton Bean by declaring the package where it resides.

Tip

> Java Beans should always be part of a package in order to prevent problems with name collisions and to limit access by other classes in the default package.

The imported packages are also defined in listing 6.1a. The awt and awt.event packages are used to build the button and its events.

Listing 6.1a: Class RoundButton—Package membership and imported classes

```
package NewRiders.beans.buttons;
import  java.awt.*;
import  java.awt.event.*;
```

Class Signature

The next part of the listing (6.1b) is the class signature. You should note several things about the class definition for the RoundButton class:

- The class is public so that it can be accessed by classes outside its package.

- The class inherits from the Canvas class. By inheriting from Canvas, the Bean is a component with all the properties, events, and methods associated with a component. The Canvas class is used to specifically denote that the Bean has a visual presentation.

- The class implements the java.io.Serializable interface so that the state of the Bean can be saved.

Listing 6.1b: Class RoundButton—Class signature

```
public class RoundButton extends Canvas implements java.io.Serializable{
```

Default Constructor for RoundButton

The default constructor for RoundButton is fairly simple. First the super class constructor is called, secondly the size of the button is set, then mouse events are enabled. The call to the *enableEvents()* method to enable mouse events is one of the more important aspects of this constructor. The mouse events are enabled at construction so that the button is immediately sensitive to mouse clicks. This is important for a button mainly because an end user may want to see what happens when the mouse is clicked. Also, this alleviates any requirement for a listener to be added before the button can be seen to operate. Because the user has the capability to manipulate the size and color of this Bean, it is important that the property changes can be immediately tested.

Listing 6.1c: Class RoundButton

```
public RoundButton () {
    super();
    setSize(40,40);
    enableEvents(MouseEvent.MOUSE_EVENT_MASK);
}
```

The paint() Method

The *paint()* method shown in listing 6.1d is used by the RoundButton class displaying a circle with the color associated with being pressed or released. If the component does not have focus, the button is drawn in the released state. The user, therefore, knows that if the mouse button is released, the button clicked event will not be generated for this component.

Listing 6.1d: Class RoundButton—The paint() method

```
/**
 * Draws an oval that fits the bounds of the canvas.
 */
public void paint (Graphics context) {
    if (down && hasFocus){
        context.setColor(pressedColor);
    }else{
        context.setColor(releasedColor);
    }
    context.fillArc(5, 5, getSize().width-10, getSize().height-10,
0, 360);
}
```

Event Processing

Event processing for the RoundButton (defined in listing 6.1e) is concerned with determining whether the button is up, down, in focus, or out of focus. This is done by processing mouse events in the case statement on line 6 in listing 6.1e. Using this information, a new state is determined and the *repaint()* method is called so that the correct color will be drawn for the mouse state.

Remember that this method is enabled as soon as the class is created because of the call to *enableEvents()* with the mouse event mask set.

The most important feature of the method occurs on line 40 where the call to the *super.processMouseEvent(e)* method is made. This call causes the mouse event to propagate to the Canvas class and into the Component class. Within the Component class, the mouse clicked events are propagated to registered MouseListener objects with the call: *super.processMouseEvent(e)* on line 40.

This propagation of events to the components super class is very important to the functionality of the RoundButton. The Component class's event handling has made it unnecessary for the RoundButton to implement its own event listener logic.

Listing 6.1e: Class RoundButton—The processMouseEvent() method

```
01.      /**
02.       * Processes the push button event to display a down or up event.
03.       */
04.     protected void processMouseEvent (MouseEvent e){
05.        switch(e.getId()) {
06.           case MouseEvent.MOUSE_PRESSED :
07.              //The mouse button was pressed.
08.              // Paint the pressed color.
09.              down = true;
10.              repaint();
11.              break;
12.           case MouseEvent.MOUSE_RELEASED :
13.              //The mouse button was released.
14.              //Paint the normal color.
15.              down = false;
16.              repaint();
17.              break;
18.           case MouseEvent.MOUSE_DRAGGED:
19.              if ((e.getX() < 0) || (e.getX() > size().width) ||
20.                  (e.getY() < 0) || (e.getY() > size().height)) {
```

continues

continued

```
21.                        if (down) {
22.                            down = false;
23.                            repaint();
24.                            }
25.                        } else if (!down) {
26.                            down = true;
27.                            repaint();
28.                        }
29.                        break;
30.                    case MouseEvent.MOUSE_ENTERED:
31.                        hasFocus = true;
32.                        repaint();
33.                        break;
34.                    case MouseEvent.MOUSE_EXITED:
35.                        hasFocus = false;
36.                        repaint();
37.                        break;
38.                }// End switch
39.                //Ensure that the event is propagated.
40.                super.processMouseEvent(e);
41.        }
```

Property Accessors

The final group of methods consist of the property set/get methods used to set and get the releasedColor and the pressedColor properties. These properties, in listings 6.1f and 6.1g are simple, unbound properties. There is probably no reason to report changes to these properties or to veto the color selected.

Listing 6.1f: Class RoundButton—releasedColor property accessors

```
01.    /**
02.     * Returns the color that the bean released event is expressed as.
03.     * @see #setReleasedColor
04.     */
05.    public synchronized Color getReleasedColor (){
06.        return releasedColor;
07.    }
08.    /**
09.     * Sets the color that the bean released event is expressed as.
10.     * @see #getReleasedColor
11.     */
```

```
12.    public void setReleasedColor (Color newColor){
13.        releasedColor = newColor;
14.        repaint();
15.    }
```

Listing 6.1g: Class RoundButton—pressedColor property accessors

```
01.    /**
02.     * Returns the color that the bean pressed event is expressed as.
03.     * @see #setPressedColor
04.     */
05.
06.    public synchronized Color getPressedColor (){
07.        return pressedColor;
08.    }
09.    /**
10.     * Sets the color that the bean pressed event is expressed as.
11.     * @see #getPressesColor
12.     */
13.    public void setPressedColor (Color newColor){
14.        pressedColor = newColor;
15.        repaint();
16.    }
```

Figure 6.2 shows the RoundButton Bean in its pressed and released states and also shows the corresponding properties for the Bean.

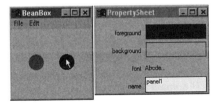

Figure 6.2

RoundButton Bean and its corresponding states and properties.

Method Fields

The final part of the RoundButton class, shown in listing 6.1h, defines the internal state of the RoundButton class. In these fields, the colors and the interpretation of the button state is kept. It is important to note that the colors, which are associated with Bean property accessor methods, are normal private fields; on the other hand, the button's down state and the focus state are defined as transients. They are also protected because that is the default protection for a field. A class inheriting from this Bean may want to have more control by accessing this variable, so it is preferable to private protection, which would prevent child classes from accessing the field. The fields are transient because the button should be initialized to the released state and assume that the mouse is not inside the bounding rectangle of the component.

Listing 6.1h: Class RoundButton—Private and protected class fields and end of class

```
    // Private data fields:
    private Color pressedColor = Color.black;
    private Color releasedColor = Color.red;
    transient boolean down = false;
    transient boolean hasFocus = false;
}
```

The RoundButton Manifest Template

The RoundButton manifest template, stored with the file name NewRidersRoundButton.mf, is extremely brief. As the following code shows, the only contents are the manifest version, the location of the RoundButton class in the template, and a property that marks the Bean as a Java-Bean. The manifest template will be used as a starting point to create the true manifest when the JAR command is called in the next section.

```
Manifest-Version: 1.0

Name:NewRiders/beans/status/RoundButton.class
Java-Bean: True
```

Building the RoundButton JAR File

Building the JAR file for RoundButton is a simple matter. The JAR name, manifest template are specified and the root directory of the package is given. The following code shows the JAR command that would be used if the manifest template is in the same directory as the root of the package:

```
jar cfm NewRidersRoundButton.jar NewRidersRoundButton.mf NewRiders
```

Building the OnOffButton Bean

The OnOffButton Bean is a little more complex than the RoundButton Bean. Where the RoundButton emulated a simple push button, the OnOffButton emulates a button that has two states: on and off (see fig. 6.3). Each time the OnOffButton Bean is clicked, the state changes from one state to the other (the RoundButton pops up when released). This type of behavior is often associated with switches or toggles. The OnOffButton also has two strings, one for the on state and another for off.

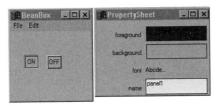

Figure 6.3

ON and OFF buttons and properties for the OnOffButton Bean.

The OnOffButton Bean has another behavior associated with it that makes it useful for a variety of purposes. Depending on the on or off state, the Bean displays an associated string. As default, when the button is up it displays OFF. When the button is depressed, the text displayed is ON. The text for both the on/off states can be controlled independently through a property sheet, so the button can serve a wide variety of purposes.

The way that this Bean is associated with other components is through property changed events. As the state changes, the button's "down" property is changed to reflect the up/down or on/off state. The down property can also be set via an IDE property sheet and is retained during serialization so that the button will be retrieved in a specific state.

The look of the button is similar to a normal AWT button, but is a custom interpretation. If another look is required, this button could be used as a base class to create other two-state buttons that have different visual attributes.

The OnOffButton example is concerned with the following issues, covered in detail in the sections that follow:

◆ Package membership

◆ Class signature

◆ Default constructor

- Text label properties

- Override of *Component.setFont()*

- Event handling

- The *paint()* method

- Resizing to fit text

- Reporting minimum and preferred size

- PropertyChangeListener support

- Bound properties

Packages Membership

Like the RoundButton Bean, the OnOffButton class is in a package that prevents a name clash with other Beans. The OnOffButton class is also associated with a wider range of imported classes. More package support is required for this Bean because of the displayed text and the property change support. Listing 6.2a shows the package membership and imported package associations.

Listing 6.2a: Class OnOffButton—Package membership and imported packages

```
package NewRiders.beans.buttons;
import java.beans.*;
import java.awt.*;
import java.awt.event.*;
import java.io.Serializable;
import java.util.Vector;
```

Class Signature

You should note several things about the class definition for the OnOffButton class (they are the same as RoundButton):

- The class is public so that it can be accessed by classes outside its package.

- The class inherits from the Canvas class. By inheriting from Canvas, the Bean is a component with all the properties, events, and methods associated with a component. The Canvas class specifically denotes that the Bean has a visual presentation.

◆ The class implements the java.io.Serializable interface so that the state of the Bean can be saved.

Listing 6.2b shows the class signature for OnOffButton.

Listing 6.2b: Class OnOffButton—The OnOffButton class signature

```
public class OnOffButton extends Canvas implements Serializable {

    /**
     * Default constructor for a two state toggle type two state button.
     * default gray color and Dialog 12 font. The label is
     * set to 'On'/'Off'.
     */
```

Default Constructor for OnOffButton

The default constructor for OnOffButton is similar to RoundButton, except that there is a little more effort required to set the text and default font to be displayed. The super class constructor of Canvas is called and the component's mouse events are enabled. The call is made to the *enableEvents()* method to enable mouse events. As stated before, it is important that a button's events be enabled when the button is created.

Another difference between OnOffButton and the RoundButton is that there is no *resize()* method call. The reason there is no sizing done in this constructor is that it is done on demand in other parts of this class based on the text that this Bean displays. Listing 6.2c shows the default constructor for OnOffButton.

Listing 6.2c: Class OnOffButton—Default constructor

```
01.    public OnOffButton() {
02.        this.onText = "ON";
03.        this.offText = "OFF";
04.        // Set to a standard font.
05.        setFont(new Font("Dialog", Font.PLAIN, 12));
06.
07.        // Give this the normal button color.
08.        setBackground(Color.lightGray);
09.
10.        // Enable events so that button can be used.
11.        enableEvents(MouseEvent.MOUSE_EVENT_MASK);
12.
13.    }
```

Specialized Constructor

An additional constructor is used for situations when this Bean is created by hand, outside a Bean-aware development environment. This constructor adds the capability to set the on/off text properties in the constructor. The rest of the constructor in listing 6.2d is essentially the same as the default constructor.

Listing 6.2d: Class OnOffButton—A specialized constructor

```
01.    /**
02.      * Create a two state button with default gray color
03.      * and Dialog 12 font.
04.      * @param label the label of the button
05.      */
06.    public OnOffButton(String OnText,String OffText) {
07.         // Initialize the canvas
08.         this.onText = onText;
09.         this.offText = offText;
10.         // Set to a standard font.
11.         setFont(new Font("Dialog", Font.PLAIN, 12));
12.
13.         // Give this the normal button color.
14.         setBackground(Color.lightGray);
15.
16.         // Enable events so that button can be used.
17.         enableEvents(MouseEvent.MOUSE_EVENT_MASK);
18.    }
```

Property Change Support Signatures

The next set of methods is concerned with the registering of interested property change listeners. These two methods enable this Bean to add and remove property change listeners. The *setDown()* method reports its state changes to these listeners. The PropertyChangeSupport class is used to lower the coding overhead required to keep track of and notify listeners. Listing 6.2e shows the property change support methods.

Listing 6.2e: Class OnOffButton—Property change support methods

```
public void addPropertyChangeListener(PropertyChangeListener l) {
     changes.addPropertyChangeListener(l);
}
```

```
public void removePropertyChangeListener(PropertyChangeListener l) {
    changes.removePropertyChangeListener(l);
}
```

Property Signatures

The next set of methods in listing 6.2f are property signatures used to set and retrieve the text displayed for the on/off states of the button. In the set methods, there is an additional call to the *sizeToFit()* method of this class. The *sizeToFit()* method (lines 3 and 7) is called in each of the set methods to ensure that the size of the button is resized to accommodate the widest of the two display strings.

Listing 6.2f: Class OnOffButton—The onText and offText property access methods

```
01.     public void setOnText(String onText){
02.         this.onText = onText;
03.         sizeToFit();
04.     }
05.     public void setOffText(String offText){
06.         this.offText = offText;
07.         sizeToFit();
08.     }
09.     public String getOnText(){
10.         return onText;
11.     }
12.     public String getOffText(){
13.         return offText;
14.     }
```

Overriding the setFont() Method

The next property method, shown in listing 6.2g, is an override of the *setFont()* method that is part of the Component class. This method must be overridden so that changes in the selected font can be immediately seen. To accomplish the instant feedback required, the super *setFont()* is called. This enables the Component class to handle the introduction of the new font. Because you do not have access to the Component private variable for the font, the set method is the only (and appropriate) procedure for accomplishing this. After the font has been set in Component, the *sizeToFit()* method is called to resize the button to fit the text and the font.

It is important to note that only one half of the property signature is expressed in this class for the font property. Because the *getFont()* method is visible in the Component base class, however, the Introspector is able to properly create a PropertyDescriptor for the font property. If there was no *getFont()* method in Canvas, there would need to be one in OnOffButton before the property would be created by the Introspector class.

Listing 6.2g: Class OnOffButton—Override of setFont() method

```
public void setFont(Font font){
    super.setFont(font);
    sizeToFit();
}
```

Event Processing

Event processing for the OnOffButton is much simpler than the RoundButton Bean. OnOffButton is concerned only with the clicked events. When clicked events are received, the button state is switched.

Remember that the *processMouseEvent()* method is enabled in the Bean's constructor with the call to the *enableEvents()* method with the mouse event mask.

Like the RoundButton event handler, line 11 in listing 6.2h has a call to *super.processMouseEvent;*. This call causes the mouse event to propagate to the Canvas class and into the Component class. Within the Component class, the mouse clicked events are propagated to registered MouseListener objects.

This propagation to the Component class is only of minor importance to this class because the actual events that clients are interested in are generated through the propertyChangedEvent rather than mouse events. Event processing for the OnOffButton is declared in listing 6.2h.

Listing 6.2h: Class OnOffButton—processMouseEvent() method

```
01.protected void processMouseEvent (MouseEvent e){
02.        switch(e.getId()) {
03.            case MouseEvent.MOUSE_CLICKED :
04.                //The mouse button was pressed.
05.                // Notify the listener.
06.                // Paint the pressed color.
```

```
07.              setDown(!isDown());
08.              break;
09.          }// End switch
10.          //Ensure that the event is propigated.
11.          super.processMouseEvent;
12.      }
```

paint() Method

The *paint()* method in listing 6.2i for the OnOffButton is much more complex than the RoundButton class. The reason is that there is a lot of code associated with creating a button with a text label. There is also logic built into the code to draw the button label for the up or down state.

Listing 6.2i: Class OnOffButton—paint() method

```
01.  /**
02.    * Paint the button including label and 3d edges
03.    *
04.    */
05.   public synchronized void paint(Graphics context) {
06.          int width = size().width;
07.          int height = size().height;
08.
09.          context.setColor(getBackground());
10.          context.fillRect(1, 1, width - 2, height - 2);
11.
12.          // Note that the down property is used to change the 3D rect.
13.          context.draw3DRect(0, 0, width - 1, height - 1, !down);
14.          context.setColor(getForeground());
15.          context.setFont(getFont());
16.          context.drawRect(2, 2, width - 4, height - 4);
17.          FontMetrics metric = context.getFontMetrics();
18.          if (down){
19.              context.drawString(onText, (width - metric.stringWidth
➥(onText)) / 2,
20.                  (height + metric.getMaxAscent() - metric.getMaxDescent
➥()) / 2);
21.          }else{
22.              context.drawString(offText, (width - metric.stringWidth
➥(offText)) / 2,
23.                  (height + metric.getMaxAscent() - metric.getMaxDescent
➥()) / 2);
24.          }
25.      }
```

The Protected SizeToFit() Method

The *sizeToFit()* method shown in listing 6.2j is called to ensure that the size of the button is resized to accommodate the widest of the two display strings. This method is protected because there is no reason for it to be called by another class, but it may be overridden by subclasses. The *sizeToFit()* method gains its size information from the current component font. Because of the use of the font and the strings of both labels, this Bean is capable of being used with multiple fonts and languages.

Listing 6.2j: Class OnOffButton—The sizeToFit() method, used to calculate a size based on label size and current font

```
protected void sizeToFit() {
        Dimension d = getPreferredSize();
        resize(d.width, d.height);
        Component p = getParent();
        if (p != null) {
            p.invalidate();
            p.layout();
        }
    }
```

Reporting Minimum and Preferred Size for OnOffButton

The next stage of ensuring that the text in this component is always visible is accomplished by properly overriding the *getPreferredSize()* and the *getMinimumSize()* methods as shown in listing 6.2k. These methods ensure that the component will be drawn at an optimal size that will fit the text and a reasonable gutter between the text and the edges of the component.

Listing 6.2k: Class OnOffButton—Override of getPreferredSize() and getMinimumSize() methods

```
01.    /**
02.     * Override of Component method to return the calculated size.
03.     */
04.    public Dimension getPreferredSize() {
05.
06.        FontMetrics metric = getFontMetrics(getFont());
07.        int maxWidth = metric.stringWidth(getOnText())
```

```
➡metric.stringWidth(getOffText()) ?metric.stringWidth(getOnText()) :
➡metric.stringWidth(getOffText()) ;
08.        return new Dimension(maxWidth + (metric.charWidth('A')*3),
09.                    metric.getMaxAscent() + metric.getMaxDescent() +
➡metric.getHeight());
10.    }
11.public Dimension getMinimumSize() {
12.        return getPreferredSize();
13.    }
```

Bound Properties

Listing 6.2l shows the final two methods in this class, which are used to set and report the up/down state of the Bean. The *isDown()* method, starting on line one is used to query the current state of the button. If the button is down, *isDown()* will return true.

The *setDown()* method (line 4) handles the switching of the state to the new state, repainting the button to reflect the change and calling *firePropertyChange()* (line 8) so that listeners are notified that the button is in a new position.

Listing 6.2l: Class OnOffButton—isDown() setDown() methods and class fields

```
01.    public boolean isDown(){
02.        return down;
03.    }
04.    public void setDown(boolean newDown){
05.        Boolean oldDown = new Boolean(down);
06.        down = newDown;
07.        repaint();
08.        changes.firePropertyChange("down",oldDown,new Boolean(down));
09.    }
10.
11.
12.    protected String onText;
13.    protected String offText;
14.
15.    protected PropertyChangeSupport changes = new PropertyChangeSupport
➡(this);
16.    protected boolean down;
17.    protected boolean sized;
18.}//End of class OnOffButton
```

Building the Nuclear Reactor Example

The NuclearReactor Bean is the core class of a collection of support classes and specialized support Beans. Only some of these classes are covered here. The complete set of classes can be found on this book's CD.

To start, you need to define what the goal is for this example. The goal of the nuclear reactor is to simulate a simple, 10-rod reactor. The simulation is only superficial in that the only thing that you are able to do with the reactor is to change the fuel rod positions and retrieve simulated power and core temperatures. The fundamental purpose here is to show how an invisible component can be connected to visual components. The NuclearReactor Bean and its corresponding PropertySheet is shown in the BeanBox application in figure 6.4.

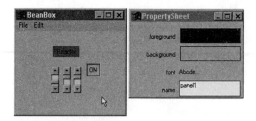

Figure 6.4

NuclearReactor Bean in the BeanBox application and its corresponding properties.

Package Membership

The package membership for the NuclearReactor Bean, as shown in listing 6.3a, has a little more meaning than the previous examples. The reason is that the support class in the NewRiders.beans.reactor package are not all available for use by other classes. This is done partially for integrity of the reactor simulator—the fewer classes available to other packages, the less likely that problems can be introduced. In addition, as stated in earlier examples, the packaging of these classes helps avoid naming conflicts.

Listing 6.3a: Class NuclearReactor—Package membership

```
package NewRiders.beans.reactor;
import NewRiders.beans.reactor.*;
import java.util.*;
import java.beans.*;
```

Class Signature

The class signature for the NuclearReactor, as shown in listing 6.3b, is quite a bit more complex than those that have been covered up to this point.

The next important features of the class signature are the two listener interfaces that are implemented. The ReactorControlListener enables a reactor to be added to a source of reactor control events. Reactor control events are simple control actions such as start, stop, and report status. The RodControlListener interface connects the reactor to rod controllers. The RodController Bean (described later in the chapter) is used to call the RodControlListener. By registering a reactor object as a listener to a rod controller, a rod in the reactor can be manipulated in the reactor.

Another interface that this class implements is the Serializable interface, which enables you to save the current configuration of the reactor. The entire state of the reactor will not be saved however. The reactor should at least start in a known, off state with all rods removed. This is where the transient modifier prevents some of the fields in the class from saving their states during serialization.

Also shown in this section of the listing are a few final constants used later in the class.

Listing 6.3b: Class NuclerarReactor

```
public class NuclearReactor
                implements  ReactorControlListener,
                            RodControlListener,
                            java.io.Serializable{
    public final int MAX_RODS = 10;
    public final double MAX_REACTOR_TEMP = 1000.0;
    public final double MAX_ROD_TEMP = 10000.0;
```

Default Constructor

The default constructor for the NuclearReactor class in listing 6.3c is mainly concerned with the initialization of the reactor rods to a known state. This initialization must be done because the initial state of the rods is undefined because the fuelRod array is transient and not restored during deserialization.

Listing 6.3c: Class NuclearReactor—Default class constructor

```
public NuclearReactor(){

    fuelRod = new FuelRod[MAX_RODS];
    for(int i= 0; i < fuelRod.length; i++){
        fuelRod[i] = new FuelRod(0.02,-1,0.0);
    }
}
```

Property Signatures

The following methods in listing 6.3d are the main property signatures of the class. There are two methods, *getPowerOutput()* on line 1 and *getCoreTemp()* on line 7, which do not have corresponding set methods. The properties that these methods access cannot be changed externally to the class. Only their current values can be read.

On line 20 and 23 *getFuelRodState()* is another set of methods that returns status from the Bean. The first method returns a specific rod while the second returns an array of all the rods in the NuclearReactor. The rod data must first be loaded into an immutable object. This prevents callers of the *getFuelRodState()* from accessing the internal data of the NuclearReactor's fuelRod array. If this data could be changed externally, the NuclearReactor Bean could be fooled into seeing the fuel rods at positions and temperatures that were not correct.

Listing 6.3d: Class NuclearReactor—property signatures

```
01.     public double getPowerOutput(){
02.         return powerOutput;
03.     }
04.
05.     public double getCoreTemp(){
06.         return coreTemp;
07.     }
08.
09.     public boolean isRunning(){
10.         return running;
11.     }
12.     public void setRunning(boolean run){
13.         running = run;
14.     }
```

```
15.    public final FuelRodState getFuelRodState(int rod){
16.        return( new FuelRodState(fuelRod[rod]));
17.    }
18.    public final FuelRodState[] getFuelRodState(){
19.        FuelRodState[] fuelRodState= new FuelRodState[fuelRod.length];
20.        for(int i= 0; i < fuelRod.length; i++){
21.            fuelRodState[i] = getFuelRodState(i);
22.        }
23.        return(fuelRodState);
24.    }
```

errorCheck() Method

The *errorCheck()* method in listing 6.3e checks when the reactor is beyond its specified limits. If it exceeds the specified limits, a NuclearReactorEvent is generated and listeners are notified with the current state of the reactor.

 Note

The state in this case is a non-mutable class that will hold the reactor status at the moment that the status was taken. If the status was a reference to the state, by the time listeners are notified, the data may be different than when first read.

Listing 6.3e: Class NuclearReactor—errorCheck method

```
01.    /**
02.     * Method to be called at periodic times to
03.     * update reactor status.
04.     * Also checks for error conditions.
05.     */
06.    public void errorCheck(ReactorState reactorState){
07.        if(reactorState.getCoreTemp() >= MAX_REACTOR_TEMP){
08.            NuclearReactorEvent event = new
➥NuclearReactorEvent(this,NuclearReactorEvent.REACTOR_ERROR,reactorState);
09.            notifyListeners(event);
10.        }
11.    }
```

The triggerStatusEvent() method

The *triggerStatusEvent()* method in listing 6.3f is called in response for a request to gather the current state of the reactor and generate a status event.

Listing 6.3f: Class NuclearReactor—triggerStatusEvent() method

```
01.    /**
02.     * Method to be called at periodic times to
03.     * update reactor status.
04.     * Also checks for error conditions.
05.     */
06.    public void triggerStatusEvent(){
07.        ReactorState reactorState= new ReactorState(this);
08.        errorCheck(reactorState);
09.        NuclearReactorEvent event = new
➡NuclearReactorEvent(this,NuclearReactorEvent.REACTOR_STATUS,reactorState);
10.        notifyListeners(event);
11.    }
```

Implementing RodControllerListener

The *setFuelRodDepth()* method receives events from a fuel rod controller. The fuel rod corresponding to the rod specified by the event is set to the requested value. Listing 6.3g shows the implementation for the RodControllerListener. The RodControllerListener's primary purpose is to connect to the RodController Bean, which will be used by the operator to manipulate the fuel rods in the reactor.

Listing 6.3g: Class NuclearReactor—Implementation for RodControllerListener—setFuelRodDepth()

```
public void setFuelRodDepth(RodControlEvent rce){
    try{
    setFuelRodDepth(rce.getRod(),rce.getDepth());
    }catch(PropertyVetoException pve){
        System.err.println("Error: Could not change rod depth!");
        System.err.println(pve);
    }
}
```

fuelRodDepth Properties

The fuelRodDepth property signature methods defined in listing 6.3h are used mainly by the *setFuelRodDepth()* method, but are made available in case the reactor is to be manipulated directly rather than through FuelRodEvent messages. The set method is also used to calculate the temperature of the reactor simulation.

Listing 6.3h: Class NuclearReactor—fuelRodDepth property signature methods

```
01.    /**
02.     * Move fuel rod in or out of reactor.
03.     * Notifies listeners if reactor is shut down
04.     * or started, based on rods.
05.     * for simulation we calculate temps & power here.
06.     */
07.
08.    public void setFuelRodDepth(int rodNumber, int rodDepth) throws
➥PropertyVetoException, IllegalArgumentException/* also ArrayIndexOutOfRange
➥*/{
09.        vChange.fireVetoableChange("rodDepth",new
➥Integer(fuelRod[rodNumber].getInsertionDepth()), new Integer(rodDepth));
10.        // update rod temp
11.        fuelRod[rodNumber].setRodTemp( rodDepth * 100.0);
12.        // update power and core temp(sychronize to keep consistent).
13.        synchronized(this){
14.            coreTemp -= fuelRod[rodNumber].getInsertionDepth() * 100;
15.            coreTemp += rodDepth * 100;
16.            powerOutput -= fuelRod[rodNumber].getInsertionDepth() * 100;
17.            powerOutput += rodDepth * 100;
18.        }
19.
20.        fuelRod[rodNumber].setInsertionDepth(rodDepth);
21.        if (rodDepth > 0 && (running == false)){
22.            running = true;
23.            ReactorState reactorState= new ReactorState(this);
24.            NuclearReactorEvent event = new
➥NuclearReactorEvent(this,NuclearReactorEvent.REACTOR_STARTED,reactorState);
25.            notifyListeners(event);
26.        }else{
27.            // check for the last rod removed.
28.            boolean rodIn = false;
29.            for (int i = 0; i < fuelRod.length; i++){
30.                if (fuelRod[i].getInsertionDepth() > 0){
31.                    rodIn = true;
32.                    break;
33.                }
```

continues

continued

```
34.                    }
35.                    if (rodIn == false){
36.                        running = false;
37.                        ReactorState reactorState= new ReactorState(this);
38.                        NuclearReactorEvent event = new
➥NuclearReactorEvent(this,NuclearReactorEvent.REACTOR_STOPPED,reactorState);
39.                        notifyListeners(event);
40.                    }
41.                }
42.
43.    public int getFuelRodDepth(int rodNumber)/* also ArrayIndexOutOfRange
➥*/{
44.            return fuelRod[rodNumber].getInsertionDepth();
45.        }
46.    }// end of setFuelRodDepth()
```

removeAllRods() Utility Method

The *removeAllRods()* method in listing 6.3i is used as part of the shutdown procedure for the Reactor. After all the rods have been removed, a REACTOR_STOPPED method is generated and all listeners are notified.

Listing 6.3i: Class NuclearReactor—removeAllRods() utility method

```
01.    /**
02.     * Removes all rods from the reactor.
03.     * Notifies listener that the reactor has shut down.
04.     */
05.    public void removeAllRods(){
06.        synchronized(this){
07.            for(int i= 0; i < fuelRod.length; i++){
08.                fuelRod[i].setInsertionDepth(-1);
09.                fuelRod[i].setRodTemp(0.0);
10.            }
11.            coreTemp = 0;
12.            powerOutput = 0;
13.        }
14.        if (running == true){
15.            running = false;
16.            ReactorState reactorState= new ReactorState(this);
17.            NuclearReactorEvent event = new NuclearReactorEvent(this,
➥NuclearReactorEvent.REACTOR_STOPPED,reactorState);
```

```
18.            notifyListeners(event);
19.        }
20.
21.    }
```

NuclearReactorListener Support Signatures

The next two methods in listing 6.3j are used to add the custom event listener—
NuclearReactorListener—to the notification list. The NuclearReactorListener objects will
be called whenever the NuclearReactor Bean generates NuclearReactorEvent objects for
status actions and errors.

**Listing 6.3j: Class NuclearReactor—add/remove NuclearReactorListener
methods**

```
01.    /**
02.     * Add listener to the listener notification list.]
03.     * If successful events will be enabled.
04.     */
05.    public void addNuclearReactorListener(NuclearReactorListener nrl){
06.        listeners.addElement(nrl);
07.    }
08.    /**
09.     * Remove a listener from the listener notification list.
10.     * If there are no more events, notification will stop.
11.     */
12.    public void removeNuclearReactorListener(NuclearReactorListener nrl){
13.        listeners.removeElement(nrl);
14.    }
```

Implementation for ReactorControlListener Methods

The following methods in listing 6.3k are implementations for ReactorControlListener.
These methods are used for the primary control of the reactor, which is the startup
(line 1), the stopping (line 9) and requesting status events (line 16).

Listing 6.3k: Class NuclearReactor—Implementation for ReactorControlListener methods

```
01.      // Implementation for ReactorControlListener
02.      /**
03.       * Called when the reactor is started.
04.       * @param reactor event.
05.       */
06.      public void reactorStart(ReactorControlEvent nre){
07.          setRunning(true);
08.      }
09.      /**
10.       * Called when the reactor is stopped.
11.       * @param reactor event.
12.       */
13.      public void reactorStop(ReactorControlEvent nre){
14.          removeAllRods();
15.      }
16.      /**
17.       * Called to force reactor to send out status.
18.       * @param reactor event.
19.       */
20.      public void reactorDoStatus(ReactorControlEvent nre){
21.          notifyListeners(new NuclearReactorEvent
     ➥(this,NuclearReactorEvent.REACTOR_STARTED,new ReactorState(this)));
22.      }
```

notifyListeners() Method

The *notifyListeners()* method defined in listing 6.3l notifies all NuclearReactorListener objects when a NuclearReactorEvent is generated. The NuclearReactorEvent is generated when the reactor is started, stopped, or encounters errors, and to report status of the reactor.

The method is primarily used to select the method in the listener interface that corresponds to the event ID it is associated with. This technique puts the logic of dispersing events in this one method. The caller of this method only needs to generate the appropriate event object with the correct event ID. There is no reason for the code that is the source of the event to also have logic for lookup of listeners and calling each of the event handler methods.

Listing 6.3l: Class NuclearReactor—The notifyListeners() method

```
01.    /**
02.     * Call each registered listener.
03.     */
04.    private void notifyListeners(NuclearReactorEvent nre){
05.        // Uses a synchronized block to prevent threads
06.        // from changing targets.
07.        Vector listenersCopy;
08.        synchronized (this) {
09.            // only continue if listeners exist.
10.            if (listeners.size() == 0){
11.                return;
12.            }
13.            // Clone listeners so that listener
14.            // list can not change while dispatching events.
15.            listenersCopy = (Vector)listeners.clone();
16.        }
17.        // Call each listener's event method.
18.        for (Enumeration e = listenersCopy.elements() ;
➥e.hasMoreElements() ;) {
19.
20.            NuclearReactorListener target = (NuclearReactorListener)
➥e.nextElement();
21.
22.            switch(nre.getEventID()){
23.                case NuclearReactorEvent.REACTOR_STARTED:
24.                    target.reactorStarted(nre);
25.                    break;
26.                case NuclearReactorEvent.REACTOR_STOPPED:
27.                    target.reactorStopped(nre);
28.                    break;
29.                case NuclearReactorEvent.REACTOR_STATUS:
30.                    target.reactorStatus(nre);
31.                    break;
32.                case NuclearReactorEvent.REACTOR_ERROR:
33.                    target.reactorError(nre);
34.                    break;
35.            }// end switch
36.        }// end for each listener
37.    }// end notifyListeners()
```

Vetoable Change Support

The remaining two methods of this class, *addVetoableChangeListener()* and *removeVetoableChangeListener()*, are used to add vetoable change listeners. Listing

6.3m defines these methods. The vetoable method in the NuclearReactor is *setFuelRodDepth()*. The *setFuelRodDepth()* is monitored by external listeners that can veto any change in rod depth that could cause an over temperature condition in the reactor.

Listing 6.3m: Class NuclearReactor

```java
public void addVetoableChangeListener(VetoableChangeListener vcl){
    vChange.addVetoableChangeListener(vcl);
}
public void removeVetoableChangeListener(VetoableChangeListener vcl){
    vChange.removeVetoableChangeListener(vcl);
}
```

Class Fields for NuclearReactor

The class fields for the NuclearReactor class are split into those that are saved by the serialization process and others that deal with the current status of the reactor. It is assumed that the reactor should start from a known point (Off), so reactor status variables are marked as transient and initialized to the off state when the object is constructed. Listing 6.3n shows the class fields for the NuclearReactor Bean.

Listing 6.3n: Class NuclearReactor—Fields

```java
private Vector listeners = new Vector(0);
// Note: reactor always begins in an off state.
private transient boolean running = false;// Note: Running true when any
➥rod is inserted.
private transient double coreTemp= 0.0;
private transient FuelRod fuelRod[] ;
private transient double powerOutput = 0.0;
private VetoableChangeSupport vChange = new VetoableChangeSupport(this);
}// end of NuclearReactor class
```

The RodController Bean

The RodController Bean controls the positions of rods in the NuclearReactor Bean. The class is a simple extension of the Scrollbar class in the AWT package. The class translates the scroll bar's processAdjustmentEvent events (the movement of the scroll bar's elevator button) to RodControlEvent events and notifies registered listeners. Each instance of a RodController represents one rod.

Package Membership

Package membership is again used to isolate the RodController class in its own namespace as listing 6.4a shows.

Listing 6.4a: Class RodController—Package membership

```
package NewRiders.beans.reactor;
import NewRiders.beans.reactor.*;
import java.util.*;
import java.awt.*;
import java.awt.event.*;
```

Class Signature

The class signature for this Bean shows that the Bean is inherited from the List component and it implements Serializable so that the current state can be saved.

Listing 6.4b: RodController class signature

```
public class RodController extends Scrollbar implements java.io.Serializable{
```

Default Constructor

The default constructor for the RodController sets the slider parameters to initial values compatible to the positions and movement of a nuclear reactor rod. The initial position is set to –1 (out). The rod being controlled is initially set to zero. To access another rod, the controller must call the *setRod()* method to change the specific rod it handles. Listing 6.4c defines the default constructor for the RodController class.

Listing 6.4c: Class RodController—default constructor

```
public RodController(){
    super( Scrollbar.VERTICAL ,-1,1,-1,10);
    this.rod = 0;
}
```

processAdjustmentEvent() method

The *processAdjustmentEvent( )* method in listing 6.4d converts the AdjustmentEvent to a RodControlEvent by creating a RodControlEvent with the position of the scroll bar's elevator button. The event is then sent to all of the registered listeners of the RodController Bean. In this example, the listener is the NuclearReactor Bean.

Listing 6.4d: Class RodController—processAdjustmentEvent() method

```
protected void processAdjustmentEvent(AdjustmentEvent e){
        RodControlEvent rce = new RodControlEvent(this, rod,e.getValue());
        notifyRodListeners(rce);
        processAdjustmentEvent;
    }
```

RodControlListener Signatures

The add and remove RodControlListener methods in listing 6.4e register reactors or other RodControlListener classes to this class. As was mentioned previously, the primary listener is the NuclearReactor Bean, which uses the event to change the positions of its fuel rods. Additional listeners could be added to display the position that the rods are set to or even to display a graphic representation of the rods in the reactor.

Listing 6.4e: Class RodController

```
01./**
02.    * Add listener to the listener notification list.]
03.    * If successful events will be enabled.
04.    */
05.    public void addRodControlListener(RodControlListener nrl){
06.       listeners.addElement(nrl);
07.       enableEvents(AWTEvent.ADJUSTMENT_EVENT_MASK );
08.    }
09.    /**
10.    * Remove a listener from the listener notification list.
11.    * If there are no more events, notification will stop.
12.    */
13.    public void removeRodControlListener(RodControlListener nrl){
14.          listeners.removeElement(nrl);
15.          if (listeners.size() == 0){
16.               disableEvents(AWTEvent.ADJUSTMENT_EVENT_MASK );
17.          }
18.    }
```

notifyRodListeners() Method

The *notifyRodListeners()* method in listing 6.4f calls all registered listeners when a control rod depth is changed by calling the scrollbar.

Listing 6.4f: Class RodController—notifyRodListeners() method

```
01.    private void notifyRodListeners(RodControlEvent rce){
02.    // Uses a synchronized block to prevent threads
03.       // from changing targets.
04.       Vector listenersCopy;
05.       synchronized (this) {
06.           // only continue if listeners exist.
07.           if (listeners.size() == 0){
08.               return;
09.           }
10.           // Clone listeners so that listener
11.           // list can not change while dispatching events.
12.           listenersCopy = (Vector)listeners.clone();
13.       }
14.       // Call each listener's event method.
15.       for (Enumeration e = listenersCopy.elements() ;
➥e.hasMoreElements() ;) {
16.
17.           RodControlListener target = (RodControlListener)
➥e.nextElement();
18.
19.           switch(rce.getId()){
20.               case RodController.ROD_MOVED:
21.                   target.setFuelRodDepth(rce);
22.                   break;
23.
24.           }
25.       }
26.    }
```

Rod Properties

The rod property accessor methods in listing 6.4g set and query the rod controlled by this object.

Listing 6.4g: Class RodController—rod property signatures

```
01.    public void setRod(int rod){
02.        this.rod = rod;
03.    }
04.    public int getRod(){
05.        return(rod);
06.    }
07.    private Vector listeners = new Vector(0);
08.    private int rod;
09.
10.}
```

Broken Beans

As with any software, you will encounter bugs while developing Java Beans. The sections that follow cover common bugs specifically related to Beans. The techniques here are generally related to how a Bean-aware application behaves in the presence of incorrectly written Java Beans.

Debugging Components Before Using the IDE

Debugging outside of the IDE is a very important task, especially for complex Beans. In most situations, Bean developers will be using a third-party Bean-aware IDE such as the BeanBox, Jbuilder, or AppletAuthor. The developer will probably not have any control over how the IDE uses the Bean, and may have limited capabilities to report on a Bean's errors or status.

First of all, Beans can be used without an IDE. There is nothing that cannot be done to a Bean from a normal Java application. After you are in an IDE, you lose the ability to directly debug the component. A programmer should first debug the Bean from a test program before using the Bean in an IDE. The reason for this is quite simple—there is much more control of the Bean in a main application. The other benefit to testing the Bean outside of the IDE is that code is created to test the Bean that can be used later for validation of new versions of the Bean.

Common Types of Errors

The following list describes the five main categories that cause many of the errors in Beans:

◆ **Public access:** the methods are either private or protected and do not appear, or they are public and appear when not needed.

◆ **Invalid signature:** an invalid signature can be caused by a series of errors, from typos to omissions of required methods. These errors are quickly discovered when a Bean is used in the IDE. The source of the error, however, can be difficult to spot.

◆ **Incorrect signature:** this type of error is nearly as bad as invalid signatures. Instead of a property or event not appearing, an event or property is added where one is not required. The most common problem is a property that should be private or protected. In such situations, the easiest remedy is to change the set/get methods to anything other than public. Another common error is to cut and paste the add/remove methods from another class. A problem can occur here because the add and remove methods may handle one type of listener class, while the code used to notify listeners may be associated with another. This error is easy to make because the event handling code may store listeners in a Vector object. Because a Vector holds generic objects, there is no way to see the error until an InvalidClassCastException is thrown when the listener is first accessed. The best solution here is to create a specific listener handler for each type of listener supported.

◆ **Invalid class hierarchy or use:** class type or base class inheritance is also an integral part of most signatures. The use of the naming part of a signature is not enough for the Introspector class to resolve a signature. An example of this type of error can be caused by not properly inheriting from the AWTEvent class when creating new events. All the code associated with listeners and event sources could be overlooked by the Introspector class if custom events are missing the AWTEvent base class.

◆ **Custom BeanInfo incorrect:** whenever a BeanInfo is created, the developer is taking on some of the tasks that the Introspector class is normally used for. The errors created in the BeanInfo are usually associated with omission. A Bean's methods, properties, and events are not added. This usually will happen if a Bean is modified without completely modifying the BeanInfo. The reverse can also occur when a method, property, or event is removed from a class, but the BeanInfo still contains a reference to it. The compiler will catch errors in the BeanInfo when the BeanInfo is compiled. The Descriptor objects contain true references back to the

Bean methods and the compiler will complain when the Bean does not have the correct method. If only the Bean is recompiled, however, and not the BeanInfo, the errors will not be caught until run time, at the point that the BeanInfo is first used to access the missing methods in the modified Bean.

Diagnosing and Curing Common Bean Problems

The following examples describe common problems encountered when developing Beans and their probable cause. Any time a Bean behaves improperly, this list should be the first place you look to help resolve the problem. This list is not exhaustive, but it is a good start.

Problem: The Bean does not appear in the IDE palette or does not get created when used.

Probable causes:

◆ The Bean class is not marked in the Manifest file as a Bean.

◆ The Bean class is private or protected.

◆ The Bean class does not have a default constructor with null parameters or is not public.

◆ An exception occurred when creating the Bean.

In this scenario, as can be seen by the first three probable causes above, the problems occur because the design signatures have not been properly followed. The fourth is the worst situation in that the Bean object could not be created. It is important that anything that can prevent your Bean from loading generate specific exceptions that can be used to pinpoint problems as quickly as possible.

One problem that can occur easily is that the CLASSPATH is not correct. Either the class is missing or there are two copies of the class in the class path. The hardest problem to diagnose is one in which the programmer is modifying one class while an older copy is always loaded instead.

Problem: Properties are not visible in the IDE property sheet.

Probable causes:

◆ Property set/get methods are not marked as public.

◆ Property set/get methods do not meet signature specification.

◆ Only one accessor method was defined.

IDE property sheets fail to show properties because part of the signature for properties requires corresponding get and set methods for a property to be recognized as such.

This situation can also occur if the Bean is only capable of reporting a property and not setting it. Two solutions remedy this problem: a custom BeanInfo, and a dummy set method. You use a custom BeanInfo to create a PropertyDescriptor object that defines the set method as null or points to a method taking the correct type, but not using it.

The best solution is to create a dummy set method that uses the vetoable change signature. The dummy set method is written so that it never modifies the property and throws a PropertyVetoException every time it is run. The thrown PropertyVetoException prevents the IDE from modifying the property.

Summary

The examples in this chapter, as well as those later in the book and on the book's CD, should form a sound basis for developing your own Beans. These examples have been somewhat simplistic. Most Beans, however, *should* be somewhat simplistic. The concept of Java Beans is that larger systems are created with smaller parts. Case in point is the Nuclear Reactor example. There are many small support classes for events and a few, special purpose Beans that create a larger entity that is more than the sum of its parts.

When creating Beans, strive for simplicity, modularity, and compatibility. Create components as generic as possible. Be aware of how a Bean is seen by the Introspector and of the capabilities of Bean-aware IDE development tools. Most importantly, document your Beans.

Another aspect of Java Beans is that they are often used out of the context of debuggers and instead, in an IDE. This often makes it difficult to diagnose problems. Often the problems are caused by a misunderstanding and application of design signatures or simple mistakes like leaving an associated class out of the CLASSPATH. In either case, the errors could be difficult to diagnose until you become comfortable with your tools and authoring Java Beans.

This chapter has served as an introduction to some simple and complex Java Beans. There are still many more issues to be addressed that will go into creating robust commercial quality Java Beans.

CHAPTER 7

Java Bean Persistence

This chapter covers the Java Persistence model and its relationship to Java Beans. The goal of this chapter is to cover the mechanics of the Java Serialization API and its use by Bean developers.

Persistence is the saving and recovery of an object's state. Persistence is not a new idea. In fact, persistence can be found in a lot of computer products. The Bookmarks menu in your web browser, for example, is a form of persistence. When you add your favorite web sites to the Bookmarks menu, the web browser retains the information after the program is terminated. When the browser is restarted, the Bookmarks menu is repopulated with the same state as it appeared before the program was terminated. The menu information *persists* between times that the program is not running.

Java implements persistence at the object level. Instead of saving and loading information to a special file, Java can traverse a tree of objects, each saving their contents into a stream, which can be a file or a storage device. When the program is restarted, the stream can be re-read, creating the original object tree containing the persistent information. If a web browser was written with Java, an array of web site URL strings could be saved using the Serialization API. The array could then be read later when the program is restarted.

The biggest difference between writing to a custom file for storage and writing serialized data is that there is very little that a programmer needs to do to implement serialized storage. In fact, a whole object tree of information can be stored by simply serializing the root node of the object tree. This is much simpler than older methods where the programmer would have to write code to iterate through all the objects and save the data depending on each object's type.

Deserialization is also much simpler than reading data files. The deserialization process is able to create objects as they are deserialized. This is automatic and does not require that the user know the exact types that are being deserialized. The process is also done at a level that is type safe. Anyone who has written a complex file loader has had problems with converting to the correct types of numbers or accounting for delimiters in strings that might be the same used to tokenize data. The Java Serialization API stores the type of data along with the data itself so that the correct logic is used to retrieve the value.

In Java, persistence is accomplished through object serialization. *Serialization* is the process of converting the state of an object into a data stream. When objects are restored, they are deserialized. This process creates the original object by first creating a blank instance and reading data from persistent storage.

For some programmers, this might seem a little strange. The idea that parts of the program appear as they did the last time they were used definitely bears little relation to what many are used to. It is also new for the 1.1 release of the JDK. The best way to look at the serialization process is that it is like taking a snapshot of objects. Deserialization is the opposite because it creates an actual object from the snapshot.

Persistence Pitfalls

A class must have two things before it can be serialized. The first is that the class must implement the java.io.Serializable or java.io.Externalizable interface. The Serializable interface is the simplest to implement because there are no methods that need to be instantiated. The interface is just used as a permission marker to tell the serialization tools that the class can be serialized. The Externalizable interface requires that specific methods be implemented to control the serialization process.

The next rule that must be followed to make a class serializable is that the class must have a default constructor that takes no arguments. The reason for this is quite simple. When an object is deserialized, it is creating a previous state. The state of an object could have been created through different constructors and methods operating on the internal state of the object. Because there is no record of what constructor was used to create the object or any log of methods called, there is no way to recreate the same sequence of events. Because there is no creation sequence, only the current state of the Bean can be stored. When retrieved, therefore, only the previous state can be read into the Bean's fields. Given that only the state matters, the default constructor is used to create a base object to be filled with data. Not having a default constructor would require the deserialization process to pick a constructor (classes can have many) and fill the parameters with meaningful information; however, as you now know, there is no way to derive such information. Therefore, the default constructor is the only choice, and must be implemented for classes that are to be serialized.

Besides the requirement for default constructors and implementations of serializable interfaces, there are other problems need to be addressed, including the following:

◆ Determining how much of an object's state needs to be saved

◆ Securing sensitive data

◆ Dealing with stream corruption

◆ Allowing for class versioning

The object of this chapter is to deal with these problems and specifically relate them to Java Beans. The Serialization API is separate from the Java Beans API, but it forms the basis of Java Beans storage. The Bean developer must be aware of the issues involved in serialization because almost all Java Beans will be used as persistent objects.

Persistent Java Beans

The persistent life of a Bean is a little different from persistence as it might be used in other situations. *Persistent Java Beans* are usually objects that have only one starting state. Java Beans get deserialized to populate the target application with components each time the application is loaded. In other words, an application programmer using a Bean just starts the deserialization process to load the Bean and then it's ready for use. The programmer does not attempt to serialize the object from an application between executions.

In other words, we are treating most Java Beans as components that have a persistent configuration. The state of a Bean is saved when the Bean is configured in an application builder tool where the Bean component has been configured to meet the needs of the current application. When the application is run, the saved state is restored and the Bean component used as if the program had created and configured the Bean with setup instructions. The state of the Bean is probably not stored before the application terminates. For example, a button Bean added to an application in an application development tool is configured with a specific color and a label. The state of the button is saved along with the state of other Java Beans that are used by the program. When the program is started by the end-user, the state of the button, including its color and label, are restored. The button is configured for the application, not for a state that represents something that is stored between execution. To return to the Bookmark example, the title of the Bookmark menu is a Bean that has a state that is originally stored when the application is built. The entries in the Bookmark menu are saved and restored in a process separate from the Bean state.

It is rare that a Bean will be saved by the end user. Beans are normally modified just by the developer. There are cases where a Bean may have a persistent state that is execution-dependent, such as a list of Bookmarks, but this is treated as a feature of a particular Bean, and not a general use of Java Beans in general.

The oddest thing about persistent Beans is that the state used in the target program is usually created in an IDE. Persistent Beans are self-contained building blocks plugged into applications configured by the developer for the specific context.

In the old component model, familiar to many developers, the state of a component is set from within a program. Beans carry their initialization with them. This enables the programmer to avoid writing initialization and configuration code. The programmer needs only to connect the component to others within the program. Now, instead of setting colors, size, and other parameters, the Bean configures itself from the persistent state set from within the developer's IDE. This is the real power of persistence. The concept can be extended to the network where applications can send anything from simple objects or plug-in software components to whole applications across the network wire with little interaction required by the main program. This means that a Bean component's state can be loaded from the network.

Serialization can also be made immune to new versions. For example, if a component adds the capability to add a background image, the component can be made to use an older serialized state that does not have a background image. The user will either see a default image or the component as it was originally configured without a background image. A need to have static programs no longer exists. The number of features and enhancements to existing programs can change dynamically over time with a user's specific configuration intact.

Bean Serialization

In the life of a Bean, serialization is the memory of how a Bean should look and/or behave. Any information set in the IDE is saved so that it can be recovered when the Bean is used in the final application.

During initialization, a serialized Bean or an application program has very little to do. Everything is done by deserializing the object. The default serialize process, however, is a very heavy-handed way of going about it. Just by implementing *java.lang.Serializable* to a new class and supporting a default constructor makes it possible to serialize an object's fields. Any primitives in this object are serializable. Any fields that are objects are also serialized if their classes implement *java.lang.Serializable* or *java.io.Externalizable* interfaces. This serialization continues until all data in an object tree is saved. The same is true for when the Bean is restored—all data in the object tree is reset with the saved information. Ways to prevent certain fields from being stored and recovered are discussed later in this chapter. For now, examine a small Bean that can use the standard mechanism without much work by the developer.

The Bean in listing 7.1 represents only a few pieces of information and has no GUI representation. It extends the *java.lang.Serializable* interface and conforms to the design signature for Bean properties:

Listing 7.1: A simple Bean to demonstrate serialization

```
01.import java.io.Serializable;
02.class BeanState1 implements Serializable{
03.     BeanState1(){
04.          state = 0;
05.     }
06.BeanState1(int beginingState){
07.state = beginingState;
08.     }
09.public int getState(){
10.return(state);
11.     }
12.public void setState(int newState){
13.state = newState;
14.     }
15.     private int state;
16.}
```

The first thing to notice about this Bean is that there are two constructors. The first constructor (line 3) contains no parameters. This default constructor is used by the deserialization mechanism to create an object to fill. The second constructor (line 6) is only used to create a new instance of the Bean. It's possible that the second constructor may never be used. The developer should also be aware that the constructor on line 6 is never called when this object is deserialized.

Controlling Serialization

Serialized Beans are never initialized via parameterized constructors. The initialization of a persistent object starts with the non-parameterized object and then the persistent state is replaced by the contents of the object stream. In listing 7.1, the state member is initialized to zero (line 4) in the default constructor (line 3), but the state member will be replaced with whatever is held in the state of the saved stream.

 Note

> Note that the *set* method is not used during the serialization of objects. Persistent values are stored directly to an object's memory space and not through any calls to an object's methods.

Serialization of primitives such as *int* and *float* are handled through the Serialization API. Objects that are not primitive or part of the standard packages must implement the *java.lang.externalizable* or *java.lang.Serializable* interfaces. Unfortunately, serialization is too good for many Beans; it stores more than you might want.

Situations occur when specific control is required for reasons of security or validation, where additional control must be added. The *ObjectOutput()* and *ObjectInput()* methods can be used to control the serialization and deserialization of a class. If these methods are implemented by a Bean's main class, the standard serialization of the Bean is not used. In the case of the short Bean in listing 7.2, the contents of all the members would be serialized when the Bean was saved.

Listing 7.2: A simple Bean that saves all internal data when serialized

```
01.Public Class KonaBean implements java.io.Serializable{
02.private int a = 0;
03.private int b = 0;
04.private int c = 0;
05.     KonaBean(){
06.a = 1;
07.b = 2;
08.c = 3;
09.     }
10.public void setA(int newValue){ a = newValue;)}
11.public void setB(int newValue){ b = newValue;)}
12.public void setC(int newValue){ c = newValue;)}
13.}
```

Sometimes an object might require complete control so that only specific amounts of the current state are to be written. An object that processes stock values may hold a day's worth of values while executing, but when exiting may save as its state the day's open, close, high, and low values only. Many Beans only save and restore configuration values and never save any other state values in normal use.

Static and transient members of objects are not written as part of an object's state, so it might become necessary to implement specific serialization of such members. Another reason to write specific serialization logic is to validate incoming data in case of file corruption or possible tampering.

The use of the *ObjectInput* and *ObjectOutput* interfaces and the Object I/O stream adds finer control by objects over their serialization. The serialization mechanism is broken into support for input and output. The interfaces and classes that make up the serialization API are included because most Beans implement the serialization signature.

Object Trees and Recursive Serialization

When an object is serialized, more is written to the stream than just the data that are members of a class. The serialization mechanism follows each object reference in an attempt to serialize each member object and its members. This is done recursively until there are no serializable members remaining.

The example in listing 7.3 illustrates how the recursive store works with simple objects. The first class, *BaseLevel*, is the class that creates an object to be serialized. *BaseLevel* contains a Date object, a Boolean primitive, and an object reference to a user-defined class called *FirstLevel object*. When the *setupTest()* method is called (line 5), the object's members are initialized.

Listing 7.3: Class BaseLevel—Example to show recursive serialization

```
01.import java.util.Date;
02.import java.io.Serializable;
03.class BaseLevel implements Serializable{
04.    BaseLevel(){}
05.    public void setupTest(){
06.        firstLevel = new FirstLevel();
07.        firstLevel.setupTest();
08.        initialized = true;
```

```
09.      }
10.      public String toString(){
11.          return("BaseLevel{\n"
12.·             "   created = "+created+"\n"
13.·             "   initialized = "+initialized+"\n"
14.·             "   firstLevel = "+firstLevel.toString()+"\n"
15.·             "}\n");
16.      }
17.      private boolean initialized = false;
18.      private Date created = null;
19.      private FirstLevel firstLevel;
20.      private FirstLevel copyOfFirstLevel;
21.}
```

The *FirstLevel* class in listing 7.4, like the *BaseLevel* class, contains a Date object and a Boolean primitive. The class creates a SecondLevel object. When the *setupTest()* method is called, the object's members are initialized.

Listing 7.4: Class FirstLevel—Example used to show recursive serialization

```
01.import java.util.Date;
02.import java.io.Serializable;
03.class FirstLevel implements Serializable{
04.      FirstLevel(){}
05.      public void setupTest(){
06.          secondLevel = new SecondLevel();
07.          refToSecond = secondLevel;
08.          secondLevel.setupTest();
09.          initialized = true;
10.          created = new Date();
11.      }
12.      public String toString(){
13.          return("FirstLevel{\n"
14.·             "   created = "+secondLevel.toString()+"\n"
15.·             "   initialized = "+initialized+"\n"
16.·             "   secondLevel = "+secondLevel.toString()+"\n"
17.·             "   refToSecond = "+refToSecond.toString()+"\n"
18.·             "}\n");
19.      }
20.      private boolean initialized = false;
21.      private Date created = null;
22.      private SecondLevel secondLevel;
23.      private SecondLevel refToSecond;
24.}
```

The *FirstLevel* class, like the BaseLevel class, contains a Date object and a Boolean primitive. When the *setupTest()* method is called, the object's members are initialized.

These classes form the object tree as shown in figure 7.1.

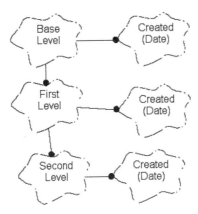

Figure 7.1

Object inheritance hierarchy.

The following code fragment in listing 7.5 creates the BaseLevel object, initializes it, and saves it to an object stream file.

Listing 7.5: Example creation and serialization of the BaseLevel class

```
BaseLevel baseLevel = new BaseLevel();
baseLevel.setupTest();
FileOutputStream fileOutputStream = new FileOutputStream("test.obj");
objectOutputStream = new ObjectOutputStream(fileOutputStream);
objectOutputStream.writeObject(baseLevel);
objectOutputStream.flush();
objectOutputStream.close();
```

The serialization process proceeds in the same sequence as the members of the classes are defined. When an object is encountered that can be serialized, *writeObject()* is called. If the object has already been saved and another reference to the object is encountered, only the reference is saved to the stream.

Deserialization occurs in the same order as serialization. In other words, objects are deserialized from the root to each node in the tree. The following code in listing 7.6 creates the BaseLevel object from the previously stored object state.

Listing 7.6: Example code fragment used to deserialize the BaseLevel class object

```
BaseLevel baseLevel;
FileInputStream fileInputStream = new FileInputStream("test.obj");
objectInputStream = new ObjectInputStream(fileInputStream);
baseLevel = (BaseLevel)objectInputStream.readObject();
objectInputStream.close();
```

The more objects that are serializable, the higher the complexity and fragility of the serialization process become. For example, references to other objects may break if the referenced objects are transient and do not exist the next time the application is started. The Bean developer must be very aware about what is happening during serialization and control it where transient information exists. Listing 7.7 creates a Bean that holds a simple integer state as well as implements the add and remove property change listener signature:

Listing 7.7: Example Bean that supports the Bound Property signature

```
01.import java.io.Serializable;
02.import java.beans.*;
03.class BeanState1WithNotify implements Serializable{
04.BeanState1WithNotify(){
05.    }
06.BeanState1WithNotify(int beginingState){
07.state = beginingState;
08.    }
09.public int getState(){
10.return(state);
11.    }
12.public void setState(int newState){
13.changes.firePropertyChange("state", new Integer(state), new
➡Integer(newState));
14.state = newState;
15.    }
16.public void addPropertyChangeListener(PropertyChangeListener
➡newListener){
17.changes.addPropertyChangeListener(newListener);
18.    }
19.public void removePropertyChangeListener(PropertyChangeListener
➡aListener){
20.changes.removePropertyChangeListener(aListener);
21.    }
22.private PropertyChangeSupport changes = new PropertyChangeSupport(this);
23.private int state = 0;
24.}
```

The code in listing 7.7 represents a whole new set of behaviors when serialization is considered. The first problem is that of member *changes*, which is a *PropertyChangeSupport* type that implements the *Serializable* interface. Therefore the changes object will be serialized and deserialized with all the PropertyChangeListener objects that were added before serialization. This could easily become a big problem if the PropertyChangeListener objects don't exist in the program that contains this Bean.

The error of a missing object will not be readily apparent for missing objects. The main reason is that the serialization process saves a copy of the object that is restored during deserialization. This object may not be referenced anywhere else in the program. If a property change event occurs, the transient object will be notified appropriately. What happens in the listeners *propertyChange()* method depends on how well the class is written. For example, if the property listener was a visual component, the component may attempt to display the new property. Because the object only exists in the changes object, the listener is not connected to a parent container. When the component attempts to repaint the display, the object may throw exceptions because there is no parent hierarchy to give context to window operations.

When this Bean is operating in the context of an end user's program, the Bean should not be saved as part of normal serialization. If event listeners are added dynamically without knowing if the added listeners will exist when reloaded, the class should be written so that serialization avoids transient data.

Java Serialization Is Not a Database

It might seem appropriate to place Java's serialization of objects into the same category as traditional databases—a hardly sustainable notion when they are compared to each other. It is also not something appropriate for Bean designs.

Serialization and RMI

The first problem is that Java serialization was originally designed as part of the RMI (Remote Method Invocation) API. This means that serialization was designed as a way of passing the state of objects across a network to other Java programs. It was not designed for long-term storage, sorting, data lookup, or any of the other attributes normally associated with databases.

Databases Have Multiple States

The idea of object persistence is far different than the concept of tables and records. An object's persistence is just the state between executions. A persistent program ends up in a similar state to that in which it was stored. A database application has a much more varied state—a mix of states depending on the number of tables and the number of records in each table. Databases are much more data-heavy, whereas a one-to-one relationship always exists between an object and its stored state. In general, database applications iterate the same objects with data from different records or queries.

Serialization Is Stream-Based

Java serialization is also inappropriate for database use because objects are in streams. Only one effective channel can be read. When started, the stream is read completely, filling in all the data for the objects in the class tree—the database equivalent of a linked read of records across several tables in a database. To do the equivalent of another record, it needs to be read from another stream file.

Avoid Using Serialization as a Database

Some readers, by now, have come up with ways to make serialization work as a database. The point is that this is more work than will be done from the context of Java Beans. Java Beans should interface with databases, not be databases themselves.

A persistent program accomplishes the same tasks as a database program. A list of addresses can be kept in a hash table object, for example. As the number of addresses grows, so does the executable image, causing more processing memory to be used. In a database application, most of the data is kept in external storage and does not garner a memory penalty. Disk storage is still cheaper than processing memory—a legacy that will most likely persist for many more years.

Use Serialization to Store Persistent State

One of the reasons that Java has become so popular is the idea that the user's machine becomes a portal to other machines that control resources. Databases are almost never small things. If a database were embedded in the persistent state of a program, it could take a very long time to move the complete database state across a network. A better design is for a client to request information from a server. This way only the information required is moved across the network.

Object state is much simpler than a database state. For a program to work correctly, the entire state is loaded and executed. Deserialization for an object should only occur at load time.

Object Databases

An object database is a different animal when compared to the Java Serialization API. *Object databases* are a cross between strict persistence and a databases that includes record lookup and multi-user access. In an object database, a record can represent an object. One thing, however, distances object databases from serialization: Only a subset of object is stored in execution memory. Objects not in scope remain in external storage.

Controlling Serialization

To keep the persistent state of objects valid, it is usually necessary to control what is to be saved and eventually restored. The proper design of a persistent object needs to take into account what is to be its starting state as well as its persistent state. The following sections describe the design decisions and techniques that can be used to develop persistent objects.

Deciding What to Serialize

A primary design task for serializable classes is determining the objects that should be serialized and those that should not. Remember that only specific information should be considered persistent. Imagine a program that saves its complete image. This can cause a multitude of problems. The following list identifies some of the more dangerous things that can occur when more data is serialized than is proper:

- ◆ State saved just prior to failure; the restored state will cause the failure again.

- ◆ Secure data is saved and available in public storage.

- ◆ Secure data is restored by anyone who next runs the program.

- ◆ The current sequence of execution is restored, regardless of whether the user wants to start from the beginning.

- ◆ Different users will start execution at points depending on where other users left off.

To counter these problems, the Serialization API has different types of control. These mechanisms range from the marking of data that is not to be serialized with the *transient* modifier, to the addition of serialization control with *readObject()* and *writeObject()* methods to the complete control of serialization with the Externalizable interface.

The most basic of these types of control is at the language level. The *transient* modifier is used to prevent the automatic serialization of fields.

Configuration Parameters

Configuration parameters are set in the IDE and never changed by the client program. Configuration parameters are safe for reading and writing of the object stream, but do not normally change their state.

Uncontrolled Configuration Parameters

An uncontrolled configuration parameter can be modified within the context of the client program. An example of this type of parameter is a string pointing to the home URL for a browser. The string may have an initial value that represents the home of the Bean designer's company. The user can change the URL string to whatever they like. As the user exits the program, the state of the Bean is stored, thus saving the new URL to be used when the program is reloaded later.

Run-Time State Variables

The run-time state members are those that are never loaded or stored as part of the serialization of an object. These variables are set to some initial value as their object is created. Examples of run-time state variables are stream objects that must be reopened for use.

Tricks for Controlling Serialization

Controlling the saving and retrieving of a class's persistent state is very important. Explicit control can alleviate problems with saving too much state information or to otherwise create a state that will be valid when restored with deserialization. There are several ways that serialization can be controlled:

- ◆ Use of the transient modifier to explicitly stop object data from being serialized.

- ◆ Use of the static modifier. By default, class level or static information is not serialized.

◆ Implementation of the ObjectInputValidation interface. The method *validateObject( )*, in the implementation of the ObjectInputValidation interface, will be called after all data in an object has been deserialized. This is a point in the deserialization process for validating that the conditions that existed at the time of serialization are still valid, or that the data is not corrupted.

◆ Serialization can be controlled with *writeObject( )* and *readObject( )* methods. These methods are optional methods that are used if they exist in classes that implement the Serialization interface.

◆ Implementing the Externalizable interface lets the developer completely control the serialization process.

Using Transient Modifiers

The simplest way to control serialization is through the transient modifier. Any member marked as transient will not be serialized. This makes it simple to partition members between those that are serialized and those that are not. Use the modifier to mark members and classes not to be serialized. The serialization process skips any transient object.

The transient modifier has been in the Java language specification since version 1.0. Until the serialization mechanism was created for the 1.1 release, many programmers have probably ignored this very useful modifier.

In listing 7.8, the OnOffButton class that was first used in the events chapter is modified to make the state (the *down* field at line 25) of the button transient. This transient modifier prevents the down member from becoming serialized. In addition to disabling serialization for the button state, three new methods have been added:

◆ **setInitialState() at line 14.** This method is used to set the initial state of the button.

◆ **getInitialState() at line 17.** This used to query the initial state of the button.

◆ **validateObject() at line 21.** A method to be called when the object is deserialized. The method is used to set the *down* property to the value in *initialState*. This method makes it possible to reset the initial state to a user configurable position.

The *setInitialState( )* and *getInitialState( )* methods are property access methods used to set and get an initial state for the button. The *validateObject( )* method is called after deserialization. The *validateObject( )* method is a perfect place for copying the saved *initialState* member field to *down* member field so that when the component is displayed it will be in the correct initial state.

Alternatively, you could have hard coded a default for the *down* field so that the button would either start as true or false. Unfortunately, such a hard coded value is not as useful as using the stored initial state value. In the original class in Chapter 5, "Java Beans and Events" the state of *down* was persistently stored and retrieved. This is not a good idea, because the developer might not realize that the button was in the up or down state when serialized. Controlling the value explicitly in this example creates a more robust version of the OnOffButton.

Listing 7.8: Class OnOffButton2—Demonstration of the transient modifier

```
01.public class OnOffButton2 extends Canvas implements Serializable,
➡ObjectInputValidation {
02.
03.     public OnOffButton2() {
04.         this.onText = "ON";
05.         this.offText = "OFF";
06.         // Set to a standard font.
07.         setFont(new Font("Dialog", Font.PLAIN, 12));
08.         // Give this the normal button color.
09.         setBackground(Color.lightGray);
10.         // Enable events so that button can be used.
11.         enableEvents(MouseEvent.MOUSE_EVENT_MASK);
12.     }
13.     // Property accessors used to access the initial state.
14.     public void setInitialState(boolean newState){
15.         initialState = newState;
16.     }
17.     public boolean getInitialState(){
18.         return initialState;
19.     }
20.     // Method called by deserialization
21.     public void validateObject() throws InvalidObjectException{
22.         // Set the button state to the initial state.
23.         down = initialState;
24.     }
25.     transient protected boolean down;//Current position of the button.
26.     protected boolean initialState;//Used to store the initial starting
➡position.
27.     .
28.     . < See listing OnOffButton2.java for additional code >
29.     .
30.}
```

Using Static Modifiers

Members that are static are also not written to the object stream. Static variables are too complex to attempt any type of automated serialization.

Static fields are not serialized. A simple example of why is provided by a class that counts copies of itself. If the static variable was stored to the object stream, it would write into the same area when any object is restored. If several instances were created of one class and then several more were loaded via serialization, the count in the static member would contain the count for deserialized objects and not total objects.

Another reason that static members are not written is because static variables are identical across objects. Should any of the collection of objects of the same class fail, no mechanism will update the static variables to keep them valid for the collection.

 Warning

> Programmers can use the static modifier as a way of protecting members from serialization, but it is not a very safe solution. There are a few problems with this method of serialization control. The first is that static members hold their values across several objects of the same class. Specifying a class member as static just to prevent serialization is not very useful, even when there is only one instance. The main problem is that it can cause problems if the class is modified to have several instances. Another problem is that static variables must be valid across objects. Code to handle such validation is probably far worse than being able to avoid serialization by adding the static modifier. Use the transient modifier instead.

Unfortunately, static variables are a part of many serialized classes. To manage static variables, three patterns can be used to keep statics valid. Management can be done in two different places: the *readObject()* (for the Serialization interface) or *readExternal()* (for the Externalizable interface) methods. In addition the implementation of the ObjectInputValidation interface will cause the *validateObject()* method or be called at the end of deserialization. These are the only methods guaranteed to execute during a valid deserialization of an object. The following examples cover the use of these methods.

Static Variable Management at Validation

Validation is the best place to control static values. Listing 7.9 shows an example of class instance counting for a serialized class. It uses the ObjectInputValidation interface to increment the instance counter. The class limits the number of instances to be 10 or less.

If an eleventh instance is attempted, the validation throws an exception that prevents the new instance from being added. This pattern can be used to control the number of instances for classes that control limited resources such as communication ports, or to limit the number of separate threads to prevent processing bloat.

Listing 7.9: Class CounterAtValidation—Example of managing static objects counting members during deserialization

```
01.import java.io.*;
02.class CounterAtValidation implements Serializable, ObjectInputValidation{
03.    CounterAtValidation(){
04.        System.out.println("Entered default construtor");
05.    }
06.    CounterAtValidation(int beginingState) throws Exception{
07.        if (counter > maxCounter){
08.            throw new Exception("Too many instances");
09.        }else{
10.            counter++;
11.            state = beginingState;
12.        }
13.    }
14.    public int getState(){
15.        return(state);
16.    }
17.    public void setState(int newState){
18.        state = newState;
19.    }
20.    public void validateObject() throws InvalidObjectException{
21.        // This method is called after an object is loaded.
22.        if (counter > maxCounter){
23.            throw new InvalidObjectException("Too many instances");
24.        }else{
25.            counter++;
26.        }
27.    }
28.    protected void finalize() throws Throwable {
29.        counter--;
30.    }
31.    private final int maxCounter = 10;
32.    private int state;
33.    private static int counter = 0;
34.}
```

In this example, the *validateObject()* method, beginning on line 20, is used to increment the class's static member. If the number of objects counted so far is greater than the maximum allowable, the method throws an InvalidObjectException.

The same scenario of using the *validateObject()* method can also be used to validate checksums or check for related objects. If the method determines that the object is not valid in the current context, the method can throw the InvalidObjectException to invalidate the serialization process. When the InvalidObjectException is thrown, the current object deserialization is aborted.

Static Variable Management at Read

Management of statics can also be accomplished by using the *readObject()* or the *readExternal()* methods. This management technique is not as preferable to using the *validateObject()* method.

Listing 7.10 is identical to the example in listing 7.9, except that it handles the static member from within the *readObject()* method. The same technique can be accomplished in Externalized objects from within the *readExternal()* method.

Listing 7.10: Class CounterAtRead—Demonstration of using the readObject() method

```
01.import java.io.*;
02.class CounterAtRead implements Serializable{
03.    CounterAtRead(){
04.        System.out.println("Entered default construtor");
05.    }
06.    CounterAtRead(int beginingState) throws Exception{
07.        if (counter > maxCounter){
08.            throw new Exception("Too many instances");
09.        }else{
10.            counter++;
11.            state = beginingState;
12.        }
13.    }
14.    public int getState(){
15.        return(state);
16.    }
17.    public void setState(int newState){
18.        state = newState;
19.    }
20.    private void readObject(ObjectInputStream stream) throws IOException,
➥ClassNotFoundException{
21.        stream.defaultReadObject();
22.        // This method is called after an object is loaded.
23.        if (counter > maxCounter){
24.            throw new IOException("Too many instances");
```

```
25.        }else{
26.            counter++;
27.        }
28.    }
29.    protected void finalize() throws Throwable {
30.        counter--;
31.    }
32.    private final int maxCounter = 10;
33.    private int state;
33.    private static int counter = 0;
34.}
```

In the *readObject()* method on line 20, the method is passed the current object input stream. The first line of the *readObject()* method is a call to the *defaultReadObject()* method (line 21) which automatically deserializes the current object. It is important to note here that the *readObject()* method is part of a signature that is used by the deserialization mechanism, as is the *defaultReadObject()* method. These entries are handled in a special way that enables the private and protected data to be written from the stream to the current object. Also note that the *readObject()* method is private. The serialization mechanism is able to call this method despite the private modifier. The point here is that the deserialization (and for that matter, serialization) happens a level lower than is evident in the code.

In lines 23 through 27 of the *readObject()* method, there is a check to see if the maximum instances of this object have been created. If the limit has been reached, the deserialization is aborted.

Object Validation

Object validation is very important for ensuring that a Bean's data is accurate and valid. Object validation is also used for the accurate initialization of non-persistent parts of objects. These transient parts must be configured prior to the completion of an object's deserialization. If there are also static members of classes, they can also be manipulated during the validation process.

The pattern for persistent object validation is accomplished with the *ObjectInputValidation* interface. The interface contains the *validateObject()* method that is guaranteed to be called after the object has been serialized, but before the object is validated. In other words, after the object's stream has been read and before the next object is read or deserialization completes. The *validateObject()* method can throw an *InvalidObjectException* if the implementation of this method determines that the object was deserialized incorrectly or some other condition exists which invalidates the new object. For example, the *validateObject()* can be used to prevent too many instances from being loaded.

The *validateObject()* method can be used to guard against corrupt object streams and to act as an entry point that signals to the object that its deserialization is complete. For example, the *validateObject()* method can be used to load an image after the information about the image's location is deserialized.

By using the *validateObject()* method, the use of specific reading and writing of object information can many times be completely avoided. Using the *readObject()* and *writeObject()* methods should be avoided and a combination of transient fields and the *validateObject()* reduce the risk that the object stream that is written is different from the one that is read. If complete control is assumed by the programmer, it is easy to make mistakes and possibly leave some members out of the serialization process. By implementing the *validateObject()* method, it is assumed that all serialized members have been restored and can now be validated for accuracy and/or the object manipulated so that it is put into a valid state.

Validation can take several forms, and it is up to the programmer to implement a scheme that applies to a particular object. The following list shows the possible validation tasks that might be applied to a persistent object:

- ◆ Verify data against a checksum

- ◆ Ensure that objects are valid in the current context

- ◆ Validate that a version number read into the object matches the expected version of the class (discussed in detail later in this chapter)

- ◆ Check that values are within their expected bounds

- ◆ Verify that arrays and collections have the correct number of elements

- ◆ Validate serial numbers

- ◆ Validate encrypted validation keys

- ◆ Validate members against defaults

- ◆ Check for null members that may not have been part of an earlier version that will need initialization in the current version

The Bean in listing 7.11 implements some of the techniques from the preceding list. The Bean validates a vector for its expected size and validates the supported versions of objects. In the *validateObject()* method (lines 42–49), there is a check to see whether there is a valid vector of stored state data (line 44). If there is not, an InvalidObject-Exception is thrown. Next, the version is validated (line 47) by calling the Bean's version conversion method that starts on line 54. In the version validation method, if the version is too old or unknown, the object is invalid. If the version is 1.5, the information required for version 2.0 is added and version 2.0 validation is started.

Finally, after validation completes, the restored information is validated against the supported range of values (line 48). If the data is out of bounds, the object creation is aborted. Note that the input object stream may have loaded data from an older version of this class, making this method necessary for validation. Such a validation is required if the older version did not perform a range check. For example, a calendar Bean, in initial versions, allowed all dates to be input. In a later version, the Bean developer has found that users are setting dates in the past instead of the future. The Bean would bomb whenever this happens. So, to prevent the problem the developer limits the Bean to future dates only. Unfortunately the developer has many clients that have the old Bean and subsequently, old serialized object streams. Some of these streams could have past instead of future dates in them. The validation mechanism described here can be used to correct the bad dates or invalidate the old object stream with a message for the user to recreate the object because it is invalid.

Listing 7.11: Class BeanWithValidation—Class to demonstrate deserialization validation and version tracking

```
01.import java.io.*;
02.import java.util.*;
03.import java.beans.*;
04.class BeanWithValidation implements Serializable, ObjectInputValidation{
05.
06.    BeanWithValidation(){
07.        state = new Vector();
08.        vectorSize = state.size();
09.        // Version initialized to class version when object created.
10.        objectVersion = classVersion;
11.    }
12.
13.    // Get indexed property
14.    public int getState(int index) throws
➥ArrayIndexOutOfBoundsException{
```

```
15.          return(((Integer)state.elementAt(index))).intValue();
16.     }
17.
18.     // set indexed PropertyVetoException property
19.     public void setState(int newState, int index) throws
➥PropertyVetoException{
20.         if ( newState > maxValue || newState < minValue ){
21.             Integer oldValue;
22.             try{
23.                 oldValue = (Integer)state.elementAt(index);
24.             }catch(ArrayIndexOutOfBoundsException aioobe){
25.                 oldValue = null;
26.             }
27.             PropertyChangeEvent change = new
➥PropertyChangeEvent(this,"state",oldValue,new Integer(newState));
28.             throw new PropertyVetoException("The requested set point is
➥out of bounds.",change);
29.         }
30.
31.         try {
32.             state.setElementAt(new Integer(newState),index);
33.         }catch(ArrayIndexOutOfBoundsException aioobe){
34.             state.setSize(index);
35.             state.setElementAt(new Integer(newState),index);
36.         }
37.         // save size for persistence validation.
38.         vectorSize = state.size();
39.     }
40.
41.     // Implementation for ObjectInputValidation interface
42.     public void validateObject() throws InvalidObjectException{
43.         // This method is called after an object is loaded.
44.         if (state == null){
45.             throw new InvalidObjectException("The state vector was
➥empty.");
46.         }
47.         checkVersion();
48.         validateRange();
49.     }
50.
51.     // Check for valid versions.
52.     // In addition handle any upgrades from old to new versions.
53.
54.     private void checkVersion() throws InvalidObjectException{
55.         switch (objectVersion){
56.           case 10: // Version 1.0 not supported by this version
```

continues

continued

```
57.               throw new InvalidObjectException("Version"
➥"+classVersion+" not compatible with "+objectVersion");
58.          case 15: // Version 2.0 is ugradable to this version
59.               // 1.0 did not have a Vector size so we set it here
60.               // so that it does not cause an exception later.
61.               vectorSize = state.size();
62.               // bump version to 2.0
63.               objectVersion = 20;
64.               // Run checkVersion() again as 2.0
65.               checkVersion();
66.               break;
67.          case 20: // This is the current version so validate that the
➥vector
68.               // is the correct size.
69.               if (state.size() != vectorSize){
70.                    throw new InvalidObjectException("Vector is not the
➥expected size.");
71.               }
72.               break;
73.          default: // Version unknown so not supported by this version
74.               throw new InvalidObjectException("Version"
➥"+classVersion+" not comatable with "+objectVersion");
75.          }//end switch (objectVersion)
76.      }
77.
78.     // Validate that all elements in a persistent array have been loaded.
79.     void validateRange() throws InvalidObjectException{
80.          for (Enumeration e = state.elements() ; e.hasMoreElements() ;) {
81.               int testValue = ((Integer)e.nextElement()).intValue();
82.               if ( testValue > maxValue || testValue < minValue ){
83.                    throw new InvalidObjectException("An element in the sate
➥array is out of bounds.");
84.               }
85.          }
86.     }
87.     private Vector state;
88.     private int vectorSize;
89.     private int objectVersion;
90.     private final static int classVersion = 20;//Version 2.0
91.     private final static int minValue = 0;
92.     private final static int maxValue = 10;
93.}
```

The Bean designer should also expect certain errors and have methods for recovering gracefully from them. In a Bean that expects to open a database at a certain URL, if the URL is missing or has moved, there should be a way for the user to reset the URL to a new location. The new location should then be updated as the application is serialized before termination. Such friendly error recovery should be applied to everything from URLs to files and available hardware. Another example is an application that expects a file at a certain location on the user's file system. If the file cannot be found (because of directory rename or moving of directories), instead of throwing exceptions or printing warnings, give the user the opportunity to locate the files.

Controlling Object Serialization

Sometimes it is necessary to control all or part of an object's serialization. For example, the object's data must be compressed, encrypted, or synched with other objects before the data is serialized. You can accomplish this in two ways. The first is used by the *java.io.Serializable* interface in conjunction with the *objectOutput()* and *objectInput()* methods. As has already been covered, the *objectOutput()* and *objectInput()* methods are specialized methods that are used for serialization processing if the class implements the Serializable interface. Remember that the *defaultWriteObject()* and *defaultReadObject()* methods can be called from their respective *writeObject()* and *readObject()* methods. These default read/write mechanisms can be used to read and write the non-transient and non-static data. This reduces the workload of reading and writing to those members of a class that need to be compressed, encrypted, or otherwise modified.

The *writeObject()* and *readObject()* methods also provide a secure method of serialization control because they are private methods with full access to the object to be serialized. Because they are private, other classes cannot access these methods, preventing a misuse or possible malicious use (for instance, a bank account class could not have its output stream diverted by another class calling the method directly).

 Warning

Do not confuse the *writeObject()* and *readObject()* methods with those of the same name in the respective *ObjectOutput()* and *ObjectInput()* methods. These are not the same. The ObjectOutput and ObjectInput interfaces should only be used when directly reading and writing object streams and not for serializing and deserializing objects.

The second method for serialization control uses the *java.io.Externalized* interface. The *Externalized* interface includes two public methods that are used to serialize and deserialize an object. Using the *Externalized* interface requires that the developer completely control the reading and writing of the objects data. The *writeExternal()* and *readExternal()* methods of this interface are called when serialization takes place.

Each of these different types of control through the Serialization interface or through the Externalizable interface are handled transparently by the serialization process. In other words, there is no difference between serializing objects that implement either interface.

Note

Although the deserialization process is controlled via these methods, it may still be important to validate objects through the java.io. ObjectInputValidation interface. The *objectValidation()* method in this interface is called *after* deserialization when the object can be completely validated.

Controlling Object Output

Listing 7.12 shows one of the simpler ways to just use the *writeObject()* method (remember this method is a private method that is called if it exists in a class the implements Serializable) to set up the object so that it is ready for serialization. This Bean holds a stack of URL strings that represent the sites that the user has visited while using the parent application. The URL stack grows as the user visits new sites; the stack, therefore, could grow quite large. To fix this potential size problem, save only the last 10 sites each time the program is terminated.

To accomplish the task, the *writeObject()* method first creates a temporary stack and copies only the top 10 URLs and replaces the existing stack. Next, the method calls the *defaultWriteObject()* method, which performs the standard writing of the object. You do not need to implement a *readObject()* method because no special handling of the object's data image has occurred.

This class implements a class that contains a stack object. The class is written so that the serialized copy of the class contains at most only the top 10 entries. In the *writeObject()* method on line 17, a copy of the top 10 items on the current stack is created (lines 19–27). Next, a new stack object is created over the old stack (line 30). The new stack is then populated with the top 10 elements that were copied from the original stack (lines 31–38). This process converts a possibly large stack to one that contains at most 10 entries.

Listing 7.12: Class BeanStateWithSerialControl—implements the writeObject() method to ready data for serialization

```
01.import java.io.*;
02.import java.util.*;
03.
04.class BeanStateWithSerialControl implements Serializable{
05.    BeanStateWithSerialControl(){
06.        URLs = new Stack();
07.    }
08.
09.    public Stack getURls(){
10.        return(URLs);
11.    }
12.
13.    public void setURLs(Stack newURLs){
14.        URLs = newURLs;
15.    }
16.
17.    private void writeObject(ObjectOutputStream stream) throws
➥IOException{
18.        // Copy the stack to a temp vector.
19.        Vector temp = new Vector(10);
20.        for (int i = 0; i< 10;i++){
21.            String URL = (String)URLs.pop();
22.            if (URL != null){
23.                temp.setElementAt(URL,i);
24.            }else{
25.                break;// Exit loop on null data.
26.            }
27.        }
28.
29.        // Create a new stack.
30.        URLs = new Stack();
31.        for (int i =0; i< 10;i++){
32.            String URL = (String)temp.elementAt(i);
33.            if (URL != null){
34.                URLs.push(URL);
35.            }else{
36.                break;// Exit loop on null data.
37.            }
38.        }
39.
40.        // Do the default write of the object.
41.        defaultWriteObject(stream);
42.    }
```

continues

```
continued
43.
44.    private Stack  URLs;
45.}
```

The code in listing 7.12 uses two serialization methods. The first is the *writeObject()* method. This method, when it exists, is used by the object stream to control an object's serialization. The other method, *defaultWriteObject()*, is called by default during normal serialization. The use of the *writeObject()* method makes it necessary to call *defaultWriteObject()* to write the object's contents.

The *writeObject()* method is defined as:

```
private void writeObject(ObjectOutputStream stream) throws IOException;
```

The *defaultWriteObject()* method is defined as:

```
private void defaultWriteObject(ObjectOutputStream stream) throws IOException;
```

Note that both of these methods are defined as private. These methods are only accessible by the *ObjectOutputStream* and *ObjectInputStream* classes. This helps to ensure that other classes are unable to access possibly sensitive information.

Controlling Object Input

Controlling object input is exactly like controlling object output. The *readObject()* method is called during deserialization and can be used to control what happens during this time. Again, it is important that anything done within the *readObject()* method is compatible with whatever happens in the *writeObject()* method. For example, if 10 objects are written in a *writeObject()* method, then 10 objects should be read, in the same order as they were written, in the *readObject()* method. Not doing so can create exception errors when the data expected in the *readObject()* method fails to match the saved object stream.

Listing 7.13 shows the *readObject()* method initializing a stack object marked as transient. The *defaultReadObject()* method loads the rest of the object's image. You do not need to implement a *writeObject()* method because no special handling of the object's data image has occurred.

In this example, a member of the *scratchURLs* class is marked as *transient* (line 32). When the object is serialized this object is not serialized. To recover, the *readObject()* method (lines 25–30) is used to recreate the scratchURLs member (line 27) before the rest of the object is deserialized by the *defaultReadObject()* method (line 29).

Listing 7.13: Class BeanStateWithSerialReadControl—Example using the readObject() method

```
01.import java.io.*;
02.import java.util.*;
03.
04.class BeanStateWithSerialReadControl implements Serializable{
05.    BeanStateWithSerialReadControl(){
06.        URLs = new Stack();
07.    }
08.
09.    public Stack getURls(){
10.        return(URLs);
11.    }
12.
13.    public void setURLs(Stack newURLs){
14.        URLs = newURLs;
15.    }
16.
17.    public Stack getScratchURls(){
18.        return(scratchURLs);
19.    }
20.
21.    public void setScratchURLs(Stack newURLs){
22.        scratchURLs = newURLs;
23.    }
24.
25.    private void readObject(ObjectInputStream stream) throws IOException{
26.        // Setup scratch URL space.
27.        scratchURLs = new Stack();
28.        // Do the default read of the object.
29.        defaultReadObject(stream);
30.    }
31.
32.    private transient Stack  scratchURLs;
33.    private Stack  URLs;
34.}
```

The code in listing 7.13 uses the other two methods new to the 1.1 version of the Java programming language. The first is the *readObject( )* method. This method, when it exists, is used by the object stream to control an object's deserialization. The other method, *defaultReadObject( )*, is called by default during normal serialization. The use of the *readObject( )* method makes it necessary to call *defaultReadObject( )* to read the object's contents.

The *readObject( )* method is defined as:

```
private void readObject(ObjectInputStream stream) throws IOException;
```

The *defaultReadObject( )* method is defined as:

```
private void defaultReadObject(ObjectInputStream stream) throws IOException;
```

Note that both of these methods are defined as private. These methods are only accessible by the object stream class. This helps to ensure that other classes are unable to access possibly sensitive information.

Handling Optional Data

Some classes might need to control optional data. Such data might be very different between objects or require special handling. Listing 7.14 implements both the *readObject( )* and *writeObject( )* methods to handle a optional transient string. A Boolean that is part of the persistent state is used to control the optional read/write of the string. For example, a program could be set to optionally save a list of URLs. The class serialization mechanism would be used to save or not save the data, depending on the setting.

Listing 7.14: Class BeanWithOptionalState—optional data and cooperating writeObject() and readObject() methods

```
01.import java.io.*;
02.import java.util.*;
03.
04.class BeanWithOptionalState implements Serializable{
05.BeanWithOptionalState(){
06.URL = null;
07.hasURL = false;
08.    }
09.
10.public String getURl(){
11.return(URL);
```

```
12.    }
13.
14.public void setURL(String newURL){
15.URL = newURL;
16.if (URL == null){
17.hasURL = false;
18.}else{
19.hasURL = true;
20.         }
21.    }
22.
23.private void writeObject(ObjectOutputStream stream) throws IOException{
24.defaultWriteObject(stream);
25.if (hasURL){
26.stream.writeObject(URL);
27.        }
28.    }
29.
30.private void readObject(ObjectInputStream stream) throws IOException{
31.defaultReadObject(stream);
32.if (hasURL){
33.try {
34.URL = (String) stream.readObject();
35.}catch(ClassNotFoundException cnfe){
36.// Handle an error if it occurs.
37.hasURL = false;
38.URL = null;
39.             }
40.}else{
41.URL = null;
42.         }
43.    }
44.
45.private boolean hasURL;
46.private transient String URL;
47.}
```

Listing 7.14 must implement both the *writeObject()* and *readObject()* methods to maintain the integrity of the persistent object. This example also uses a specific call to read
and write the string object.

The order of read and write must also be correct (a very important point). The state of the
hasURL Boolean in this example must be written before the optional string. When
deserializing the state of the hasURL, Boolean must be read before it is known that an
URL string is available on the *ObjectInputStream*.

Externalized Objects

Objects that implement the externalization interface have complete control of the data in the object stream. They must implement the *readExternal()* and *writeExternal()* methods. Externalized objects have the most control over their serialization. Externalized objects are usually those that require a high degree of control over their persistent state. These objects include specially compressed objects such as images, or secure data that is encrypted.

Unlike standard serialized objects, that use software patterns to define private read/write methods, the read/write methods in externalized objects are defined by the *Externalized* interface. This means that the two methods are public and can be called by classes other than the I/O methods of the Object stream classes. This could become a security or safety issue. For such problems, classes with the *Externalizable* interface should not be public classes. They should be marked using the protected modifier or have no modifier, which makes them default protected. To serialize an object in a protected class, a public class in the same package can be used as a container for the protected class's object. The public container can then be serialized along with the data in the protected object.

The *defaultWriteObject()* method can be used to write most of the serializable data. It is not required for externalized objects, but it does reduce the work to be done for saving information in objects that are always saved. The *defaultWriteObject()* method saves all non-static and non-transient fields to the object stream. After this has been done, the remaining information in the object can be saved.

Bean Versioning

The problem with the delivery of programs and their data is keeping a customer's data compatible with newer versions of the software. The addition of just one value can cause a user to discard old data. The format of the new data will have a different format and could be incompatible with older files. The designers of Java's object serialization expected classes to evolve over time. They have supplied guidelines, behaviors, and methods to ensure most programs continue working as versions change.

Imagine a Java Bean that implements a button that has an animated icon called *AnimatedButtonBean*. It is delivered to the customer who installs it into his IDE. The customer builds an application by using AnimatedButtonBean and uses the IDE to configure the Bean with his animation, a rotating corporate logo. The designer also routes a button press message to another part of the program. The IDE serializes the state of AnimatedButtonBean to a JAR file to be used to deliver the complete application to end users.

Everything has been working fine, but the Bean manufacturer redesigns its AnimatedButtonBean and adds the capability for the button to play a little tune every time the button is pressed. This change adds some code and new parameters for selecting the tune as well as volume. The AnimatedButtonBean now has two more pieces of information associated with the AnimatedButtonBean's serialized object stream.

The customer receives a new Bean and reinstalls it in his IDE. The customer then reloads the application for a couple of changes that have nothing to do with AnimatedButtonBean, but the new Bean is now in the class path. The IDE causes the state of the AnimatedButtonBean to be loaded. But, what happens when the Bean is expecting to now see a sound and a volume object as part of the object stream?

The answer to this problem is that it requires some work to make each version compatible with the previous. Luckily, most of the work required for versioning happens only to newer versions of classes and not by adding control code to original versions. Many rules need to be followed, but if done correctly, program integrity should not be compromised by loading older object data into newer versions of classes.

To load an old object into a newer object, the rules in the following sections must be followed.

Changes That Are Valid

Valid changes are those that will either add data to classes or entail no change to the state of serialization. The following is a list of the changes that are compatible:

- ◆ Adding new methods added to a class
- ◆ Adding new fields to a class
- ◆ Removing classes
- ◆ Adding *writeObject( )/readObject( )* methods
- ◆ Removing *writeObject( )/readObject( )* methods
- ◆ Adding the Serializable interface
- ◆ Removing the Serializable interface
- ◆ Changing the Access modifiers of a field

Adding New Methods to a Class

Because methods are not serialized as data, they do not affect serialization. The same is true for the addition and deletion of code within methods.

Adding New Fields to the Class

As an object is deserialized, any field not in the stored stream is unaffected by the deserialization process. If such new fields are not in the object stream, the initial value specified by their class default is used. This applies to both new primitives and new class references. In listing 7.15, the first class is the original followed by the enhanced version that has an extra field initialized at creation.

Listing 7.15: Adding new fields to a class

```
01.//Original class
02.class Foo extends Serializable{
03.void setA(int newA){
04.a  = newA;
05.     }
06.int getA(){
07.return(a);
08.     }
09.int a;
10.//New class
11.class Foo extends Serializable{
12.void setA(int newA){
13.a  = newA;
14.     }
15.int getA(){
16.return(a);
17.     }
18.void setB(int newB){
19.b  = newB;
20.     }
21.int getB(){
22.return(b);
23.     }
24.int a;
25.int b = 0;//default value for new versions.
26.}
```

For fields that must have more complex initialization, new fields can be initialized either in *readObject()*, *readExternal()*, or the *validateObject()* methods. These methods should compare an invalid default value to the current value to determine whether the field requires initialization. Listing 7.16, for example, is the original class to be extended:

Listing 7.16: Version 1 of class MyBean

```
class MyBean implements Serializable{
MyBean(){
     }
private String BaseURL;
}
```

The new class in listing 7.17 adds an additional string that adds an alternate URL to the class. In addition, to have a valid backup URL, the primary URL is used to load the correct value.

Listing 7.17: Version 2 of class MyBean

```
01.class MyBean implements Serializable, ObjectInputValidation{
02.MyBean(){
03.     }
04.public String readBackupURL(){
05.// Support for reading URL backup
06.
07.          // detail deleted for clarity
08.
09.     }
10.public void validateObject() throws InvalidObjectException{
11.if (backupURL == null){
12.backupURL = readBackupURL()
13.     }
14.     }
15.private String BaseURL;
16.private String backupURL = null;
17.}
```

Removing Classes

Removing classes from the object stream causes the read process to still read objects, but prevents them from being assigned to references. The objects become garbage collected. Do not confuse the deletion of classes from streams with the deletion of fields within classes. Deletion of classes is at the level of *writeObject()* calls that are not part of the recursive write of objects.

Adding writeObject()/readObject() Methods

When control is added via the *writeObject()/readObject()*, the object stream control passes from the default process to that described by these methods. As long as these new methods read the stream in a compatible way, the new version remains valid. This means that the *defaultReadObject()* method and *defaultWriteObject()* methods are called before any new optional data is read or written.

Removing writeObject/readObject Methods

Because the *writeObject()* and *readObject()* methods use the *defaultReadObject()* method and *defaultWriteObject()* methods, the integrity of the objects data in relation to the base object data remains intact. This causes the reading of optional data to be discarded.

Adding the Serializable Interface

Classes that become serializable are written to the stream. Conversely, if a class is converted to be serialized, it should not exist in an older version of the object stream. The newly serializable class will be initialized to its defaults. If the class becomes serializable, it is also required that the class has a constructor without arguments. If such a constructor is missing, the *NotSerializableException* will be thrown.

Removing the Serializable Interface

Making a class so that is no longer serializable is equivalent to removing a class. The data for the class will be discarded in the same way. If the class is used as a required, non-optional part of another serialized class, it will break versioning.

Changing the Access Modifiers of a Field

Access modifiers public, package, protected, and private do not affect the serialization process and cannot break versioning. Care should be taken when reducing visibility when such access reduction might break other parts of a program.

Changing a Field from Static to Non-Static

Moving a field from static to non-static is the same as adding a field to a class, and is perfectly legal as long as the default for the value is valid or properly initialized.

Changing Transient Fields to Non-Transient Fields

Moving a field from transient to non-transient is the same as adding a field to a class, and is perfectly legal as long as the default for the value is valid or properly initialized.

Changes That Break Versioning

The following sections detail all things that cause a new version of a class to fail. In general, changes that cause fields that are non-optional to turn up missing in the stream are the things that make serialization fail. The following list details the changes that break versioning. Each procedure is covered in the sections that follow.

- ◆ Changing the class name
- ◆ Changing the inheritance tree
- ◆ Deleting fields
- ◆ Promoting or demoting classes in the hierarchy
- ◆ Changing a non-static field to a static field
- ◆ Changing a non-transient field to transient
- ◆ Changing the declared type of a primitive field
- ◆ Changing default writes in *writeObject( )* method
- ◆ Changing default writes in *writeObject( )* method
- ◆ Changing a class from Externalizable to Serializable

Changing the Class Name

If a class name is changed, any assignment from the object stream to target class will fail. Object classes are resolved by name.

Changing the Inheritance Tree

If base classes are changed, base data changes along with class signatures. These changes make the object stream incompatible to older versions of the class.

Deleting Fields

Deletion of non-static or non-transient fields will be disposed because they are read into a class in pwhich they do not exist. Deletion of such fields does not cause a breakage in the new version, but an older class reading the newer stream needs to use the default value in its class. This default value may not be valid given the new state of the remaining class and could cause the entire object to become invalid. Any deletion is considered an incompatible change, therefore, because it is not valid for backward-compatibility.

Promoting or Demoting Classes in the Hierarchy

Moving classes so that they appear in different places in the object tree is not allowed. This is an error in the sequence of the stream. When moved in the hierarchy, there is no way to create a context that allows the state of such objects to be read.

Changing a Non-Static Field to a Static Field

Converting a field from non-static to static is the equivalent of deleting the field from the class. In other words, the field is no longer available for serialization. Such deletions can cause backward-compatibility problems because the field may not be properly initialized.

Changing a Non-Transient Field to Transient

Converting a field from non-transient to transient is the equivalent of deleting the field from the class. This causes the field to be deleted from those that can be serialized. Such deletions can cause backward-compatibility problems because the field may not be properly initialized. Such behavior may cause the class to fail in unexpected ways.

Changing the Declared Type of a Primitive Field

Changing the declared type of a primitive breaks the backward-compatibility of older classes that expect data of a specified type. For example, if a field is an int in one version and a long in another, the two versions are incompatible.

Changing Default Writes in writeObject() Method

Modification of default writing of data in any way causes compatibility problems between versions. Default data must always be written in a way that is fully compatible to different versions. If version 1 of a class writes default data and version 2 does not, for example, the stream for version 2 will not contain the correct data for version 1. This causes version 1 to rely on default values for all serialized fields. Such behavior will probably cause a version 1 class to behave inappropriately.

Changing Default Reads in readObject() Method

Changing the default read is also inappropriate and invalidates the stream between versions. If a class no longer reads default data, it cannot rewrite default data when it is serialized. When this occurs, an earlier version of the class will not find the default part of the stream and will throw a NoDefaultDataException.

Changing a Class from Serializable to Externalizable

The move between *Serializable* and *Externalizable* interfaces causes a class to be in full control of serialized data. This means that there will not be any default data written or read from externalized classes. This is okay when moving from version 1 to version 2 of a class only if the *defaultReadObject()* and *defaultWriteObject()* are still used in the newer version. If this is not true, the older version will throw a *NoDefaultDataException* when a newer version of the stream is read.

Changing a Class from Externalizable to Serializable

Changing from Externalizable to Serializable is inappropriate in most cases. This is because externalized classes usually do not call *defaultReadObject()* and *defaultWriteObject()* methods to store their default fields. In a Serializable class, there must always be a default data section. Such a change is possible only if all older versions that implement Serializable had no default data (such a class should have been designed as Externalizable instead).

Summary

In this chapter, the basics of object persistence have been covered. The process for serialization and deserialization has been described and the techniques for controlling this process have been covered.

This chapter has covered a very important subject for Java Beans developers as well as for any type of persistence programming. The conservative approach should be taken to avoid the possibly unnecessary serialization of objects. In other words, study each field member in a class and determine on a case-by-case basis if the member really needs to be serializable. The developer should be aware of situations that may require special handling. The class may require explicit validation of deserialized data or the partial or complete control of the serialization process.

In general, most Java Beans can be safely serialized. In some cases, using the transient modifier may be the only form of control over serialization. However, the programmer should be wary. Serialization can be implemented with very little effort by the developer, as is the case with anything that is almost free, caveat emptor.

CHAPTER 8

Java Bean Introspection and Core Reflection

One of the important features of the Java Bean component model is the ability for Java Beans-aware applications to connect components and to configure their parameters. Traditionally, component-aware applications used definition files to publish a component API so that it could be programmatically understood by an application development tool. Instead of being read from separate definition files, Java Beans classes are read directly with the Core Reflection API using the Introspector class.

The Core Reflection API is a set of classes that enables Java to dynamically read the class and method definitions directly from a class file. These definitions can then be used to create objects. Objects can also be manipulated dynamically because the method definitions can be used to create and call the object's methods.

The Introspector class, part of the Java Beans API, is used to create a representation of Java Bean's classes. The class data found by the Introspector is used to create the data in a BeanInfo object that gives programmatic access to the Bean's API. The information accessible through the BeanInfo includes properties, events, and all the accessible methods.

If Beans could not be manipulated and examined by a Bean-aware IDE, programmers would need to write definition files or generate these files with special tools. Instead, Bean-aware applications are able to read a Bean's API directly from the Java class file. By automating the configuration tasks in the IDE, programs using Beans can be created more quickly and with fewer mistakes, usually with just a few mouse clicks.

This chapter covers the Core Reflection API and the process of introspection that enables Bean-aware applications or components to examine Beans so that they can be displayed, their properties modified, and connected to other components and the base application. Several examples are given that read class files containing Java Beans and connect them programmatically. Creating a complete Bean-aware application is beyond the scope of this book, but a few examples of how it is done will help you understand how an IDE works. The techniques described can also be used to create Java Beans or specialized applications that can contain or manipulate Beans. A specialized container Bean, for example, could sort or arrange components based on their attributes. In fact, Core Reflection and the Java Beans Introspector class can be used in combination to create plug-and-play type applications. For instance, a graphics package could be written that would have plugable components for displays, filters, algorithms, file format converters, and so on. By extending the information retrieved by the Introspector class, specific APIs can be easily recognized and used to trigger specific application-specific behaviors. After a Bean-aware framework is in place, an application can be easily extended by adding components. In fact, because the capability to read standard Java Beans components exists in the core Java API, any application can be written to be Bean-aware.

This chapter is not overly difficult to understand. It does present a challenge, however, because it describes how to write software that reads code. You may find the programming constructs a little hard to follow at first because, as a programmer, you are well-versed in reading APIs and using them in your own software. You should already be familiar with the AWT package, for example, and have used the API in your own software. When you change the background color of a Button you simply write the following line of Java code:

```
Button myButton = new Button();
myButton.setBackground(Color.red);
```

Human beings have a great deal of pattern matching software in their brains that make short work of such tasks. Nevertheless, programmers have a lot going on in their heads to do this simple task.

1. The programmer has to first read the API for the Button.

2. Then, in the code, the programmer creates a button from a default constructor.

3. The programmer must then realize that to change a button's background color requires implementing the *setBackground()* method of the base component class.

4. The programmer must also remember that the *setBackground()* method takes one parameter, the color, has no return method, and throws no exceptions that need to be caught.

The preceding steps are very simplified, and do not come close to explaining all of the complexities of learning and problem solving that are actually performed by the human mind. But, for the experienced Java programmer, the process happens almost as if it were a reflex. If we understood this process, artificial intelligence would be a reality. Unfortunately, we can only accomplish some of these tasks in software. With a constrained task like setting the background color of a Bean, we can easily write software with enough built-in intelligence to handle the job.

Setting a background color of a button in a Bean-aware application is straightforward as was previously stated. But, as can be seen by the following steps (and the code in listing 8.1), the task takes several more steps and quite a lot more code to accomplish.

1. Load the Button's class object (Line 2).

2. Using the Bean's class, create a BeanInfo object that contains the Bean's API (line 5).

3. Create an instance object of the button (line 8).

4. Locate the background property in the BeanInfo object (line 11).

5. Get the write method object used to set the background (line 12).

6. Create a parameter list that contains a new color object (line 15).

7. Call the *setBackground()* method for the Bean with the parameter list containing the new background color (line 16).

Listing 8.1: Code fragment example showing how to use Introspection and Core Reflection APIs to create a button and set its background color to red

```
01.        // Create a class object for a button
02.        Class classButton = Class.forName("Button");
03.
04.        // Get BeanInfo object for the Button class
05.        BeanInfo myButtonBeanInfo =
➡Introspector.getBeanInfo(classButton,null);
06.
07.        // Create new instance of the button.
08.        Object myButton = classButton.newInstance();
09.
10.        //create a setBackground() method for component2
11.        PropertyDescriptor
➡background=getPropertyDescriptor(myButtonBeanInfo,"background");
12.        Method setBackground = background.getWriteMethod();
13.
```

continues

```
continued
14.        // Set the background colors of the button
15.        args[0] = Color.red;
16.        setBackground.invoke(myButton,args);
```

This chapter focuses on code similar to this example, but the emphasis will be on creating software that performs these tasks in a very generic way, similar to the BeanBox application or other Bean-aware products like application development tools. For example, instead of creating and manipulating a button, the code in listing 8.1 could be applied to any class that had a background property. You will learn how to create software that manipulates classes and objects that use specific signatures like those for Java Beans and others.

The Programmatic View

Components are manipulated by understanding their API. Traditionally, the API was expressed as a text file or special binary file that is either hand-written or generated by a component builder tool. The component-aware tool reads the definition file and uses it to generate code to present the component in the IDE and to generate code. Programmatically viewing components is the equivalent of reading the component's documentation.

In Java Beans, this reading of the API is done with the Core Reflection API and the Introspector class. The Core Refection API is a set of classes that can read a class object and retrieve class, method, and field information. This information, in the form of language objects, can be used to instantiate classes, call methods, and access an object's fields.

The Introspector class, in the Java Beans API, uses the Core Reflection API to examine Java Beans. The Introspector applies signature matching rules against the information retrieved with the reflection classes. This information is used to build FeatureDescriptor classes that group the methods matching the signatures into the feature categories, which are Properties, Event Sets, and the remainder as simply methods.

The best way to think of the Core Reflection API is that it enables a program to examine itself or others and from this data build accessor objects to instantiate classes and call methods. The programmatic examination allows IDE tools to interpret components without human intervention. This gives the IDE much more information about plugable components, and reduces the amount of preparation that component developers normally need to interface with an IDE. For reflection to work properly, the Java Beans developer must follow certain patterns of programming. These patterns enable the IDE to recognize, for instance, setFoo(int fooValue), which means that foo is set with an integer. The pattern that the IDE looks for is the "set" in the method name. After this method is recognized, the IDE can continue to use reflection to determine the type of the value to be set. This information can be used to create property sheets or to be used by scripting languages to access components.

Because there is no code generated, the problems of an IDE keeping track of generated and user created code is eliminated. Most configuration tasks are performed on live objects with their persistent state saved for loading when the application is actually used. If the GUI adds any code to a user's program, it is only the instantiation of the component by loading its persistent state and adding it to the current panel or canvas. The only other code that needs to be created is event adapters, which are very simple and have no impact on developers' custom classes.

The BeanInfo Interface

In addition to the automated process of building a BeanInfo, the BeanInfo class can be used to override or extend the information. The BeanInfo, used as an override, is similar to Component Definition Files. The big difference with a BeanInfo is that the information is 100 percent Java. The BeanInfo for a Java Bean component is type checked and validated as a compiled class, eliminating problems that could occur in proprietary Component Definition Files that are usually not written in a type checked language.

The BeanInfo object can be created in three different ways:

- ◆ Using the Introspector class to populate the minimum information through Core Reflection.

- ◆ By the Bean developer creating the BeanInfo object by writing a class that implements BeanInfo.

- ◆ Combined developer information of specific parts of a BeanInfo object with the Introspector class, using Core Reflection to obtain the remaining data.

Java Bean Introspector Class

The Introspector class is a utility provided in the Java Beans package. It aids in creating a view of a Bean's API. The Bean API in Part III of this book covers the class in detail.

This chapter, however, pays special attention to the *getBeanInfo()* method. The *getBeanInfo()* method may at first seem to be linked with a BeanInfo class associated with a Bean, but this is only partially true. What *getBeanInfo()* does is far more powerful:

1. *getBeanInfo()* creates a BeanInfo object by first retrieving a BeanInfo object for a class.

2. *getBeanInfo()* then analyzes the target class with Core Reflection for information not supplied by the designated BeanInfo.

3. If there is no supplied BeanInfo class, *getBeanInfo()* analyzes all the methods and events to create event set descriptors, method descriptors, and property descriptors. The BeanInfo object is then ready to be examined as the API representation of a Java Bean.

Using the Core Reflection API

Before covering how the BeanInfo and Introspector class is used, you first need to understand what is happening inside of the Introspector class. This information is important for two reasons: first, as mentioned previously, Java Beans must conform to software signatures. By understanding how they are found, the patterns themselves should become more clear. Each signature needs to follow a layout that can be searched for and used; understanding this process helps in debugging and design of Java Beans.

The second reason for understanding the Core Reflection API and its ability to find and manipulate specific classes and methods is so that extensions to the Introspector can be created. Extensions are appropriate when creating specific components that have more signatures than just properties or event sets. For example, there is no explicit pattern for a container in the Java Beans API. A container signature is simply a class that inherits from the Container base class. This is obvious, and it is simple to look up the base class using core reflection. After the class is known to be a container, it is a simple matter to cast the Bean to a container object whenever container functionality is required.

To extend the container example further, the container might need to examine each class that is added to it. For instance, a smart container could be used to link related objects.

The following sections detail how the Core Reflection API is used to find Java Beans design signatures.

Recognizing Class Name Design Signatures

One of the simplest ways to determine a design signature is to parse a Bean's class name. The class name could be very important in several situations. It is mainly used as a way of implying that other classes exist. For instance, the BeanInfo class for a Bean is found by appending "BeanInfo" to the Bean's name. The Bean Foo may have a BeanInfo named FooBeanInfo. The classes used to edit properties are also found by appending the class name of the property type to the word "Editor." So a property of type Color would have a custom property editor named ColorEditor.

As a rule, naming signatures are usually string combinations. The name is formed from its true name and a type name. As was shown for the ColorEditor class, the name is "Color" while the type of the signature is "Editor." The same is true for FooBeanInfo where Foo is the name and BeanInfo is the type.

Usually, the name of the class is designated where the Bean signature discovery process starts, so the name can be used immediately to search for related classes. There are times, however, when Beans are encountered as objects. To obtain the name of the class that the object was created from, use the *getClass()* method of the object and then use the *getName()* method on the resulting class object. For example, listing 8.2 shows a method that returns the class name of a given object.

 Note

> Remember any class can be operated on by the Core Reflection API or the Introspector class. There is no need for the class to be a Bean.

Listing 8.2: Method used to retrieve the name of an object's class

```
01.    /**
02.     * Return the class name of an object.
03.     */
04.    public static final String getName(Object anObject){
05.
06.        // Get the class of the object.
07.        Class theClass = anObject.getClass();
08.
09.        // Get the name of the object and return it.
10.        return(theClass.getName());
11.    }
```

Recognizing Class Inheritance Design Signatures

The next aspect of the Bean to be matched against design signatures is the class hierarchy. This level of inspection gives context to the methods in the Bean. For example, if a Bean was a child of a component, then only component type signatures need to be searched for (such as *set Foreground()*). Whereas if the Bean did not inherit any AWT classes then the Bean would need to be treated as an invisible component.

Creating Classes by Name

If a class to be studied is specified by name rather than by object, the class can be loaded via the *forName()* method. The example in listing 8.3 shows how this is accomplished. Note that this is a Class object, not an instantiation of the object. To create an object of a class, the *newInstance()* from the Class object or a Constructor object must be called.

Listing 8.3: Method used to get a class object from a class name

```
/**
 * Return the class object given the class's name.
 */
public static Class getClass(String className) throws
➥ClassNotFoundException{
    return (Class.forName(className));
}
```

Remember that the name of the class should be fully qualified. In other words, the class name should include the package name.

Retrieving Parent Classes

In addition to the class type and name, sometimes the parent class may be part of the pattern. For example, a component of a Bean may inherit from the Component class. An IDE can look for the SimpleBeanInfo class by using the *getClasses()* method in the Class class. The method in listing 8.4 does exactly that, given an object to inspect.

Listing 8.4: Method used to check if a class's parent is SimpleBeanInfo

```
01.    /**
02.     * Returns true if the class parent is equal to SimpleBeanInfo.
03.     */
```

```
04.    public static boolean isSimpleBeanInfo(Class aClass){
05.
06.        // Get the super class.
07.        Class superClass = aClass.getSuperclass();
08.
09.        // Get the name and return true if it is a SimpleBeanInfo class.
10.        return(superClass.getName().equals("java.beans.SimpleBeanInfo"));
11.    }
```

Looking at All Classes and Interfaces

An additional method in the Class class is *getClasses()*. The *getClasses()* method returns an array of all classes inherited and all interfaces implemented by a class. Listing 8.5 uses *getClasses()* to search for a specific class name. This method can be used to quickly locate a specific class that fits part of a pattern.

The method is static because it is not associated with any object data. Another reason for setting this method as static is to use it without creating an object. The method is part of the class ReflectionTools (found on the book's CD).

Listing 8.5: ReflectionTools.hasClass()—Method to locate a specified superclass or interface in a target class

```
01.    /**
02.     * Returns true if the class targetToSearch inherites
03.     * or implements an interface specified by searchFor.
04.     * Note: getClasses() is part of the new Java 1.1 API.
05.     */
06.    public static boolean hasClass(Class targetToSearch, Class
    ⇒searchFor){
07.
08.        // Get the super classes and interfaces.
09.        Class classes[] = targetToSearch.getClasses();
10.
11.    // For each superclass or interface, look for the search class.
12.        for (int i = 0; i< classes.length;i++){
13.
14.            // If the class is the same as the one being searched, return
    ⇒true.
15.            if(classes[i].equals(searchFor)){
16.                return true;
17.            }
```

continues

continued

```
18.         }
19.         // If we got here then there was no match.
20.         return false;
21.         }
```

The *hasClass()* method simply takes a target class and a class to search for as arguments. On line 9, the *getClasses()* method is called for the test class. In lines 12 through 18, the target's classes and interfaces are each compared to the class to search for. If the class is either extended or implemented by the target class, then this class returns true. If the class to find did not exist, this method will return false.

This class can be used as the first stage of a design signature-matching tool. For example, this class could be used to search for the extension of the Component class. If the class extended Component then the class would be a visual component, otherwise it would be an invisible component.

The *hasClass()* method can also be used to look for interfaces that signal specific design signatures, too. For example, if the PropertyChangeListener interface is implemented by a class, then objects of the class can be added to property change source Java Beans.

For interfaces, the methods supported are used by signature matching software directly. In contrast, many signatures are not directly associated with an extended class. The signature-matching tool must be able to find signatures by examining methods or groups of methods. The easiest signature characteristic to match is the method's name. The next section details how to write a method to do exactly that.

Finding Design Signatures by Method Name

The next level that can be used to discover design signatures is by method name. Like classes, the name can either be an exact match to a string or a partial match, matching either the beginning or the end of the method name. The Action source method patterns are an example of a pattern that is a complete match. For example, a class meets the Bound PropertyAction Source signature if it implements the *addPropertyChangeListener()* and the *removePropertyChangeListener()* methods. For such a signature, the existence of both methods implies that any property change can be bound to by a class that implements the PropertyChangeListener interface.

The other method of matching a pattern is through a partial match of the name of a method. An example of a partial match is the parameter patterns where methods to access parameters start with "set" and retrieval starts with "get." For example, the *setColor()* method would match the "set" property signature, while *getColor()* would match the "get" property signature.

Listing 8.6 shows an example method that searches a class for the first occurrence of a method with the specified name. The *getDeclaredMethods()* method returns an array of all methods in a class. This method is useful only for situations where there should only be one method in the class with the specified name. If there were two methods with different sets of parameters, this method would only return the first one encountered.

Listing 8.6: ReflectionTools.getMethodForName()—Utility function to locate the first occurrence of a method with the specified name

```
01.    /**
02.     * Find a named method in a class and return its method object.
03.     * @param target Class to search.
04.     * @param methodName Name of the method to find.
05.     * @returns the method of the matched name or null if none found.
06.     */
07.    public static Method getMethodForName(Class target,String
➥methodName){
08.          // Hashtable to temporarily store the Properties.
09.          Hashtable hashedProperties=new Hashtable();
10.
11.          Method[] methods;
12.          // Get the declared methods for the target class.
13.          try{
14.              methods = target.getDeclaredMethods();
15.          }catch( SecurityException se){
16.              // If this failed, there is no reason to continue.
17.              // Return a null.
18.              return (null);
19.          }
20.
21.          // For each method, test for the method name.
22.          for (int i = 0; i < methods.length; i++){
23.
24.              // Get the name of this method and check against target.
25.              if(methodName.equals(methods[i].getName())){
26.                  // Return matched method
27.                  return methods[i];
28.              }
```

continues

```
continued
29.        }// End for each method
30.        // If we got here then there were no matches.
31.        // Return null
32.        return null;
33.    }//End of getMethodForName()
```

Searching by name is useful mainly if the properties of a method are unknown. Such a method signature is sometimes quite useful. Searching by name enables the developer to create scenarios where the action specified by the name of the method is the characteristic of the signature, while the parameter type is arbitrary and depends on the implementation of the component. For example, a design signature for a store command might be:

```
public void store(<class type>)
```

In this signature, the type is not resolved until it is used. In other words, the program would first catalog that the classes support the *store()* function. Then, when an object of a particular type needs to be stored, the program would search for the specific class in its catalog of classes that support the same type object as the object. For example, there might be a class with store(GIF gifObject) and another class with the method store(BMP bmpObject). The program would use the object and method that matched the type to be stored, either BMP or GIF.

Such signatures are very useful because there is no other way to describe such dynamically different signatures. The only other way of doing this is to force the parameters to be of class Object. Using Object is not as clear as using the actual type. Also, the class typing is enforced at the method call instead of from within the method where it would be cast from an object to its required type. Such signatures are also of more benefit when used in application development tools because the tool can enforce the interconnection of methods due to the exact type match. This can prevent exceptions later when the methods are actually called. In general, builder tools will also choose exact types over those that are cast to base classes like Object.

Locating Fully Qualified Methods

A fully qualified method, a method signature that specifies both the name and types of method parameters, is used in many of the Java Bean design signatures. Both the property change source and the vetoable change source patterns require that specific patterns need to be defined in a class. To find these methods, a specialized form of the *getDeclaredMethod( )* method is used. Unlike the previous example of *getDeclaredMethod( ),* this method returns the single method that matches the name and specifies a parameter type list.

Listing 8.7 shows one way to locate a property change source. The *FindPropertyChangeSourceClasses( )* is given a vector of classes to search and returns the classes that match the property change source design signature. The design signature consists primarily of the class supporting add and remove property change listener objects. Assuming that the methods are specifically named "addPropertyChangeListener" and "removePropertyChangeListener," the methods can be easily located.

Listing 8.7: ReflectionTools.hasClass()—Method to locate property change source classes.

```
01./**
02.    * Given a list of classes this method locates and returns
03.    * any classes that have the property change source design signature.
04.    * The action source design signature must implement the
05.    * addActionListener() method.
06.    * @param classes Vector of classes that are to be searched.
07.    * @returns Classes that has property change source design signature.
08.    */
09.
10.    static final Vector findPropertyChangeSourceClasses (Vector classes){
11.        // Create a Vector to store the source classes.
12.        Vector foundClasses= new Vector();
13.
14.        // Create an argument list that contains the
15.        // PropertyChangeListener class.
16.        Class[] arguments = new Class[1];
17.        try{
18.            arguments[0] =
➥Class.forName("java.beans.PropertyChangeListener");
19.        }catch(ClassNotFoundException cnfe){
20.            System.err.println("Error: PropertyChangeListener not found");
21.        }
22.
23.        // For each class look for the addActionListener() method design
➥signature.
24.        for (Enumeration e = classes.elements() ; e.hasMoreElements() ;){
25.            Class aclass = (Class)e.nextElement();
26.
```

continues

```
continued
27.              // Attempt to locate the add method in the class.
28.              // If the getDeclaredMethod() fails it will
29.              // throw an exception. The current loop is aborted
30.              // in the catch blocks by using 'continue'.
31.              try{
32.aclass.getDeclaredMethod("addPropertyChangeListener",arguments);
33.aclass.getDeclaredMethod("removePropertyChangeListener",arguments);
34.              }catch(NoSuchMethodException nsme){
35.                  continue;
36.              }catch(SecurityException se){
37.                  System.err.println();
38.                  Sustem.err println("Error finding add/remove property");
39.                  System.err.println("Methods might be private, they must
    ➥be public to be used.");
40.                  System.err.println(aclass);
41.                  System.err.println(se);
42.                  System.err.println();
43.                  continue;
44.              }
45.              // If we got here then add the class.
46.              foundClasses.addElement(aclass);
47.
48.          }// End of for each class
49.          return(foundClasses);
50.    }//End of findPropertyChangeSourceClasses
```

Verifying Parameters and Return Types of Methods

After a method name that matches a known pattern has been located, the next step is to verify that the return type and parameters match the rest of the pattern. The pattern may include the lack of parameters. A get pattern, for example, may be for an indexed parameter or singleton parameter like these:

```
MyType getMyParameter();//Single value parameter pattern.
MyType getMyParameter(int index);//Indexed value parameter pattern.
```

Also, the class of the parameter or return type can be used to build the specific pattern. The return type of a get method and the parameter type of a *get()* method defines the type of a property signature. For example, the following *setBackground()* and *getBackground()* methods are associated with the class Color.

```
void setBackground(Color newColor);// Set a color parameter.
Color getBackground();// Get a color parameter.
```

An IDE recognizes the Color class in these methods as a Color property. Further, the Color class is used in the Bean property editor to display the current color or to pop up a color editor dialog.

Compare this to a very similar signature where the only difference is the type of property, in this case, an Image:

```
void setBackground(Image newImage);// Set a background image parameter.
Image getBackground();// Get the background image parameter.
```

As you can see, this creates a very different property. To go with this property, we would also need to add a custom property editor. The property editor would be used to edit the Image to be used.

Implemented Interfaces

Interfaces provide very easily recognized patterns. After an interface has been found to be implemented by a class, an IDE can use its information about the interface to cast an object to an interface object and access its methods.

The example in listing 8.8 shows a method for testing that a class implements the BeanInfo interface. By using this method, the program can then cast an object of this class to a BeanInfo and use all of its methods. Compared to matching methods, matching to interfaces is mainly for signatures that have very stable and distinct APIs. The BeanInfo interface, for example, is a very stable API for Java Beans. Specific event listener interfaces are also stable for Java Beans because they should match exactly the type of event that they are to listen for.

Listing 8.8: ReflectionTools. implementsBeanInfo ()—Method to test a class for BeanInfo implementation

```
01./**
02.    * Check a class to see if it implements the BeanInfo interface.
03.    *
04.    * @param targetToSearch Class to test.
05.    * @returns true if the class implements BeanInfo interface.
06.    */
```

continues

continued

```
07.    public static boolean implementsBeanInfo(Class targetToSearch) throws
➡ClassNotFoundException{
08.
09.        // Create a class of BeanInfo to use in search.
10.        Class searchFor = Class.forName("java.beans.BeanInfo");
11.
12.        // Get the super classes and interfaces.
13.        Class interfaces[] = targetToSearch.getInterfaces();
14.        // For each interface, look for BeanInfo interface.
15.        for (int i = 0; i< interfaces.length;i++){
16.
17.            // If the class is the same as the one being searched, return
➡true.
18.            if(interfaces[i].equals(searchFor)){
19.                return true;
20.            }
21.        }
22.        // If we got here then there was no match.
23.        return false;
24.    }
```

Getting a Bean's BeanInfo

The example in listing 8.8 of testing for a BeanInfo's interface implementation leads you to how a BeanInfo should be found. In the Java Beans specification, the primary way a BeanInfo is found is by searching for a class that has the same name as a Bean, but with the text "BeanInfo" appended to the text. So, a Bean class Foo would have a BeanInfo class called FooBeanInfo.

In the *getBeanInfo()* method shown in listing 8.9, the parameter passed into the method is the class name and the result is the BeanInfo object, if it exists. Just to be sure that the class is actually implementing the BeanInfo interface, the *implementsBeanInfo()* method is used from listing 8.8.

Note that there are several exceptions thrown in this method. The exceptions are ignored here because you are only interested in finding a valid BeanInfo. If any part of this method failed to work, then the BeanInfo is not valid and a null is returned.

Listing 8.9: Method to locate a BeanInfo for a target class name

```
01.    /**
02.     * Returns a BeanInfo object given a bean's class name.
03.     */
04.    public static BeanInfo getBeanInfo(String beanName){
05.        try{
06.            Class beanInfo = Class.forName(beanName+"BeanInfo");
07.            if (ReflectionTools.implementsBeanInfo(beanInfo)){
08.                return((BeanInfo)beanInfo.newInstance());
09.            }else{
10.                return null;
11.            }
12.        }catch(InstantiationException ie){
13.            return null;
14.        }catch(IllegalAccessException iae){
15.            return null;
16.        }catch(ClassNotFoundException cnfe){
17.            return null;
18.        }
19.    }
```

Locating and Using Patterns

Now that the foundation of some key areas of Core Reflection is understood, the next step is to understand how to recognize and use a few Java Bean patterns. The following sections cover the following software patterns: Action Source and Action Listener. Action Source implements the *addActionListener( )* and optionally the *removeActionListener( )* methods. Because these methods are not part of a class, they must be searched for by their method names. Action Listeners are quite different because they do implement an interface. Action Listeners can be found by searching through the implemented interfaces for the Action Listener interface.

An Action Source is a type of event. The Action event is the event that signals that a primary action has occurred on an object. For example, a Button class generates an Action event whenever the button is pressed or released. An Action Listener is a class that implements the ActionListener interface. The interface has one method, *actionPerformed( )*, which is called by the Action Source when an action event is generated.

After these Action Sources and Action Listeners are identified, the objects implementing them will be dynamically connected. What this example demonstrates is the ability to write software using Core Reflection that is capable of performing complex programming tasks, with some advanced knowledge of design signatures and the names of classes that fit the signature characteristics.

Finding Classes That Are Action Sources

The pattern for an Action Source is that the class implements the *addActionListener()* method and the *removeActionListener()* method. (For the sake of simplicity, however, the *removeActionListener()* method option is not examined here.) The *findActionSourceClasses()* method, in listing 8.10, returns a Vector of classes that implement the *addActionListener()* method.

Here are the steps that the *findActionSourceClasses()* method takes:

1. Create a Vector to store the source classes.

2. Create an argument list that contains the ActionListener class.

3. For each class, attempt to locate the method in the class by using the *getDeclaredMethod()* method. The method takes the argument list with the ActionListener class that was created in step 2.

4. For each class, if the *getDeclaredMethod()* fails, it will throw an exception. The current loop is aborted in the catch blocks by using "continue." Otherwise, if the call succeeds and no errors are thrown, add the class to the Vector of Action Sources.

The primary method used here is *getDeclaredMethod()*, called on the Class object that is being tested. By successfully calling *getDeclaredMethod()*, you prove that the method you are looking for exists.

Listing 8.10: Method findActionSourceClasses()

```
01.    /**
02.     * Given a list of classes this method locates and returns
03.     * any classes that have the Action Source pattern. The
04.     * Action Source pattern must implement the addActionListener()
05.     * method.
06.     * @param classes Vector of classes that are to be searched.
07.     * @returns Classes that have addActionListener() method pattern.
08.     */
```

```
09.
10.static final Vector findActionSourceClasses (Vector classes){
11.     // Create a Vector to store the source classes.
12.     Vector actionClasses= new Vector();
13.
14.     // Create an argument list that contains the
15.     // ActionListener class.
16.     Class[] arguments = new Class[1];
17.     try{
18.         arguments[0] = Class.forName("java.awt.event.ActionListener");
19.     }catch(ClassNotFoundException cnfe){
20.         System.err.println("Error");
21.     }
22.
23.     // For each class look for the addActionListener() method pattern.
24.     for (Enumeration e = classes.elements() ; e.hasMoreElements() ;) {
25.         Class aclass = (Class)e.nextElement();
26.
27.         // Attempt to locate the method in the class.
28.         // If the getDeclaredMethod() fails it will
29.         // throw an exception. The current loop is aborted
30.         // in the catch blocks by using 'continue'.
31.         try{
32.             System.err.println(aclass);
33.             aclass.getDeclaredMethod("addActionListener",arguments);
34.         }catch(NoSuchMethodException nsme){
35.             continue;
36.         }catch(SecurityException se){
37.             continue;
38.         }
39.         // If we got here then add the class.
40.         actionClasses.addElement(aclass);
41.
42.     }
43.     return(actionClasses);
44.}
```

Like many of the methods described in this chapter, the main loop of the *findActionSourceClasses().*method attempts to perform a Core Reflection method on a class. In this example, the Class.*getDeclaredMethod()* method attempts to create a Method object from the class being tested. The method that *getDeclaredMethod()* is attempting to create is an *addActionListener()* method. If the creation fails, the current iteration of the loop is aborted via continue statements in the exception catch blocks. If the *getDeclaredMethod()* call succeeds, the class that succeeds is added to the vector of classes that support the addActionListener design signature.

Now that you know how to find an Action Source, the next step is to locate a corresponding class that implements the ActionListener interface.

Finding Classes That Are Action Listeners

Locating classes that are Action Listeners is quite different from locating an Action Source, but it is a similar type of search because the end results in a method fitting a pattern that needs to be found. The operation to locate the pattern is different here, because the method pattern is found by locating an implemented interface. The interface in this case has the method pattern for which you are looking. It is also required that the interface is used rather than just a method pattern because the Action Source class uses the interface explicitly.

The following steps detail how to get a list of listener classes:

1. Create a Vector to hold the confirmed listeners.

2. For each class to be tested, get the interfaces for this class.

3. For each interface to be tested, if name of the interface is an ActionListener, add the class that contains the interface.

This class accepts a list of classes to search and returns any classes that have the Action Listener pattern. The Action Listener signature is a class that implements the ActionListener interface. The *findActionListenersClasses()* method in listing 8.11 is similar to a previous method called *implementsBeanInfo()*. The primary difference here is that a list of classes is searched for a specific interface and a list of classes that have the interface are returned.

Listing 8.11: Method findActionListenersClasses()

```
01.    /**
02.      * Given a list of classes this method locates and returns
03.      * any classes that have the Action Listener pattern. The
04.      * Action Listener pattern must implement the
05.      * ActionListener interface.
06.      *
07.      * @param classes Vector of classes that are to be searched.
08.      * @returns Classes that have ActionListener interface.
09.      */
10.static final Vector findActionListenersClasses (Vector classes){
11.
```

```
12.     // Create a vector to hold the confirmed listeners.
13.     Vector actionClasses= new Vector();
14.
15.     //For each class to be tested:
16.     for (Enumeration e = classes.elements() ; e.hasMoreElements() ;) {
17.         Class aclass = (Class)e.nextElement();
18.
19.         //Get the interfaces for this class;
20.         Class[] interfaces = aclass.getInterfaces();
21.
22.         //Check each interface for a match to ActionListener.
23.         for (int i = 0;  i < interfaces.length ; i++) {
24.             if
➥(interfaces[i].getName().equals("java.awt.event.ActionListener")){
25.                 // If we got here then add the class that contains the
➥interface.
26.                 actionClasses.addElement(aclass);
27.             }
28.         }// End of interfaces.
29.
30.     }// End of for classes.elements()
31.
32.     // Return list of action classes.
33.     return(actionClasses);
34.
35.}// End of findActionListenersClasses()
```

Now that the Action Source and the Action Listener classes can be found, the next major operation is to connect an Action Listener to an Action Source. To do this, the *addActionSource()* method must be created as a Method object.

Adding an Action Listener to an Action Source

Because the code in listings 8.10 and 8.11 provides a way to locate Action Listeners and Action Sources, you need a way to programmatically add a listener to a source. The code in listing 8.9 does exactly that. The code is not too difficult to understand, but it is very different from how the code would have been written if you were to do it explicitly. The code is different primarily because there is no way to just write something like:

```
object.addActionListener(listener);
```

The *addActionListener()* cannot be called because there is no way to cast an object to an object that implements the method. The preceding statement may seem a little odd, but it is quite simple to grasp if you understand that *addActionListener()* is a design signature, not a method in an interface or a method in an inherited base class.

The *addActionListener()* method is essentially unique to any class that implements the Action Listener pattern.

If you are still confused, remember that this discussion assumes that the method in listing 8.12 is written to understand the *addActionListener()* method as a signature only, not the class that contains it. In other words, the method is able to call the *addActionListener()* method on any class, regardless of any other class extension or interface implementation. If the target Action Source object contains the *addActionListener()* method, the *AddActionListenerToSource()* method can call it.

The technique for executing a method of a class by name is simple, but it does require several steps, implemented in listing 8.12, to accomplish the desired result, as follows:

1. Build an argument list that defines the ActionListener class. The argument list is used along with the method name to request a Method class object for the class with which you are working.

2. Construct an argument list made up of the objects to be passed in the *addActionSource()* method. In this case, there is only one argument, the Action Listener.

3. Call the *invoke()* method to give the Action Source object as the context and the argument list that contains the Action Listener object. The *invoke()* method performs the equivalent *addActionListener()* call for you.

It is also important to understand that the *AddActionListenerToSource()* method in listing 8.12 throws several exceptions. These several exceptions result because of the methods being called. The methods in the Class and Method classes are both performing operations susceptible to security constraints and to errors caused by classes not being in the current CLASSPATH. It is also possible that the objects being passed in for processing are not the same as those expected, because they are treated as base Object types.

Listing 8.12: Method addActionListenerToSource()

```
01./**
02. * Add Action Listener to Action Source by calling the
03. * addActionListener() method of the source object.
04. *
05. * @param source Source of action events.
06. * @param listener Action listener.
07.    */
```

```
08.static void addActionListenerToSource(Object source,Object listener)
09.throws NoSuchMethodException,
10.        SecurityException,
11.        IllegalArgumentException,
12.        InvocationTargetException,
13.        ClassNotFoundException{
14.
15.    //Create argument list for addActionListener() method.
16.    Class[] arguments = new Class[1];
17.        arguments[0] = Class.forName("java.awt.event.ActionListener");
18.
19.        //create an add listener method object
20.        Method addListener =
➥source.getClass().getDeclaredMethod("addActionListener",arguments);
21.
22.        // Create the argument list and add the lister to it.
23.        Object args[] = new Object[1];
24.        args[0] = listener;
25.
26.        // invoke the addActionListener method of a source object.
27.        addListener.invoke(source,args);
28.
29.    }// End of addActionListenerToSource()
```

Assuming that an Action Listener can be added to an Action Source, you need to also enable the removal of an Action Listener from a source. The next example deals with the removal of a listener.

Removing an Action Listener from an Action Source

Removing an Action Listener is almost completely identical to adding one. As listing 8.13 shows, the only difference is in the name or the method requested in the *getDeclaredMethod()* command in line 21.

The code that calls *removeActionListenerFromSource()* needs to handle the throws from this function slightly differently. Exceptions may occur if the Action Source class implements the *addActionListener()*, but might not have a *removeActionListener()*. This combination could occur (but should not occur if the code were written correctly), so code using the *removeActionListenerFromSource()* method should just pop up a warning that the *removeActionListener()* method did not exist or could not be called.

```
Listing 8.13: Method removeActionListenerFromSource()

01./**
02. * Add Action Listener to Action Source by calling the
03. * addActionListener() method of the source object.
04. *
05. * @param source Source of action events.
06. * @param listener Action listener.
07.    */
08.
09.static void removeActionListenerFromSource(Object source,Object listener)
10.throws NoSuchMethodException,
11.        SecurityException,
12.        IllegalArgumentException,
13.        InvocationTargetException,
14.        ClassNotFoundException{
15.
16.        //Create argument list for addActionListener() method.
17.        Class[] arguments = new Class[1];
18.        arguments[0] = Class.forName("java.awt.event.ActionListener");
19.
20.        //create an add listener method object
21.        Method addListener =
⇒source.getClass().getDeclaredMethod("removeActionListener",arguments);
22.
23.        // Create the argument list and add the lister to it.
24.        Object args[] = new Object[1];
25.        args[0] = listener;
26.
27.        // invoke the removeActionListener method of a source object.
28.        addListener.invoke(source,args);
29.
30.    }// End of removeActionListenerFromSource()
```

Now that you know how to interconnect classes programmatically with events, the next task is to be able to programmatically access the properties of classes. Remember that properties are the attributes of classes. See Chapter 4, "Java Bean Design Signatures" to review the types of properties that can be found. The next example locates the different types of property access with logic provided by the PropertyDescriptor class.

Locating set() and get() Methods

An important reflection task is the retrieval of property access methods. The property access signature is found by looking for pairs of methods that start with 'set' and 'get' (or 'set' and 'is' for boolean properties) that manipulate the same class of data. The set and get property methods are the primary way that a class is configured. Locating these methods begins with the calling of the *getDeclaredMethods()* method on the target class.

For each method returned by *getDeclaredMethods(),* if the prefix of the method is "set," the IndexedPropertyDescriptor is created with the name of the test method minus the "set" prefix given as the property's name. Remember that part of the property's design signature is that the property must have a corresponding "get" (or "is" for boolean properties) method signature. You can exploit this design rule and only search for the "set" method signature. If creation of the IndexedPropertyDescriptor passes and does not throw an exception, then the property exists. Otherwise, a PropertyDescriptor object is created with the suspected property name. If PropertyDescriptor creation also fails, then the property is not valid and is not added to the property list.

Listing 8.14 shows the *getProperties()* method that returns an array of PropertyDescriptor objects for get/set pairs. The PropertyDescriptor class is a convenient way of storing parameter methods and is part of the java.bean package. As discussed previously, the steps are simple. The *getProperties()* method includes a check for the number of parameters. The number of parameters is important because this utility needs to create PropertyDescriptor and IndexedPropertyDescriptor objects.

Listing 8.14: Method getProperties()

```
01.    /**
02.     * This method is used to locate set/get of properties in a class.
03.     */
04.    public static PropertyDescriptor[] getProperties(Class bean){
05.        // Hashtable to temporarily store the Properties.
06.        Hashtable hashedProperties=new Hashtable();
07.
08.        Method[] methods;
09.        // Get the declared methods for the bean.
10.        try{
11.            methods = bean.getDeclaredMethods();
12.        }catch( SecurityException se){
13.            // If this failed, there is no reason to continue.
14.            // Return an array of zero.
15.            return (new PropertyDescriptor[0]);
16.        }
17.
18.        // For each method, look for set/get patterns.
19.        for (int i = 0; i < methods.length; i++){
```

continues

continued

```
20.
21.              // Get the name of this method.
22.              String fullName = methods[i].getName();
23.              // Get the parameter name(starting after get/set).
24.              // Check to see if we have a 'set' or 'get'signature.
25.              if fullName.startsWith("set"){
26.
27.                  // Get the parameter name(starting after get/set).
28.                  // Note that we decapitalize it per the Bean API.
29.                  String propertyName =
➥Introspector.decapitalize(fullName.substring(3));
30.
31.                  try{//Trap for IntrospectionException from
32.                      // new IndexedPropertyDescriptor().
33.
34.                      //Attempt to create an IndexedPropertyDescriptor
➥object.
35.                      hashedProperties.put(propertyName,new
➥IndexedPropertyDescriptor(propertyName,bean));
36.                  }catch(IntrospectionException ie1){
37.
38.                      try{//Trap for IntrospectionException from
39.                          // new PropertyDescriptor().
40.
41.                          //Attempt to create a PropertyDescriptor object.
42.                          hashedProperties.put(propertyName,new
➥PropertyDescriptor(propertyName,bean));
43.                      }catch(IntrospectionException ie2){
44.                          // Quietly ignore this exception
45.                          // because we were not intended to
46.                          // ever use the parameter.
47.                      }
48.                  }
49.              }//end if not already processed or a get/set pattern.
50.          }// end for each method.
51.
52.          // Array of PropertyDescriptor to be returned.
53.          PropertyDescriptor properties[] = null;
54.
55.          // If we have any parameters in the hashtable
56.          // then copy them into an array. Note that this
57.          // method returns an array so it can be returned by
58.          // custom code in a BeanInfo. Note 2: If there were no
59.          // properties found then this function returns an array
60.          // of zero length just like BeanInfo.getProperties() does.
61.          properties = new PropertyDescriptor[hashedProperties.size()];
```

```
62.
63.        //Add properties from Hashtable
64.        int i = 0;
65.        for (Enumeration e = hashedProperties.elements() ;
➥e.hasMoreElements() ;) {
66.            properties[i++] = (PropertyDescriptor) e.nextElement();
67.        }
68.
69.        // Return the list of set/get properties.
70.      return(properties);
71.    }// End of getProperties()
```

It is important to remember that this is just one example of how to locate property descriptors. The primary way to locate properties is with the Introspector class's *getBeanInfo()* method. The method returns the properties that are valid for the particular Bean. The example *getProperties()* method indiscriminately attempts to find all properties. A Bean developer might not want all of these methods to be available for use. It is also possible that the developer has created a special BeanInfo that maps methods that are for property access, but do not follow the property signature into a property descriptor. The previous method considers none of this. It should not be used to locate properties in a Bean.

The previous examples should provide you with an understanding of some of the functionality available in the Introspector class. You can now use their capabilities to perform other tasks.

Now that events and properties can be located and manipulated, the next section in the overview of Core Reflection and Introspection is the actual programmatic manipulation of Java Beans.

Programmatic Manipulation of Java Beans

This section shows how some simple Java Beans are accessed programmatically and connected to other classes or components. The process used is essentially programming with programs. In fact, one of the examples is a program, given only the names of classes, which connects Action SourceAction Sources to Action ListenerAction Listeners.

Programming without writing code is far different from the normal assumptions about how programming is done. Normally when writing a program, the code is developed by first studying classes and then carefully connecting them with code that is typed in or generated with an IDE.

A Simple Java Bean: RoundButtonBean

Now it's time to further your understanding with an example. Listings 8.15 and 8.16 are two simple Java Beans that will be connected programmatically. Listing 8.15 has the RoundButtonBean class. RoundButtonBean is a very simple button that follows the Action Source pattern. The Action Source is the clicked button event monitored by the Bean. In addition to the Action Source, there are also parameter patterns for the colors of the button in its pressed and released states. Listing 8.15 presents the code for the RoundButtonBean class.

Listing 8.15: RoundButton class

```
001.import   java.awt.*;
002.import   java.awt.event.*;
003.import   java.beans.*;
004.
005./**
006. * A simple bean to demonstrate Core Reflection
007. *
008. */
009.
010.public class RoundButton extends Canvas implements java.io.Serializable
011.{
012.    /**
013.     * Construct a round button.
014.     */
015.    public RoundButton () {
016.        super();
017.        setSize(40,40);
018.        enableEvents(MouseEvent.MOUSE_EVENT_MASK);
019.    }
020.    /**
021.     * Draws an oval that fits the bounds of the canvas.
022.     */
023.    public void paint (Graphics context) {
024.        System.out.println("RB paint called");
025.        if (down && hasFocus){
026.            context.setColor(pressedColor);
027.        }else{
028.            context.setColor(releasedColor);
029.        }
030.        context.fillArc(5, 5, getSize().width-10, getSize().height-10, 0,
031.);
032.    }
033.
```

```
034.     /**
035.      * Processes the push button event to display a down or up event.
036.      */
037.     protected boolean processMouseEvent (MouseEvent e){
038.         System.out.println("Event:"+e);
039.         switch(e.getId()) {
040.             case MouseEvent.MOUSE_PRESSED :
041.                 //The mouse button was pressed.
042.                 // Notify the listener.
043.                 if (listener != null){
044.                     listener.actionPerformed(new
➥ActionEvent((Object)this,e.getId(),"RoundButton"));
045.                 }
046.                 // Paint the pressed color.
047.                 down = true;
048.                 repaint();
049.                 break;
050.             case MouseEvent.MOUSE_RELEASED :
051.                 //The mouse button was released.
052.                 // Notify the listener.
053.                 if (listener != null){
054.                     listener.actionPerformed(new
➥ActionEvent((Object)this,e.getId(),"RoundButton"));
055.                 }
056.                 //Paint the normal color.
057.                 down = false;
058.                 repaint();
059.                 break;
060.             case MouseEvent.MOUSE_DRAGGED:
061.                 if ((e.getX() < 0) || (e.getX() > size().width) ||
062.                     (e.getY() < 0) || (e.getY() > size().height)) {
063.                     if (down) {
064.                         down = false;
065.                         repaint();
066.                     }
067.                 } else if (!down) {
068.                     down = true;
069.                     repaint();
070.                 }
071.                 break;
072.             case MouseEvent.MOUSE_ENTERED:
073.                 hasFocus = true;
074.                 repaint();
075.                 break;
076.             case MouseEvent.MOUSE_EXITED:
077.                 hasFocus = false;
```

continues

continued

```
078.              repaint();
079.                break;
080.        }// End switch
081.
082.        //Ensure that the event is propigated.
083.        return(super.processMouseEvent(e));
084.    }
085.
086.    /**
087.     * Returns the color that the bean released event is expressed as.
088.     * @see #setReleasedColor
089.     */
090.    public synchronized Color getReleasedColor (){
091.        return releasedColor;
092.    }
093.    /**
094.     * Sets the color that the bean released event is expressed as.
095.     * @see #getReleasedColor
096.     */
097.    public void setReleasedColor (Color newColor){
098.        releasedColor = newColor;
099.        repaint();
100.    }
101.    /**
102.     * Returns the color that the bean pressed event is expressed as.
103.     * @see #setPressedColor
104.     */
105.    public synchronized Color getPressedColor (){
106.        return pressedColor;
107.    }
108.    /**
109.     * Sets the color that the bean pressed event is expressed as.
110.     * @see #getPressesColor
111.     */
112.    public void setPressedColor (Color newColor){
113.        pressedColor = newColor;
114.        repaint();
115.    }
116.    /**
117.     * Action source pattern:addActionListener()
118.     * @param listener the PropertyChangeListener
119.     */
120.    public void addActionListener (ActionListener aListener){
121.        listener = aListener;
122.    }
123.
```

```
124.    /**
125.     * Action source pattern:removeActionListener()
126.     * @param aListener the ActionListener
127.     */
128.    public void removeActionListener (ActionListener aListener){
129.        if (aListener==listener){
130.            listener = null;
131.        }
132.    }
133.
134.    // Private data fields:
135.    private ActionListener listener = null;
136.    private Color pressedColor = Color.black;
137.    private Color releasedColor = Color.red;
138.    boolean down = false;
139.    boolean hasFocus = false;
140.
141.}//End of class RoundButton.
```

A Bean That Listens to Buttons: ButtonStatusBean

To test your ability to connect components, another Bean is needed that will listen to the RoundButtonBean events. The class must be usable in the *addActionListener()* method of RoundButtonBean. The second Bean, shown in listing 8.16, is a label that changes its text in response to action events. This Bean is quite simple. The important feature of this Bean is the ActionListener interface. The ActionListener has the *actionPerformed()* method, called by an Action Source whenever the button is pressed or released. The implementation of *actionPerformed()* causes the label to be changed depending on the event ID.

Listing 8.16: ButtonStatus class

```
01.class ButtonStatus extends Label implements ActionListener
02.{
03.    /**
04.     * Create a new ButtonStatus Bean.
05.     */
06.    ButtonStatus (){
07.        super("Released",CENTER);
08.        resize(40,70);
```

continues

```
continued
09.    }
10.    /**
11.     * Reset the text of the button depending on the button state.
12.     */
13.    public void actionPerformed (ActionEvent e){
14.        // Repaint the text to reflect the monitored state.
15.        if (e.getId() == MouseEvent.MOUSE_PRESSED ){
16.            setText("Pressed");
17.            repaint();
18.        }else if (e.getId() == MouseEvent.MOUSE_RELEASED){
19.            setText("Released");
20.            repaint();
21.        }
22.    }
23.
24.}// end of class ButtonStatus.
```

Using RoundButton and ButtonStatus in an Applet

Now that you understand the two Beans in this example, you should also understand how they would be used to make an application by hand. In the example in listing 8.17, the RoundButton and the ButtonStatus Java Beans are used in an applet. This example will accomplish the tasks of creation of the two Java Beans, and the interconnection of the ActionEvent from the Action Source Bean (RoundButton) to the listener Bean (ButtonStatus). Each part of this example will be automated with core reflection in the example later.

The first task is to create each of the Beans and add them to the current canvas. The code also adds the ButtonStatus Bean to the RoundButton Bean.

Listing 8.17: Test1 class—Application showing manual connection of Beans

```
01.import java.awt.*;
02.import java.applet.*;
03.import java.awt.event.*;
04.import RoundButtonBean;
05.import ButtonStatusBean;
06./**
07.  * Demonstration of action events.
08.  */
```

```
09.public class Test1 extends Applet {
10.    RoundButtonBean roundButton;
11.    ButtonStatusBean buttonStatus;
12.
13.    public void init() {
14.        super.init();
15.        setLayout(new FlowLayout());
16.        resize(100,100);
17.
18.        // Create and add button Bean to applet canvas.
19.        roundButton=new RoundButtonBean();
20.        add("Center",roundButton);
21.
22.        // Create and add button status Bean to applet canvas.
23.        buttonStatus = new ButtonStatusBean();
24.        add("South",buttonStatus);
25.
26.        // Connect button actions to button listener.
27.        roundButton.addActionListener((ActionListener)buttonStatus);
28.    }// end of init()
29.
30.}// End of Test1
```

The applet in listing 8.17 is quite simple, as are the Beans that it uses. The process that a programmer goes through to write the applet is also simple. A programmer only needs to understand how to create the two Beans and to add the listener Bean to the source Bean. In summary, the following steps are required:

1. Study each Bean and confirm that it is a component

2. Determine how to call the constructor for each Bean

3. Create the Bean (Lines 19 & 23)

4. Look for ActionEvent source patterns

5. Look for ActionEvent listener patterns

6. Connect Action Listener to Action Source (line 27)

To accomplish the preceding steps is somewhat simple for an experienced Java programmer. To develop code that accomplishes the steps is more complex and, as you will see, takes more code to implement. The benefit of Core Reflection-based programming is that it is capable of accepting Bean patterns in other classes with little or no need for additional programming. This is quite different from the normal programming tasks where you need to recreate the code by hand each time depending on the components added.

An example of such reuse can be seen especially with buttons and button listeners. Any button listener can be connected to any button. This is very powerful because it can be done without explicitly compiling the button or button listener in relation to the code that connects them. Another example of the power of Core Reflection is the use of class parameters. Class parameters that follow the set and get patterns can be programmatically accessed and presented or connected to other Bean components.

Connecting Beans with Core Reflection

Connecting Beans via Core Reflection requires several steps. The code in listing 8.18 takes advantage of the code that has already been covered in this chapter (listings 8.2 through 8.9).

This example implements the following steps:

1. Create a Frame object to work in (lines 15–18).

2. Create a temporary place to hold objects (line 20).

3. Load a list of Beans to play with and attempt to create classes from the names (lines 25–31).

4. Find all classes that might be buttons (line 34).

5. Find all classes that might be listeners of buttons (line 37).

6. Create button objects (lines 40–44).

7. Add buttons to the Frame (line 47).

8. Add button components to the list of objects (line 50).

9. Create listener objects (lines 60–66).

10. Add button listener components to the Frame (line 69).

11. Add components to the list of Listener objects (line 71).

12. Add button listener for each button source (lines 82–110).

The remainder of the class is standard window event handling to close down the application when the window is closed.

Listing 8.18: class ReflectTest. Application showing Core Reflection connection of Beans

```
001.import  java.awt.*;
002.import  java.applet.*;
003.import  java.awt.event.*;
004.import  java.util.*;
005.import  java.lang.reflect.*;
006.import  java.lang.*;
007.import  ReflectionTools;
008./**
009. * Class used to test core reflection tools.
010. */
011.public class ReflectTest{
012.    Frame myFrame;
013.
014.    public ReflectTest(){
015.        myFrame = new Frame("Test2");
016.        myFrame.setLayout(new FlowLayout());
017.        myFrame.resize(100,100);
018.        myFrame.addWindowListener(new MyWinEvents());
019.
020.        // Create a temporary place to hold objects.
021.    Vector classes = new Vector();
022.
023.        // Load a list of beans to play with and attempt
024.        // to create classes from the names.
025.        try{
026.            classes.addElement(Class.forName("RoundButtonBean"));
027.            classes.addElement(Class.forName("ButtonStatusBean"));
028.        }catch(ClassNotFoundException cnfe){
029.            System.err.println("Could not load classes");
030.            return;
031.        }
032.
033.        // Find all classes that might be buttons.
034.        Vector actionSources =
➡ReflectionTools.findActionSourceClasses(classes);
035.
036.        // Find all classes that might be listeners of buttons.
037.        Vector actionListeners =
➡ReflectionTools.findActionListenersClasses(classes);
038.
039.        // Create button objects.
040.        Object[] sources= new Object[actionSources.size()];
041.        int i = 0;
```

continues

continued

```
042.         for (Enumeration e = actionSources.elements() ;
➥e.hasMoreElements() ;) {
043.            try{ //  Create the Button
044.                Object obj = ((Class)e.nextElement()).newInstance();
045.
046.                // Add component to the Frame
047.                myFrame.add((Component)obj);
048.
049.                // Add component to our list of objects.
050.                sources[i++] = obj;
051.            }catch(IllegalAccessException iae){
052.                System.err.println("Unable to create new instance.");
053.                return;
054.            }catch(InstantiationException iae){
055.                System.err.println("Unable to create new instance.");
056.                return;
057.            }
058.        }// End for each action object.
059.
060.        // Create listener objects
061.        Object[] listeners= new Object[actionListeners.size()];
062.
063.        i = 0;
064.        for (Enumeration e = actionListeners.elements() ;
➥e.hasMoreElements() ;) {
065.            try{ //Create the listener object
066.                Object obj = ((Class)e.nextElement()).newInstance();
067.
068.                // Add button listener components to the Frame
069.                myFrame.add((Component)obj);
070.                System.out.println("Listener added");
071.                listeners[i++] = obj;
072.            }catch(IllegalAccessException iae){
073.                System.err.println("Unable to create new instance.");
074.                return;
075.            }catch(InstantiationException iae){
076.                System.err.println("Unable to create new instance.");
077.                return;
078.            }
079.        }
080.        // For Each source add listeners
081.
082.        Class[] arguments = new Class[1];
083.        try{
084.            arguments[0] =
➥Class.forName("java.awt.event.ActionListener");
```

```
085.          }catch(ClassNotFoundException cnfe){
086.              System.err.println("Error-
➥ClassNotFoundException=java.awt.event.ActionListener");
087.          }
088.
089.          // Add listener to source by calling the addActionListener()
➥method.
090.          Method addListener = null;
091.          try{
092.              //create an add listener method
093.              addListener =
➥sources[0].getClass().getDeclaredMethod("addActionListener",arguments);
094.          }catch(NoSuchMethodException nsme){
095.              System.err.println("Error-NoSuchMethodException");
096.          }catch(SecurityException se){
097.              System.err.println("Error-SecurityException");
098.          }
099.
100.          // Add all the listeners to the one source
101.          for (i = 0; i <listeners.length ; i++) {
102.              // copy the listener to a listener object
103.              try{
104.                  addListener.invoke(sources[0],listeners);
105.              }catch(IllegalArgumentException iae){
106.                  System.err.println("Error-IllegalArgumentException");
107.              }catch(InvocationTargetException ite){
108.                  System.err.println("Error-InvocationTargetException");
109.              }
110.          }// End for each listener.
111.
112.          myFrame.show();
113.      }
114.
115.      /**
116.       * main() method used to start this test.
117.       */
118.      public static void main (String args[])    {
119.          new Test2();
120.      }
121.
122.      /**
123.       * Inner class to handle termination.
124.       */
125.      class MyWinEvents implements WindowListener{
126.          MyWinEvents(){}
127.          public void windowClosed(WindowEvent e){}
```

continues

```
           continued
128.           public void windowOpened(WindowEvent e){}
129.           public void windowIconified(WindowEvent e){}
130.           public void windowDeiconified(WindowEvent e){}
131.
132.           public void windowClosing(WindowEvent e){
133.               System.out.println("windowClosing");
134.               // Note references to the current this.myFrame
135.               myFrame.hide();
136.               myFrame.dispose();
137.               System.exit(0);
138.           }
139.     }//End of inner class MyWinEvents
140.
141.}// End of ReflectTest class
```

As you can see, the code has swelled tremendously from listing 8.17. This class also uses the code from the ReflectionTools class created earlier in this chapter. Much of this can be done away with if the BeanInfo is used to locate signatures.

The Introspection Class and BeanInfo Interface

Now that you understand the nature of Core Reflection and how to use it to obtain information on classes, the next step is to use the Introspection class to examine a Bean for you. In the previous sections, you covered many tasks that are accomplished by just calling the *getBeanInfo()* method in the Introspection class. The Introspection class is part of the java.bean package and is primarily used to do most of the reflection work normally required.

To show the power of this class, listing 8.19 shows the *printBeanInfo()* method that prints the BeanInfo created by the Introspection class for a Java Bean class.

Listing 8.19: Method used to print key information in a BeanInfo object

```
01.    /**
02.     * Prints the Bean Info for a bean class.
03.     * @param bean Class to be examined.
04.     * @param stopBefore Class to stop introspection at.
05.     */
```

```
06.    public static void printBeanInfo(Class bean,Class stopBefore){
07.        try{
08.            //Get the BeanInfo object for the class
09.            BeanInfo beanInfo = Introspector.getBeanInfo(bean,
➥stopBefore);
10.            System.out.println("BeanInfo for "+bean.getName());
11.
12.            // Get Bean Property Descriptors.
13.            PropertyDescriptor[] properties =
➥beanInfo.getPropertyDescriptors();
14.
15.            // Print bean Properties
16.            System.out.println(" Property Descriptors:");
17.            for (int i = 0 ;i < properties.length;i++){
18.                System.out.println("  "+properties[i].getName());
19.            }
20.
21.            // Get Bean eventSetDescriptors
22.            EventSetDescriptor[] eventSetDescriptors =
➥beanInfo.getEventSetDescriptors();
23.
24.            // Print Bean eventSetDescriptors
25.            System.out.println(" Event Descriptors:");
26.            for (int i = 0 ;i < eventSetDescriptors.length;i++){
27.                System.out.println("  "+eventSetDescriptors[i].getName());
28.            }
29.
30.            // Get Bean methodDescriptors
31.            MethodDescriptor[] methodDescriptors =
➥beanInfo.getMethodDescriptors();
32.
33.            // Print Bean methodDescriptors
34.            System.out.println(" Method Descriptors:");
35.            for (int i = 0 ;i < methodDescriptors.length;i++){
36.                System.out.println("  "+methodDescriptors[i].getName());
37.            }
38.        }catch( IntrospectionException ie){
39.            System.err.println("Error getting Bean
➥Info:"+ie.getMessage());
40.        }
41.    }// End of printBeanInfo()
```

The BeanInfo class holds a great deal of information about the subject class—the most important being the PropertyDescriptor objects. The BeanInfo *getBeanInfo()* method has obtained all the properties of the Bean. Listing 8.20 shows the output of the *printBeanInfo()* method for the RoundButtonBean in listing 8.19.

Listing 8.20: Result of printBeanInfo(Class.forName("RoundButtonBean"), Class.forName("java.awt.Component"))

```
01.BeanInfo for RoundButtonBean
02. Property Descriptors:
03.   pressedColor
04.   releasedColor
05. Event Descriptors:
06.   action
07. Method Descriptors:
08.   paint
09.   removeActionListener
10.   addActionListener
11.   addNotify
12.   setPressedColor
13.   getPressedColor
14.   getReleasedColor
15.   setReleasedColor
```

The BeanInfo Interface

In addition to the capability for any component to be understood through Core Reflection, the Java Bean API includes an interface class called BeanInfo. The BeanInfo class is used similarly to the way that Component Definition Files are used. The big difference with a BeanInfo is that the information is 100 percent Java. The BeanInfo for a Java Bean component is type checked and validated as a compiled class, eliminating problems that could occur in proprietary Component Definition Files.

The bad news is that if you were to completely implement all the possible information for a complex Bean, the amount of work could take some time to complete. The scope of the possible data that can be described is detailed in figure 8.1 and tables 8.1 through 8.6. Each of the tables describes information that can be read from a BeanInfo and objects that it contains. Figure 8.1 is a road map of the BeanInfo information. Each block in the figure represents a different class in the object tree of the BeanInfo interface.

The BeanInfo interface contains information about events, methods, and properties as well as the icon used to represent the Bean in an IDE. There is also information about the default event and default property that a user is likely to use. Figure 8.1 covers the complete breakdown of the BeanInfo data. As this figure shows, all Descriptor classes have information derived from the FeatureDescriptor class.

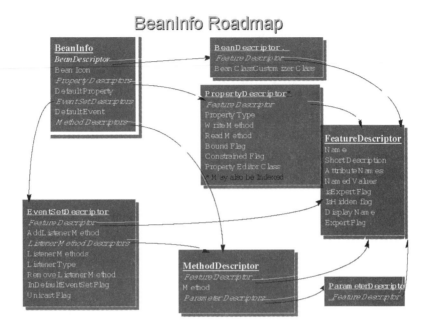

Figure 8.1

Road map to information in a BeanInfo.

The primary way that a Bean's API is found is through information contained in a BeanInfo object. The BeanInfo object is built using the BeanInfo interface. The developer can override each of the methods in the interface or simply return a null for information that should be found by the Introspector class. It is in this descriptor that the Bean's icon and feature descriptors for methods, event sets, and properties are found. Many developers are confused by the BeanInfo interface because it has no facility for setting any of the information that it contains. It is odd that there is no equivalent set method for each of the get methods, but the concept of a BeanInfo is that it is an override for information found through introspection. In other words, the BeanInfo data is created internally to the object that implements the BeanInfo interface. Therefore, if the data is internally created there should not be any methods to override the information. This is primarily a safety feature that prevents external manipulation of a BeanInfo object that might have been created to specifically hide certain details from the tool reading the BeanInfo.

Unfortunately, the fact that the BeanInfo interface, and therefore BeanInfo objects do not have set methods, the developer is forced to implement the BeanInfo interface to add information about the Bean. The simplest task is to add an Icon to a Bean's representation. The only way this can be done is to specifically implement the BeanInfo to have the *getIcon()* method return icons for the specific Bean when called. The remaining methods can be overridden to simply return null so that the remaining information about a Bean will be automatically generated by the Introspector class.

Table 8.1: Information Held in a BeanInfo

Property	Description
BeanDescriptor	See table 8.3 for the information controlled by the BeanDescriptor super class.
Bean Icon	The icon used by the IDE to represent the Bean.
Property Descriptors	The set/get property methods supported by the Bean. See table 8.4 for PropertyDescriptor information.
Default Property	The default property is the most likely to be modified by a user in an IDE (like the label text of a button component).
Event Set Descriptors	Events called or accepted by the Bean.
Default Event	The default event most likely to be interfaced with (like the button pressed event for a button component). This information is in table 8.6
Method Descriptors	Methods of the Bean that can be called. This information is described in table 8.5

FeatureDescriptor Information

Table 8.2 shows the information in a FeatureDescriptor, which is the basis all other objects that end with the postfix "Descriptor" that are returned by methods in a BeanInfo. For example, BeanDescriptor extends the FeatureDescriptor to add information that pertains to Beans.

The information in the FeatureDescriptor details common information of components features. This common information includes the features name, descriptions, design flags, and named attributes that can be used for various purposes.

Table 8.2: Information in the FeatureDescriptor

Property	Description
Name	Name for the parameter. Note that this is the programmatic name, not a name that changes based on locale.
Short Description	A short description of the parameter. May be the localized description if internationalization is supported.

Property	Description
Attribute Names	List of named attributes associated with this parameter. Note that these are programmatic names, not a name that changes based on locale.
Named Values	Associated named attributes.
isExpert Flag	The "expert" flag is used to distinguish between those features intended for expert users from those intended for normal users.
IsHidden Flag	The Hidden flag is used to identify intended only for internal use. They should not be exposed from within the IDE to the user.
Display Name	Name used when displaying this parameter. May be the localized name if internationalization is supported.
Expert Flag	The Expert flag is used to distinguish between features intended for expert users from those intended for normal or novice users.

BeanDescriptor Information

Table 8.3 shows the BeanDescriptor information. The BeanDescriptor, as previously mentioned, extends the FeatureDescriptor class and adds information to specifically describe the Bean. The extended information includes the class type and the class that is used as the Bean's customizer. Remember that a Bean customizer is a class that is used to edit a Bean as a single object.

Table 8.3: Method Information Held in a BeanDescriptor

Property	Description
Feature Descriptor Information	See table 8.1 for the information controlled by the FeatureDescriptor super class.
Bean Class	The Class object for the bean.
Customizer Class	The Class object for the bean's customizer. This may be null if the bean doesn't have a customizer.

PropertyDescriptor Information

The next FeatureDescriptor type is the PropertyDescriptor. As the name implies, this class is used to describe a Bean property. The extended information in a PropertyDescriptor is specific to the description of the type of the property (Like Color,

Image, or int). Also included is the read/write methods used to access the property which map to the set/get or set/is property accessor signatures, and information about whether the class is bound and/or constrained.

Table 8.4: Property Information Held in a PropertyDescriptor

Property	Description
Feature Descriptor Information	See table 8.1 for the information controlled by the FeatureDescriptor super class.
Property Type	The class for the property. Note that the "Class" object may describe a built-in Java type such as "int". The result may be "null" if this is an indexed property that does not support non-indexed access.
Write Method	The method that should be used to write the property value. May return null if the property can't be written.
Read Method	The method that should be used to read the property value. May return null if the property can't be read.
Bound Flag	Updates to "bound" properties cause a "PropertyChange" event to get fired when the property is changed.
Constrained Flag	Attempted updates to "Constrained" properties cause a "VetoableChange" event to get fired when the property is changed.
Property Editor Class	Any explicit PropertyEditor Class that has been registered for this property. If none is registered, the IDE can attempt to locate a standard editor for the class of parameter.

MethodDescriptor Information

The MethodDescriptor class, again an extension of the FeatureDescriptor class, is used to describe the methods in a Bean. The default behavior of the Introspector class is to return all publicly available methods of a Bean. These methods include those that are used as part of event sets and property access signatures.

The extended information available in a MethodDescriptor is the Method object used to call the method dynamically and parameter descriptors that are used to document the methods API.

Table 8.5: Method Information Held in a MethodDescriptor

Property	Description
Feature Descriptor Information	See table 8.1 for the information controlled by the FeatureDescriptor super class.
Method	The Method class of the Bean method.
Parameter Descriptors	The locale-independent names of the parameters. May return a null array if the parameter names are not known. See table 8.1 for the information contained in each ParameterDescriptor class.

EventSetDescriptor Information

The final descriptor available from the BeanInfo is the EventSetDescriptor. The EventSetDescriptor describes an event that the Bean is a source. This should not be confused with the events that a Bean is capable of being a listener. The primary way to find the events a Bean can listen for is by searching the implemented interfaces for those that end in the postfix 'Listener' and are an implementation of a EventListener base interface.

The EventSetDescriptor contains all the information required to locate classes that might be listeners. The EventSetDescriptor has the class type of the specific listener just for this type of operation. The EventSetDescriptor also contains the Method objects for adding and removing listeners as well as information pertaining to whether the event is unicast or if it is a default event for the Bean.

Table 8.6: Event Set Information Held in an EventSetDescriptor

Property	Description
Feature Descriptor Information	See table 8.1 for the information controlled by the FeatureDescriptor super class.
AddListener Method	Method used to add a listener interested in events from the Bean.
Listener Method Descriptors	Descriptors for the listener methods contained within this Bean.
Listener Methods	Methods in the Bean that listen for events.
Listener Type	Class or Interface type that the listener must implement so that it can be added as a listener to this Bean.

continues

Table 8.6: Event Set Information Held in an EventSetDescriptor, Continued

Property	Description
Remove Listener Method	Method object used to remove a listener from the Bean.
InDefaultEventSet Flag	Marks an event set as being in the "default" set (or not).
Unicast Flag	Designates an event set as unicast or multicast.

Exploiting the BeanInfo Interface

BeanInfo is oriented so that the developer needs only to specify information that could not be located through reflection. The developer needs to define only specific information such as methods that do not fit the standard Java Bean component model; the rest of the Java Bean is still defined strictly through reflection.

The BeanInfo interface can also be used to safely extend the data an IDE can present to the user. The safety comes from the fact those methods and events are type checked during compile and during runtime to ensure that names and types are correct. This is much safer than component description files used by other component technologies that are usually written in a vendor specific component-description language that does not have full type safety.

Using BeanInfo in an Application

Listing 8.21 that follows is essentially the same example as listing 8.18, except that the code uses the BeanInfo class to obtain information about Bean classes. Also, a few changes make the code a little more readable. These changes include grouping exception traps and also making the code a little less generic.

Finding Methods with the InfoBean Class

Two new methods are also added to listing 8.21 (*getMethod()*)and 8.19 (*getPropertyDescriptor()*) to help encapsulate some of the generic work required. The first method in listing 8.21 retrieves the Method object for a named method.

The method in listing 8.21 uses the *getMethodDescriptors()* method of the BeanInfo class to get an array of methods in the Bean's class. The list is searched until the named method is found. The object returned is the matching Method object.

The *getMethod()* method is used by the example to get the *addActionListener()* method in the RoundButtonBean class.

Listing 8.21: getMethod() method used to get a named Method object from a BeanInfo object

```
01.    /**
02.     * get a Method object from a BeanInfo object that matches the method
03.     * name.
04.     */
05.    Method getMethod(BeanInfo beanInfo,String methodName){
06.        // Get Bean methodDescriptors
07.        MethodDescriptor[] methodDescriptors =
    ↪beanInfo.getMethodDescriptors();
08.        // Locate the named method
09.        for (int i = 0 ;i < methodDescriptors.length;i++){
10.            if (methodDescriptors[i].getName().equals(methodName)){
11.                return(methodDescriptors[i].getMethod());
12.            }
13.        }
14.        return null;
15.    }
```

The next utility method retrieves a named PropertyDescriptor object.

Finding Property Descriptors with BeanInfo

The PropertyDescriptor holds a lot of useful information about Bean properties, including the *set()* and *get()* methods and property editor classes.

The method in listing 8.22 accesses the background color property. PropertyDescriptor is used here to change the color of the RoundButton.

Listing 8.22: getPropertyDescriptor() method used to get a named PropertyDescriptor object from a BeanInfo object

```
01.    /**
02.     * get a PropertyDescriptor from a BeanInfo object that matches the
    ➥property name.
03.     */
04.    PropertyDescriptor getPropertyDescriptor(BeanInfo beanInfo,String
    ➥propertyName){
05.         // Get Bean Property Descriptors.
06.         PropertyDescriptor[] propertyDescriptor =
    ➥beanInfo.getPropertyDescriptors();
07.         // Locate the named property.
08.         for (int i = 0 ;i < propertyDescriptor.length;i++){
09.             if (propertyDescriptor[i].getName().equals(propertyName)){
10.                 return(propertyDescriptor[i]);
11.             }
12.         }
13.         return null;
14.    }
```

Creating, Connecting, and Manipulating Beans with BeanInfo

In the code that uses the BeanInfo object, the actions performed are pretty much identical to the example in listing 8.23. The design of this example has been greatly simplified and no longer attempts to deal with the components as truly generic. This example assumes that the first component is a button and the second is a button listener. In addition, the background color of the listener is changed. Here are the steps performed as they appear in the test constructor:

1. Create a Frame to work in (lines 4–7)

2. Load a list of beans to use and attempt to create classes from the names (lines 11–12)

3. Get BeanInfo objects for the Beans (lines 15–16)

4. Create new instance objects of the Beans (lines 19–20)

5. Add the Beans to the Frame (lines 23–24)

6. Create an *addActionListener()* method by calling the *getMethod()* method described in listing 8.21 (lines 27–28)

7. Add listener to source by calling the *addActionListener()* method (lines 31–33)

8. Create a *setBackground()* method for Bean 2 by calling the *getPropertyDescriptor()* method described in listing 8.22 (lines 36–37)

9. Set the background colors of Bean 2 by using the Method object for the *setBackground()* method (lines 40–41)

10. Show the Frame (line 44)

The remainder of the constructor uses catch blocks to trap errors if any of the functions fail to operate. The catch blocks have been left blank in this example for brevity.

Listing 8.23: Constructor from BeanInfoTest2 used to show BeanInfo usage

```
01.public BeanInfoTest2 (){
02.     try{
03.         // Create a Frame to work in.
04.         myFrame = new Frame("BeanInfoTest2");
05.         myFrame.setLayout(new FlowLayout());
06.         myFrame.resize(100,100);
07.         myFrame.addWindowListener(new MyWinEvents());
08.
09.         // Load a list of beans to play with and attempt
10.         // to create classes from the names.
11.         Class component1 = Class.forName("RoundButtonBean");
12.         Class component2 = Class.forName("ButtonStatusBean");
13.
14.         // Get BeanInfo objects
15.         BeanInfo component1Info =
➥Introspector.getBeanInfo(component1,null);
16.         BeanInfo component2Info =
➥Introspector.getBeanInfo(component2,null);
17.
18.         // Create new instances.
19.         Object obj1 = component1.newInstance();
20.         Object obj2 = component2.newInstance();
21.
22.         // Add components to the Frame
23.         myFrame.add((Component)obj1);
24.         myFrame.add((Component)obj2);
25.
26.         //create an addActionListener() method
27.         Method addListener = null;
28.         addListener = getMethod(component1Info,"addActionListener");
29.
```

continues

continued

```
30.        // Add listener to source by calling the addActionListener()
➡method.
31.        Object[] args = new Object[1];
32.        args[0]=obj2;
33.        addListener.invoke(obj1,args);
34.
35.        //create a setBackground() method for component2
36.        PropertyDescriptor
➡background=getPropertyDescriptor(component2Info,"background");
37.        Method setBackground = background.getWriteMethod();
38.
39.        // Set the background colors of component2
40.        args[0] = Color.green;
41.        setBackground.invoke(obj2,args);
42.
43.        // Show the frame.
44.        myFrame.show();
45.
46.        // Error control consolidated here for clarity.
47.        // You should place try/catch code as close as possible
48.        // to where errors are thrown.
49.    }catch(IntrospectionException ie){
50.        System.err.println("Could not load BeanInfo");
51.    }catch(ClassNotFoundException cnfe){
52.        System.err.println("Could not load classes");
53.    }catch(IllegalAccessException iae){
54.        System.err.println("Unable to create new instance.");
55.    }catch(InstantiationException iae){
56.        System.err.println("Unable to create new instance.");
57.    }catch(IllegalArgumentException iae){
58.        System.err.println("Error-IllegalArgumentException");
59.    }catch(InvocationTargetException ite){
60.        System.err.println("Error-InvocationTargetException");
61.    }catch(SecurityException se){
62.        System.err.println("Error-SecurityException");
63.    }
64.
65.}//End of constructor
```

Summary

This chapter covered some of the classes and methods available for the examination and manipulation of Java classes and objects, primarily Java Beans. As a Java Beans developer, you may never use any of these methods, but it is helpful to understand how the IDE might be using the methods discussed to examine and manipulate your code.

The information in this chapter can also be used to create Bean-aware components or applications too. Also, the Java Beans API can be extended to add increased functionality for specific component types. For example, a specialized application could be written that is a plug-and-play graphics tool. Such an application would have code to examine Beans for specific signatures associated with drawing objects, file formats, and graphic filters.

The Core Reflection API is a very powerful set of tools. These tools can be used to create easily extensible component-based programs. Core Reflection can be used in the same way that the Java Beans API is capable of manipulating very diverse types of components in an application builder tool. In addition, the Java Beans API can be used as a basis for any component extension.

Unfortunately, there is also the burden that the Core Reflection API is so powerful that there is a possibility that a new component API could be created that is incompatible with the Java Beans API. It is for that reason that any attempt at creating such software should first start with the minimum of the Java Beans API. Not using Java Beans is wasteful, because many functions are already available for use. Moreover, using the API also ensures that components are created with a minimum Java Beans capability. Without a component's conformity to the Java Beans API, the components cannot be connected using application builder tools. The developer should create applications that extend the functionality without sacrificing compatibility.

CHAPTER 9

Building Custom Component Editors for Java Beans

This chapter covers custom editors for Java Beans and their properties. Custom editors extend IDEs and Bean-aware applications such as the BeanBox. Without customization, the properties that would be editable in a Bean-aware IDE would be limited to class types that were supported. This means that you might be limited to numbers, strings, color, fonts, images, and possibly sound. It is definitely probable that such an IDE would not be capable of editing a class of your own invention.

Remember that a Bean is meant to be used regardless of which IDE it is installed in, so there has to be a way for the developer of a Bean to also supply editors for parts of the Bean about which the IDE developer cannot have any advanced information. Through the use of interfaces, naming conventions, and behavior patterns, custom editors can be recognized by an IDE and used to modify the Bean as a single entity or to just modify the Bean's properties.

To start with, you should know the types of editor that might be written. Figure 9.1 shows the relationship of IDE and Bean with the Bean Customizer and the Bean PropertyEditor. In the diagram, you can see that the Bean Customizer is used to edit a Bean directly, and that PropertyEditor classes are used to edit data obtained through the IDE. Property Editors in turn, control the entries in the property sheet as well as spawn and control custom editor components. Custom editor components are usually panels or canvases used outside the property sheet. A custom editor is used to give more control over the presentation used to edit classes that cannot be fully edited in the limited space and capabilities available in property sheet. A property sheet is only capable of displaying a small amount of text, numbers, or a dropdown list. The property sheet can also display a small amount of graphics, but the size of the graphic is only useful as an icon. Using a custom editor, the limitations of the property sheet are bypassed because the property can be edited in its own panel that can have any representation.

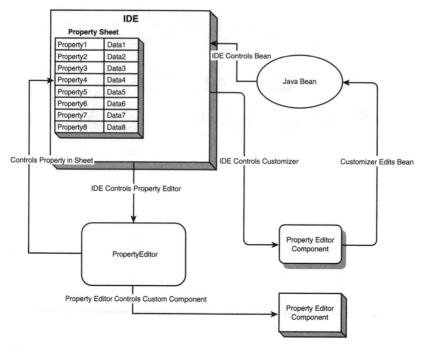

Figure 9.1

Relationship of Beans, the IDE, and custom editors.

PropertyEditor Interface

The PropertyEditor interface is a standard way to control the the behavior of the IDE's property sheet. There are many reasons for augmenting the way a property sheet handles a component. The primary uses are validation, display of an image or icon, adding a list, and generation of custom editor components.

Control of Validation

The validation of user input is very important. Invalid data, if it reaches the Bean, can adversely affect a Bean's behavior. Bad data can cause exceptions to be thrown or the Bean to react in an unknown manner. The IDE and the user may not understand that there is a problem. In fact, it is possible that the Bean will be edited with bad data and the user will never know it until something goes wrong in the final product in which the Bean is used.

Validation can be performed in the Bean by having set method throw exceptions when invalid data is recognized. Trapping such exceptions will necessarily need to happen in the IDE. Trapping errors in the IDE limits the amount of information that can be supplied to the user and may not be as informative as desired. If the error is trapped in the PropertyEditor, however, there is much more capability to present errors or warnings. The editor also acts as a gatekeeper, preventing changes that are illegal. Such a gatekeeper is important for properties that do not have any error control. The custom editor can also display dialogs that can give the user information about why the data was incorrect.

Validating input from the PropertyEditor can also enable Java Beans to be smaller, because strong validation and presentation of errors is kept in the PropertyEditor and not the Bean. A Bean should have some safeguards when in normal operation. Many Java Beans, however, have many methods that are only called by an IDE during setup and configuration. If validation is necessary during the configuration stage of a Bean only, the validation should occur in a custom editor. Code space dedicated to the validation is not part a physical part of the Bean and should not be delivered with a finished application using the Bean. For example, a Bean might have a property that is an address for an URL connection. The PropertyEditor could be used to validate the URL by connecting to it. This connection logic would normally be supplied by another Bean in the final program, so there is no reason to have the logic a physical part of the Bean. Instead the validation logic is kept in the PropertyEditor, which reduces the amount of code that becomes part of the final application.

Displaying Images in the Property Sheet

There are innumerable reasons to display an image in the property sheet. Take for instance the standard editor for properties of the Color class. The editor displays both the text that defines the color and a rectangle that the user can use to visually interpret the color. Without the color being displayed, the user would be unaware of whether the text "0,0,255," which is what is displayed in the BeanBox property sheet, was the color red, blue, or green. With the image, there is no way that the user could mistake the color chosen. Figure 9.2 shows a property sheet with the color that was picked by a custom property editor that edits properties of type color.

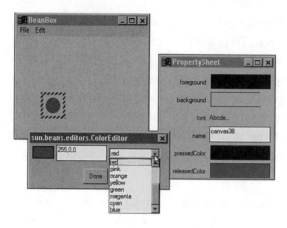

Figure 9.2

Property sheet with color icon.

Another way that images can be used in a property sheet is to mark certain properties with icons so that the user can better understand the component's class or function. A sound property, for example, might have a musical note icon; a mouse setting may have a mouse; and a directory may have a folder. Such visual representations can make understanding a component much simpler. A button that has sounds for being pressed and released, for instance, will have properties for both of these events. By having speaker icons displayed in the property sheet, the user can quickly spot the attribute to change. Alternatively, the user is forced to scan the property sheet looking for a property called PressedSound, SoundPressd, or even worse, PressedAudioClip, or possibly PressedNoise.

 Tip

> Using icons also goes a long way toward internationalizing your application. By having icons, there is less reason to add multiple language interpretations for all your properties.

An obvious reason for showing an image is for properties of the class image. Having the image displayed in a property sheet becomes important for a Bean where the image is hidden. A button that has a pressed and a released image, for example. The pressed image can only be seen if the button is pressed. In many IDEs, because the Bean is actually running, it is not too hard for the user to just press the button to see the image displayed.

Displaying a Text List in a Property Sheet

Whenever a property has a fixed list of possible alternatives, there should be a property editor. In fact, displaying a list is one of the easiest ways to change the look of a property in the property sheet.

Examples of list properties include colors, short ranges of numbers, named modes of operation (such as start, stop, and pause), and selections of state file (such as the molecule files used in the Molecule Bean in the BDK).

One advantage of list properties is that the user is limited to a set list of data. Having only a list of valid choices means that the PropertyEditor does not need to validate value changes because, by default, the entries in the list are already validated.

Generating a Custom Component Editor

One of the more useful features in the Bean model is the capability of a Property editor to generate a panel or canvas that represents a unique grouping of components to serve as a custom editor to edit a property. This enables complex property types to be expressed and edited in a way that makes the most sense to the user. Graphics can be edited in a panel that combines a file dialog and a graphics preview, for instance, and colors can be chosen from color palettes, and so on. This frees the Bean developer from the property sheet that is limited to a small graphic area, small lists, and generally text-based information.

Custom component editors are much different from their predecessors in other visual development environments. There is no standard or limitation to what the Bean developer can present. The only rules are that the custom component editor be derived from a component that is either a canvas or panel. Extending canvas or panel allows the IDE to place the editor in a dialog controlled by the IDE. The other rule is that the PropertyEditor only communicates with the IDE, and not the Bean. This communication barrier between the Bean and a PropertyEditor is done mainly to ensure that the Bean is not part of the editing process (thus reducing the edit oriented code delivered in a final Bean). Because of the Bean developer's freedom to present the editor in almost any way, the end user profits because the property will be edited exactly as it needs to be. This is in stark contrast to older visual environments where editors have limited sizes and limited functionality.

Bean Customizers

A Bean Customizer is used when a property sheet is inappropriate. There are many reasons for not using a property sheet to edit a Bean. The Bean or a major part of it may need to be represented in a specific way that is more understandable to users, or the Bean must be configured in a specific sequence. Such changes cannot be performed with a property sheet because the IDE is in control of the property sheet. The IDE has no foreknowledge of your Bean and therefore cannot perform actions that are appropriate. By using a Customizer, the Bean developer is usurping control over the Bean's edit process from the IDE.

 Note

> The property editor is still active in the presence of a Customizer object. Use the BeanInfo to either hide or prevent edits. This also means that properties that can be edited in the property sheet do not need to be controlled in the Customizer.

The Bean Customizer is an editor that has full access to the Bean to edit it in part or in whole. Usually a customizer is in the same package as a Bean. This package membership is useful for manipulating protected (package) member functions of a Bean that cannot be accessed by the IDE. Customizers are also important for representing an editable view. When manipulating a Bean associated with a database, for example, the Bean Customizer could be used to graphically present tables and fields for the user to choose and apply filter criteria to. Such database manipulations would be impossible in a standard property sheet, and confusing if the same information was presented in multiple custom editor components.

Another example is a Bean that contains animation. To properly edit the animation, the animation cells, their sequence, and rate should be presented in a single panel because all of these properties are interrelated. In addition, the animation can be previewed, by starting and stopping the animation. This is in contrast to the Juggler demo supplied in the BDK where no customizer was supplied, forcing the developer to hook up the Bean to start and stop buttons just to preview the animation.

 Tip

> A good rule of thumb is that if multiple parameters affect the behavior of a Bean, a Customizer should be created to preview and edit the changes.

Changing a Bean's Properties

One of the more important aspects of making a custom editor work seamlessly is to understand rules about the expected behavior of Java Beans and their editors. The following guidelines apply to changing Bean behavior and are covered more thoroughly in the sections that follow:

◆ Never access a Bean from a PropertyEditor

◆ Only customizers and IDEs should have access a Bean directly

◆ Ensure change notification

◆ Never accept bad data

◆ Evaluate property change control

◆ Provide an editor for every class

◆ Provide default property editors

Never Access a Bean from a PropertyEditor

The first rule is that a PropertyEditor should never modify the contents of an object still held by a Bean. The reason for this is that any change to the internal state of an object will cause an immediate change to the Bean. This circumvents any handling that might be executed for normal changes through a "set" property method of the Bean. Even if a property does not have any processing in the "set" method, the property sheet is also involved and requires notification to update its display. For example, if a PropertyEditor modifies part of a mutable object type, MyShape in a Bean that controls its shape, the Bean is unaware of the change. The Bean would expect the *setMyShape()* where it has code to redraw the Bean. Instead, the Bean will not be redrawn until the Bean's paint mechanism is called (if at all).

A key feature of isolating the PropertyEditor from the actual Bean is that the PropertyEditor can be used with other Beans that may need the same type of property edited. This proves especially useful when developing collections of Beans that have the same types of properties. Also, because the editor modifies only the one property type, the editor can be reused for multiple properties in the same Bean that have the same class. A Bean with several images, for instance, can use a single ImageEditor class.

The most important reason for isolating the editor from the Bean is that the IDE may not have a live Bean. In other words, the IDE would only show a graphic representation of the Bean rather than the Bean itself. Because the Bean is not running, the custom editor cannot manipulate the Bean directly, because the Bean does not exist. In situations such as this, the IDE would probably be set up as a code generator and therefore would generate Java instructions to set up Beans. It is situations such as this, where the Bean is not serialized, where the *getAsText( )* method (covered later in this chapter) will be used to generate the required Java instructions.

A class implementing the CustomEditor interface is only concerned with the copy of the object. The IDE is responsible for affecting changes to the Beans parameter by calling the set accessor method. The IDE will be notified of changes, because it registers itself with the PropertyEditor's *addPropertyChangeListener( )* method. Whenever the PropertyEditor causes the original value to change, the IDE will be notified, causing the IDE to call the Bean's set property method.

Only Customizers and IDEs Should Have Direct Access to a Bean

A Customizer class can always access a Bean directly, either through methods or via direct object access. However, the Customizer needs to be written such that the Bean is aware that data has changed. Otherwise the Bean could be set into a state where a change is made in one part of a Bean, but is not reflected in other areas.

An IDE is in charge of calling 'set' and 'get' property methods of a Bean. The IDE does this for the property sheet as well as for PropertyEditor objects.

Ensure Change Notification

As discussed in the preceding section, the property editor is responsible for the notification of changes. Without change notification, there is no way for the IDE to know whether a change has taken place. Because the Bean-enabled IDE is usually working with a live and running copy of the Java Bean, there is the expectation that when a property editor's value changes, the corresponding property will change in the Bean. The change should then take place both in the property sheet and in the running Bean. If the background color of a button Bean is changed in a custom component editor, for example, the new color should be immediately updated in the property sheet and in the target Bean.

Never Accept Bad Data

Filtering user input is an important job of property editors. There are many ways that a user might mistakenly attempt to update a Bean with incorrect data. The property editor should stop such data by not calling the change listener's *propertyChange( )* method. By trapping errors at their source and preventing their propagation to the IDE and therefore the Bean, exceptions and unpredictable behavior are avoided.

Unfortunately, the way that JavaSoft has configured the BeanBox does not bode well for trapping bad data. The problem is in the frequency that the BeanBox property sheet changes are sent to the Bean. The BeanBox updates a property at the end of each character typed. What this means is that if the property is a file name or similar object that is invalid until completely typed, the property will be invalid for 99% of the users input. This can wreak havoc if the PropertyEditor object or the Bean is attempting to do a validation or actual operation based on the interim changes. For example, a property that is an image file name will attempt to load the file after each keystroke (this could really slow down a computer with all the attempts at loading the file). In such cases, use a PropertyEditor that does not attempt to validate the object until the user has completed the entry.

Evaluate Property Change Control

Figure 9.3 summarizes the flow of data between the Bean, the IDE, and the PropertyEditor class in a graphical fashion.

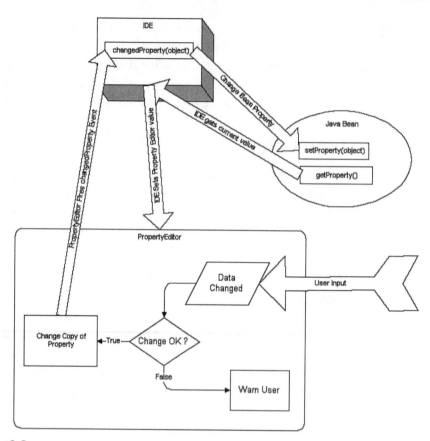

Figure 9.3

Data flow between Bean, IDE, and CustomEditor.

As figure 9.3 shows, the Java Bean is accessed with set and get methods by the IDE. The IDE sends the state of the property to the property editor. When the property has its data changed by user input, the property editor first validates the new data. If the data is invalid, the user is warned of the problem. If the data is valid, the *propertyChanged()* method in the IDE is called. The *propertyChanged()* method in the IDE sets the new value of the property in the Bean. Note that there is no direct interaction between the property editor and the Java Bean. All interactions are channeled through the IDE.

Provide an Editor for Every Class

The Java Bean scenario essentially requires that every property type to be edited has a corresponding PropertyEditor. The four types of editors are as follows:

◆ Default

◆ Augmented property editor

◆ Property editor with custom editor component

◆ Bean Customizer classes

The Bean Customizer classes catch any properties not handled by property editors and for property edition that needs to be done in the context of the Bean.

Provide Default Property Editors

Default property editors are provided by the IDE for the Java built-in types: Boolean, byte, short, int, long, float, and double. There should also be editors for the classes java.lang.String, java.awt.Color, and java.awt.Font. These base types and classes are common property types that should cover most property entries of Java Beans. There may be others supported depending on the particular IDE (like Locale, Image, AudioClip, and many more). You should expect to see the minimum set, so there should be no reason to add editors for these types unless explicit control of ranges or other conditions is required.

The PropertyEditor Interface

The PropertyEditor interface defines property editors in a predictable way. A class implementing PropertyEditor can pick and choose the type of representation for a property in the property sheet and also give an IDE a customized editor component that can be used to edit the property.

The following sections describe in detail each of the PropertyEditor interface methods.

setValue() Method

The *setValue()* method sets the value of the property to be viewed and edited by this editor. This should be the only way that an editor is able to set the value of a property in a Bean. When this method is called, the property editor should update its component view (if it exists). The syntax for this method is as follows:

```
void setValue(Object value)
```

The object passed into this method should never be modified. If the property editor needs to modify the value, the editor should instead clone a copy and modify the copy. Alternatively, the property editor can create a new object. The reason why the original should never be modified is that the Bean will not know that the value has changed, and yet will still have access to changed data. This is important if the Bean is running within a thread periodically accessing the value. As a matter of safety, the Bean's get method for any property should return a copy of the internal object unless the object is immutable (like String or Color, where new values can only be set during construction).

The *setValue()* method only accepts Object class, so built-in types such as int and float should be wrapped in their class types. Variables of type int, for example, should be wrapped in Integer, and variables of type float should be wrapped in the class Float.

getValue() Method

This method is used by the IDE to retrieve the current value of the object to which the property editor is set. If there is any danger of the value being changed outside the control of the editor, this method should return a copy of the object. The syntax for this method is as follows:

```
Object getValue()
```

isPaintable() Method

The *isPaintable()* method is used by the IDE to determine whether the editor supports the *paintValue()* method also in this class (see the following section). Paintable editors are those that display their state as within a graphical window inside the IDE's property editor. The syntax for this method is as follows:

```
boolean isPaintable()
```

void paintValue() Method

Component editors implement this method to paint a graphical representation in the IDE's property sheet. This method is given a graphic context to paint with and a rectangle to draw in. The IDE uses this method to update the property editor when it is displayed or when the internal state of the property editor changes, thus causing a propertyChanged event to be fired. When the editor gets the event, it calls this method if the value of the *isPaintable()* method returns true (see the preceding section for the *isPaintable()* method). The syntax for this method is as follows:

```
void paintValue(Graphics context, Rectangle box)
```

The rectangle that the image is to be drawn within is not guaranteed to be square. If the image to be displayed requires a certain height to width ratio, use the minimum dimension to resize to. Figure 9.4 shows a Bean drawn in a rectangle in the BeanBox application and the PropertySheet that dictates the Bean's properties.

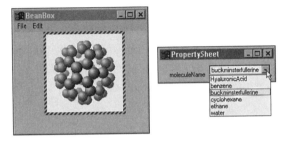

Figure 9.4

Property editor with an image in the property sheet.

 Warning

When an Image class object is resized, the original information is lost. This can cause problems if the image is to be used again at a larger size. Therefore, use a copy of the image and resize the copy.

getJavaInitializationString() Method

This method is used by an IDE to generate code to create an object of the current value. This method is used as an alternative to serializing the data of a Bean, including the value of the property represented by a property editor. This method would be used by an IDE to directly set the value of the property with generated code. The syntax for this method is as follows:

```
String getJavaInitializationString()
```

This method is intended for use when generating Java code to set the value of the property. It should return a fragment of Java code that can be used to initialize an object with the current property value.

If the class of the object is a Color class, for example, the return value should be something like: "new Color(0,255,0)."

getAsText() Method

The *getAsText()* method returns the value of the object as text. The text is used to populate the entry in the Bean's property sheet. If there is no way to represent the object as text, this method should return null. The syntax for this method is as follows:

```
String getAsText()
```

The text in the property sheet can be modified by the user. If this method is supported, therefore, the *setAsText()* method should also be supported. The *setAsText()* method accepts the same text as is presented by this method.

setAsText() Method

The *setAsText()* method is used to change the value of a property by parsing the string and attempting to create an object from it. This method should throw the java.lang.IllegalArgumentException if the text cannot be converted into a valid object. The syntax for this method is as follows:

```
void setAsText(String text) throws IllegalArgumentException
```

getTags() Method

The *getTags()* method is used to get an array of strings that represent a list of states for a property from which the user can select. The IDE uses this list to populate a Choice, List, or PopupMenu component in a Bean's property sheet. The syntax for this method is as follows:

```
String[] getTags()
```

If the property does not support a selectable list, this method should return null.

getCustomEditor() Method

The *getCustomEditor()* method is pivotal for enhancing the editable view of a Bean property. The method returns a component that contains the user interface for modifying the component. The component should be a panel or canvas so that the IDE can place it into a window or integrate it into another panel used as a target for custom editors. The component should be very reactive to the size of container it will be placed in and support minimum and maximum size information about itself. The syntax for this method is as follows:

```
Component getCustomEditor()
```

The *supportsCustomEditor()* method should return true if *getCustomEditor()* actively returns an editor component. Conversely, *supportsCustomEditor()* should return false if *getCustomEditor()* returns null.

If there is a state when the component cannot be edited, this method should still return a valid component. The component should have a message stating the reason why the component cannot be edited or have its child components disabled. The method should return null if a custom editor is never available.

supportsCustomEditor() Method

This method should return true if the PropertyEditor returns a component when *getCustomEditor()* is called. The syntax for this method is as follows:

```
boolean supportsCustomEditor()
```

addPropertyChangeListener() Method

The *addPropertyChangeListener()* method is used to add listener objects interested in changes to the component. The primary listener is the IDE, which needs to know when the value controlled by the PropertyEditor has changed. Once the IDE receives a PropertyChangeEvent it calls the Bean's 'set' method with the new value. This event mechanism between IDE and PropertyEditor is the only way in which a Property editor can cause a Bean to change state. The syntax for this method is as follows:

```
void addPropertyChangeListener(PropertyChangeListener listener)
```

removePropertyChangeListener (PropertyChangeListener listener) Method

The *removePropertyChangeListener()* method removes a listener interested in the PropertyChange event (usually the IDE). The listener should be removed just after the IDE stops editing the Bean. The syntax for this method is as follows:

```
void removePropertyChangeListener(PropertyChangeListener listener)
```

PropertyEditors in Action

Now that the details of the PropertyEditor interface have been discussed, you can now use it to create custom editors for a Java Bean. In the following sections, you will first create a Bean that needs to have custom editing. Then you will create the custom editors. Finally, you will learn how the BeanBox displays the Bean, its property sheet, and custom editor components.

Creating the SoundImageButton Bean

The example Bean is a simple multimedia push button. The custom button has a pressed sound, a released sound, an up image, and a down image. The shape of the custom button is rectangular and its size is completely configurable. Images used for the custom button will be resized to fit.

The custom button's state can be saved through serialization. Editors that you will create later will set the Image and AudioClip types of properties by object rather than a file name, so there is no need for the custom button to read sounds and images or store their file names.

The base class of the custom button is a canvas, so the user can be a listener to any event that a canvas supports, including the mouse clicked event. Because of this, there is no need to clutter the Bean with any further add or remove listener methods.

The up and down images to be drawn are each stored as rendered copies and as sized-to-fit copies. The reason for keeping the original, as well as the currently sized image, is that after an image is resized, it loses the original data. A button that was resized many times, therefore, would eventually lose too much detail to be of much use. In this Bean, whenever it is resized, a new copy of the image is created from the original. This method is a horrible waste of space, especially if the original was very large. To prevent saving the originals, the private data members have been marked as transient and code is provided to account for any post serialized resizing of the button by using the current images. This keeps the button as flexible and as lean as possible without too much sacrifice.

Declaring the SoundImageButton Base Class

In listing 9.1, besides the transient images, the state of the button is also transient. This ensures that the button is not reloaded in its pressed state. Keep in mind that if this was a toggle button, you would want to save the toggle position persistently.

Listing 9.1: Class SoundImageButton—Packages, class definition, object data

```
01.import  java.awt.*;
02.import  java.awt.event.*;
03.import  java.beans.*;
04.import  java.applet.*;
05.
06./**
07. * A simple bean to demonstrate Custom Bean Editors
08. *
09. */
10. public class SoundImageButton extends Canvas implements
➥java.io.Serializable{
11.     // Sounds to play
12.     AudioClip releasedSound = null;
13.     AudioClip pressedSound  = null;
14.
15.     // Images resized to fit canvas.
16.     Image upImageFixed   = null;
17.     Image downImageFixed = null;
18.     int scaleHint = Image.SCALE_DEFAULT;
19.
20.     // Marked transient because we do not want to save original images.
21.     transient Image upImage   = null;
22.     transient Image downImage = null;
23.
24.     // marked trasient because we do not want to save button state
25.     transient boolean down = false;
26.     transient boolean hasFocus = false;
```

Constructors for SoundImageButton

There are two constructors for this class. The first in listing 9.2 is the required null constructor. This constructor is used by a Bean IDE to create a new object. The most that is done in this method is to set a default size and to enable mouse events.

Listing 9.2: Class SoundImageButton—SoundImageButton () class constructor I

```
/**
 * Construct Blank button.
 */
public SoundImageButton () {
```

continues

```
continued

        super();
        setSize(new Dimension(40,40));
        enableEvents(MouseEvent.MOUSE_EVENT_MASK);
    }
```

The second constructor, in listing 9.3, has everything in its parameters for setting all properties of the Bean in the one call. This constructor is provided for the use of developers who do not have a Bean IDE to edit properties. If there was only the default constructor, the developer would be forced to write several lines of code to set up the Bean. Instead, this method makes it easier to create and configure the Bean in one line.

Note that the method in listing 9.3 also enables the mouse events. Remember that in the Java 1.1 event model, that Canvas or Panel components cannot receive events until the *enableEvents()* method is called with the event mask for the events of interest. If the *enableEvents()* method is not called, the button will not react to button click events.

Events are enabled in the constructors because it is highly unlikely that a developer would create a button where the clicked event was ignored. In this Bean, the fact that events are enabled here enables the button to only switch images and play sounds. No automatic notification of other components occurs until a listener is added.

Listing 9.3: Class SoundImageButton—SoundImageButton () class constructor 2

```
01.    /**
02.     * Construct button with image and sound.
03.     */
04.    public SoundImageButton (int width,int height,int scallingHint, Image
➥up, Image down,AudioClip pressed,AudioClip released ) {
05.        super();
06.        scaleHint = scallingHint;
07.        upImage = up;
08.        downImage = down;
09.
10.        pressedSound = pressed;
11.        releasedSound = released;
12.        setSize(width, height);
13.        enableEvents(MouseEvent.MOUSE_EVENT_MASK);
14.    }
```

Resizing the SoundImageButton

The *setSize()* method in listing 9.4 is a very important method to consider for any Bean to be edited in an IDE. From within an IDE, the component can be resized at any time regardless of the state of the Bean. Therefore, careful attention must be paid to possibly unconfigured parts. In this Bean, the images could possibly not exist. In fact, the default is that no images are available.

This method is also part of the logic required to resize the button after the original images were lost through serialization. If the transient images are null, the current images are copied so that they become the basis for further resizing. If this copy was not made, the component would not behave properly when resized.

Listing 9.4: Class SoundImageButton—setSize() method

```
01.     public void setSize(Dimension size){
02.         // Set up images to be scaled for the new size.
03.         // If we don't have the originals, make copies
04.         // of the current images first.
05.         if (upImage != null){
06.             upImageFixed   = upImage.createScaledImage( size.width,
    size.height,scaleHint);
07.         }else{
08.             if (upImageFixed != null){
09.                 upImage = upImageFixed;
10.                 upImageFixed   = upImage.createScaledImage( size.width,
    size.height,scaleHint);
11.             }
12.         }
13.         if (downImage != null){
14.             downImageFixed = downImage.createScaledImage( size.width,
    size.height,scaleHint);
15.         }else{
16.             if (downImageFixed != null){
17.                 downImage = downImageFixed;
18.                 downImageFixed = downImage.createScaledImage( size.
    width, size.height,scaleHint);
19.             }
20.         }
21.
22.         // Send the resize up the chain.
23.         super.setSize(size);
24. }// End of setSize()
```

Drawing the SoundImageButton

The *paint()* method in listing 9.5 is where the actual drawing of the up and down versions of the Bean are drawn. By placing all drawing within this function, the normal *repaint()* method will keep the image refreshed whenever the canvas is invalidated.

Note that this method makes certain that images exist before attempting to use them. The default is to print "Up" or "Down" inside the button if there is no corresponding image available. By painting default values, the user can see results of pressing the button without adding images first. This can be very important if the user is just creating a quick mockup and is not worried abut the aesthetics of the images.

Listing 9.5: Class SoundImageButton—paint() method

```
01.    /**
02.     * Draws an Image that fits the bounds of the canvas.
03.     */
04.    public void paint (Graphics context) {
05.         //System.out.println(" paint called");
06.          Dimension size = getSize();
07.        if (down && hasFocus){
08.            // draw down image
09.            if (downImageFixed != null){
10.                context.drawImage(downImageFixed,0,0,size.width,size.
   ➥height,this);
11.            }else{
12.                // Default is to draw a string if the button image is
13.                // not initialized.
14.                context.setColor(Color.red);
15.                context.drawRect(0,0,size.width-1,size.height-1);
16.                context.setColor(Color.blue);
17.                context.drawString("Down",1,size.height/2);
18.            }
19.        }else{
20.            //Draw up image
21.            if (upImageFixed != null){
22.                context.drawImage(upImageFixed,0,0,size.width,size.
   ➥height,this);
23.            }else{
24.                // Default is to draw a string if the button image is
25.                // not initialized.
26.                context.setColor(Color.red);
27.                context.drawRect(0,0,size.width-1,size.height-1);
28.                context.setColor(Color.blue);
```

```
29.                    context.drawString("Up",1,size.height/2);
30.            }
31.        }
32.    }
```

Accessing SoundImageButton Parameters

The next method is a Parameter accessor. Listing 9.6 shows the method for getting the current up image for the Bean. An important feature of this method is that it returns the original image or the resized image if the original is unavailable. The design rule here is that the image with the most data should be returned.

Listing 9.6: Class SoundImageButton—getUpImage() method

```
01.    /**
02.     * Get the non resized Image for the 'up' image.
03.     * @returns non resized Image for the 'up' image.
04.     */
05.    public Image getUpImage(){
06.    if (upImage != null){
07.            return (upImage);
08.        }else{
09.            return (upImageFixed);
10.        }
11. }
```

Setting the Up Image

Listing 9.7 is the complement of the *getUpImage()* method. It is used to set the original copy of the up image. If the image is valid, a copy is created that equals the current size. The button is then repainted so that the user can immediately see the change. This immediate update is a very important behavior. Without it there would be no way to see the updated image after the IDE called this function.

Listing 9.7: Class SoundImageButton—setUpImage() method

```
01.    /**
02.     * Set the non resized Image for the 'up' image.
03.     * Creates an image for the current size of the component.
```

continues

```
continued
04.       * @param non resized Image used for the 'up' image.
05.       */
06.      public void setUpImage(Image up){
07.           upImage = up;
08.
09.           // Set up images to be scaled for the new size.
10.           Dimension size = getSize();
11.           if (upImage != null){
12.               upImageFixed   = upImage.createScaledImage( size.width,
     ⇒size.height,scaleHint);
13.           }else{
14.               upImageFixed = null;
15.           }
16.           repaint();
17.      }
```

Setting the Down Image

Listing 9.8 and 9.9 are the mirror of the previous two methods. The *getDownImage()* and *setDownImage()* methods are used to set the image to be displayed when the component receives a mouse down event.

Listing 9.8: Class SoundImageButton—getDownImage() method

```
01.      /**
02.       * Get the non resized Image for the 'down' image.
03.       * @returns non resized Image for the 'down' image.
04.       */
05.
06.      public Image getDownImage(){
07.           if (downImage != null){
08.               return (downImage);
09.           }else{
10.               return (downImageFixed);
11.           }
12. }
```

The *setDownImage()* method in listing 9.9 contains a call to the *repaint()* method like the *setUpImage()* method, but this repaint is not as important. It will be very rare that the button will be down at the same time that the image is changed. It can happen, however, so the possibility is accounted for.

Listing 9.9: Class SoundImageButton—setDownImage() method

```
01.    /**
02.     * Set the non resized Image for the 'down' image.
03.     * Creates an image for the current size of the component.
04.     * @param non resized Image used for the 'down' image.
05.     */
06.
07.    public void setDownImage(Image down){
08.        downImage = down;
09.
10.        // Set up images to be scaled for the new size.
11.        Dimension size = getSize();
12.        if(downImage != null){
13.            downImageFixed = downImage.createScaledImage( size.width,
➥size.height,scaleHint);
14.        }else{
15.            downImageFixed = null;
16.        }
17.         repaint();
18.    }
```

Retrieving SoundImageButton Sounds

The *getReleasedSound()* method in listing 9.10 is used to retrieve the current released sound AudioClip. This is much simpler than the *getUpmage()* or the *getDownImage()* methods, because there is only one possible sound available.

Listing 9.10: Class SoundImageButton—getReleasedSound() method

```
public AudioClip getReleasedSound(){
    return (releasedSound);
}
```

Setting SoundImageButton Sounds

The *setReleasedSound()* method in listing 9.11 is also simpler than its image counterpart for the same reasons as previously stated. All that is needed by this call is the current AudioClip.

Listing 9.11: Class SoundImageButton—setReleasedSound()

```
public void setReleasedSound(AudioClip released){
    releasedSound = released;
}
```

Setting and Retreiving the Pressed Sound

Listings 9.12 and 9.13 are the mirror of listings 9.9 and 9.10. These methods are used to set and get the AudioClip to be played when the button is pressed.

Listing 9.12: Class SoundImageButton—getPressedSound() method

```
public AudioClip getPressedSound(){
    return (pressedSound);
}
```

Listing 9.13: Class SoundImageButton—setPressedSound() method

```
public void setPressedSound(AudioClip pressed){
    System.err.println("setPressedSound");
    if (pressed==null)System.err.println("setPressedSound ERROR");

    pressedSound = pressed;
}
```

Capturing SoundImageButton Mouse Events

The last method in this Bean class is the *processMouseEvent()* method, shown in listing 9.14. This method is used to capture mouse events so that the sounds can be played and the button images can be drawn. Notice here again the caution exercised regarding Bean properties that might be null.

Also, the last line in this method contains a call to the super class *processMouseEvent()* method. This statement is required so that the registered listeners are serviced by the parent class.

Listing 9.14: Class SoundImageButton—processMouseEvent() method

```
01.    /**
02.     * Processes the push button event to display a down or up event.
03.     */
04.
05.    protected void processMouseEvent (MouseEvent e){
06.        // System.out.println("Event:"+e);
07.        switch(e.getId()) {
08.            case MouseEvent.MOUSE_PRESSED :
09.                //The mouse button was pressed.
10.                // Play the sound!
11.                if (pressedSound != null){
12.                    pressedSound.play();
13.                }
14.                // Paint the pressed color.
15.                down = true;
16.                repaint();
17.                break;
18.            case MouseEvent.MOUSE_RELEASED :
19.                //The mouse button was released.
20.                // Play the sound!
21.                if (releasedSound != null){
22.                    releasedSound.play();
23.                }
24.
25.                //Paint the normal color.
26.                down = false;
27.                repaint();
28.                break;
29.            case MouseEvent.MOUSE_DRAGGED:
30.                if ((e.getX() < 0) || (e.getX() > size().width) ||
31.                    (e.getY() < 0) || (e.getY() > size().height)) {
32.                    if (down) {
33.                        down = false;
34.                        repaint();
35.                    }
36.                } else if (!down) {
37.                    down = true;
38.                    repaint();
39.                }
40.                break;
41.            case MouseEvent.MOUSE_ENTERED:
42.                hasFocus = true;
43.                repaint();
```

continues

```
    continued
44.              break;
45.           case MouseEvent.MOUSE_EXITED:
46.              hasFocus = false;
47.              repaint();
48.              break;
49.       }// End switch
50.
51.       // Use superclass to dispatch mouse events to registered
 ↪listeners
52.       super.processMouseEvent(e);
53.    }
54.}// End of class SoundImageButton
```

ImageEditor

Now that you know the working philosophy behind the SoundImageButton Bean, the editors can now be examined. The first PropertyEditor is ImageEditor. As its name implies, this class is used to edit parameters of the Image type.

The ImageEditor class is treated as two separate entities: a PropertyEditor and a custom component editor. The PropertyEditor is used to augment the processing in the property sheet. Secondly, the class is the custom component editor. The reason this is done is because of the tight coupling involved in accessing the methods and data by both the custom component editor and the PropertyEditor interface.

Some of the interactions are confusing, so the two entities could be split into two classes. There is no reason why this is not possible. This discussion, however, deals with the two entities in the single class because it is the common practice employed by Sun for their components.

Declaring the ImageEditor Base Class and Constructor

Listing 9.15 begins the examination of the ImageEditor with the class definition and the default constructor. First note that the class extends panel and implements Property-Editor. Because of this, the class may be seen as a custom editor component or as a property editor.

The class also implements the FilenameFilter and MouseListener interfaces. These will be used to support other parts of this class later.

The class constructor begins the setup of the object as a panel with components added to control the retrieval and display of the image. The actual sizing of the button is put off until the component has access to the font metrics that reside in the button's peer.

 Note

Because this is the creation stage of the component, it has yet to be added to a tree of components leading to the toolkit where system-specific information becomes available.

Listing 9.15: Class ImageEditor—Packages, class definition and constructor

```
01.import java.awt.*;
02.import java.beans.*;
03.import java.applet.*;
04.import java.net.*;
05.import java.awt.event.*;
06.import java.io.*;
07./**
08.* ImageEditor class is used to load Images for a Java Bean.
09.* <p>
10.* This class is used by a Bean aware IDE to edit Bean properties
11.* that are of the type Image.  This editor handles the locating
12.* and loading of GIF files. The client Bean should serialize the
13.* resulting Image object if it is to be used again.
14.* <p>
15.* This class is both a PropertyEditor and a custom editor component.
16.*
17.* @see PropertyEditor
18.* @see Image
19.*/
20.public class ImageEditor extends Panel implements
➥PropertyEditor,FilenameFilter, MouseListener{
21.
22.    //Current value of the edited object
23.    private Image target =null;
24.
25.    /**
26.     * ImageEditor Class constructor.
27.     * This class is used by a Bean aware IDE to edit Bean properties
28.     * that are of the type Image.  This editor handles the locating
29.     * and loading of AU files. The client Bean should serialize the
30.     * resulting Image object if it is to be used again. Alternatively the
```

continues

continued

```
31.      * IDE can use the getJavaInitializationString() to load the
32.      * image resource by name.
33.      * <p>
34.      * This constructor has no parameters because of a the pattern for
35.      * PropertyEditor classes must have a null constructor.
36.      *
37.      * @see PropertyEditor
38.      */
39.     public ImageEditor() {
40.          setLayout(null);
41.          ourWidth = hPad;
42.
43.          // Create a sample color block bordered in black
44.          Panel p = new Panel();
45.          p.setLayout(new FlowLayout());
46.          p.setBackground(Color.black);
47.
48.          // Create a place to draw the image.
49.          sample = new Canvas();
50.          p.add(sample);
51.          sample.reshape(2, 2, sampleWidth, sampleHeight);
52.          add(p);
53.          p.reshape(ourWidth, 2, sampleWidth+4, sampleHeight+4);
54.          ourWidth += sampleWidth + 4 + hPad;
55.
56.          // Create a text field to view and edit the resource name.
57.          text = new TextField("", 14);
58.          add(text);
59.          text.reshape(ourWidth,0,100,30);
60.          ourWidth += 100 + hPad;
61.
62.          // Create a button to popup a file dialog.
63.          fileButton = new Button(label);
64.
65.          // Add the mouse listener to the button so that
66.          // the FileDialog can be popped up when a
67.          // button clicked event is see.
68.          fileButton.addMouseListener((MouseListener)this);
69.            add(fileButton);
70.
71.
72.          // Note that no sizing of the button has been done here.
73.          // This is so that we can size it according to its font.
74.          // Since the Font cannot be found until after the peer is
75.          // known, we hold off until we are sure(see getMinimumSize())
76.
```

```
77.          // Resize to current (tough not final) size.
78.          resize(ourWidth,40);
79.      }
```

Implementing the FileFilter's accept() method

The first true method in this class is the *accept()* method, shown in listing 9.16. This method is an implementation for the FilenameFilter that will be used later by a FileDialog object used to retrieve the locations of GIF files.

Listing 9.16: Class ImageEditor—accept() method

```
01.
02.      /**
03.       * Implementation for  FilenameFilter.
04.       * <p>
05.       * Used to filter files from the FileDialog.
06.       *
07.       * @see FilenameFilter
08.       */
09.      public boolean accept(File dir, String name){
10.          if (name.toUpperCase().endsWith(".GIF")){
11.              return true;
12.          }else{
13.              return false;
14.          }
15.      }// end of accept()
```

Displaying the FileDialog

The next method is also an implementation. In this case, it is the implementation for the MouseListener interface. The *mouseClicked()* method in listing 9.17 is used to listen to the get file button. When called, this method pops up a file dialog for the user to browse for images to use. When the dialog is closed, the file name is extracted and the *setAsText()* method is called. The *setAsText()* method is part of the PropertyEditor implementation. The purpose is to change the internal state to a new one based on the text. In this case, it is the file name. The *setAsText()* method eventually causes a PropertyChangeEvent to occur so that the client Bean property can be updated.

Listing 9.17: Class ImageEditor—mouseClicked() method

```
01./** Used to trap button clicks for the file button.
02.    * This method dispalays a FileDialog to be used to
03.    * retrieve images.
04.    */
05.    public void mouseClicked(MouseEvent e) {
06.
07.    //Button pressed
08.    FileDialog fileDialog = null;
09.
10.        // Create a new file dialog. Note that
11.        // a plain Frame is used here because there
12.        // is no easy way to find the editor frame.
13.        fileDialog = new FileDialog(new Frame(),"Get
    ➥Image",FileDialog.LOAD);
14.
15.        // Set the file filter to our implementation.
16.        fileDialog.setFilenameFilter((FilenameFilter)this);
17.        fileDialog.setMode(FileDialog.LOAD);
18.
19.        // Show the file dialog.
20.        // Because it is model, execution is suspended here until
21.        // the file dialog returns.
22.        fileDialog.show();
23.
24.
25.        // Get current directory
26.        String base = (new File(".")).getAbsolutePath();
27.
28.        // Remove '.' char from end.
29.        base = base.substring(0,base.length()-1);
30.
31.        System.out.println(base);
32.
33.        String newBase = fileDialog.getDirectory();
34.        System.out.println(newBase+fileDialog.getFile());
35.        if (newBase.startsWith(base)){
36.            // Change the current value of the target.
37.            setAsText(newBase.substring(base.length())+fileDialog.
    ➥getFile());
38.        }
39.
40.    }// End of mouseClicked()
```

The methods in listing 9.18 are excess mouse event handlers that this method does not care about. These excess mouse event handlers need to exist, however, for the MouseListener interface implementation to be complete.

Listing 9.18: Class ImageEditor—unused mouse event handlers

```
/** unused method */
public void mouseEntered(MouseEvent e) {}
/** unused method */
public void mouseExited(MouseEvent e) {}
/** unused method */
public void mousePressed(MouseEvent e) {}
/** unused method */
public void mouseReleased(MouseEvent e ){}
```

Implementing setValue()

The next step is to implement the *setValue()* method of the PropertyEditor interface. This is a key method that is used to set the initial value of the property that this class will manipulate. The primary caller of this method will be the IDE. The *setValue()* method in listing 9.15 is also part of the PropertyEditor implementation, shown in listing 9.19. This method is used to set the value of the property to display and edit. For safety, defaults are set up in case the object set is null.

Listing 9.19: Class ImageEditor—setValue() method

```
01.    public void setValue(Object o) {
02.        if (o == null){
03.            System.out.println("set text field.");
04.            text.setText("t1.gif");
05.            text.repaint();
06.            setAsText(text.getText());
07.
08.            System.out.println("leaving set as text field.");
09.
10.        }
11.        changeImage((Image)o);
12.    }// End of setValue()
```

Overriding SoundImageButton Component Size

The next method in this class is an override of the components *preferredSize()* method. This method is called by the parent so that it knows the size of panel or window to be used for the custom editor component. The opportunity is taken here to complete the resizing of the get file button. At this point, the component should be a member of a component hierarchy that knows what the font is. The button is resized and the minimum desired width recalculated.

Listing 9.20: Class ImageEditor—preferredSize() method

```
01.    /**
02.     * New implementation used to ensure that the minimum
03.     * size is presented by the IDE.
04.     * <p>
05.     * This method also resize the file button to match
06.     * the text in the button at the current font metric.
07.     */
08.    public Dimension preferredSize() {
09.            // Put our button size logic here because we have the peer to
➥get
10.            // the Font and Metric by this time
11.         try{
12.             String label = "Find Image";
13.             FontMetrics fm =
➥fileButton.getFontMetrics(fileButton.getFont());
14.
15.             fileButton.reshape(ourWidth, 2, fm.stringWidth(label)
➥+(fm.charWidth('A')*3), fm.getHeight() *2);
16.         }catch(Exception ex){
17.             System.err.println("Error creating button:"+ex);
18.         }
19.         resize(ourWidth+(fileButton.getSize()).width+hPad,40);
20.         invalidate();
21.         repaint();
22.         return new Dimension(ourWidth+(fileButton.getSize()).
➥width+hPad, 40);
23.     }// End of preferredSize()
```

Detecting Keystroke Events

The *keyUp()* method in listing 9.21 is used to detect keystroke events. When a key up event is detected, the current value of the TextField is used as the file name of the image. The *setAsText()* method does the actual work of attempting to load the image.

Tip

The *keyUp()* method is poorly written. It would have been better to delay the call to *setAsText()* until the user presses a tab or return key.

Listing 9.21: Class ImageEditor—keyUp() method

```
01.     public boolean keyUp(Event e, int key) {
02.         if (e.target == text) {
03.             try {
04.                 setAsText(text.getText());
05.             } catch (IllegalArgumentException ex) {
06.                 // Quietly ignore.
07.                 //ex.printStackTrace();
08.
09.             }
10.         }
11.         return (false);
12.     }// End of keyUp()
```

Converting Text to Images

The *setAsText()* method in listing 9.22 is used to convert a text representation to a value. In this case, it is a file name converted to an image. This method is also part of the PropertyEditor implementation. The method will throw an IllegalArgumentException if the method fails to convert the text to the desired property value.

Listing 9.22: Class ImageEditor—setAsText() method

```
01.     public void setAsText(String s) throws
➥java.lang.IllegalArgumentException {
02.         try {
03.             //System.out.println("Loading image:"+s);
04.             Image c = loadImage(s);
05.             changeImage(c);
06.         } catch (Exception ex) {
07.             System.err.println("ImageEditor.setAsText()"+ex);
08.             System.err.println(ex);
09.             ex.printStackTrace();
10.             IllegalArgumentException iae = new
➥IllegalArgumentException(s);
```

continues

```
continued
11.              iae.fillInStackTrace();
12.              throw iae;
13.          }
14.     }// End of setAsText()
```

Loading Images by Name

Because this class concerns itself with images, the method in listing 9.23 is used to load images by their name. The *loadImage()* method uses the current class loader to load a resource object by name and convert it to an image. If the name does not resolve to an image, an exception is thrown. The exception propagates back to the *setAsText()* method so that an IllegalArgumentException is finally thrown, completely aborting any possible changes.

 Note

Note that the MediaTracker is used to ensure that the component is completely loaded before continuing. The reason for this is that there is no guarantee that the client Bean has any media tracking logic available.

Listing 9.23: Class ImageEditor—loadImage() method

```
01.    /**
02.     * Load GIF Images from via the resource file.
03.     * It takes the name of a resource file associated with the
04.     * current object's class-loader and loads a GIF image
05.     * from that file.
06.     * <p>
07.     * @param imageName    A pathname relative to the base
08.     *          directory of the current class-loader.    For example
09.     *          "NewRiders/ch14/t1.gif".
10.     * @return    Image object.
11.     */
12.    public Image loadImage(String imageName) throws Exception{
13.        URL url= null;//Url to use as a base to find images.
14.        try {
15.            url = getClass().getResource(imageName);
16.            Image tempImage = (Image) url.getContent();
17.            MediaTracker tracker = new MediaTracker(this);
18.            tracker.addImage(tempImage, 0);
```

```
19.            try{
20.                tracker.waitForAll();
21.            }catch( InterruptedException ie){
22.                // Quietly ignore
23.                ie.printStackTrace();
24.            }
25.            return tempImage;
26.        } catch (Exception ex) {
27.            System.err.println("Exception loading image in
➡ImageEditor.loadImage()");
28.            System.err.println("     URL:" + url);
29.            System.err.println("     Attempting to load '"+imageName +
"'");
30.            System.err.println("     " + ex);
31.            ex.printStackTrace();
32.            throw ex;
33.        }
34.    }
```

Generating Java Code to Instantiate Target Objects

The *getJavaInitializationString()* method in listing 9.24 is quite a departure from most other methods in the PropertyEditor Interface implementation. This method is used to generate Java code to instantiate the current target object. In this case, the object is an Image object created by loading a resource by its name. This method would be called by an IDE when the serialization of a Bean is not possible and step-by-step property initialization is preferred.

Listing 9.24: Class ImageEditor—getJavaInitializationString()

```
01.    /**
02.     * Returns the equivalent text required to initialize
03.     * the target object handled by this property editor.
04.     * <p>
05.     * The supported initialization is to return the named target
06.     * from resources.
07.     *
08.     * @see PropertyEditor
09.     */
10.    public String getJavaInitializationString() {
11.        // System.out.println("getJavaInitializationString() called");
```

continues

continued

```
12.        return "(Image)
  (Image.class.getResource("+text.getText()+")).getContent()";
13.     }// End of getJavaInitializationString()
```

Updating the Image Display

The *changeImage()* method in listing 9.25 is used to perform the housekeeping functions required whenever the target object changes either by setting the text value or by the IDE setting the current image obtained from the Bean. This method updates the custom property component and also fires a property change event.

Listing 9.25: Class ImageEditor—changeImage() method

```
01.    /**
02.     * Sets the value of the target that is currently being edited.
03.     * <p>
04.     * If the value is null then a default string is used.
05.     * Fires a property change event to notify the IDE.
06.     * <p>
07.     * This method also updates the display to show an
08.     * icon of the original image.
09.     *
10.     * @see PropertyEditor
11.     */
12.    private void changeImage(Image c) {
13.        if (sample == null || c == null) return;
14.        target = c;
15.
16.        // Get a context to paint with
17.        Graphics context = sample.getGraphics();
18.
19.        // Get the bounds for the sample box.
20.        Rectangle size = sample.getBounds();
21.
22.        // Use the PropertyEditor method to draw.
23.        paintValue(context,size);
24.
25.        // Fire a property change event.
26.        support.firePropertyChange("", null, null);
27.    }
```

Retrieving the Result of an Editing Session

Listing 9.26 shows the *getValue()* method used by the IDE to obtain the current value of the object being edited. The primary way that the IDE uses the *getValue()* method to obtain this value is through the PropertyChangedEvent that should be thrown when the property value changes. This method returns the current state. The *getValue()* method is another part of the PropertyEditor interface implementation.

Listing 9.26: Class ImageEditor—getValue() method

```
/**
 * Returns the value of the target that is currently being edited.
 *
 * @see PropertyEditor
 */
public Object getValue() {
    return target;
}
```

Implementing paintValue() to Force IDE to Paint

Listing 9.27 is also another part of the PropertyEditor interface implementation. The *isPaintable()* method is used to query the PropertyEditor to learn whether the *paintValue()* method is active. If this is true, the IDE reserves a portion of the property sheet for the PropertyEditor to draw into. The drawing is triggered by the method in listing 9.28.

Listing 9.27: Class ImageEditor—isPaintable() method

```
01.    /**
02.     * Returns true if PropertyEditor.paintValue() is used.
03.     * This method is called by the IDE to populate an image into
04.     * the property sheet.
05.     * <p>
06.     * Paintable because we have an Icon displayed in the property sheet.
07.     *
08.     * @see PropertyEditor
09.     */
10.    public boolean isPaintable() {
11.        return true;
12.    }
```

Painting the Image in the Property Sheet.

Listing 9.28, another part of the PropertyEditor interface implementation, is used to query the PropertyEditor to paint within a rectangle at the IDE's request. The method will only be called by the IDE if the *isPaintable()* method in listing 9.27 returns true.

Because the IDE may have a rectangle, and most images are somewhat square, this method uses the target rectangle's shortest dimension to create a target square. If this was not done, the possibility exists that the image will be too distorted to serve a useful purpose. You may see a black border showing around part of the image. The reason for this is that the *isPaintable()* method does not have access to the parent container to query the background color properly. If this were rewritten it would be better to add a distinct border and properly center the image in the property sheet. Unfortunately, there does not seem to be a published standard for the image target dimensions or methods to retrieve background colors.

This method does double duty in this class because it is also used to draw the sample into the custom editor component's panel.

Listing 9.28: Class ImageEditor—paintValue() method

```
01.   /**
02.    * Draw representation of target value into a specified location.
03.    * <p>
04.    * This method is called by the IDE to populate an image into
05.    * the property sheet.
06.    * <p>
07.    * This editor uses the image space to display an icon to
08.    * help the user visually understand that this is a sound
09.    * component.
10.    *
11.    * @see PropertyEditor
12.    */
13.   public void paintValue(java.awt.Graphics context, java.awt.Rectangle
➥box) {
14.
15.        // May be drawing before a context
16.        // becomes available.
17.        if (context == null) {
18.            return;
19.        }
20.        // Get the minimum dimension of the box.
21.        int min = (box.width < box.height)? box.width:box.height;
```

```
22.
23.        if (target != null){
24.             // Draw a copy of the image.
25.             context.drawImage(target,box.x,box.y,min,min,0,0,target.
26.                     getWidth(null),target.getHeight(null),null);
27.        }else{
28.             // Draw a default
29.             context.setColor(Color.pink);
30.             context.fillRect(box.x,box.y,min,min);
31.        }
32.    }// End of paintValue()
```

Converting the Image to Text

The *getAsText()* method in listing 9.29 is part of the implementation for PropertyEditor and a functional mirror of the *setAsText()* method. The *getAsText()* method should therefore return the same value as was set by the *setAsText()* method or a string that is functionally equivalent. Because the main repository of the string is the TextField component, it is retrieved from that point.

Listing 9.29: Class ImageEditor—getAsText() method

```
01.    /**
02.     * Get text vlaue of the parameter.
03.     * <p>
04.     * For this editor, the text is in the
05.     * text field.
06.     *
07.     * @see PropertyEditor
08.     */
09.    public String getAsText() {
10.             return text.getText();
11.    }
```

Disabling the List Drop-Down Menu

The only part of the PropertyEditor interface implementation not meant to contribute to the behavior of the PropertyEditor is the *getTags()* method shown in listing 9.30. This method would normally return a list of text settings (such as the MoleculeEditor class, for instance). In this class, however, there is no reason for a list, and so a null is returned.

Listing 9.30: Class ImageEditor—getTags() method

```
01.    /**
02.     * Get the list of valid entries for  this parameter.
03.     * <p>
04.     * This ParameterEditor does not support tags so
05.     * this method returns null.
06.     *
07.     * @see PropertyEditor
08.     */
09.    public String[] getTags() {
10.        return null;
11.    }
```

Indicating Custom Editor Support

The *supportsCustomEditor()* method in listing 9.31 is very important in that it signals to the IDE that the PropertyEditor has a custom editor component associated with it. The IDE will therefore make a part of the property sheet that the ImageEditor class is associated with and cause the custom editor component to be displayed when triggered. The panel or canvas containing the editor is obtained by calling the *getCustomEditor()* method.

Listing 9.31: Class ImageEditor—supportsCustomEditor() method

```
01.    /**
02.     * Returns true if a custom editor component is supported.
03.     * <p>
04.     * This ParameterEditor is itself the editor component
05.     * so always return true.
06.     *
07.     * @see PropertyEditor
08.     */
09.    public boolean supportsCustomEditor() {
10.        return true;
11.    }
```

Giving the IDE Access to the Custom Property Editor Panel

The *getCustomEditor()* method in the case of this property editor is the class itself. Because this class derives from Panel, it is a simple manner to return the this reference to the current object. Listing 9.32 shows the *getCustomEditor()* method.

Listing 9.32: Class ImageEditor—getCustomEditor() method

```
01.   /**
02.    * Get a custom editor component.
03.    * <p>
04.    * This ParameterEditor is itself the editor component
05.    * so we return a reference to 'this'.
06.    *
07.    * @see PropertyEditor
08.    */
09.   public java.awt.Component getCustomEditor() {
10.       return this;
11.   }
```

Registering Property Change Listeners

The remaining methods in this class in listing 9.33 are used to support the registering of property change listeners. Without this registering, there would be no way to inform the IDE that changes have taken place.

By now you should reognize the pattern of add and remove listener methods with the PropertyChangeSupport class is used to make the addition of these methods easy to maintain.

Listing 9.33: Class ImageEditor—Property change support methods and misc. data

```
01.   // Used to support property change listener interface.
02.   private PropertyChangeSupport support = new
➥PropertyChangeSupport(this);
03.
04.   /**
05.    * Adds a PropertyChangeLister to monitor changes to the target.
06.    *
07.    * @see PropertyEditor
08.    * @see PropertyChangeListener
09.    */
10.   public void addPropertyChangeListener(PropertyChangeListener l) {
11.       support.addPropertyChangeListener(l);
12.   }
13.
14.   /**
```

continues

```
continued
15.    * Removes a PropertyChangeLister.
16.    *
17.    * @see PropertyEditor
18.    * @see PropertyChangeListener
19.    */
20.    public void removePropertyChangeListener(PropertyChangeListener l) {
21.         support.removePropertyChangeListener(l);
22.    }
23.    private Canvas sample;
24.    private int sampleHeight = 40;
25.    private int sampleWidth = 40;
26.    private int hPad = 5;
27.    private int ourWidth;
28.    private TextField text;
29.    private String label = "Find Image";
30.    private Button fileButton;
31.}// End of class ImageEditor
```

AudioClipEditor Class

The AudioClipEditor class is almost identical to the Image Editor class except that it deals with AudioClip objects rather than with images. Also, the AudioClipEditor class uses the image area of the property sheet to display a musical note to designate that the property is a sound as shown in figure 9.5.

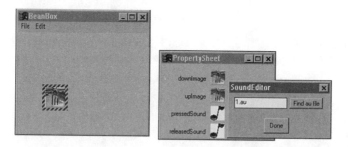

Figure 9.5

Using the PropertySheet image area to designate a specific type of property.

The class is also slightly less complex than the ImageEditor because the only image is a musical note icon, which never changes. The icon is used to help the user of the Bean recognize that the property is a sound.

Because the Bean is very similar to the ImageEditor, please refer to the code on the book's CD-ROM.

PropertyEditorSupport Class

The PropertyEditorSupport class is an implementation of the PropertyEditor interface. Every method in the PropertyEditor interface has been implemented to provide a minimal implementation to use as a basis for simple property editors. PropertyEditorSupport should be used as a base for a property editor to reduce the implementation of of dummy methods that a developer might normally have to implement for simple property edit classes. A property that returns values with the *getTags()* method, for example, will probably not require any other methods to have a functional implemented.

Another excellent use of PropertyEditorSupport can be seen in the section titled, "Displaying Images in the Property Sheet," where there are more methods overridden. There are still, however, fewer method implementations than would normally be required if the PropertyEditor interface was implemented by the example.

PropertyEditorSupport should not be used in every case, however. The more complex a property editor gets, the more methods of the PropertyEditor interface need to be overridden. When complexity drives the count of overridden methods toward 100 percent, the PropertyEditor interface should be implemented directly (as was done with the ImageEditor class). And, if the property editor is also acting as the custom editor component, the PropertyEditor interface must be used because a class can only have one parent class. For a custom editor component, that class must inherit from a component class. For a custom editor component, the base class must be Panel or Canvas with the implementation of the PropertyEditor interface.

IDEs or other programs that introspect on Beans should never assume that property editor classes inherit from the PropertyEditorSupport class. Property editors should only be searched for based on their implementation of the PropertyEditor interface.

Using List Properties

In listing 9.34, the PropertyEditorSupport is very useful because only the *getTags()* method needs to be overridden to return a list that is used to populate the drop-down list menu as shown in figure 9.6.

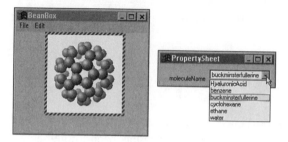

Figure 9.6

Displaying a drop-down list in the property sheet.

Listing 9.34: Class MoleculeNameEditor—getTags() method

```
01.package sun.demo.molecule;
02.
03./**
04. * Special case property editor for molecule names.
05. */
06.
07.public class MoleculeNameEditor
08.        extends java.beans.PropertyEditorSupport {
09.
10.    public String[] getTags() {
11.    String result[] = {
12.        "HyaluronicAcid",
13.        "benzene",
14.        "buckminsterfullerine",
15.        "cyclohexane",
16.        "ethane",
17.        "water"};
18.    return result;
19.    }
20.}
```

The Customizer Interface: An Editor for the Whole Bean

A customizer class provides a complete custom GUI for customizing a target Java Bean. The Customizer interface only consists of three methods, one that sets the customizer to the value of the Bean that is to be edited. The add and remove listeners are used to register the IDE as a listener so that the Customizer can signal that changes to the Bean have been made.

A class implementing Customizer should inherit from the Panel class so that it can be displayed in a dialog that the IDE creates. Also, the customizer must have a null constructor so that the IDE can create the customizer without any other information except the Customizer interface and the Panel base class.

setObject() Method

This method sets the object to be customized. This method should be called only one time, before the Customizer has been added to any parent AWT container. The syntax for this method is as follows:

```
void setObject(Object bean);
```

addPropertyChangeListener() Method

This method registers a listener for the PropertyChange event. The customizer should fire a PropertyChange event whenever it changes the target Bean in a way that might require the displayed properties to be refreshed. The syntax for this method is as follows:

```
void addPropertyChangeListener(PropertyChangeListener listener);
```

removePropertyChangeListener() Method

This method removes a listener so that it no longer receives PropertyChange events. The syntax for this method is as follows:

```
void removePropertyChangeListener(PropertyChangeListener listener);
```

Customizer Interface Example

The OurButton class is a fully functional equivalent of a normal AWT button. This class derives itself from Canvas, where an image of a button is drawn. The class handles events just like a button. It also draws the button in a depressed position when the button is pressed, and draws the button in an up position when released.

Of all the demos that come with the BDK, this example is the most complete in its implementation of a complete component that is also Bean-compatible.

The OurButtonCustomizer Class

The customizer for OurButton is very simplistic. The only thing that the customizer does is allow a label to be set for the button. This example is a little overkill. In fact this operation could have been handled with just the support of the property sheet.

The guts of the code are completely handled in the *handleEvent()* (line 28) method in listing 9.35, where the new value is read from the customizer's text field and copied to the target object (in this case, an instance of OurButton). In addition, the property changed event is fired so that the IDE can propagate the changes.

Listing 9.35: Class OurButtonCustomizer—Example from Sun BDK

```
01.package sun.demo.buttons;
02.
03.import java.awt.*;
04.import java.beans.*;
05.
06.public class OurButtonCustomizer extends Panel implements Customizer {
07.
08.    public OurButtonCustomizer() {
09.      setLayout(null);
10.    }
11.
12.    public void setObject(Object obj) {
13.      target = (OurButton) obj;
14.
15.      Label t1 = new Label("Caption:", Label.RIGHT);
16.      add (t1);
17.      t1.reshape(10, 5, 60, 30);
18.
19.      labelField = new TextField(target.getLabel(), 20);
20.      add(labelField);
21.      labelField.reshape(80, 5, 100, 30);
22.    }
23.
24.    public Dimension preferredSize() {
25.      return new Dimension(200, 40);
26.    }
27.
28.    public boolean handleEvent(Event evt) {
29.      if (evt.id == Event.KEY_RELEASE && evt.target == labelField) {
30.          String txt = labelField.getText();
31.          target.setLabel(txt);
```

```
32.            support.firePropertyChange("", null, null);
33.        }
34.        return (super.handleEvent(evt));
35.    }
36.
37.    //--------------------------------------------------------------
38.    // Since we're the OurButton customer we get to specify its
➥externally
39.    // visible behaviour.  But we instead return "null" indicating that
40.    // the information should be obtained elsewhere.
41.
42.    public PropertyDescriptor[] getTargetPropertyInfo() {
43.     return (null);
44.    }
45.
46.    public EventSetDescriptor[] getTargetEventInfo() {
47.     return (null);
48.    }
49.
50.    public MethodDescriptor[] getTargetMethodInfo() {
51.     return (null);
52.    }
53.
54.    //--------------------------------------------------------------
55.
56.    public void addPropertyChangeListener(PropertyChangeListener l) {
57.      support.addPropertyChangeListener(l);
58.    }
59.
60.    public void removePropertyChangeListener(PropertyChangeListener l) {
61.      support.removePropertyChangeListener(l);
62.    }
63.
64.    private PropertyChangeSupport support = new
➥PropertyChangeSupport(this);
65.
66.    //--------------------------------------------------------------
67.
68.    private OurButton target;
69.    private TextField labelField;
70.}
```

Custom Editors for Text Properties

To some readers, this may at first seem to be a useless idea (surely the IDE's property sheet handles text properties without further help). The fact is, the IDE can handle text properties, but certain tasks may need to be explicitly handled that the property sheet will not be aware of. A text property, for example, can represent an image. The custom property editor, for text selection of an image, can display the corresponding image in the property sheet (an example of this exact situation is covered later in the SoundImageButton).

PropertyEditorManager Class

The PropertyEditorManager class is for use by an IDE or a Bean-aware application such as the BeanBox. The class is used to find property editors associated with Beans. The PropertyEditorManager class is not intended for use by Beans, but is supplied so that a uniform method for looking up property editors can be implemented by using the class.

Reusing Property Editors

Reusing property editors is relatively easy and conserves a lot of time. In addition, improvements made to one property editor will improve the editability of all the Beans that use the same editor. Remember that component editors are written based on the type of parameter that they edit, not any particular Bean. An example of this is the editor for bytes, sun.beans.editors.ByteEditor, which is used for all properties of type byte. You can also reuse the ImageEditor class.

Bean Editor Aesthetics

It is important to remember that Bean editors are for use from within another manufacturer's IDE. Because of this, the developer of a custom editor should attempt to keep within the bounds of normal behavior, look, and feel that the IDE conforms to. If the behavior, look, or feel is different from other editors, the user may be confused about how to use your editor to edit your Bean.

Keep the user in mind when developing editors. Be as conservative in your approach as possible by creating editors that avoid logos and gaudy colors. Keep to black, white, and gray. Only use more colors when you are certain that the user needs something more to differentiate between different types of data. Never change the default background, button colors, or stray from system fonts. Even when using more colors or fonts, be careful about ensuring that colors are properly contrasted to prevent eye-strain.

Avoiding complex editors also reduces the final code size of your packaged Bean. Size is still important, especially if users are downloading from the web. The size of an editor also affects its response time when used in an IDE. Imagine having to wait for an animation every time an editor loaded. The rule of thumb: keep editors simple, small, and purely functional.

Summary

As a Bean developer, it is almost certain that at some time you will design and develop a custom editor for a Java Bean. This chapter supplied the necessary information, but there are many more examples that are supplied in the BDK as well as by the libraries of Beans that come with Bean-aware IDEs.

Like most of the Bean API, custom editors are useful in their own right as well as a starting point for other uses. In addition to their use in IDEs, property editors and customizers can be used in a wide range of applications from debuggers to production applications. The developer needs only imitate some of the actions of an IDE, which is not difficult (look at the source code for the BeanBox application in the BDK for how Sun does it).

Make every effort to stay within the boundaries when creating these editors, as described in this chapter and in the Java Bean API. Straying from the established standards will lead to Beans that may not be editable in some IDEs and that may be difficult to use in others.

The reason that editors and customizers exist is to enable the Bean developer to extend an IDE to make it capable of editing a Bean that has more than the standard set of Java base classes. The developer is not prevented from presenting any type of property or groups of properties from within an IDE environment. Use this to your advantage to create useful and easily understood and *editable* Beans!

CHAPTER 10

Packaging Java Beans

Java Beans are primarily components delivered to other users. For the most part, only Java Beans will be accessed from within a Java Bean-compliant editor, but Java Beans can be used in a program through hand-coding techniques. This chapter begins by covering the features of Java Beans that should be considered prior to their delivery to end users. The steps described should help ensure that your Java Beans will be robust and easy to use.

This chapter concludes with coverage of the JAR files—the primary medium for delivering Java Beans. JAR files are similar to ZIP archive files that contain compressed copies of multiple files in an easily transportable single file. You will learn about the types of data in the file and how to build a JAR file for a Java Bean. You will also learn how to access the JAR file contents when a Java Bean Compliant-editor is not available.

Evaluating Java Beans for Real-World Readiness

The first step toward packaging a Java Bean is to verify that its design is complete, accurate, and ready to be used. To some developers, this has usually just meant that the current version works okay for them; there is, however, a lot more work to do. The fundamental issues of Bean readiness are addressed in a series of questions covered in the following sections. These questions should be used as a checklist to verify that your Bean is ready for packaging.

Understanding the End User

To some developers, this may not seem very important. Besides, the user is always a programmer, right? Well, in fact, the Java Beans technology has opened up a whole new field of design and development that can be accomplished by relatively unsophisticated users. Currently, one Java Beans development tool, AppletAuthor, is based solely on the interaction of Java Beans and some tool-generated code. AppletAuthor from IBM has no way to write Java code, but produces sophisticated applets for distribution on the web. Examples of the type of application that can be built by just connecting a collection of Java Beans together is endless. The only caveat is that the component needs to be robust enough that it can be easily manipulated in an IDE and have an action-oriented interface.

An applet can be built to query an employee database for telephone numbers, for instance, by combining just a few Java Beans in an applet. Imagine an applet that presents a little instructional text, a text field to enter the name to be searched, and a text box. Figure 10.1 shows the Java Beans involved. These Java Beans are covered in greater detail in the bulleted list that follows.

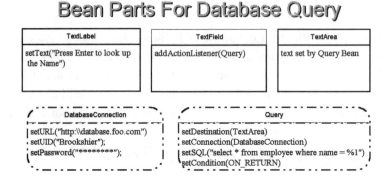

Figure 10.1

Bean components used to perform database query.

♦ **TextLabel:** a standard AWT component, loaded as a Bean. Asks the user to enter a name in the TextField and press the enter key to start the search.

- **TextField:** a standard AWT component, loaded as a Bean. The TextField holds the name of an employee to be searched for.

- **TextArea:** another AWT component, the TextArea returns the results of the query.

- **DatabaseConnection:** this Bean is a custom invisible component built to connect to a JDBC-compatible database server. This component is manipulated in the IDE to set the URL of the database, the ID, and password used to log on. The component has a parameter such as *getCurrentConnection( )* that is passed to the next component (Query) after it is initialized.

- **DatabaseQuery:** the final Bean in this example is an invisible component triggered by the key press events coming from the TextField component. In an IDE, the component is set up with the SQL code to be performed when triggered. After the DatabaseQuery component sees a carriage return, it takes the contents of the TextField, integrates it into the query string, and then using the current setting of the DatabaseConnection Bean it squirts the query to the database server. The Bean waits for the return information and presents it by calling the *setText( )* method of the TextArea component.

The example is fictitious, but very possible. Anybody with access to a database could build the applet in a couple of minutes without ever knowing that they were dealing with Java code.

There are many more existing examples of codeless Java Beans, and many yet to be imagined. The point here is to start by working on how your component could fit into a codeless scenario. If it can fit into this scenario, be aware that your user may not understand a lot of complicated language. Explain your Bean in terms of what it does and not necessarily the details of how it achieves these results.

You should also be aware of when a Bean can only be used in an environment where some Java coding is required. A Bean may have all or part of its API unavailable to the IDE (remember that this is accomplished by marking the methods, events, or properties as hidden in the customized BeanInfo class). A Bean that simulates a neural net, for example, may need a lot of code to set it up and use the results. Even in this case, however, another Bean could be written as a neural net manager and be used to generically manipulate and connect it to other Java Beans in a codeless Bean. The lesson here is that non-Java programmers can use a Bean in a codeless IDE like AppletAuthor.

Providing Configurable Parameters for Java Beans

The parameters of a Java Bean need to be properly formed both as set/get patterns, properly documented in HTML documentation, and if necessary, the BeanInfo class. The get and set methods should be public unless they are available only from a custom editor class, where they may be declared public or protected.

Careful consideration should be made as to whether the parameters need to be exposed. Be careful not to expose access to parameters that the user has no reason to modify such as fields that are only used by the Bean or accessed only by a Customizer class.

Synchronization Issues

One of the many features of Java that is both a boon and a curse to programmers is built-in support for concurrent programming—threads. Threads are great for providing a program with a look of virility by enabling the programmer to add animation and sound, and yet not unduly affecting the main thread of execution. Threads also simplify many tasks that require separate threads, like a web server where multiple tasks are performed concurrently. Despite the benefits, writing software that will behave appropriately in a concurrent environment takes some extra effort. The inherent nature of Java Beans, being components, is that they are only pieces of a larger program. There is no guarantee that the Bean is accessed by only one thread or by many. Because there is no way to predict the environment, the best defense is to design the Bean to run in a multithreaded environment.

As part of Bean planning, a developer should consider the following rules for concurrency patterns:

- ◆ **Rule 1:** use non-mutable data types whenever possible.

- ◆ **Rule 2:** synchronize blocks of code or methods that could be interrupted by another thread before a data change or data read is complete.

- ◆ **Rule 3:** disable events of a component related to changing data. Enable events after changes are made and the component reflects changed data.

- ◆ **Rule 4:** synchronization blocks and synchronized methods should be as short as possible.

Using Non-Mutable Data

Non-mutable types are those that once created, cannot be changed. An example of a non-mutable data type is a String. Once created, the String object cannot be modified. Any class can be made non-mutable by not including any method that changes the state of the Bean and that returns no mutable types that are either non-mutable or copies of internal data. An example of a mutable type is the StringBuffer class. The reasoning behind this rule is that an object that cannot change will not have a synchronization conflict. This is where one thread modifies at the same time another writes. This rule eliminates the need for synchronized methods and code blocks for changes to simple class properties.

In contrast, mutable types can be manipulated after they have been created. This means that information in a mutable object could be modified by different threads causing synchronization problems. A mutable class contains methods to set the internal state of the Bean or returns another mutable object. Another problem with a mutable type is that data in the object could be modified that points back to the originating class. In the case of a Bean, this could be a problem if the references changed affect the size, shape, or color of the Bean. If these properties are not changed in the context of the Bean then there is no way for the Bean to act upon the new changes. Therefore mutable types should be avoided.

A String object, for example, either exists or it does not. There is no such thing as a partially constructed String. Because of this, set and get methods for string properties do not need to be synchronized. Both set and get methods must be synchronized, however, if the property is a StringBuffer. The contents of the StringBuffer can be changed at any time between multiple threads (unless synchronization is enforced in the software).

Synchronizing Reads and Writes

Synchronizing blocks of code and methods prevents other threads from running while data in the current thread is being modified. This is very important when the integrity of the data could be corrupted if another thread accesses the information before the data is completely changed.

An example of code that could cause synch problems is the manipulation of an indexed property in a Bean. Remember that an indexed property is accessed by its index, similar to an array (and probably is an array within the Bean). This example assumes a Bean that shows a list of items, and the indexed property is the list of items to be displayed and selected.

Figure 10.2 shows the Bean represented as the 3D box. Actions are performed on the box as separate threads on the left and on the right of the box. The diagram shows two concurrent threads being performed on the Bean. The loop on the left represents the flow of a *setItem()* call to the Bean. The flow on the right is caused by the user selecting an entry from the graphic representation of the list.

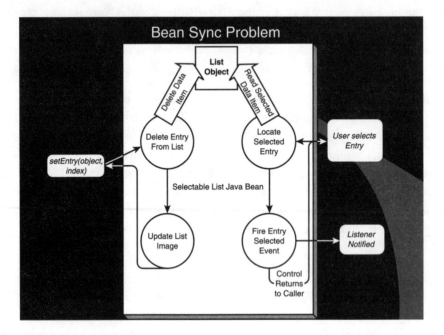

Figure 10.2

Bean sync problem.

The diagram show both threads can access the Bean's internal state at the same time. The end result is that the user may select an item that will either not exist or has changed to a state that was not expected. If the list contained a list of possible actions to be performed, and the user selected an entry that is being deleted, for example, the action is no longer possible. The user may have selected the event just before it was deleted. By beating the deletion thread, the selection thread is capable of getting a copy of the reference and passing it on to the action listener. The action listener is then capable of performing the action, but the context to perform it is no longer possible. Two possibilities exist at this point: Either the action is performed incorrectly, but succeeds despite this; or, the action fails because of related objects being deleted.

A concrete example of an application that could have this problem is an editor where the list stores a record of all open windows. When the user clicks on entries in the list, the selected window is raised to the top of the display. If the user deletes a window, the list will be updated to remove its entry. If, just as the list is updated, the user clicks on the deleted item in the list, the possibility arises that the program will attempt to redisplay the deleted window. One of two things could occur: either a null pointer exception will be generated because the window no longer exists; or the window will be displayed, but the internal state of the program will be unable to delete it a second time. This is because the entry no longer exists to manipulate it further.

Fixing this problem is relatively easy. All that is required is that the synchronized keyword be used on the get and set methods that affect the representation of the list. In addition, if the item is related to events, the processing of events on the component should be suspended and any events in the queue should be flushed if a change is made to the data.

Synchronization is very important. You do not have any guarantee of how a Bean will be accessed or how many threads will attempt to access it at any one time.

Disabling Changing Components

Disabling changing components is similar to using non-mutable data, but the process relates to the visual part of the component and events such as mouse and keyboard events. The previous example of the editor list is a good place to exercise this rule. The graphic representation of the list is also a point of conflict. A user could select an item after the internal state has changed, but before the display has completed its update.

Minimizing Synchronization Time

Minimizing your synchronization time helps to avoid problems where synchronization may be held too long by one thread, preventing other threads from executing. Short synchronization is also important when using the AWT because the user cannot interact with components while a synchronization lock is enforced.

The rule of thumb is to block other threads only while reading or writing mutable properties that are available to other threads and not while performing other processing. The only time a lock is held for processing is when the processing is referencing data that should not change while reading or writing a property. In figure 10.2, for example, you would first disable events to the list component and then place a synchronization block around the change to the list's array. The list's graphic representation can then be changed after which the component's events are enabled. The added benefit to the synchronize and event disable/enable sequence is that the AWT can begin the process of changing the list view before the method returns. If there was a lot of work performed by the set method, other threads can also execute concurrently.

If, after the list entry was modified, the method goes on to sort the list, the synchronize block should include the sort process. The reason is that the data is still changing state. After the sort, the lock should be ended before the visual part of the component is updated.

Concurrency Rules Summary

Concurrency is a fact that all Java Beans must be able to operate within. Java Beans that do not behave appropriately in a multithreaded environment can create hard to debug errors that might make the Bean unusable. The four rules of concurrent programming described in the previous sections must be enforced before a Bean is delivered—preferably designed into the Bean from the beginning. To summarize, the best defense against multiple thread access is to synchronize any part of a method that changes the internal state of a Bean and to synchronize the reading of a parameter that might be interrupted by a change. Whenever possible, avoid synchronization by using non-mutable objects that cannot be modified as they are read. Also, synchronization locks should be kept as short as possible and/or be implemented by disabling events and actions related to the changing state.

The rules given here should be sufficient for most components. Many more rules and patterns of programming may be necessary for very complex and interrelated components. The book *Concurrent Programming in Java*, by Doug Lea, is a good source of information concerning Java and multithreaded applications.

Implementing Complete and Balanced Java Bean Design Signatures

Java Bean Design Signatures are key to a Bean being recognized and used properly by an IDE. For many signatures, several pieces are necessary. Of particular importance is the balancing and completeness of these signatures. For lack of a better word, balancing refers to the existence of both halves of a particular design signature that is required to exist in order for the Introspector class to recognize the signature. If a Bean has a set method for a parameter such as *setColor()*, for example, the Bean should also have a corresponding *getColor()* method. The same is true for the event source pattern where there needs to be an *addEventListener() and removeEventListener()* method.

Be certain that all design signatures that a Bean supports are recognizable by an IDE either through the Introspector or through a custom BeanInfo object. Typos in names or improperly formed patterns can prevent an IDE from making decisions about the use of methods and events.

Evaluating Java Beans for Usability

A key question that should be asked is whether users can actually use the Bean. Tests should be performed to ensure that others can successfully understand and use the Bean in an application. It is often insufficient to have the programmer of the Bean test his own work; a second- or third-party tester is a more accurate measurement of usability.

Usability should be measured from all aspects of the Bean. The documentation should be understandable and complete as well as accurate. The BeanInfo should be validated in an IDE to prove that a developer can understand the descriptions and uses of methods, events, and properties.

In addition to the usability by a developer, the Bean should also be looked at from the perspective of end users that use an application built using the Bean. Usability by end users also includes descriptive warning messages and appropriate look and field issues.

Beans Should Be AWT Friendly

Being AWT friendly is a primary feature of visible components. The Bean should properly respond to containers into which it is placed. The most important behavior is the Bean's response to resize and paint events. The parent container should be notified that a resize has taken place if the Bean is the source of the resize. If the container is not notified, other components may be overlapped. Also, if something occurs that could change the size, the size should change. A label button, for instance, should reset its minimum size to a height and width at least equal to the rectangle of the label as described by its metric. Another example is an image button Bean that needs to be as big as its image.

Chapter 11, "Java Bean Internationalization" and Chapter 9, "Building Custom Component Editors for Java Beans" have examples of AWT friendly Java Beans.

Evaluating Bean Error Control

The plethora of possible exceptions that can be thrown by Java Beans can be quite large. A Bean should avoid throwing any exception that could halt or cripple a running application. The Bean should trap expected exceptions and either deal with them or pop up a message box that gives a detailed explanation of the problem.

Special care should be taken with any code that uses parameters set from an application program or through an IDE. When dealing with such external input, the Bean developer should first prevent data that could compromise the integrity of the Bean. This includes preventing settings from causing executions such as divide by zero or null pointer exceptions. The user should be forced to supply a valid parameter, otherwise the current or default setting should be substituted.

Evaluating Bean Serialization

Most Java Beans have a persistent state because they are configured through editors that directly access parameter methods. This primarily means that code that uses a Bean will probably not access data that makes up the state of a Bean. Because of this, the developer should verify that the persistent state of the Bean is stored and retrieved correctly. Problems can occur if too much or too little is stored in the persistent data store.

There are also design considerations about versions of serialized states with which to deal. If you are delivering a second version of a Bean, for example, you must consider whether the serialized state is compatible with an older Bean. Or is the new Bean compatible with older persistent states created with older versions of Java Beans? The rule should be that the newer Bean should, as a minimum, be able to read an older serialization file. The reason for this is because a user has already created a specific persistent state for the Java Beans currently in use. If you make the persistent state incompatible, the user is forced to redesign the application that uses your Bean. If you cannot make compatible serialization possible within the Bean, include a utility that will read old serializations and convert them to those compatible to the new version.

Validating the BeanInfo Class

If a BeanInfo class is supplied, it should probably define all the parameters, event sets, and methods of the Java Bean. The more information supplied in the BeanInfo class, the more information about a Bean can be represented in an IDE. Remember that short descriptions of parameters and methods are stored in the BeanInfo object so that they can be used to make an IDE's presentation clear. Also, the BeanInfo class holds the icon that an IDE uses in its palette of components. This chapter contains a descriptive example of how to design a complete BeanInfo object.

Internationalization Considerations

As is discussed in Chapter 11, Java Beans should support internationalization. When packaging Java Beans, there are several points where international support can be added. Primarily the BeanInfo can be customized to present different languages during the Bean's design presentation in the property sheet, Customizer, and PropertyEditor. In addition, the Bean itself should be written so that text, numbers, dates, and sometimes images and audio clips can be changed to meet a specific locale. Remember that once a Bean has been designed to support two locals, the Bean can add support for new locales easily.

If you do support additional languages, every aspect of the deliverable Bean should have versions written for each locale. If your Bean supports French and English, for example, the HTML help files delivered with your Bean should also have a French and English version.

Custom Component Editor Associations

Any parameter that is not a Java primitive type or does not have an editor specified by a Java Bean Editor IDE should have a specific custom editor associated with it. This means that there must be a class that will display an editor in a Frame object whenever the user desires a change to the particular component. Also, the parameter will need an entry in the BeanInfo class to associate the parameter to its editor.

Providing Bean Support Files

Support files for Java Beans can be almost anything from sounds, images, or custom data to parameter and internationalization support files. Each file needs to be properly documented with examples so that there can be little question about its format and layout.

Providing Sample Configurations of Java Beans

A good form of documentation is a set of examples of configured Java Beans. The examples should be as complete as possible and should be related to real-world use of the Bean. These examples should be stored in a directory of the JAR file called EXAMPLE_SER. JAR files are covered extensively in the latter half of this chapter.

Providing Sample Applications of Java Beans

As far as documentation goes, the best documentation is a complete example that uses the Bean. There should be as many examples as is reasonable to show how to use the Bean. The examples should cover the range from a Bean's most simplified use to the more complex usage in a complex situation. Each example should be delivered in its own JAR file.

Providing Bean Documentation

Bean documentation comes in three forms:

- messages displayed by a Bean
- BeanInfo
- HTML documents that describe how to configure and use the Bean

The better a Bean is documented, the easier it will be understood and used.

The error and status messages of a Bean are primarily intended for consumption by the end user who sees the messages from the context of a running application. The messages may also be displayed in response to a programmer configuring a Bean from within an IDE. In either case, the messages should be as clear and descriptive as possible. If the message relates to an error, the context of the error conditions should be included. If a Bean is attempting to load a sound file and it fails, for example, the message should state that an error was made loading a sound file and it should also include the full path and name that was attempted.

The BeanInfo object is the second level of documentation. An IDE not only uses the BeanInfo for manipulating Bean, but also to present the view of the Bean to the user.

The third level of documentation is the HTML documentation. This can come in two types. The first type of HTML document is used by a programmer to configure and use Java Beans. The second type of HTML documentation is a user-oriented document that informs a user on how the Bean functions in a running application. A developer using your Bean in his application can add this documentation to the final product's documentation delivered to the end user.

The following sections explain the types of information that should be in your documentation.

set/get Property Methods

Properties of Java Beans fall into three categories that should be explicitly described in your documentation. These categories are as follows:

- **Setup:** parameters set from an IDE only or by a developer using the Bean without an IDE. This type of parameter is usually only for setup of a Bean. After the setup is complete, the set/get methods are rarely called. Examples of setup parameters are labels on buttons, images, sounds, size, and color information.

- **Runtime:** parameters used to set and get the state of a Bean. These state type parameters are integral to something that the Bean does. Examples of runtime parameters are current selections from list components, text from text fields and text areas, button states, and so on.

- **Setup/Runtime:** some parameters are used both at development time and at runtime. A list Bean, for example, has a *getCurrentSelection()* method. The CurrentSelection could be set initially. This type of parameter should always be visible in an IDE.

Default Property

The default property is found by calling the *getDefaultPropertyIndex()* method of the Bean's BeanInfo and using the index returned to find the specific property in the array of properties returned from the BeanInfo's *getProperyDescriptors()* method. The default property is the most likely modified property when setting up a Bean within an IDE. Examples of default properties are labels, colors, and images.

Supported Events

Events are very important to most Java Beans. Events are usually how a Bean interacts with other components in a program. List the events that the Bean is a source for and the events that the bean can be a listener for.

Default Event

The default event is found by calling the *getDefaultEventIndex()* method of the Bean's BeanInfo and using the index returned to find the specific property in the array of properties returned from the BeanInfo's *getEventSetDescriptors()* method. The default event is the event most likely used to connect to other components. Examples of a default events are property changes, mouse events, and window events. The following should be documented for each event set:

- ◆ **Event Set Name:** the programmatic name of the event set

- ◆ **Event Conditions:** the conditions that will cause events to be generated

- ◆ **Listener Interface Type:** the Class for the listener interface

- ◆ **Listener Method Descriptors:** an array of MethodDescriptor objects describing each of the event handling methods in the target listener

- ◆ **Add Listener Method:** the method on the event source that can be used to register an event listener object. This should also include any exceptions thrown by the method if the event set is unicast.

- ◆ **Remove Listener Method:** the method on the event source that can be used to deregister an event listener object

- ◆ **Listener Type:** the Class object for the target interface that will get invoked when the event is fired

- ◆ **Unicast/Multicast Type:** description of the event as multicast or unicast

- ◆ **In Default Event Set:** description of an event set as being in the "default" set or not

- ◆ **Concurrency:** concurrency includes the creation of threads, synchronization blocking, waits, and notifies. With events, this includes information about whether the event is generated from within a thread owned by the component. This information is very important for developers to know during debugging.

Supported Methods

These are the methods returned by the *getMethodDescriptors()* method of the Bean's BeanInfo. These are the public methods of the Bean not covered by the properties or by the event set descriptors.

The documentation for methods should include the following:

- ◆ **Processing:** the processing that a method performs

- ◆ **Concurrency:** concurrency includes the creation of threads, synchronization blocking, waits, and notifies. This information is very important for developers to know during debugging.

- ◆ **Parameters:** the type and description of parameters used to call the method

- ◆ **Returns:** the type and information returned from a method call. This should include the reason and values returned for errors as well as normal return values.

- ◆ **Exceptions Thrown:** the type and reasons for exceptions generated by a method

- ◆ **Related Information:** this is any other information that a developer needs to understand about a method. Such information includes related functions, patterns, or reference material.

Java Bean Naming Conventions

Naming is a very important subject for Java Beans. As has already been covered in this book, names are an integral part of the signature matching logic used to examine and manipulate Java Beans. The naming conventions for Bean packages, base classes, BeanInfo classes, and custom editor classes are covered in the following sections.

Naming Packages

The primary method to prevent name collisions is through the grouping of classes into packages. Developers should always use packages when developing Java Beans. Java Bean components are often small and usually have a specific function or use. Java Beans, for example, can be buttons, sliders, data viewers, text containers, data base connections, and others. With very specific tasks, Java Beans are likely to be called similar names by developers. It is very possible that name collisions could occur among different packages of components. It is very likely that if two manufacturers create round buttons, for example, that the class names will be RoundButton. If each manufacturer places its Bean in a package that includes the manufacturer's domain name and the name of the component, the names will not collide. With two separate packages, both RoundButton Java Beans can be added to a developer's IDE and used without problems in the same application. Having access to both Java Beans can be very important if the RoundButton Bean class is very different between manufacturers.

A Java Bean is made up of a minimum of the one Bean class file, but can consist of several files. These files can include the BeanInfo, custom editors, data files, and documentation. It is recommended, therefore, that the package name also include the name of the Bean. This way the directory structure enforced by the package will contain all the related classes for the Bean as well as serve as a location for storing related data files. If desired, additional directories can be used to store classes of data used by a Bean.

Naming Bean Classes

The class name of your Bean is very important. The name should convey what the Bean is. Simply calling a Bean class "Button" is less meaningful than something more expressive that clearly defines that the class is a component and that it is a button and it is round. The more expressive the name, the better. Be careful to not overdo it, however. A name such as "RoundButtonWithHappyFaceAndSqueaksWhenPressed" might be overdoing it. "ImageSoundButton" might be a better choice.

Naming BeanInfo Classes

The name of the class that is your BeanInfo should be the name of your class plus the string "BeanInfo" appended to it. If the class was named "RoundButton," for example, the BeanInfo class should be named "RoundButtonBeanInfo." This naming convention is required by the Introspector class when *getBeanInfo()* is called for a Bean class. If class is improperly named, the BeanInfo will not be found and the default introspection will be used instead. Without access to the BeanInfo, the IDE will be unable to present information explicitly provided by one.

Naming Custom Editor Classes

A clear convention exists for naming custom editor classes for components in Java Beans. The name of a custom editor class should be the name of the property the editor is for, followed by the word "Editor." If the custom editor is for the whole Bean, append "Editor" to the name of the Bean's class. A custom editor for the Color class, for example, would be called ColorEditor. The name is used by the IDE to locate the class for the property. This helps to avoid setting a custom editor in a BeanInfo class.

JAR Files

JAR files are the primary method for delivering Java Beans. A JAR file should contain one Bean, or a set of closely related Java Beans, and the support files and classes.

The command to create JAR files and to extract information from them is simple to understand. It is used similarly to other archive tools such as those from PKWARE, with the exception that it supports fewer options and has an optional specification for a manifest template. The command is specified as follows:

```
jar [ctxvfm] [jar-file] [manifest-file] files ...
```

Option flags are as follows:

Flag	Function
c	Create a new archive
t	List table of contents for archive
x	Extract named (or all) files from archive
v	Generate verbose output on standard error
f	Specify JAR file name
m	Use manifest template file

If any file is a directory, it is automatically processed recursively. Recursive reading is very useful because packages are stored in directories that have the same name as the package name. All files in a package can be added to a JAR file by specifying the root of the package directory.

The package directory structure is very important for locating classes too. The class loader, when searching a JAR file, will use the directory structure to locate classes in the JAR file exactly like it would on a hard disk. It is very important that when specifying files for inclusion in a JAR file, that you do specify packages by their root directory so that the class loader will be able to locate your classes. If you had a class file that was part of a package called "my.tools," for example, the JAR command "jar cf myTools.jar my" would read and store files into the archive properly.

 Note

> As of the beta-2 version of the JAR specification, a JAR file is not readable by a standard ZIP utility. When files are extracted via a tool such as Unzip from PKWARE, the resulting files are empty. To extract files from JAR files, use the JAR command (for example, JAR xf <jarfile>).

Understanding JAR Files

To understand how to use the JAR file, start with a simple JAR file. The Bean that you will use for the first example is the RoundButton Bean. To deliver the RoundButton Bean to a customer, you need only the RoundButton.class file. There is no need to have a serialized version of the Bean because this Bean is simple enough to be created from its default class settings. Figure 10.3 illustrates the JAR file for the RoundButton Bean.

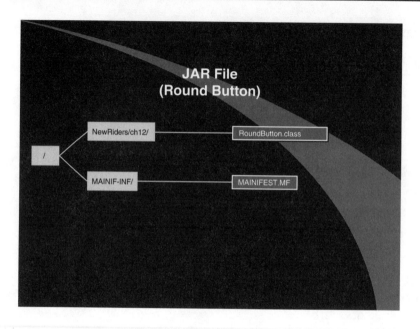

Figure 10.3

JAR files for the RoundButton Bean example.

The files required for the SoundImageButton are much more complex. As can be seen in figure 10.4 there are many more files involved including images and sounds.

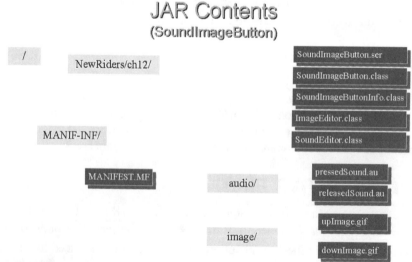

Figure 10.4

JAR files for the SoundImageButton Bean example.

Examining JAR File Contents

Many times a JAR file will need to be examined to determine its contents or to create an inventory of contents for documentation. The process is very simple, requiring only the following command:

```
jar tf <JAR File>
```

The contents of the JAR file in figure 10.3, for example, can be listed with the following command:

```
jar tf RoundButton.jar
```

The output for the preceding command is shown in the following lines of code:

```
META-INF/MANIFEST.MF
NewRiders/ch12/RoundButton.java
NewRiders/ch12/RoundButton.class
```

Package java.util.zip

The java.util.zip package holds all the classes used to create and access JAR files. The Checksum interface is the only interface for this package. java.util.zip consists of the following classes:

- **Adler32:** used to calculate an Adler 32 bit checksum

- **CRC32:** used to calculate an CRC 32 bit checksum

- **CheckedInputStream:** input stream that calculates a checksum

- **CheckedOutputStream:** output stream that calculates a checksum

- **Deflater:** compression utility

- **DeflaterOutputStream:** uses a Deflater compression tool to deflate data in a stream

- **GZIPInputStream:** uses GZIP format to decompress data in a stream

- **GZIPOutputStream:** uses GZIP format to compress data in a stream

- **Inflater:** tool to decompress data that was compressed with the Deflater class

- **InflaterInputStream:** uses Inflater class to decompress data in a stream

- **ZipEntry:** entry in a zip file

- **ZipFile:** zip file read/write utility class

- **ZipInputStream:** used to read a zip file

- **ZipOutputStream:** used to write a zip file

This package also contains the following exceptions:

- **DataFormatException**

- **ZipException**

JAR Manifest Files

The manifest file is the standard method for cataloging JAR file contents. The manifest file indicates which of the potential Java Beans in the JAR archive are actual Beans as well as signature and checksum information. If there is no manifest file, the IDE may not be able to properly locate Java Beans. Also, there will be no checksum to compare any of the JAR contents to (possibly stopping the read process entirely).

The name of the manifest file in the JAR is META-INF/MANIFEST.MF. This naming is automatic if you use the JAR tool. The JAR tool automatically builds the manifest file for you based on the files that are added. Optionally, a manifest template is specified for specific information to be associated with the JAR contents. The template file closely follows the format of the actual manifest file, the only difference is that the template file does not contain checksum information.

Marking Java Beans in a Manifest Template File

To designate a Bean or a serialized Bean as an actual Bean, the key "Java-Bean: True" must follow the name of the class or serial file. The following lines of code show an example manifest template of how the RoundButton Bean class would be designated as a Java Bean:

```
Name: newRidersBeans/RoundButtonBean.class
Java-Bean: True
```

These two lines of code show the contents of the manifest file that gets written for the template in the final manifest file for RoundButton Bean class as follows:

```
Manifest-Version: 1.0
Name: RoundButtonBean.class
Java-Bean: True
Hash-Algorithms: MD5 SHA
MD5-Hash: S2+dpTzNIk/xn7Q5TqzPxw==
SHA-Hash: E+XYVoHTwz5YR71KK8FKjljWB6k=
Name: RoundButtonBean.class
Hash-Algorithms: MD5 SHA
MD5-Hash: S2+dpTzNIk/xn7Q5TqzPxw==
SHA-Hash: E+XYVoHTwz5YR71KK8FKjljWB6k=
```

Notice that there are two entries for the RoundButtonBean.class. The first version has the
"Java-Bean: True" entry, and the second does not. The reason for this is that the JAR
program first matches a file to an entry in the manifest template and then adds other files
to the manifest. Why it does this is not clear, and may in fact be a bug in the early implementations of the JAR tool. According to the manifest documentation from JavaSoft,
when duplicate entries do occur, only the first is recognized. In the preceding listing,
therefore, only the first entry, which thankfully specifies that the class is a Bean, will be
used.

HTML Documentation

HTML documentation is stored in the JAR file as *<locale>/<bean-name>.html*. If there
is only one locale, or an additional default locale the file would be named *<bean-
name>.html*. The default documentation for the RoundButtonBean would be
RoundButtonBean.html. (If the documentation is only available for a single locale, the
initial *<locale>/* may be omitted.)

Serialized Prototypes

If the Bean supports serialization, a serialized prototype of a Bean is required to initialize
the Bean. Serialization files have names ending in ".ser." newRidersBeans/
SoundImageButton.ser, for example, would hold the default serialization of the
SoundImageButton Bean.

Resource Files in JAR Files

Another part of a Bean's JAR file may also include resources and resource bundle files.
These files may be sounds, images, and any other data that a Bean may need to access. A
Bean that plays a sound when pressed, for example, may be delivered with several sound
files to be selected from (see the example in Chapter 9 "Building Custom Component
Editors for Java Beans" for a complete example on how resources are loaded).

Note

> Don't worry about the size of a Bean JAR file. Only the Bean class and its serialized persistent state will be included in a user's application. In Chapter 9, "Building Custom Component Editors for Java Beans" for example, the SoundImageButton had a large JAR file with many images, sounds, and several custom component editor classes. When added to an application, the Bean only has two images (pressed and released) and one sound that are part of the serialized state of the Bean.

Bean JAR Files and the IDE

Now that a JAR file has been created, the JAR will have to be installed into an IDE environment. An IDE will need to do several things to process the JAR in order to install the Bean successfully into the IDE's palette of components. There are also issues that developers need to understand about the process and the end results.

The first thing that an IDE will probably do is extract all the files from the JAR into a specific directory. The directory should be in the CLASSPATH. Also, because JAR files are extracted this way, the manifest file will end up in the same directory and file name as other manifest files. The manifest file will also be read directly from the JAR file or extracted and copied to a file that is the same name as the JAR file. Additionally, the contents of the manifest will be added to the system manifest for the IDE. The information in the manifest will be used to validate the contents by comparing the checksums in the file to the calculated checksums of the files pulled from the JAR.

The scenario above is only one possibility, however. An IDE may not extract any files to local storage, but only read the file. There is some overhead to reading a list of JAR files every time the IDE initializes. However this does allow the IDE to work in a web browser across the Internet.

The BeanBox tool included in the BDK extracts JAR files into a directory called unjar. The manifest from each JAR is stored here by the same name as the JAR file from which they were extracted. Also, each JAR's manifest is appended to the MANIFEST file, also stored in the unjar directory.

The class files, including custom editor classes and BeanInfo for each Bean, are stored in directories made up from the package names of the components. Any support files such as data, images, or sounds are also saved in these directories or in sub-directories.

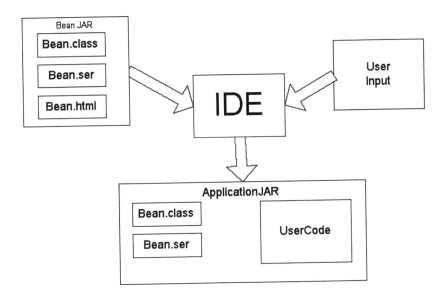

Figure 10.5

Bean components and the IDE.

Using JAR Files without an IDE

One possibility that must be considered is that the user may use your Java Bean component in a hand-coded applet or application. This will remain especially true for a couple of years, because Java Beans are quite new and all IDE's may not currently support Bean integration.

The most that can be done is to document how to configure a Bean without a Customizer or PropertyEditor. If the user does not have a Bean-aware IDE then there is no way for the user to configure the Bean. Another alternative is to provide a utility that presents the Customizer and a simple property sheet so that the Bean can be configured and a serialized copy of the customized Bean can be generated.

Summary

This chapter covered the information that should be considered before a Java Bean is packaged and delivered to users. You have also learned about naming issues and documentation. In addition, you should now be familiar with how to use the jar command to create JAR files so that Java Beans can be delivered in a manner expected by most IDEs.

The information in this chapter is the final step for Bean developers. You should now be able to create and deliver components that can be used in a Java Bean-aware IDE.

One last comment of advice that all developers should heed: Test until you are certain that the component is ready. Testing is the crux of most development; for components, however, testing is very important. Because Java Beans are used in other programs, they should be free of bugs and be well documented.

Creating Java Beans is very rewarding. The component that you create may be used in thousands of programs, and those programs could be used by thousands of end users. With the rewards also comes the responsibility that the component you create will not be the source of bugs or a confused user.

Java Bean Internationalization

Not writing an international Bean any time soon? That's okay, the information in this chapter and its related API in the appendix is useful for tasks other than internationalization. This chapter covers the tools in Java for formatting text, parsing, and manipulating times and dates.

In general, the Internationalization API is a very good package of text manipulation and formatting tools. Even if there is no intention to create an international Bean or application, these classes and interfaces should be used to reduce the amount of formatting that would have to be developed without them.

The "World" Wide Web

The Internet makes the world smaller every day. People and companies are a click away. There is no longer a need to update your passport to meet new people in far away lands. The same is true for commerce. Now it is possible to shop for products from all over the world.

All you need is a credit card or an account with the new Internet banks that are appearing on the web. Unfortunately, the world does not speak one language yet. If you order a bike from France with your credit card, the bicycle will be delivered to your home. The bike's assembly instructions might be written in ten foreign languages including English, so there is no problem assembling the bike.

The same is not always true for software purchased from other countries. If you purchase a spreadsheet program from France, the program and manuals might be written only in French.

Beans and International Retail

Companies all over the world are moving toward selling their software over the Internet. Instead of buying software at a retailer such as CompUSA or Fry's Electronics, you can now purchase it from the web. Instead of a French bicycle, you could order a 3D-rotating button Java Bean from a software company in France. With the software component from France, however, the instructions, the help screens, and all the dialog boxes for the Bean's IDE view would be written in French. Most American programmers—at least those who can't read French—would be unable to use this 3D-rotating button Java Bean from France.

Java Beans have two areas where language becomes a problem. The first is the Bean's representation in a client program. This includes label text, dates, and times that populate panels or are used to display status or help to a user. The second area of concern is the Bean's representation in an IDE. The IDE is like any other program and is sometimes written to run in other countries and display its information in differing languages. An IDE running in France will use French. This means that your Bean's representation should switch to French when running in a French IDE.

Because most of the readers of this book do not speak French, imagine an IDE running in an English-speaking country (United Kingdom, for example). Although the "English" language is used, the language differs somewhat from that used in the United States. Many words are spelled differently in United Kingdom than they are in the United States. A button Bean written in the U.S., for example, would have a "Color" setting. In most countries where the Queen's English is spoken, the spelling would need to be "Colour."

Java's capacity for switching languages is made possible through the Internationalization API. The API is made up of several classes scattered in the packages that make up the core Java classes. The Internationalization API was added to the Java specification as of version 1.1. This API does not translate between different languages, but switching between them is very easy.

It should be general practice to build Beans that access all data used for presentation through the Internationalization API. Adding the extra code is not too difficult and eliminates any rewriting later as the Bean is deployed to different countries. Creating a Bean's user interface so that it can be laid out in various languages and countries is a little harder to do, but should be done to prevent hard-to-solve layout problems later. The benefit is enormous for software that is to be sold in other countries. The only added expense for each country is the translation and testing required after substituting existing text.

This chapter reviews the Internationalization API and how to use it to create international Beans. The Internationalization API does not completely automate everything required. It is, after all, only a set of classes that help make the job easier. You will learn how to integrate the API features into Beans so that the process is understood.

The first step toward internationalizing Beans is to grasp the problems that multiple languages create. These problems involve the user interface, language management, presentation, and font management.

Multi-Lingual User Interfaces

The problems that affect the user interface are the most daunting for multi-language programs. Consider the problem of word length for a moment.

Figure 11.1 shows a very simple dialog box with a short message and a Done button. This dialog box looks fine in English. Compare that to the same dialog box written in Pig Latin. Because each word has two extra characters, the text of the message is truncated and cannot be completely read. The Done button is completely unreadable because the text was centered, causing the word to be cut off at the beginning and end.

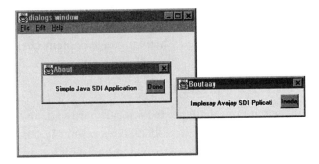

Figure 11.1

Two About boxes—one written in English, the other written in Pig Latin.

The section titled "Making International Text Fit" at the end of this chapter introduces an internationalized label and internationalized text button. These internationalized components can be used to solve the problems previously mentioned. Figure 11.2 shows the same dialog boxes, except they are built with internationalized Bean components.

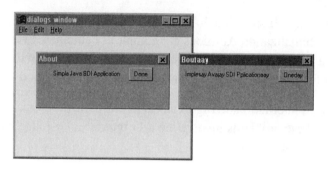

Figure 11.2

Properly formatted About box translated into Pig Latin. Text and button resize themselves to fit international text.

Language Management

Language management is also a big headache for the designer of multilingual systems. When dealing with international programs, the locale-sensitive data needs to be easily accessible and easily modified within the proper context. Problems with incorrect translations can easily occur as new features are added or new languages are supported. Although the Java Internationalization API does not eliminate these problems, it does enable the programmer to manage the differing resources separately from the software, eliminating the need to recompile classes when language content changes.

Locale/Platform Management

In addition to the management of language, the various hardware and operating system platforms also differ. The platform-specific differences primarily deal with keyboard mapping. These keyboard mappings can also change based on locale. A Microsoft Windows key mapping, for example, will be different in the United States than it will be in Japan. Japanese characters are formed using combinations of keys, so there will be a larger valid character set.

In Java, all characters coming from the keyboard have already been converted from the keyboard ASCII to Unicode. So a character on a Japanese keyboard will automatically be converted to its proper Unicode equivalent.

But how would Java know that the keyboard was generating Japanese? When the Java initializes the input system it reads the font.properties file for the locale. To set the default locale in the program to Japanese use the following line of code (Note: you won't see Japanese characters unless you are running a Japanese-enabled PC):

```
Locale.setDefault(Locale.JAPANESE);
```

In the U.S., the default would be the font.properties file (file is located in the Java lib directory). In Japan the properties file loaded would be based on the Japanese default locale, which is "ja." The file fonts.properties.ja would be loaded. At the end of the font properties file for Japanese, the last line designates the correct language character set to use:

```
# charset for text input
#
inputtextcharset=SHIFTJIS_CHARSET
```

For the U.S., the default character set is standard ANSI:

```
# charset for text input
#
inputtextcharset=ANSI_CHARSET
```

Font Management

Another of the very nasty problems involved with different languages is special characters and fonts. Decoding the keyboard, as we've seen, is quite easy; displaying the results is a different problem. Chinese, for example, has no equivalent to the letters that are used in English. Other languages such as Spanish have mostly the same characters, with a few special ones such as the character ñ.

Java, from its very first release, used the Unicode specification to define its character set. Both the String and BufferedString classes use Unicode characters. Fonts that support the Unicode character set can be used to print Unicode-encoded characters. This means that as long as a character to be printed is equal to its Unicode equivalent, the correct character will be printed. In the section titled "International Fonts" later in this chapter, we will cover the basic issues that must be resolved to acquire and use the correct fonts for the specific languages.

MultiLingual Presentation

One of the difficulties in international programs is that certain patterns used to build compound strings become very difficult. In Java, for example, a string that is a combination of strings would be written like the code in listing 11.1:

Listing 11.1: A String in U.S.-style English

```
String fruitColor = "red";
String fruit = "apple";
String displayThis = "The color of the " + fruit + " is " + fruitColor +".";
```

This preceding code is fine for English in the United States, but it needs to be different in the United Kingdom. Listing 11.2 shows the difference.

Listing 11.2: A String in the Queen's English

```
String fruitColor = "red";
String fruit = "apple";
String displayThis = "The colour of the " + fruit + " is " + fruitColor
  +".";
```

An English speaker in the United States wrote the code above, so the variable fruitColor is still spelled in its U.S. form. The printed text includes the word "colour," which is used by English speakers in the U.K.

When writing in some languages, not only do words change, but so does the positioning of the words in a sentence. Many languages reverse the order in which the sentence is presented. Think about the way that a foreign speaker, new to the English language, would say the same sentence. The words would be the same, but the order could be different. Translating only the position of words, for example, the code may need to read like listing 11.3:

Listing 11.3: English sentence reformatted by a foreign speaker

```
String fruitColor = "red";
String fruit = "apple";
String displayThis = fruitColor + "is the color of the " + fruit + ".";
```

Such differences between English and other languages are quite prevalent. In fact, it is this ordering of words within sentences that makes translations between languages very difficult. The positioning of accent marks, subjects, and connecting words may also be completely different between languages. In the case of languages such as Chinese and Japanese, groups of ideograms may be used to either represent one language concept, or a single character may represent several at one time.

Presentation of complex sentences is discussed in the section titled "Formatting Messages" later in this chapter.

The Internationalization API

To support the internationalization of Java software, a collection of classes was added to the standard JDK package. A few additions were also made to the original 1.02 classes to support their interaction with the Internationalization API. The Internationalization API can be broken into the following four types of functionality:

◆ **Locale information:** where the program is running and in what language

◆ **Font information and support:** used to load and display fonts for different languages

◆ **Text iteraters:** used to traverse text containers

◆ **Time and date interfaces and containers:** used to represent the time and date of particular locals

In Java, several classes are used to support internationalization. Most of these are covered in the following sections, but please refer to Chapter 17 for a complete reference of the entire Java Internationalization API. The Internationalization API consists of the classes described by topic in the following sections.

Locale Class

The Locale class represents the locale—where the code is being used. Locale is defined to the language, country, and variants (see table 11.1 for a list of the currently supported locals). The Locale class is the basis for most internationalization tasks because it contains a static reference that other classes can use to determine the correct presentation for the default locale. New Locale objects can also be created and passed into classes that support internationalization so that a multilingual or multi-local application can also be created.

Component Class

The Component class, though not an explicit part of internationalization, contains methods to get/set the locale and get/set the font.

Font Class

By using the Font class and font members of AWT classes, components can be changed to load either default system/locale fonts or the font can be loaded to meet specific language needs. Bean authors should be aware that the font of a component could be changed at any time by the end user. It is the Bean programmer's responsibility to ensure that the Bean is resized properly so that text is not occluded if a larger font is used. Resizing can also happen even if the point size does not change. A font may have a different descent or ascent than a font currently in use, for example.

FontMetrics Class

A font metric is the description of the font height, width, ascent, and descent. The FontMetrics class also has utility methods for determining these characteristics for particular strings of characters. Of all the classes that make up the Internationalization API, the FontMetrics class is the most important. This class is used to determine the true area that a piece of text will occupy. Such information is used in buttons, labels, and other components that have a text representation.

CharacterIterator Interface

The CharacterIterator interface is used to give a class acting as a text container a standard method for iterating through text. The locale or internationalization characteristics are not readily apparent in this interface. Internationalization, when iterating through text, is important when considering word, sentence, and other text boundaries. In many languages, for example, text reads right to left rather than left to right as it does in English. In addition, punctuation is used differently in various languages. Such punctuation will determine whether a word, phrase, sentence, or paragraph is searched, selected, or presented.

By using this interface, the developer can create a locale-sensitive iteration to fulfill specific tasks, such as text selection or pattern searching.

StringCharacterIterator Class

The StringCharacterIterator class implements the CharacterIterator interface for a string. This class is the most basic type of text iterator because it is at the smallest granularity of the character. A class reading text would use this class to iterate through the text to find the next higher level of interest like words or sentences.

Collation Abstract Base Class

The Collation class is an abstract class used as a base to create a collation or comparitor. A comparitor is used during the sorting of characters to determine if a character is greater or less than another character. Simply comparing the numeric value of ASCI values usually works well for sorting standard English. Unfortunately, different Unicode character sets are not organized in a way that lends itself to sorting numerically.

Collation is important to sorting and ordering. Sorting and ordering are very different between character sets and languages. The main language differences arise from different locations of characters in the character set. For standard English, the positions in the character set correspond to the correct ordering, but other languages do not map to the same sequence or may be different based on accents or capitalization. There are different forms of sort within a language. Text containing numbers, for instance, can be treated as their location in the character set or by the numeric value and whether the calculation of the value is done left to right or right to left.

CollatedString Class

The CollatedString class is used to collate strings. With this class, strings can be compared and localized variations of hash keys can be created to represent the order of an international string. Hash keys are used to reduce the time to collate by converting text to an equivalent positional number.

CollationElementIterator Class

The CollationElementIterator is used to retrieve keys that make up words. In standard English, the keys are the letters, in other languages the keys may be more complex, possibly consisting of multiple characters that represent special symbols or accented characters. Iterating through German, for example, "äb" would return three keys: a, e, and b. In some languages, adjacent characters in words may even be considered as single keys. Iterating through the Spanish text "cha," for example, would return two keys: ch and a.

The CollationElementIterator class uses a TableCollation object to do the actual map of text to keys. There should be no need to create localized versions of this class. The correct, localized TableCollation does need to be provided for this class to function properly.

SortKey Class

The SortKey class represents the order of a string. The Collation class generates SortKey objects for strings. Sort keys are used to make comparing strings faster when done multiple times. Therefore, instead of using a collator to build a comparison between two strings, the strings' collation keys are first found and then the keys are compared. Using SortKey objects is faster because, after a string is converted, the comparison is numeric. Sort keys do take some effort to build, however, so just using the Collator class is adequate for many comparisons. Only use the SortKey class when a string is to be compared many times, thus preventing multiple passes to find the string position in the collation sequence.

TableCollation Class

The TableCollation class is used to map localized text to keys suitable for comparison during collation. TableCollation is an implementation of the Collation class. By supplying a table of rules (see Chapter 17), a collation sequence can be defined for use in the CollationElementIterator class.

Format Abstract Base Class

The Format class is the base class for string formatting tasks. The Format class is used to convert from one type of object to another type of object or to combine various objects to form a single object. When constructed with the ParseStatus class, the Format class is also useful for larger conversions such as translating streams.

FormatStatus Class

The FormatStatus class is slightly misnamed. In actuality, this class is used to specify alignment of an object. The class is taken in the context of the subclass of the Format.

ParseStatus Class

The ParseStatus class is used to keep track of the current position in a format or parsing task. This proves particularly useful when a parse returns at intermediate points in a parse task. A formatter for paragraphs, for instance, might be given a large text object to break into paragraphs. The formatter would return each time a paragraph was found, keeping track of the current position with the ParseStatus.

DateFormat Abstract Base Class

The DateFormat abstract base class creates localized time and date formatters.

DateFormatData Class

The DateFormatData class holds locale-dependent formatting data. DateFormatData is used by DateFormat and SimpleDateFormat to control their output.

SimpleDateFormat Class

The SimpleDateFormat class is a locale-independent date format class. This class is primarily for applications that require that date and time presentations must be the same. A primary use for this class is when the date will be read by another program. If the other program was non-localized, it will expect a specific format for date and time. Another example is for saving and retrieving information. If the date was saved in one country and loaded in another, the format could be unreadable by a localized version. This class is also very useful for programs or components that do not require localization or for those that require that, although a program may run in different locales, the date and time formats must agree.

Calendar Abstract Base Class

The abstract Calendar class is the base for concrete classes that represent specific calendars. An example of a concrete calendar is the GregorianCalendar class. A specific calendar implements functions in the abstract class in ways that correct system dates and times to match the specific calendar. The Gregorian calendar, for example, accounts for month, week, and time changes. There can also be information on leap days and other corrections. Many other types of calendars can also be expressed by concrete calendars, from Mayan to Lunar.

GregorianCalendar Class

The GregorianCalendar class is an implementation of the standardized Gregorian calendar. This class should be used for most locales—western Europe and the United States. This class is very useful for representing dates prior to 00:00:00 GMT Jan 1, 1970 (a limitation of the original Date class). In fact, this class can be used to represent dates in eras A.D. and B.C. This class can also calculate the correct time on the Gregorian calendar based on the current or a specific locale. The locale includes the specific time zone.

This is important for applications that need to know the local time in different parts of the world. A stock trading program, for example, would need to know the time for the market close in each country with which it is concerned.

TimeZone Abstract Base Class

The TimeZone class is used as an abstract base for creating specific time zones. A time zone is the offset from GMT (Greenwich Mean Time) to the specific locale. The TimeZone class also includes the capability to use daylight savings time.

SimpleTimeZone Class

The SimpleTimeZone class is used to create a time zone that can be used with the GregorianCalendar class.

MessageFormat Class

The MessageFormat class is used to mix text based on a format specification. This class is one of the more useful classes—not just for internationalization, but for many standard formatting tasks. When combined with resource bundles, choice formatter, number formatter, and date format classes, the MessageFormat class can create specific, localized messages.

ChoiceFormat Class

The ChoiceFormat class is used to associate numbers with text. The most obvious use is to associate the number of the day of the week with the string name for the day of the week.

NumberFormat Abstract Base Class

The NumberFormat class is the base class for all number formatting. NumberFormat is used as the standard base for formatting and parsing numbers. This class is also used to obtain the default NumberFormat implementation as well as formats for specific locales.

NumberFormatData Class

NumberFormatData is used with classes that subclass NumberFormat to specify specific information about representing data. The types of information represented by this class primarily are concerned with the textual representations of items such as the character used to show decimal place or sign and the definitions of characters for patterns used in formatting and parsing.

DecimalFormat Class

The DecimalFormat class is a concrete class based on NumberFormat used to format and parse decimal numbers. The NumberFormatData class is used to control parsing and formatting by this class.

FormatException Class

Format exceptions are a special case thrown by formatters when errors are encountered.

StringCharacterIterator Class

StringCharacterIterator is a utility class used to iterate through strings.

TextBoundary Abstract Base Class

The TextBoundary class is an abstract base class used to define the interface used to locate boundaries in text. Text boundaries include characters, words, sentences, and line-breaks. Localized concrete classes based on this class are used for parsing, selecting, and interpretation of text.

ResourceBundle Abstract Base Class

The ResourceBundle class is used to access objects based on locale. Resource bundles contain lists of objects associated with key words. The resource bundle, given a key word, will return the associated object. If the key word is not found in the bundle, a parent resource bundle will automatically be searched for the key word. With parent searching, it is easy to create a specialized resource that adds only the necessary information to override or augment the main resources.

 Note

It is important to note that resource bundles are found by name. The static method *getResourceBundle()* method is a utility used to locate a named bundle for a locale. If the locale is not found, baser locales are searched.

ListResourceBundle Abstract Base Class

The ListResourceBundle class is another level of abstraction above the ResourceBundle class used to represent lists of key words and object associations. Classes override the *contents( )* method to implement a specific list of resource associations.

PropertyResourceBundle Class

The PropertyResourceBundle class is a concrete specialization of a resource bundle that obtains its contents from an input stream. This class is very useful for managing localized text because it can use text files that can be edited and modified by users that do not need to recompile a class to add internationalization (as is the case with the ListResourceBundle).

Properties Class

The Properties class is used to associate keys to objects. The Properties class is similar to a resource bundle, except that properties are a non-localized association of keys and objects. The Properties class also has functions to load and store properties using an I/O stream.

Supporting Localization in a Bean

Any base class, including Beans, that is capable of supporting various locals must provide minimum static methods. These methods (listed in the following text) are used to determine the supported locales as well as provide a means for display of the localized name of the class in an IDE.

```
// Get a list of locales that this class supports.
public static Locale[] getAvailableLocales();\

// Get the programatic(non localized name).
public static String getName();

// Get the display of class localized name.
public static String getDisplayName(Locale objectLocale,
                                     Locale displayLocale);
public static final String getDisplayName(Locale objectLocale);
```

Selecting the Language: the Locale Class

The Locale class is the keystone of most of the Internationalization API. Locale is used to designate a language and a country to be used for representation. Table 11.1 shows the languages and regions supported in Java 1.1.

Table 11.1: Locales Supported by JDK 1.1

Locale	Language	Region
da_DK	Danish	Denmark
DE_AT	German	Austria
DE_CH	German	Switzerland
DE_DE	German	Germany
el_GR	Greek	Greece
en_CA	English	Canada
en_GB	English	United Kingdom
en_IE	English	Ireland
en_US	English	United States
es_ES	Spanish	Spain
fi_FI	Finnish	Finland
fr_BE	French	Belgium
fr_CA	French	Canada
fr_CH	French	Switzerland
fr_FR	French	France
it_CH	Italian	Switzerland
it_IT	Italian	Italy
ja_JP	Japanese	Japan
ko_KR	Korean	Korea
nl_BE	Dutch	Belgium

continues

Table 11.1: Locales Supported by JDK 1.1, Continued

Locale	Language	Region
nl_NL	Dutch	Netherlands
no_NO	Norwegian (Nynorsk)	Norway
no_NO_B	Norwegian (Bokmål)	Norway
pt_PT	Portuguese	Portugal
sv_SE	Swedish	Sweden
tr_TR	Turkish	Turkey
zh_CN	Chinese (Simplified)	China
zh_TW	Chinese (Traditional)	Taiwan

In addition to the language and the region, there is also a "variant." Variants are used to designate a platform- or browser-specific variation of the presentation. If a Bean were running on a Macintosh, for instance, its mouse would have only one button; on PCs there would be two; and on Unix workstations, the mouse would have three buttons. Messages could be written for each of the three platforms and refer to their specific uses. In the previous table the only entry with a variant is "no_NO_B" where the "_B" denotes a second form of the Norwegian language. Variants can be used for just about anything. The variant used in this book, for example, will be "PL" to designate Pig Latin for test purposes later in this chapter.

Many classes that return values based on Locale will often implement a method that specifies a locale object and one without. The NumberFormat class, for example, has the following two methods:

Listing 11.4: Static functions that return different locale-specific NumberFormat objects

```
static NumberFormat NumberFormat.getDefaultCurrency();
static NumberFormat NumberFormat.getDefaultCurrency(Local myLocale);
```

The first method in listing 11.4 retrieves the currency formatter for the current locale. The second method retrieves a specific currency formatter for the specified locale.

Platform/Locale Key Resolution: The awt.properties File

Listing 11.5 displays the contents of the awt.properties file for the Microsoft Windows platform in the United States. The fundamental things to keep in mind are that this file displays AWT keyboard properties for a specific platform (Windows) in a particular locale (the United States). This file would differ given a different platform (Mac or Unix) and locale (France or the Czech Republic).

Listing 11.5: Contents of the Java's awt.properties file for the Microsoft Windows platform in the United States

```
01.# @(#)awt.properties    1.1 97/01/06 1.1, 06 Jan 1997
02.
03.#
04.# AWT-specific properties
05.#
06.
07.# Modifier names
08.AWT.shift=Shift
09.AWT.control=Ctrl
10.AWT.alt=Alt
11.AWT.meta=Meta
12.
13.# Key names
14.AWT.enter=Enter
15.AWT.backSpace=Backspace
16.AWT.tab=Tab
17.AWT.clear=Clear
18.AWT.pause=Pause
19.AWT.capsLock=Caps Lock
20.AWT.escape=Escape
21.AWT.space=Space
22.AWT.home=Home
23.AWT.end=End
24.AWT.pgup=Page Up
25.AWT.pgdn=Page Down
26.AWT.up=Up
27.AWT.down=Down
28.AWT.left=Left
29.AWT.right=Right
30.AWT.f1=F1
31.AWT.f2=F2
32.AWT.f3=F3
```

continues

continued

```
33.AWT.f4=F4
34.AWT.f5=F5
35.AWT.f6=F6
36.AWT.f7=F7
37.AWT.f8=F8
38.AWT.f9=F9
39.AWT.f10=F10
40.AWT.f11=F11
41.AWT.f12=F12
42.AWT.multiply=NumPad *
43.AWT.add=NumPad +
44.AWT.separater=NumPad ,
45.AWT.subtract=NumPad -
46.AWT.decimal=NumPad .
47.AWT.divide=NumPad /
48.AWT.printScreen=Print Screen
49.AWT.scrollLock=Scroll Lock
50.AWT.numLock=Num Lock
51.AWT.insert=Insert
52.AWT.delete=Delete
53.AWT.help=Help
54.AWT.backQuote=Back Quote
55.AWT.quote=Quote
```

Converting Key Codes to Text Equivalents

Listing 11.6 looks up information in the awt.properties file. This file is automatically read when the AWT initializes the Toolkit. The code in this listing, though lengthy, is quite simple. The *getKeyText()* method is used mainly to convert key codes. It should be noted, however, that this method is assuming a somewhat standard keyboard, with the keycodes for special characters like SHIFT being variable enough to warrant this converter method.

Listing 11.6: Method to convert key codes to a text equivalent

```
001./**
002.    * Returns a String describing the keyCode, such as "HOME", "F1" or
➥"A".
003.    * These strings can be localized by changing the awt.properties
➥file.
004.    */
005.   public static String getKeyText(int keyCode) {
006.       if (keyCode >= VK_0 && keyCode <= VK_9 ||
```

```
007.              keyCode >= VK_A && keyCode <= VK_Z) {
008.              return String.valueOf((char)keyCode);
009.          }
010.
011.          // Check for other ASCII keyCodes.
012.          int index = ",./;=[\\]".indexOf(keyCode);
013.          if (index >= 0) {
014.              return String.valueOf((char)keyCode);
015.          }
016.
018.          case VK_ENTER: return Toolkit.getProperty("AWT.enter",
➥"Enter");
019.          case VK_BACK_SPACE: returnToolkit.getProperty("AWT.backSpace",
➥"Backspace");
020.          case VK_TAB: return Toolkit.getProperty("AWT.tab", "Tab");
021.          case VK_CANCEL: return Toolkit.getProperty("AWT.cancel",
➥"Cancel");
022.          case VK_CLEAR: return Toolkit.getProperty("AWT.clear",
➥"Clear");
023.          case VK_SHIFT: return Toolkit.getProperty("AWT.shift",
➥"Shift");
024.          case VK_CONTROL: return Toolkit.getProperty("AWT.control",
➥"Control");
025.          case VK_ALT: return Toolkit.getProperty("AWT.alt", "Alt");
026.          case VK_PAUSE: return Toolkit.getProperty("AWT.pause",
➥"Pause");
027.          case VK_CAPS_LOCK: return Toolkit.getProperty("AWT.capsLock",
➥"Caps Lock");
028.          case VK_ESCAPE: return Toolkit.getProperty("AWT.escape",
➥"Escape");
029.          case VK_SPACE: return Toolkit.getProperty("AWT.space",
➥"Space");
030.          case VK_PAGE_UP: return Toolkit.getProperty("AWT.pgup", "Page
➥Up");
031.          case VK_PAGE_DOWN: return Toolkit.getProperty("AWT.pgdn",
➥"Page Down");
032.          case VK_END: return Toolkit.getProperty("AWT.end", "End");
033.          case VK_HOME: return Toolkit.getProperty("AWT.home", "Home");
034.          case VK_LEFT: return Toolkit.getProperty("AWT.left", "Left");
035.          case VK_UP: return Toolkit.getProperty("AWT.up", "Up");
036.          case VK_RIGHT: return Toolkit.getProperty("AWT.right",
➥"Right");
037.          case VK_DOWN: return Toolkit.getProperty("AWT.down", "Down");
038.
039.          case VK_MULTIPLY: return Toolkit.getProperty("AWT.multiply",
➥"NumPad *");
```

continues

continued

```
040.          case VK_ADD: return Toolkit.getProperty("AWT.add", "NumPad
➡+");
041.          case VK_SEPARATER: return Toolkit.getProperty("AWT.separater",
➡"NumPad ,");
042.          case VK_SUBTRACT: return Toolkit.getProperty("AWT.subtract",
➡"NumPad -");
043.          case VK_DECIMAL: return Toolkit.getProperty("AWT.decimal",
➡"NumPad .");
044.          case VK_DIVIDE: return Toolkit.getProperty("AWT.divide",
➡"NumPad /");
045.
046.          case VK_F1: return Toolkit.getProperty("AWT.f1", "F1");
047.          case VK_F2: return Toolkit.getProperty("AWT.f2", "F2");
048.          case VK_F3: return Toolkit.getProperty("AWT.f3", "F3");
049.          case VK_F4: return Toolkit.getProperty("AWT.f4", "F4");
050.          case VK_F5: return Toolkit.getProperty("AWT.f5", "F5");
051.          case VK_F6: return Toolkit.getProperty("AWT.f6", "F6");
052.          case VK_F7: return Toolkit.getProperty("AWT.f7", "F7");
053.          case VK_F8: return Toolkit.getProperty("AWT.f8", "F8");
054.          case VK_F9: return Toolkit.getProperty("AWT.f9", "F9");
055.          case VK_F10: return Toolkit.getProperty("AWT.f10", "F10");
056.          case VK_F11: return Toolkit.getProperty("AWT.f11", "F11");
057.          case VK_F12: return Toolkit.getProperty("AWT.f12", "F12");
058.          case VK_DELETE: return Toolkit.getProperty("AWT.delete",
➡"Delete");
059.          case VK_NUM_LOCK: return Toolkit.getProperty("AWT.numLock",
➡"Num Lock");
060.          case VK_SCROLL_LOCK: return Toolkit.getProperty
➡("AWT.scrollLock", "Scroll Lock");
061.          case VK_PRINTSCREEN: return
➡Toolkit.getProperty("AWT.printScreen", "Print Screen");
062.          case VK_INSERT: return Toolkit.getProperty("AWT.insert",
➡"Insert");
063.          case VK_HELP: return Toolkit.getProperty("AWT.help", "Help");
064.          case VK_META: return Toolkit.getProperty("AWT.meta", "Meta");
065.          case VK_BACK_QUOTE: return Toolkit.getProperty
➡("AWT.backQuote", "Back Quote");
066.          case VK_QUOTE: return Toolkit.getProperty("AWT.quote",
➡"Quote");
067.        }
068.
069.        if (keyCode >= VK_NUMPAD0 && keyCode <= VK_NUMPAD9) {
070.            String numpad = Toolkit.getProperty("AWT.numpad", "NumPad");
071.          char c = (char)(keyCode - VK_NUMPAD0 + '0');
072.            return numpad + "-" + c;
```

```
073.        }
074.
075.        String unknown = Toolkit.getProperty("AWT.unknown", "Unknown
➥keyCode");
076.        return unknown + ": 0x" + Integer.toString(keyCode, 16);
077.    }
078.
079.    /**
080.     * Returns a String describing the modifier key(s), such as "Shift",
081.     * or "Ctrl+Shift". These strings can be localized by changing the
082.     * awt.properties file.
083.     */
084.    public static String getKeyModifiersText(int modifiers) {
085.        StringBuffer buf = new StringBuffer();
086.        if ((modifiers & Event.META_MASK) != 0) {
087.            buf.append(Toolkit.getProperty("AWT.meta", "Meta"));
088.            buf.append("+");
089.        }
090.        if ((modifiers & Event.CTRL_MASK) != 0) {
091.            buf.append(Toolkit.getProperty("AWT.control", "Ctrl"));
092.            buf.append("+");
093.        }
094.        if ((modifiers & Event.META_MASK) != 0) {
095.            buf.append(Toolkit.getProperty("AWT.alt", "Alt"));
096.            buf.append("+");
097.        }
098.        if ((modifiers & Event.SHIFT_MASK) != 0) {
099.            buf.append(Toolkit.getProperty("AWT.shift", "Shift"));
100.            buf.append("+");
101.        }
102.        if (buf.length() > 0) {
103.            buf.setLength(buf.length()-1); // remove trailing '+'
104.        }
105.        return buf.toString();
106.    }
```

Accessing International Text with the ResourceBundle Class

The ResourceBundle class is the basis for most internationalization tasks. Resource bundles enable you to retrieve strings and objects based on the locale.

The ResourceBundle encapsulates a great deal of code that must normally be written by a programmer. To make a button that will have the name Color in the U.S., or Colour in the United Kingdom, and Olorcay in Pig Latin, for example, requires the code in listing 11.7.

As you can see, the code required to implement just three different languages is simple, but it is not easy to read or very extensible. Any new language would need to be added via another if statement.

Listing 11.7 Internationalization without ResourceBundle

```
01.Button color;
02.String buttonName;
03.if (locale == "EN,GB"){// English, Great Briton
04.     buttonName = "Colour";
05.}else if (locale == "EN,US"){// English, United States
06.     buttonName = "Color";
07.}else if (locale == "EN,US,PL"){// English, United States (Pig
➥Latin Âvarient)
08.     buttonName = "Olorcay";
09.}else{
10.     // default name to use if locale criteria does not match.
11.     buttonName = "Color";
12.}
13.color = new Button(buttonName);
```

In listing 11.8, the same internationalization is accomplished by using a ResourceBundle. The mapping of the text for the locale is accomplished by loading a resource file (shown in listing 11.9). The resource file contains the information required for the mapping of a key word to the supported locale. Also notice that the locale is retrieved from the panel because all AWT components also have a *getLocale()* method. Because *getLocale()* is part of all components, after they have been created, components are aware of the country in which they reside. Such knowledge is very useful because the component may change over time and may need to generate information that needs to be translated to the locale.

Listing 11.8: Internationalization using ResourceBundle

```
ResouceBundle myResouces = ResourceBundle.load(new MyResourceLoader(),
➥"myPackage.MyBean",myPanel.getLocale());
color = new Button(myBeanResources.getString("Color"));
```

When using the *getString()* method, the only language dependence is in the use of the key. The locale of such keys is known as the programmatic locale.

Listing 11.9: Property file used by AppletViewer

```
01.# @(#)appletviewer.properties    1.3 96/06/11 1.3, 11 Jun 1996
02.
03.#
04.# AppletViewer-specific properties follow
05.#
06.
07.appletloader.destroyed=Applet destroyed.
08.appletloader.loaded=Applet loaded.
09.appletloader.started=Applet started.
10.appletloader.inited=Applet initialized.
11.appletloader.stopped=Applet stopped.
12.appletloader.disposed=Applet disposed.
13.
14.# —AppletViewer/HotJava start—
15.#
16.# The lines that follow are shared between the AppletViewer and HotJava
17.# Add ONLY shared AppletViewer/HotJava properties after this line!
18.
19.#
20.# Applet status messages
21.#
22.appletloader.nocode=APPLET tag missing CODE parameter.
23.appletloader.notfound=load: class %0 not found.
24.appletloader.nocreate=load: %0 can't be instantiated.
25.appletloader.noconstruct=load: %0 is not public or has no public
➥constructor.
26.appletloader.death=killed
27.appletloader.exception=exception: %0.
28.appletloader.exception2=exception: %0: %1.
29.appletloader.error=error: %0.
30.appletloader.error2=error: %0: %1.
31.appletloader.notloaded=Init: applet not loaded.
32.appletloader.notinited=Start: applet not initialized.
33.appletloader.notstarted=Stop: applet not started.
34.appletloader.notstopped=Destroy: applet not stopped.
35.appletloader.notdestroyed=Dispose: applet not destroyed.
36.appletloader.notdisposed=Load: applet not disposed.
37.appletloader.bail=Interrupted: bailing out.
38.appletloader.filenotfound=File not found when looking for: %0
39.appletloader.fileformat=File format exception when loading: %0
40.appletloader.fileioexception=I/O exception when loading: %0
41.appletloader.fileexception=%0 exception when loading: %1
42.appletloader.filedeath=%0 killed when loading: %1
43.appletloader.fileerror=%0 error when loading: %1
44.
```

continues

```
continued
45.#
46.# Signed Applet class loading
47.#
48.appletviewer.security.allowUnsigned=true
49.
50.# Add ONLY shared AppletViewer/HotJava properties before this line!
```

The layout of this resource file follows the same naming conventions that would normally be used for packages, with the exception of a locale identifier appended to the class name. The ResourceBundle class locates the correct package and then locates the class name that fits the locale. If the locale could not be matched exactly, the ResourceBundle strips the tokens from the locale string one at a time until a match is made. So, for example, if the locale had been the English for the United Kingdom, the locale string would be "en_UK". In the resource file shown in listing 11.10, line 3 would be the resource matching the locale. If instead, the locale was for French speakers in Canada, line 1 would be chosen because none of the locale matches so that the resource without a specified local is selected.

 TIP

Always include default resources in a resource bundle. Default resources do not specify language or locale so they can be used when the user's locale does not exist in the resource bundle.

Listing 11.10: Resource file used by ResourceBundle

```
MyPackage.MyBean_Color:Colour
MyPackage.MyBean_en_US_Color:Color
MyPackage.MyBean_en_UK_Color:ColouUr
MyPackage.MyBean_en_US_PL_Color:Olourcay
```

The ResourceBundle class is used to store and retrieve data associated with a locale. A name string associates data in a resource bundle. A two-character ID (as listed in table 11.1) specifies each language-specific version of each resource bundle, an additional two-character region identifier further specifies the object to be returned. The language and region can be specified directly or via the Locale class. A third optional identifier can also be used to further specify the item. In the Locale column in table 11.1, the Norwegian language is split into two types "NO_NO" for the Norwegian Nynorsk and

"NO_NO_B" for Norwegian, Bokmål variant. What is happening with these different identifiers is that the language, country, and a variant that exists for the same language and country are specified. We can add additional variants to existing language and country codes to extend the locale to meet specific sub-regions too. In listing 11.10 a resource bundle defines four variants for the word "color" by defining a combination of language, country, and region codes. In this case we use Pig Latin as the variant and specify it by adding "PL" to the locale identifier. Listing 11.11 has a default version used when the current locale does not match any other defined locale, which is U.S. English. There are also English versions for the United Kingdom and the United States. The United States version also has another regional variant for Pig Latin.

Property File-Based Resources

The easiest way to create and manage resources is through property resource files, using the PropertyResourceBundle to read the files. By using property resource files, the text may be edited with a standard editor. The reason for this is that the resources may change over time. Imagine someone correcting a spelling mistake made to a string used for a menu title resource. If that text was embedded in a class, the class would need to be recompiled. If the menu title is in a properties file, only a Unicode editor is required to make the change without the requirement of a recompile.

Another useful feature of the ResourceBundle class is that its *getResourceBundle()* methods are written to look for resource property files. This means that property files do not need to be written for all supported languages ahead of time. Just add a properly named resource bundle for the new language and country as it is needed. In fact, end users can add their own resource bundles for their specialized locale without ever recompiling your code. This means that even though the code does not support French, a French developer can add a MyResource.properties.fr_FR file to override your MyResources.properties.en_US file.

In listing 11.12, several resource bundles for the MyResources bundle are created pro-grammatically. These files could have been created by hand but we are also showing how to write a bundle. You might need to write a bundle if you are translating data to be used by other programs that need to access data in a locale based manner. It is a good idea, however, to have a way to automatically generate a default properties file. A default file will give the user something to work with in case the original property files are lost.

The first thing to do in the *main()* method is to create some string lists used to represent the key/value pairs. Then each property file is created in the *createPropertyFile()*

method. The *createPropertyFile()* method takes the string list and creates a Properties class object that is then written to the disk. The method also reads and then prints the properties so that the process can be validated.

After all the property files have been written, you need to attempt to load the MyResource file for the United Kingdom and for English.

 NOTE

> The "??" wildcard forces the bundle loader to look for the base language because the "??" locale does not exist.

To prove that the United Kingdom resource is capable of finding the base English resource, the English keys are printed, while passing the keys to the UK resource bundle. The result is that the OK and Quit keys are printed, along with the UK's resource override for the color key value: "Colour"(see listing 11.12 for the output).

Listing 11.11: BuildResources class demonstrates the creation and use of property files and ResourceBundle class

```
01.import java.text.*;
02.import java.util.*;
03.import java.io.*;
04.class BuildResources{
05.     public static void main(String args[]){
06.         String propertyFile = "MyResource.properties";
07.         String[][] defaultResource = {
08.             {"color", "color"},
09.             {"OK", "OK"},
10.             {"quit", "Quit"}
11.         };
12.         String[][] UKResource = {
13.             {"color", "colour"},
14.         };
15.         String[][] UKResource_PL = {
16.             {"color", "Olourcay"},
17.             {"OK", "Koay"},
18.             {"quit", "Uitqay"}
19.         };
20.         String[][] USResource_PL = {
21.             {"color", "Olorcay"},
23.             {"quit", "Uitqay"}
24.         };
```

```
25.            createPropertyFile("MyResources",defaultResource);
26.            createPropertyFile("MyResources_en",defaultResource);
27.            createPropertyFile("MyResources_en_US",defaultResource);
28.            createPropertyFile("MyResources_en_UK",UKResource);
29.            createPropertyFile("MyResources_en_UK_PL",UKResource_PL);
30.            createPropertyFile("MyResources_en_US_PL",USResource_PL);
31.
32.            //Test the UK resource as a loaded bundle
33.        System.out.println("Resources read via
➥ResorceBundle:MyResources_en_UK");
34.             ResourceBundle  resourceBundle =
➥ResourceBundle.getResourceBundle("MyResources",new Locale("en","??"));
35.         // Iterate through the keys in the base bundle
36.         // but call the UK bundle to search for the key.
37.         // This proves that if a key is not found, the base bundle is
38.         // searched.
39.         ResourceBundle  resourceBundle2 =
➥ResourceBundle.getResourceBundle("MyResources",new Locale("en","US"));
40.         for (Enumeration e = resourceBundle2.getKeys() ;
➥e.hasMoreElements() ;) {
41.                 String key = (String)e.nextElement();
42.                 // Note that we are looking at the parent through the
➥child.
43.                 System.out.println(key + "="+resourceBundle.getString(key));
44.         }
45.
46.
47.     }// End of main()
48.
49.     /**
50.      * Utility method used to write, then read a property file.
51.      */
52.     public static void createPropertyFile(String propertyFile,
➥String[][] contents ){
53.             Properties props = new Properties();
54.             for (int i = 0; i < contents.length; ++i) {
55.                     props.put(contents[i][0],contents[i][1]);
56.             }
57.             try {
58.                     FileOutputStream file = new
➥FileOutputStream(propertyFile+".properties");
59.                     props.save(file, "Default Properties");
60.                     file.close();
61.             }catch(IOException ioe){
62.                     System.err.println("Error creating resource
➥file:"+propertyFile+".properties");
```

continues

```
continued
63.                    System.err.println(ioe);
64.                    return;
65.          }
66.        } // end of createPropertyFile()
67.}// End of BuildResources
```

Lines 11 through 23 of the example are the resource bundle strings to be created. Lines 25 through 30 create each of the property files by calling the static utility function *createPropertyFile()* that we have created on line 52. In *createPropertyFile()* we create a new Properties object (line 53) and then fill the properties object with the locale-specific data. Note that the resources are looked up by name so there is no reason for any of these different property files to be in any particular order. The code continues on line 58 where an output stream is created. Looking back to lines 25 through 30 we can see that the file name that is created is made from "MyResources," a locale identifier, and ".properties." For a properties file that is English in the UK the file name would be "MyResources_en_UK.properties". On line 59 the properties object is written to the stream using the *save()* method.

Reading properties is very simple as demonstrated by line 39. All that is needed is to specify the name of the bundle and the Locale that is required. All that is then required to access data in the bundle is to supply the appropriate key for the object required.

 Tip

Any serializable object can be saved in a resource file.

Listing 11.12: Output of BuildResources program

```
Resources read via ResorceBundle:MyResources_en_UK
color=colour
OK=OK
quit=Quit
```

Formatting Messages for International Display

As discussed previously, the problems of formatting a sentence with embedded data can vary wildly among languages. Now that you are familiar with the retrieval of language-specific information, listing 11.1 can be rewritten as listing 11.13 to use a resource bundle.

Listing 11.13: Rewriting English text from listing 11.1 using ResourceBundle

```
String fruitColor = "red";
String fruit = "apple";
String displayThis = myRes.getString("The color of the") +" "
                              + myRes.getString(fruit) + " "
                              + myRes.getString("is")+" "
                              + myRes.getString(fruitColor) +".";
```

As you can see, the string will translate equally well in American or British English, creating either "The color of the apple is red." or "The colour of the apple is red." Converting to another language may not be readable. As in listing 11.3, for example, the resulting sentence may need to read: "Red is the color of the apple." To prevent positional dependencies, the FormatMessage class is used to dynamically build strings from keyed patterns and parameters. The way FormatMessage works can be easily seen in the code of listing 11.14.

Listing 11.14: Printing two differently formatted messages with FormatMessage

```
01.String fruitColor = "red";
02.String fruit = "apple";
03.Object[] argumentList = new Object[2];
04.
05.// Add variant language converted data to argument list;
06.argumentList[0] = myRes.getString(fruitColor);
07.argumentList[1] = myRes.getString(fruit);
08.
09.// Create format strings for two different sentence structures.
10.String englishFormat = "The colour of the %0 is %1."
11.String otherFormat   = "%1 is the color of the %0.";
12.
13.// Create and print the different sentences.
14.String englishSentence = MessageFormat.format(englishFormat,arguments);
15.String otherSentence   = MessageFormat.format(otherFormat,arguments);
```

The example in listing 11.14 uses the static member function of the MessageFormat class to perform the substitutions and to build a string. This is the easiest to use and does not require an object of the MessageFormat class to be created. It is, however, not very efficient for some applications. A message and list of numbers, for example, would use the FormatMessage as an object. The pattern would only be set one time, and the arguments would change each time the message is to be printed (as listing 11.15 shows).

Listing 11.15: Printing multiple messages using a MessageFormat object

```
01.Object[] argumentList = new Object[1];
02.
03.// Create a format with a pattern.
04.MessageFormat fmt = new MessageFormat("The number is %0.");
05.StringBuffer temp;// String scratch space to write the message
06.
07.for (int index = 1; index <11; index++){
08.    // Set the argument list.
09.    argumentList[0] = new Integer(index);
10.    // Create a formatted string and place it in the
11.    // string buffer.
12.    fmt.format(argumentList,temp, null);
13.    // Print the message in the string buffer.
14.    System.out.println(temp);
15.}
```

Listing 11.15 sets the pattern for the message when it is created. As each new message is created, the *format()* method that uses a StringBuffer is used. The reason that the buffer variant of *format()* is used is to save time creating new objects. Another variant only takes the arguments and creates a String object. Using the StringBuffer avoids the creation of a String object each time the loop is executed.

Many more methods exist in the FormatMessage class. Each can be used in various ways for different situations. Read the section of the Internationalization API in Chapter 17 for the complete definition of the MessageFormat class and apply the most efficient methods for each particular task.

Using ChoiceFormat

Another task that is simplified by a class in the Internationalization API is the ChoiceFormat class. ChoiceFormat can be used to convert a numeric range to an object. In listing 11.16 the NumberOfThings class simply converts a number to a string that gives the number's approximate size. The ChoiceFormat is created by combining a range of numbers (starting at line 25) to a list of messages that are to be printed for a number in the specified range (line 39). This example prints the results of a few numbers just to prove that it does what is intended.

Listing 11.16: NumberOfThings class

```
01. import java.text.*;
02. /**
03.  * Class used to return text approximation of a number.
04.  * For internationalization, override the limits and messages methods.
05.  */
06. public class NumberOfThings{
07.     // Test main for this class
08.     public static void main(String args[]){
09.         for (double i = -1; i < 5; i++){
10.             System.out.println(i+" =
➡'"+NumberOfThings.getMessage(i)+"'");
11.         }
12.         double x =0.5;
13.         System.out.println(x+" = '"+NumberOfThings.getMessage(x)+"'");
14.         x =100;
15.         System.out.println(x+" = '"+NumberOfThings.getMessage(x)+"'");
16.         x =400;
17.         System.out.println(x+" = '"+NumberOfThings.getMessage(x)+"'");
18.         x =4000;
19.         System.out.println(x+" = '"+NumberOfThings.getMessage(x)+"'");
20.         x =4000000;
21.         System.out.println(x+" = '"+NumberOfThings.getMessage(x)+"'");
22.
23.
24.     }// End of main()
25.     static double[] getLimits(){
26.         double[] limits = {      -1.0,
27.                                   0.0,
28.                                   0.0001,
29.                                   1.0,
30.                                   2.0,
31.                                   3.0,
32.                                  24.0,
33.                                 200.0,
34.                                2000.0,
35.                             2000000.0,
36.                          2000000000.0 };
37.         return (limits);
38.     }
39.     static String[] getMessages(){
40.         String[] messages = {"are a negative number",
41.                              "are none",
42.                              "is less than one",
43.                              "is one",
44.                              "are two",
```

continues

```
continued
45.                                       "are many",
46.                                       "are dozens",
47.                                       "are hundreds",
48.                                       "are thousands",
49.                                       "are millions"
50.                                       };
51.             return (messages);
52.       }
53.     /**
54.       * returns a string that is formatted depending on the number of
↪items
55.       */
56.       public static String getMessage(double numberOf){
57.           ChoiceFormat choiceFormat = new ChoiceFormat(getLimits(),
↪getMessages());
58.           return choiceFormat.format(numberOf);
59.
60.     }// End of getMessage()
61.}//End of class NumberOfThings
```

Telling Time with the SimpleTimeZone Class

The SimpleTimeZone class is used to create a context for a specific time zone. SimpleTimeZone is a child class of the TimeZone class that implements most of its functions.

The purpose of the SimpleTimeZone class is to store time information for a specific locale. The class is also used to calculate times and dates that are locale-dependent and that follow the rules of the Gregorian calendar.

A string designating the requested time zone specifies the specific time zone created. Table 11.2 lists the time zone strings supported in Java 1.1.

Table 11.2: Time Zones Supported in Java 1.1

Time Zone	Hours from GMT
GMT	0
ECT	1
EET	2
EAT	3

Time Zone	Hours from GMT
MET	3
NET	4
PLT	5
IST	5
BST	6
VST	7
CTT	8
JST	9
ACT	9
AET	10
SST	11
NST	12
MIT	-11
HST	-10
AST	-9
PST	-8
PNT	-7
MDT	-7
CST	-6
EST	-5
PRT	-4
CNT	-3
AGT	-3
BET	-3
CAT	-1

The example in listing 11.17 shows how to create a date by using the SimpleTimeZone class.

Listing 11.17: Examples of creating time zones

```
// Time zone for the current location.
SimpleTimeZone myTimeZone = SimpleTimeZone.getDefault();

// Time zone for London, England, using offset to GMT.
SimpleTimeZone myTimeZone = SimpleTimeZone(0,"GMT");
```

International Dates: The GregorianCalendar Classes

The Gregorian calendar embodies all the rules of time and dates that most westerners are accustomed to. This includes leap years and the fact that dates are calculated in reverse prior to the year 0 A.D. This class is much more useful than the standard Java Date class because it properly calculates dates before 1970.

This class would be used for most time/date representations. If another calendar is required (the Arabic calendar, for instance), the abstract class Calendar would be used through inheritance to create the new calendar (like Lunar, Aztec, Muslim, Old Chinese, and so on). Creating another calendar is beyond the scope of this book. Don't worry, though, most of the world agrees on the Gregorian calendar.

The GregorianCalendar class inherits its base functionality from the abstract base class Calendar. A SimpleTimeZone date is used to give the calendar locale context to calculate time and date based on the offset from GMT and whether Daylight Savings Time is in effect. Listing 11.18 shows a simple example that retrieves the day of the week for the current locale and time.

Listing 11.18: Retrieving the Day of the Week index

```
// Time zone for the current location.
SimpleTimeZone myTimeZone = SimpleTimeZone.getDefault();
GregorianCalendar currentTime = new GregorianCalendar(myTimeZone);
int day of week = currentTime.get(Calendar.DAYOFWEEK);
```

Printing Dates and Times: The DateFormat Class

Many people do not realize it, but the presentation of dates can be very regional. Days of the week, for example, are different in most languages. Also, the order of dates differs between regions. In the United States, for example, the order of dates is month/day/year. In most of western Europe, the order is day/month/year. There are also differences between time zones and the use of Daylight Savings Time.

DateFormat is an abstract base class used as a base to create other classes that format dates based on locale. DateFormat also has static functions used to retrieve the specific format objects. Listing 11.19 shows how the time and date can be printed for the U.S. and for the United Kingdom:

Listing 11.19: Examples of creating time zones

```
01.// Format a time/date string for the current locale.
02.DateFormat localDateFormat = DateFormat.getDateTimeFormat();
03.System.out.println("Local format of Time/Date
04.format"+localDateFormat(System.currentTimeMillis());
05.
06.// Format a timeDate string for London.
07.DateFormat londonDateFormat =
08.DateFormat.getDateTimeFormat(DateFormat.DEFAULT,local.UK);
09.System.out.println("London format of Time/Date
10.format"+localDateFormat(System.currentTimeMillis());
```

Printing Dates and Times: The SimpleDateFormat Class

Another way to create locale-dependent time/date strings is by using the SimpleDateFormat class. SimpleDateFormat gives complete control for formatting times and dates. By simply creating a string containing the format keys of table 11.3 any specific time format can be created.

Table 11.3: Symbols Used to Format Date and Time Strings

Symbol	Meaning	Presentation	Example
G	Era designator	Text	AD
y	Year	Number	1996
M	Month in year	Text & Number	July & 07
d	Day in month	Number	10

continues

Table 11.3: Symbols Used to Format Date and Time Strings, Continued

Symbol	Meaning	Presentation	Example
h	Hour in am/pm (1–12)	Number	12
H	Hour in day (0–23)	Number	0
m	Minute in hour	Number	30
s	Second in minute	Number	55
S	Millisecond	Number	978
E	Day in week	Text	Tuesday
D	Day in year	Number	189
F	Day of week in month	Number	2 (2nd Wed in July)
w	Week in year	Number	27
W	Week in month	Number	2
a	am/pm marker	Text	PM
k	Hour in day (1–24)	Number	24
K	Hour in am/pm (0–11)	Number	0
z	Time zone	Text	Pacific Standard Time
'	Escape for text	None	None
''	Single quote	Text	None

International Numbers: The NumberFormat Class

The NumberFormat class is used to display numbers properly based on locale. In the United States, for example, a number would be printed as 3,123.00. Conversely, in parts of Europe the number could be written as 3.123,00 or as 3123.00. Listing 11.20 shows how to display numbers properly based on locale.

Listing 11.20: Example showing use of NumberFormat classes

```
01.Locale[] locales = NumberFormat.getAvailableLocales();
02.double myNumber = -1234.56;
```

```
03.NumberFormat format;
04.// Print out a number with the locale format for number, currency and
⇒percent classes.
05.for (int locale = 0; locale < locales.length; ++locale) {
06.        if (locales[i].getCountry().length() == 0) {
07.            // skip blank locals
08.            continue;
09.        }
10.        System.out.print(locales[locale].getDisplayName() +" : ");
11.
12.format = NumberFormat.getDefault(locales[locale]);
13.system.out.print("Number:"+format.format(myNumber));
14.
15.format = NumberFormat.getDefaultCurrency(locales[locale]);
16.system.out.print("Number:"+format.format(myNumber));
17.
18.format = NumberFormat.getDefaultPercent(locales[locale]);
19.system.out.print("Number:"+format.format(myNumber));
20.system.out.println()
21.}
```

International Fonts

Getting fonts from different languages to display properly in Java does not require much work. Java uses the Unicode character set. The key to proper formatting is the preservation of Unicode in the characters used for each of the language presentations.

Preservation of characters is not as easy as it sounds, however. The problem with many text editors on the market today is that they do not conform to Unicode standards. The reason for this is that Unicode is rather young. Many editors were written long before the Unicode specifications were written. Another problem is that some operating systems do not directly support the mapping between Unicode characters and their fonts. These problems usually create an insurmountable problem because Java requires the Unicode character to map to the index in the font for a language. Be certain that an editor that supports the Unicode standard is used whenever typing language-specific text. Most Java IDE editors should support Unicode directly.

The only other language-specific feature to know about fonts is which character set you use for a particular language and machine. Table 11.4 shows the specific character sets and their encoding. The encoding column designates a character set as either ISO, meaning platform-dependent, or as a platform-dependent character set.

Table 11.4: JDK 1.1 Character Encoding

Java Name	Standard	Character Set Name
8859_1	ISO	Latin-1
8859_2	ISO	Latin-2
8859_3	ISO	Latin-3
8859_4	ISO	Latin-4
8859_5	ISO	Latin/Cyrillic
8859_6	ISO	Latin/Arabic
8859_7	ISO	Latin/Greek
8859_8	ISO	Latin/Hebrew
8859_9	ISO	Latin-5
Cp1250	Windows	Eastern Europe / Latin-2
Cp1251	Windows	Cyrillic
Cp1252	Windows	Western Europe / Latin-1
Cp1253	Windows	Greek
Cp1254	Windows	Turkish
Cp1255	Windows	Hebrew
Cp1256	Windows	Arabic
Cp1257	Windows	Baltic
Cp1258	Windows	Vietnamese
Cp437	PC	Original
Cp737	PC	Greek
Cp775	PC	Baltic
Cp850	PC	Latin-1
Cp852	PC	Latin-2
Cp855	PC	Cyrillic
Cp857	PC	Turkish

Java Name	Standard	Character Set Name
Cp860	PC	Portuguese
Cp861	PC	Icelandic
Cp862	PC	Hebrew
Cp863	PC	Canadian French
Cp864	PC	Arabic
Cp865	PC	Nordic
Cp866	PC	Russian
Cp869	PC	Modern Greek
Cp874	Windows	Thai
EUCJIS	EUC	Japanese
MacArabic	Macintosh	Arabic
MacCentralEurope	Macintosh	Latin-2
MacCroatian	Macintosh	Croatian
MacCyrillic	Macintosh	Cyrillic
MacDingbat	Macintosh	Dingbat
MacGreek	Macintosh	Greek
MacHebrew	Macintosh	Hebrew
MacIceland	Macintosh	Iceland
MacRoman	Macintosh	Roman
MacRomania	Macintosh	Romania
MacSymbol	Macintosh	Symbol
MacThai	Macintosh	Thai
MacTurkish	Macintosh	Turkish
MacUkraine	Macintosh	Ukraine
SJIS	PC and Windows	Japanese
UTF8	Standard	UTF-8

The following method in listing 11.21 can be used as a utility to select the correct font for the specified language. If there is no font available, the method returns null for the font.

Listing 11.21: Utility Class to get a font for a locale

```
01. import java.awt.*;
02. class LanguageFontHelper{
03.       static Font getFont(){
04.             return (getFont(Local.getDefaultLocal()));
05. }
06.       static Font getFont(Local){
07.             Font[] = Toolkit.GetDefaultToolkit().getFontList();
08.             .
09.             .
10.             .
11.             . ??? To be completed after 1.1 is available.
12.             .
13.             .
14.             .
15. }
16. }// End of class LanguageFontHelper
```

Creating an International BeanInfo

This section takes you through the steps necessary to create an international BeanInfo class for a Java Bean. Essentially a BeanInfo should cause the IDE to present localized information for the names of properties in a property sheet as well as properly localize dates and numbers. In addition, any PropertyEditor or Customizer classes also need to present localized information.

BeanDescriptor Class

The BeanDescriptor Class is the basis for creating locale representations of Java Beans. As has been discussed earlier in this book, the BeanDescriptor class can be used by an IDE to retrieve the names of methods, parameters, fields, and their documentation. The International API can be used for retrieving locale-dependent information. All that is required is that any textual information presented through the BeanDescriptor class be based on localized resources (feature descriptors, parameter descriptors, method descriptors, and so on).

An added benefit accrues from this internationalization. The text presented is maintained separately from the code. This becomes important as documentation on particular aspects of a Bean improves or evolves. This also proves particularly useful when quickly prototyping a Bean. A Bean could be developed so quickly that the programmer does not have a good idea of how to document methods and parameters, for example. After the design is complete, the programmer can just edit the resource bundle file associated with the Bean.

It should be general practice to access, through the resource bundle file, all strings used for presentation. Adding the extra code is not too difficult and eliminates any rewriting later.

Feature Descriptors

The next step toward making the Bean Internationalized is to modify all the feature descriptors so that the text they present is pulled from the Bean's resource bundle. This is probably the simplest to do because FeatureDescriptor returns strings that can be easily replaced. The simplest method is to store keys in these strings that are then replaced with the text looked up from a resource bundle.

Making International Text Fit

A big problem with multi-language programs is the user interface text. Because the text displayed can vary its font and the number of characters depending on the locale, you need to design the user interface to be aware of the size of strings to be drawn.

To accomplish this task, the size of text must be queried. This is accomplished with the FontMetrics class. With the measurements available, it is a simple manner to reset the minimum and/or current size of a component to the size that provides enough room for the text to be displayed.

In listing 11.22, the InternationalButton class uses the FontMetrics class to calculate the minimum size of the total button. This function overrides the *getPreferredSize()*, *getMinimumSize()*, *setFont()*, and *getSize()* methods. These overridden methods ensure that all aspects of the button's size meet the minimum requirements for the current text and font.

Listing 11.22: InternationalButton Class: setting the minimum size of a component with the FontMetrics class

```
01.import java.awt.*;
02.class InternationalButton extends Button implements java.io.Serializable{
03.    public InternationalButton(String label){
04.         super(label);
05.    }
06.    public void setFont(Font f) {
07.     super.setFont(f);
08.     sizeToFit();
09.    }
10.    private void sizeToFit() {
11.     Dimension d = getPreferredSize();
12.     resize(d.width, d.height);
13.     Component p = getParent();
14.     if (p != null) {
15.         p.invalidate();
16.         p.doLayout();
17.     }
18.    }
19.    public Dimension getPreferredSize() {
20.
21.
22.         FontMetrics fm = getFontMetrics(getFont());
23.         return new Dimension(fm.stringWidth(getLabel()) +
24.(fm.charWidth('A')*3),
25.               fm.getMaxAscent() + fm.getMaxDescent() +
➥fm.getHeight());
26.    }
27.
28.    public Dimension getMinimumSize() {
29.         return getPreferredSize();
30.    }
31.public Dimension getSize(){
32.         FontMetrics fm = getFontMetrics(getFont());
33.         Dimension dim  = super.getSize();
34.         int minHeight  = fm.getMaxAscent() + fm.getMaxDescent() +
35.fm.getHeight();
36.          int minWidth   = fm.stringWidth(getLabel()) +
37.(fm.charWidth('A')*3);
38.             // Return minimum width or real width (what ever is bigger).
39.         return new Dimension((dim.width > minWidth ? dim.width:
➥minWidth),
40.(dim.height > minHeight ? dim.height : minHeight));
41.    }
42.
43.}// End of class InternationalButton
```

Using Layout Containers

Changing the size of components can cause many problems. The text may grow too large and appear to be overlapped with other components, for example. Therefore it is always preferable to use layout containers that will properly change their size. Never use a null layout unless the internal logic of the component calls *invalidate()* and then calls *getParent()* and *validate()* to cause the parent container to be properly sized around the component.

Summary

The most important attribute of Java Beans is their capability to be reused. Adding the capability to use Beans in different locales increases a Bean's developer audience as well as increases the number of users that developers can support with your Java Beans.

The Internationalization API is not just a paradigm for localizing data. It is also a paradigm for parsing and formatting of text, dates, and numbers. As an added benefit, when used correctly, these features add the capability of creating internationalized versions of the original.

The guidelines in this chapter should be followed for Beans as well as for whole applications. Besides internationalization, the capability to change a program's behavior between locales in the same country is also important (time zones, for example).

Chapter 17 covers the technical content of classes for the Java Internationalization and should serve as a pretty good reference for developers of International Beans.

Part III

Beans and Related APIs

Core Java Beans API

The package java.beans contains several different classes and interfaces that are used by Java Beans. According to the official Java Beans Specification by JavaSoft, a "Bean is a reusable software component that can be manipulated visually in a builder tool." Of course this covers a wide variety of possibilities all of which are addressed at one level or another by this API.

BeanInfo Interface

The BeanInfo interface provides a mechanism for the implementor of a Bean to provide explicit information about the methods, properties, and events that the Bean implements to any interested third party that wants to know about it. This is accomplished by providing, with the distribution of the Bean, a class which implements the BeanInfo interface and which provides the desired information. When a class that implements this interface is included with a Bean, it should be named by adding "BeanInfo" to the Bean's class name.

Even though a BeanInfo object is the official way to describe a Bean, it is possible for a component developer to use private Bean descriptor files of their own choosing behind the scenes and simply provide a BeanInfo class that knows how to manipulate these private files. Also, it is important to note that if there are implementation details in a Bean that a developer does not want exposed through Introspection, a BeanInfo object can be provided which only provides the information that developer wants to be known to a user of BeanInfo.

An object which implements this interface does not need to provide an exhaustive set of attributes. You can selectively define what information that you want to provide and the rest can be obtained via automatic analysis using low-level reflection of the Bean's class methods. This is accomplished by returning a null object from those methods that you don't want to define. When the Introspector sees a null value, it automatically applies analysis to the Bean to determine for itself the attributes in question. The class SimpleBeanInfo is an implementation that does exactly this. It returns null for each of the methods in this interface allowing the developer to inherit from it and only override those methods that need to be defined.

See Also: Introspector, SimpleBeanInfo

ICON_COLOR_16×16 Variable

Constant indicating a 16 by 16 pixel color icon.

Syntax: `static int ICON_COLOR_16x16`

ICON_COLOR_32×32 Variable

Constant indicating a 32 by 32 pixel color icon.

Syntax: `static int ICON_COLOR_32x32`

ICON_MONO_16×16 Variable

Constant indicating a 16 by 16 pixel monochromatic icon.

Syntax: `static int ICON_MONO_16x16`

ICON_MONO_32×32 Variable

Constant indicating a 32 by 32 pixel monochromatic icon.

Syntax: `static int ICON_MONO_32x32`

getAdditionalBeanInfo() Method

This method allows a BeanInfo object to return any number of additional BeanInfo objects which provide information about the Bean that this BeanInfo describes. In cases of conflict between the descriptions contained in BeanInfo objects, the parent definition is authoritative.

Syntax: `BeanInfo[] getAdditionalBeanInfo()`

Returns: An array of BeanInfo objects. This method may return null if there are no additional BeanInfo objects which describe this Bean.

getBeanDescriptor() Method

This method returns a BeanDescriptor object which provides overall information about a Bean such as (but certainly not limited to) its displayName and its Customizer.

Syntax: `BeanDescriptor getBeanDescriptor()`

Returns: A BeanDescriptor object. This method may return null if the information should be obtained via automatic analysis.

getDefaultEventIndex() Method

A Bean may have a particular event which is the one that will most commonly be used by a human programmer using the Bean.

Syntax: `int getDefaultEventIndex()`

Returns: The integer index of the default event in the EventSetDescriptor array. This method may return -1 if there is no default event for this Bean.

getDefaultPropertyIndex() Method

A Bean may have a particular property which is the one that will most commonly be used by a human programmer customizing the Bean.

Syntax: `int getDefaultPropertyIndex()`

Returns: The integer index of the property in the PropertyDescriptor array. This method may return -1 if there is no default property for this Bean.

getEventSetDescriptors() Method

The array of EventSetDescriptors returned by this method describes the kinds of event which can be fired by this Bean.

Syntax: `EventSetDescriptor[] getEventSetDescriptors()`

Returns: An array of EventSetDescriptors. This method may return null if the information should be obtained via automatic analysis.

getIcon(int) Method

This method returns an image object which can be used by toolboxes, toolbars, and other such widgets to represent the Bean. Icon images initially expected to be in the GIF format, but in the future other formats may be allowed. Beans are not required to provide their own icons and therefore may return null from this method.

It is recommended that the icons utilize the "transparent background" feature of GIF images to allow them to be rendered seamlessly onto an existing background.

Syntax:　　　**`Image getIcon(int iconKind)`**

Parameters:　　iconKind: An integer value representing the icon to be returned. This should be one of the constant values defined by this class (ICON_COLOR_16x16, ICON_COLOR_32x32, ICON_MONO_16x16, ICON_MONO_32x32).

Returns:　　　An Image object or null.

getMethodDescriptors() Method

Every Bean has a set of externally visible methods which it supports. This method returns an array of these methods.

Syntax:　　　**`MethodDescriptor[] getMethodDescriptors()`**

Returns:　　　An array of MethodDescriptors. This method may return null if the information should be obtained via automatic analysis.

getPropertyDescriptors() Method

This method returns an array of PropertyDescriptors which describes the editable properties of this Bean. If a property is indexed, then its entry in the array will belong to the IndexedPropertyDescriptor subclass of PropertyDescriptor.

Syntax:　　　**`PropertyDescriptor[] getPropertyDescriptors()`**

Returns:　　　An array of PropertyDescriptors. This method may return null if the information should be obtained via automatic analysis.

Customizer Interface

A class implementing this interface provides a complete custom graphical user interface for customizing a target Bean. Each object implementing this interface should also inherit from java.awt.Component so that it may be instantiated safely within an AWT dialog or panel. It is also important to note that every class which implements this interface should have a constructor which takes no arguments.

addPropertyChangeListener(PropertyChangeListener) Method

This method registers a listener for the PropertyChange event. A Customizer should fire a PropertyChange event anytime it changes the target Bean in a way which might require the refresh of displayed properties.

Syntax: `void addPropertyChangeListener(PropertyChangeListener listener)`

Parameters: listener: the object to be invoked when a PropertyChange event is fired

removePropertyChangeListener(PropertyChangeListener) Method

This method removes a listener from the set of objects which receive the PropertyChangeEvent.

Syntax: `void removePropertyChangeListener(PropertyChangeListener listener)`

Parameters: listener: the object removed from the notification of PropertyChange events

setObject(Object) Method

This method sets the Bean object which is to be customized. This method should only be called once and before the Customizer has been added to any parent Container.

Syntax: `void setObject(Object bean)`

Parameters: bean: the object which is to be customized

Customizer

PropertyChangeListener Interface

This interface extends EventListener. Every time a Bean has a "bound" property changed, it fires a PropertyChange event. A class that implements this interface can register events with a class that implements the addPropertyChangeListener() method.

propertyChange(PropertyChangeEvent) Method

In a class implementing this interface, this is the method that gets called whenever a bound property in and object it has registered for is changed.

Syntax: `void propertyChange(PropertyChangeEvent evt)`

Parameters: evt: the PropertyChangeEvent object describing the event source and the property which has been changed

PropertyEditor Interface

A class implementing this interface provided support for graphical user interfaces which want to allow their users to edit a property of a given type. The PropertyEditor interface supports a wide variety of different ways of displaying and updating property values however, most implementations of this interface need only to support a subset of the different options available.

Simplistic PropertyEditors need only support the getAsText and setAsText methods and ignore support for some of the fancier methods such as paintValue or getCustomEditor.

Every PropertyEditor, however, must support one or more of three simple display styles. It can either (1) support isPaintable, (2) return a non-null String array from getTags and return a non-null value from getAsText, or (3) return a non-null String from getAsText(). Every PropertyEditor must also support the setValue method when the argument object is of the type for which this is the corresponding PropertyEditor and must support either a custom editor or setAsText.

Each PropertyEditor should have a null constructor.

addPropertyChangeListener(PropertyChangeListener) Method

Registers an object for receiving PropertyChange events. Whenever a PropertyEditor changes its value, it should fire a PropertyChange event on all registered PropertyChangeListeners.

Syntax: `void addPropertyChangeListener(PropertyChangeListener listener)`

Parameters: listener: the object to be invoked when a PropertyChange event is fired

getAsText() Method

This method returns the property value as a String which can be edited. The PropertyEditor should be prepared to parse the String back in the setAsText() method. This method returns null if the property can't be expressed as an editable string.

Syntax: `String getAsText()`

Returns: A String of the property value or null.

getCustomEditor() Method

A PropertyEditor may have available a full custom Component that can edit its property value. It is the responsibility of the PropertyEditor to hook itself up to its editor Component and to report property value changes by firing a PropertyChange event whenever necessary.

This method returns null if there is no Custom Editor associated with this property value.

Syntax: `Component getCustomEditor()`

Returns: A java.awt.Component or null.

getJavaInitializationString() Method

This method is intended to be used when generating Java code to set the value of the property. It returns a fragment of Java code that can be used to initialize a variable with the current property value.

Syntax: `String getJavaInitializationString()`

Returns: A String of Java code.

getTags() Method

If the property value that this PropertyEditor is operating on must be one of a set of known tagged values, then this method should return a String array of the tags values.

If a PropertyEditor supports tags, then its setAsText method should support the use of tags as a way of setting the property value.

Syntax: `public abstract String[] getTags()`

Returns: A String array of the Tags.

getValue() Method

This method returns the value of the property. Primitive types such as "int" will be wrapped in their corresponding object type such as "java.lang.Integer".

Syntax: `Object getValue()`

Returns: The Object property value.

isPaintable() Method

Syntax: `boolean isPaintable()`

Returns: True if the class will honor the paintValue method.

paintValue(Graphics, Rectangle) Method

This method paints a representation of the property value into a given area. It is important to note that the PropertyEditor is responsible for clipping itself to fit into the Rectangle given.

If the PropertyEditor does not honor paint requests, this method should be implemented as an empty method performing no tasks.

Syntax:	**public abstract void paintValue(Graphics gfx, Rectangle box)**
Parameters:	gfx: the java.awt.Graphics object to paint into
	box: the Rectangle inside the Graphcis object within which painting is to occur

removePropertyChangeListener(PropertyChangeListener) Method

Removes the specified PropertyChange event listener from this PropertyEditor.

Syntax:	**void removePropertyChangeListener(PropertyChangeListener listener)**
Parameters:	listener: the Object which has been listening

setAsText(String) Method

Sets the property value by parsing the String given. This method may raise an IllegalArgumentException if either the String is badly formatted or if this property cannot be expressed as text.

Syntax:	**void setAsText(String text)**
Parameters:	text: the String to be parsed
Throws:	java.lang.IllegalArgumentException.

setValue(Object) Method

This method sets the object that is to be edited. Primitive types such as "int" will be wrapped in its corresponding object wrapper such as "java.lang.Integer".

Syntax:	**void setValue(Object value)**
Parameters:	value: the new target object to be edited

PropertyEditor

supportsCustomEditor() Method

Syntax: `boolean supportsCustomEditor()`

Returns: True if the PropertyEditor is capable of providing a custom editor.

VetoableChangeListener Interface

Extends: java.util.EventListner

Whenever a Bean changes a "constrained" property, a VetoableChange event will be fired. A VetoableChangeListener can be registered with a Bean so as to be notified whenever a VetoableChange event is fired.

vetoableChange(PropertyChangeEvent) Method

This method will be called in a Listener whenever a constrained property is changed. The recipient may throw a PropertyVetoException if it wishes to roll back the property change.

Syntax: `void vetoableChange(PropertyChangeEvent evt)`

Parameters: evt: a PropertyChangeEvent object describing the event source and the property that has changed

Throws: PropertyVetoException.

Visibility Interface

In some circumstances, such as a web server, a Bean may be run where a GUI is not available. This interface can be used to query a Bean in order to determine whether or not it absolutely needs a GUI and to advise a Bean whether or not a GUI is available for its use.

This interface is marked for use by expert developers by JavaSoft and should not be needed for simple Beans. To further emphasize the non-standard usage of this interface, the standard getXXXX and setXXXX design patterns are not used in this Interface.

avoidingGui() Method

This method should be used to determine whether or not a Bean is avoiding the use of a GUI (possibly due to the use of the dontUseGui() method).

Syntax: `boolean avoidingGui()`

Returns: True if the Bean is currently avoiding the usage of a GUI.

dontUseGui() Method

This method tells the code using this Bean that it should not graphically represent the Bean. This method can be used to override the Bean's implementation of the Component class. By changing the value returned form this method, the Bean can be made to have two states, invisible or visible.

Syntax: `void dontUseGui()`

needsGui() Method

If the Bean absolutely, positively has to have a GUI in order to work, then it should implement this method to return true. Otherwise, it should be implemented to return false.

Syntax: `boolean needsGui()`

Returns: True if the Bean absolutely needs a GUI in order to do its job.

okToUseGui() Method

This method notifies the Bean that the use of a Graphical User Interface is permitted.

Syntax: `void okToUseGui()`

BeanDescriptor Class

This class extends FeatureDescriptor. A BeanDescriptor provides overall information about a Bean. It is one of the descriptors which can be returned by a BeanInfo object.

BeanDescriptor(Class) Constructor

Creates a BeanDescriptor for a Bean.

Syntax: `BeanDescriptor(Class beanClass)`

Parameters: beanClass: the Class which implements the Bean

BeanDescriptor(Class, Class) Constructor

Creates a BeanDescriptor for a Bean which has an associated Customizer.

Syntax: `BeanDescriptor(Class beanClass, Class customizerClass)`

Parameters: beanClass: the Class which implements the Bean
CustomizerClass: the Class which implements the Bean's Customizer

getBeanClass() Method

Syntax: `Class getBeanClass()`

Returns: A Class object for the Bean.

getCustomizerClass() Method

Syntax: `Class getCustomizerClass()`

Returns: A Class object for the Bean's Customizer or null if the Bean does not have a Customizer.

Beans Class

A general class which contains a collection of some static Bean control methods.

getInstanceOf(Object, Class) Method

For a given Bean and target type, this method will return an instance of the Bean. If the requested target view is not available, then the Bean that was given to this method will be returned.

Syntax: `static Object getInstanceOf(Object bean, Class targetType)`

Parameters: bean: the Bean object from which to obtain a view
                 targetType: a Class object representing the type of view to return

Returns: An Object representing a specific type view of the source Bean.

instantiate(ClassLoader, String) Method

This static method instantiates a Bean based on a name relative to a ClassLoader. The name should be a standard java "dot" seperated name such as "COM.newriders.bookbean".

When this method attempts to instantiate the Bean, it first tries to treat the given beanName as a serialized object or class, then it tries to load it as if it were a normal class name. For example, if you give this method a beanName of COM.newriders.bookbean, this method would first try to read a serialized object from the resource COM/newriders/bookbean.ser and if that failed, it would then try to load COM.newriders.bookbean from the classpath and create an instance of that class.

Syntax: `static Object instantiate(ClassLoader cls, String beanName)`

Parameters: cls: a ClassLoader
                 beanName: the String of a Bean resource

Returns: The instantiated Bean.

Throws: java.io.IOException, java.lang.ClassNotFoundException.

isDesignTime() Method

A simple test to see if the current environment is an application construction environment.

Syntax: `static boolean isDesignTime()`

Returns: True if the current environment is an application construction enviroment.

isGuiAvailable() Method

A test to see if the current enviroment is one where a Bean can behave as though an interactive GUI is available so that dialog boxes and the like can be employed. Normally, this will return true in a client windowing environment and false in a server environment.

Syntax: `static boolean isGuiAvailable()`

Returns: True if a GUI can be used.

isInstanceOf(Object, Class) Method

A test to see if a Bean can be viewed as a given target type. The result will be true if the Beans.getInstanceof method can be used on the Bean to obtain an object which represents the specified targetType view.

Syntax: `static boolean isInstanceOf(Object bean, Class targetType)`

Parameters: bean: the Bean from which the view is to be obtained
               targetType: the type of View that is being testing for

Returns: True if the Bean supports the targetType.

setDesignTime(boolean) Method

Used to set the DesignTime flag. This method security checked and is not available to untrusted code.

Syntax: `static void setDesignTime(boolean isDesignTime)`

Parameters: isDesignTime: the desired flag

Throws: java.lang.SecurityException.

setGuiAvailable(boolean) Method

Used to set the GuiAvailble flag. This method security checked and is not available to untrusted code.

Syntax: `static void setGuiAvailable(boolean isGuiAvailable)`

Parameters: isGuiAvailable: the desired flag

Throws: java.lang.SecurityException.

EventSetDescriptor Class

This class extends FeatureDescriptor. An EventSetDescriptor describes a group of events that a Bean can fire. This group is delivered as method calls on a single EventListener interface. An object which implements the EventListener interface can be registered via a call on a registration method supplied.

EventSetDescriptor(Class, String, Class, String) Constructor

This constructor is used to create an EventSetDescriptor given the Bean class that is the source of events, the event name, the type of listener that can be registerd to receive events, and the method of the event listener to call when the event is generated.

Syntax: `EventSetDescriptor(Class sourceClass, String eventSetName, Class`
                `listenerType, listenerMethodName)`

Parameters: sourceClass: the Class which fires the event
                eventSetName: the name of the event
                listenerType: the target interface that events will be delivered to
                listenerMethodName: the method which is called when the event gets
                delivered to its target listener interface

Throws: IntrospectionException.

EventSetDescriptor(Class, String, Class, String[], String, String) Constructor

This constructor creates an EventSetDescriptor without making assumptions.

Syntax: `EventSetDescriptor(Class sourceClass, String eventSetName, Class listener, String listenerMethodNames[], String addListenerMethodName, String removeListenerMethodName)`

Parameters: addListenerMethodName: the name of the event source method that can be used to register an event listener object

eventSetName: the name of the event

listenerType: the target interface that events will be delivered to

listenerMethodNames[]: an array of the names of the methods that will be called when the event is delivered to its target interface

RemoveListenerMethodName: the name of the event source method that can be used to unregister an event listener object

sourceClass: the Class which fires the event

Throws: IntrospectionException.

EventSetDescriptor(String, Class, Method[], Method, Method) Constructor

This constructor creates an EventSetDescriptor using java.lang.reflect.Method and java.lang.Class objects.

Syntax: `EventSetDescriptor(String eventSetName, Class listenerType, Method listenerMethods[], Method addListenerMethod, Method removeListenerMethod)`

Parameters: addListenerMethod: the method of the event source that can be used to register an EventListener object

eventSetName: the name of the event set

ListenerMethods[]: an array of Method objects describing each of the event handling methods in the target listener listenerType: the Class of the listener interface

removeListenerMethod: the method of the event source that can be used to unregister an EventListener object

Throws: IntrospectionException.

EventSetDescriptor(String, Class, MethodDescriptor[], Method, Method) Constructor

This constructor creates an EventSetDescriptor using java.beans.MethodDescriptor and java.lang.Class objects.

Syntax:
```
EventSetDescriptor(String eventSetName, Class listenerType,
MethodDescriptor, listenerMethodDescriptors[], Method
addListenerMethod, Method removeListenerMethod)
```

Parameters: addListenerMethod: the method of the event source that can be used to register an EventListener object

eventSetName: the name of the event set

ListenerMethodDescriptors[]: an array of MethodDescriptor objects describing each of the event handling methods in the target listener

listenerType: the Class of the listener interface

removeListenerMethod: the method of the event source that can be used to unregister an EventListener object

Throws: IntrospectionException.

---

getAddListenerMethod() Method

This method returns a Method object representing the event source method which is used to register a EventListener.

Syntax: `Method getAddListenerMethod()`

Returns: A java.lang.reflect.Method object.

getListenerMethodDescriptors() Method

This method returns a set of MethodDescriptor objects for the event listener interface which will be called when events are received from the event source.

Syntax: `MethodDescriptor[] getListenerMethodDescriptors()`

Returns: An array of MethodDescriptor objects.

getListenerMethods() Method

This method returns a set of Method objects for the methods in the event listener interface which will be called when events are received from the event source.

Syntax: `Method[] getListenerMethods()`

Returns: An array of java.lang.reflect.Method objects.

getListenerType() Method

This method returns a Class object for the target interface which will be invoked when the event is fired.

Syntax: `Class getListenerType()`

Returns: A java.lang.Class object.

getRemoveListenerMethod() Method

This method returns a Method object representing the method which is used to register an event listener at the event source.

Syntax: `Method getRemoveListenerMethod()`

Returns: A Method object.

isInDefaultEventSet() Method

Verifies if an event is in the default set. The return value for this method defaults to true.

Syntax: `boolean isInDefaultEventSet()`

Returns: boolean true or false.

isUnicast() Method

By default, event sources are multicast. However, there are some sources that are only unicast. This method tests for this case.

Syntax: `boolean isUnicast()`

Returns: boolean true or false.

setInDefaultEventSet(boolean) Method

Mark an event set (or not set) as being in the default event set. The default value for this property is true.

Syntax: `void setInDefaultEventSet(boolean inDefaultEventSet)`

Parameters: inDefaultEventSet: the boolean value to set this property to

setUnicast(boolean) Method

This method marks an event set as being unicast or not.

Syntax: `void setUnicast(boolean unicast)`

Parameters: unicast: boolean value

FeatureDescriptor Class

This class is the superclass for all of the descriptor methods in this package. It suppports some common information that can be set and retrieved for any of the introspection descriptors. Also, it provides an extension mechanism allowing arbitrary attribute/value pairs that can be associated with a design feature.

FeatureDescriptor() Constructor

Syntax: `FeatureDescriptor()`

attributeNames() Method

This method returns an Enumeration of the locale-independent names of the attributes that have been registered with *setValue()*.

Syntax: `Enumeration attributeNames()`

Returns: A java.lang.Enumeration object.

getDisplayName() Method

This method returns the localized display name for the property, name, or event that this descriptor describes. This value defaults to the same value as its programmatic name that is returned by *getName()*.

Syntax: `public String getDisplayName()`

Returns: A String containing the name.

getName() Method

This method returns the programmatic name of the property, name, or event that this descriptor describes.

Syntax: `String getName()`

Returns: A String containing the name.

getShortDescription() Method

This method returns a localized short description associated with the property, name, or event that this descriptor describes. This value defaults to be the display name.

Syntax: `String getShortDescription()`

Returns: A String containing the description.

getValue(String) Method

This method retrieves a named attribute with a specified feature. This method may return null if the attribute is unknown.

Syntax: `Object getValue(String attributeName)`

Parameters: attributeName: the local-independent name of the attribute

Returns: A String containing the description or null.

isExpert() Method

This method returns a boolean value indicating whether or not this feature is intended for use by experts only and should not be used by normal users.

Syntax: `boolean isExpert()`

Returns: boolean true or false.

isHidden() Method

This method identifies if this feature is intended for internal Bean use only and should hidden from humans. Candidates that return true might also be manipulated in a Bean's Customizer.

Syntax: `boolean isHidden()`

Returns: boolean true or false.

setDisplayName(String) Method

This method sets the localized display name for this property, method, or event.

Syntax: `void setDisplayName(String displayName)`

Parameters: displayName: a string containing the localized display name

FeatureDescriptor

setExpert(boolean) Method

The expert flag is used to distinguish those features which are intended only for use by expert users rather than normal users.

Syntax: `void setExpert(boolean expert)`

Parameters: expert: boolean flag indicating if this feature is for experts only

setHidden(boolean) Method

The hidden flag is used to identify those features which are intended only for use by tools and which should not be exposed to human programmers.

Syntax: `void setHidden(boolean hidden)`

Parameters: hidden: boolean flag indicating that this feature should be hidden

setName(String Method)

This method sets the programmatic name of a Bean property, method, or event.

Syntax: `void setName(String name)`

Parameters: name: string containing the programmatic name

setShortDescription(String) Method

This method associates a descriptive string with a Bean feature. It is recommended that these descriptions be less than 40 characters in length.

Syntax: `void setShortDescription(String text)`

Parameters: text: string containing the localized description

setValue(String, Object) Method

This method associates a named attribute with this Bean feature.

Syntax: `void setValue(String attributeName, Object value)`

Parameters: attributeName: the local-independent name of the attribute
value: the value

IndexedPropertyDescriptor Class

This class extends PropertyDescriptor. IndexedPropertyDescriptors describe properties that act like an array and have an indexed read or write method to access specific elements in the array. Indexed properties may also provide simple non-indexed read and write methods.

IndexedPropertyDescriptor(String, Class) Constructor

Constructs an IndexedPropertyDescriptor for a property that follows the standard software pattern of having getXXXX and setXXXX accessor methods. If the property name given is "wired," the constructor will assume that there is an indexed read method "getWired," a non-indexed read method "getWired," and indexed write method "setWired," and a non-indexed write method "setWired."

Syntax: `IndexedPropertyDescriptor(String propertyName, Class beanClass)`

Parameters: beanClass: class object for the target bean
propertyName: string containing the name of the property

Throws: IntrospectionException.

IndexedPropertyDescriptor(String, Class, String, String, String, String) Constructor

Constructs an IndexedPropertyDescriptor for a property using the method names for reading and writing to the property given in the constructor signature.

Syntax: `IndexedPropertyDescriptor(String propertyName, Class beanClass,`
`String getterName, String setterName, String indexedGetterName,`
`String indexedSetterName)`

Parameters: beanClass: class object for the target bean
getterName: string containing the name of the method used for reading the property values as an array. This may be set to null if the property is write-only or must be indexed.

indexedGetterName: string containing the name of the method used for reading an indexed property value. This may be set to null if the property is write-only.

indexedSetterName: string containing the name of the method used for writing an indexed property value. This may be set to null if the property is read-only
propertyName: string containing the name of the property
SetterName: string containing the name of the method used for writing the property values as an array. This may be set to null if the property is read-only or must be indexed

Throws: IntrospectionException.

IndexedPropertyDescriptor(String, Method, Method, Method, Method) Constructor

Constructs an IndexedPropertyDescriptor for a property using the given Methods for reading and writing to the property.

Syntax: `IndexedPropertyDescriptor(String propertyName, Method getter, Method setter, Method indexedGetter, Method indexedSetter)`

Parameters: getter: method object representing the method used for reading the property values as an array. This may be set to null if the property is write-only or must be indexed.
indexedGetter: method object representing the method used for reading an indexed property value. This may be set to null if the property is write-only.
indexedSetter: method object representing the method used for writing an indexed property value. This may be set to null if the property is read-only.
propertyName: string containing the name of the property
setter: Method object representing the method used for setting the property values as an array. This may be set to null if the property is read-only or must be indexed.

Throws: IntrospectionException.

getIndexedPropertyType() Method

This method returns the type of object that will be returned by the indexedReadMethod. It is important to note that this method may return a Class which describes a Java primitive such as "int."

Syntax: `Class getIndexedPropertyType()`

Returns: Class object for the indexed properties type.

getIndexedReadMethod() Method

Syntax: `Method getIndexedReadMethod()`

Returns: Method object representing the method that should be used to read an indexed property value. This method may also return null if the property is not indexed or is write-only.

getIndexedWriteMethod() Method

Syntax: `Method getIndexedWriteMethod()`

Returns: Method object representing the method that should be used to write an indexed property value. This method may also return null if the property is not indexed or is write-only.

Introspector Class

The Introspector provides a standard way for tools and enviroments to learn about the properties, events, and methods supported by a target Bean. For each of these three kinds of information, the Introspector will analyze the Bean's class and superclass definitions for either explicit or implicit information in order to build a BeanInfo object that describes the target Bean in a comprehensive manner.

Explicit information can be obtained if there is a corresponding BeanInfo class which returns a non-null value when queried for the information. The Introspector looks for a BeanInfo class by taking the full package-qualified name of the target Bean class and appending BeanInfo to form a new classname. If this fails, then the final classname component of the class is taken and used as class name to be looked for in each of the packages specified in the BeanInfo package search path.

For an example bean of COM.beans.CoolButton, the Introspector would look for a BeanInfo class named COM.beans.CoolButtonBeanInfo. If this failed, the Introspector would look for CoolButtonBeanInfo in each package in the BeanInfo search path. When running in the default environment, the Introspector would look for sun.beans.infos. CoolButtonBeanInfo.

If a class has explicit information provided by a BeanInfo class, the Introspector adds this information to that which may have been obtained from analyzing any derived classes. The Introspector will regard the explicit information as being definitive for the current class and all of its base classes and will not proceed with analysis any further up the superclass chain.

If explicit information is not found, then low-level reflection is used to study the methods of the given Class and standard design patterns are used to identify property accessors, event sources, and public methods. The Classes superclass is then analyzed and the information found from this examination is added to the BeanInfo. This upward progression up the superclass chain proceeds until an explicit BeanInfo object is returned or the top of the chain is reached.

decapitalize(String) Method

This is a utility method used to take a String and convert it to normal Java variable name capitalization. In normal practice this means converting the first character from upper case to lower case except in the case where the first and second characters are upper case, in which case no translation is made.

Syntax:	`static String decapitalize(String name)`
Parameters:	name: string containing the name to be decapitalized
Returns:	String containing the translated name.

getBeanInfo(Class) Method

The method Introspects a Bean in order to learn about all of its properties, exposed methods, and events.

Syntax: `static BeanInfo getBeanInfo(Class beanClass)`

Parameters: beanClass: class object of the Bean to be analyzed

Returns: A BeanInfo object describing the Bean.

Throws: IntrospectionException.

getBeanInfo(Class, Class) Method

The method Introspects a Bean in order to learn about all of its properties, exposed methods, and events. This method will stop introspection at a specified Class in the superclass chain of the Bean Class. Any methods, properties, or events in the stopClass or in its base classes will be ignored in the analysis and will not be reflected in the resulting BeanInfo object.

Syntax: `static BeanInfo getBeanInfo(Class beanClass, Class stopClass)`

Parameters: beanClass: class object of the Bean to be analyzed.
                   stopClass: class object of the baseclass at which analysis should stop

Returns: A BeanInfo object describing the Bean.

Throws: IntrospectionException.

getBeanInfoSearchPath() Method

This is a utility method which will return an array of the package names which will be searched to find a BeanInfo class by the Introspector.

Syntax: `static String[] getBeanInfoSearchPath()`

Returns: An array of package names.

setBeanInfoSearchPath(String[]) Method

This is a utility method which sets the list of package names which will be used by the Introspector in finding BeanInfo classes.

Syntax: `static void setBeanInfoSearchPath(String path[])`

Parameters: path: an array of package names

MethodDescriptor Class

This class extends FeatureDescriptor. A MethodDescriptor describes a specific method that a Bean supports for access from external components.

MethodDescriptor(Method) Constructor

This constructor is used to automatically generate a MethodDescriptor based on the given Method object. The object created by this constructor only contains the data related to the method and its parameters as can be derived through Core Reflection.

Syntax: `MethodDescriptor(Method method)`

Parameters: method: method object describing the low level information about the method

MethodDescriptor(Method, ParameterDescriptor[]) Constructor

In addition to generating the name for the specified method, this constuctor allows for the explicit setting of specific information in the ParameterDescriptor arrary.

Syntax: `MethodDescriptor(Method method, ParameterDescriptor parameterDescriptors[])`

Parameters: method: method object describing the low level information about the method

            parameterDescriptors[]: array of ParameterDescriptors describing each of the methods parameters

getMethod() Method

This method returns the method object for the method described by this MethodDescriptor.

Syntax: `Method getMethod()`

Returns: Method object describing the low level information about the method.

getParameterDescriptors() Method

The *getParameterDescriptors()* method returns an array of ParameterDescriptor objects that describe each of the parameters in the method described by the current MethodDescriptor object.

Syntax: `ParameterDescriptor[] getParameterDescriptors()`

Returns: Array of ParameterDescriptors describing the parameters. This method may return null if the parameter names are not known.

ParameterDescriptor Class

This class extends FeatureDescriptor. ParameterDescriptors allow Beans to provide additional information on each of their parameters above and beyond the low level type information provided by the java.lang.reflect.Method class. As implemented by Javasoft, this class has no implementation beyond that of the superclass FeatureDescriptor.

Please refer to the FeatureDescriptor class.

PropertyChangeEvent Class

This class extends java.util.EventObject. A PropertyChangeEvent is delivered whenever a bound or constrained property of a Bean is changed. Typically, PropertyChangeEvents are accompanied by the old and new value of the property which has been changed. If the value is a primitive type (such as int or char) it must be wrapped in the corresponding Object type (such as java.lang.Integer or java.lang.Character).

If null values are provided for the old or new values, it means that the true values for the property is not known. In addition, an event source may send a null object as the name to indicate that an arbitrary group of its properties has been changed. In this case, the old and new values should be specified as null as well.

PropertyChangeEvent(Object, String, Object, Object) Constructor

The PropertyChangeEvent constructor creates an event object that specifies that a Bean property has been modified. The constructor uses a reference to the object creating the event, the property name, and the old/new values to give context to the change. The PropertyChangeEvent object should be created in the assumption that the change has already occurred. The sequence around the creation of a PropertyChangeEvent should follow this sequence:

1. Copy the current property value into a temporary location.

2. Change the property to the new value.

3. Create a PropertyChangeEvent object using the temporary and the new value.

4. Notify listeners.

In general, the PropertyChangeSupport class should be used to create the PropertyChangeEvent and notify all registered listeners.

The old/new parameters are Object class references so changes to primitives like int or float must be converted to their object equivalents like Integer and Float. The old/new parameters should be immutable objects (objects that once constructed cannot be changed) or copy the old/new values to new objects. The primary goal is to not pass values in the old/new parameters that can be used to modify the property directly.

Syntax:
```
public PropertyChangeEvent(Object source, String propertyName,
Object oldValue, Object newValue)
```

Parameters: newValue: the new value of the property
oldValue: the old value of the property
propertyName: string containing the name of the property that was changed
source: Bean that fired the event

getNewValue() Method

Returns the new value of the property that was modified. Note, this new value is also the current value of the object generating the event.

Syntax: `Object getNewValue()`

Returns: The new value of the property.

getOldValue() Method

Returns the old value of the property that was modified. Note, this old value is no longer in use by the object generating the event.

Syntax: `Object getOldValue()`

Returns: The old value of the property.

getPropagationId() Method

The propagationId field is reserved by JavaSoft for future use. In Beans 1.0, the only requirement is that if a listener issues a PropertyChangeEvent due to receiving a PropertyChangeEvent, then it should take care to propagate the propagationId to the outgoing event from the incoming event.

Syntax: `Object getPropagationId()`

Returns: PropagationId object associated with a bound or constrained property update.

getPropertyName() Method

The *getPropertyName()* method returns the string that was set by the object generating the property change event. This name should be the decapitalized name of the property that was changed.

Syntax: `String getPropertyName()`

Returns: String containing the name of the property that was changed. This value
                  may be null if multiple properties have been changed.

setPropagationId(Object) Method

The method sets the propagationId field of a PropertyChangeEvent.

Syntax: `setPropagationId(Object propagationId)`

Parameters: propagationId: the PropagationId object for the event

PropertyChangeSupport Class

This class implements java.io.Serializable. PropertyChangeSupport is a utility class that can
be used by Beans to support bound properties. This class can be inherited, or an instance of
this class can be used as a member field of a Bean and have work delegated to it.

PropertyChangeSupport(Object) Constructor

The constructor for PropertyChangeSupport is used to create a property change support object
that is associated with a specified source object that generates property change events.

Syntax: `PropertyChangeSupport(Object sourceBean)`

Parameters: sourceBean: the object that generates property change events

addPropertyChangeListener(PropertyChangeListener) Method

The method adds a PropertyChangeListener to the listener list.

Syntax: `synchronized void addPropertyChangeListener(PropertyChangeListener
                  listener)`

Parameters: listener: the PropertyChangeListener to be added

firePropertyChange(String, Object, Object) Method

Reports a bound property update to any registered listeners. No event is fired if the oldValue parameter and newValue parameter are equal.

Syntax: `void firePropertyChange(String propertyName, Object oldValue, Object newValue)`

Parameters: newValue: the new value of the object
oldValue: the old value of the object
propertyName: string containing the name of the property that was changed

removePropertyChangeListener(PropertyChangeListener) Method

This method removes a PropertyChangeListener from the listener list.

Syntax: `synchronized void removePropertyChangeListener(PropertyChangeListener listener)`

Parameters: listener: the PropertyChangeListener to be removed

PropertyDescriptor Class

This class extends FeatureDescriptor. A PropertyDescriptor describes one property that a Bean exports through a pair of get and set accessor methods.

PropertyDescriptor(String, Class) Constructor

Constructs a PropertyDescriptor for a property that follows the standard design pattern by having getXXXX and setXXXX accessor methods. If the property name is given as "wired," the constructor will assume that the read method is "getWired" and the write method is "setWired." It is important to note that the property name should start with a lower case character as it will be capitalized appropriately to match the design pattern.

Syntax: `PropertyDescriptor(String propertyName, Class beanClass)`

Parameters:	beanClass: class object for the Bean
	propertyName: string containing the name of the property
Throws:	IntrospectionException.

PropertyDescriptor(String, Class, String, String) Constructor

Constructs a PropertyDescriptor given the name of a property, the Class object of the Bean, and the method names for reading and writing the property.

Syntax:	`PropertyDescriptor(String propertyName, Class beanClass, String getterName, setterName)`
Parameters:	beanClass: class object for the Bean.
	getterName: string containing the name of the method used for reading the property value. This value may be set to null if the property is write only.
	propertyName: string containing the name of the property
	SetterName: string containing the name of the method used for writing the property value. This value may be set to null if the property is read only.
Throws:	IntrospectionException.

PropertyDescriptor(String, Method, Method) Constructor

Constructs a PropertyDescriptor given the name of a property and the Method objects for reading from and writing to the property.

Syntax:	`PropertyDescriptor(String propertyName, Method getter, Method setter)`
Parameters:	getter: method object representing the method used for reading the property value. This may be set to null if the property is write-only.
	propertyName: string containing the name of the property
	Setter: method object representing the method used for setting the property value. This may be set to null if the property is read-only.

getPropertyEditorClass() Method

The method returns a PropertyEditor class that has been explicitly registered for editing of this property. Normally, this method will return a null value which indicates that no special editor has been registered. This indicates that the PropertyEditorManager should be used in order to determine a suitable PropertyEditor.

Syntax: `Class getPropertyEditorClass()`

Returns: Any PropertyEditor that has been registered for this property.

getPropertyType() Method

This method returns the type of object that will be returned by the result of the property's ReadMethod. The result of this operation may be null if this is an indexed property that does not support non-indexed access.

Syntax: `Class getPropertyType()`

Returns: A Class object describing the type info for this property.

getReadMethod() Method

Syntax: `Method getReadMethod()`

Returns: A Method object which represents the method used to read the property's value. This value may be null if the property cannot be read.

getWriteMethod() Method

Syntax: `Method getWriteMethod()`

Returns: A Method object which represents the method used to read the property's value. This value may be null if the property cannot be written.

PropertyDescriptor

isBound() Method

This method indicates whether or not this is a bound property. Bound properties will fire a PropertyChangeEvent whenever they are updated.

Syntax: `boolean isBound()`

Returns: boolean True if this property is a bound property.

isConstrained() Method

This method indicates whether or not this is a constrained property. Updates to a constrained property will result in the firing of a VetoableChange event.

Syntax: `boolean isConstrained()`

Returns: boolean True if this property is a constrained property.

setBound(boolean) Method

This method sets whether or not this is a bound property. Bound properties will fire a PropertyChangeEvent whenever they are updated.

Syntax: `void setBound(boolean bound)`

Parameters: bound: boolean indicating whether or not this property should be bound

setConstrained(boolean) Method

This method sets whether or not this is a constrained property. Updates to a constrained property will result in the firing of a VetoableChange event.

Syntax: `void setConstrained(boolean constrained)`

Parameters: bound: boolean indicating whether or not this property should be constrained

setPropertyEditorClass(Class) Method

In normal practice, PropertyEditors will be found using the PropertyEditorManager. However, it can be advantageous to associate a particular PropertyEditor with a given property. This method allows this.

Syntax: `void setPropertyEditorClass(Class propertyEditorClass)`

Parameters: propertyEditorClass: class object of the property editor

PropertyEditorManager Class

The PropertyEditorManager is used to locate a property editor for any given property type. This class uses the following method to locate and editor for a given type: First, it looks to see if an editor has been registered for the type. Second, it tries to locate a suitable class by adding the string "Editor" to the fully qualified classname of the given type. Finally, it takes the simple classname with "Editor" postpended and looks for a Class with this name in the search path.

A property editor must implement the PropertyEditor interface.

Default property editors for the Java primitive types and for the classes java.lang.String, java.awt.Color, and java.awt.Font are provided in the sun.beans.editors package.

findEditor(Class) Method

This method locates an editor for a given value type.

Syntax: `static PropertyEditor findEditor(Class targetType)`

Parameters: targetType: class object for the property type to be edited

Returns: An editor object for the given property type. The result may be null if no suitable editor can be found.

PropertyEditorManager

getEditorSearchPath() Method

A utility method which will return an array of the package names which will be searched to find a property editor.

Syntax: `static String[] getEditorSearchPath()`

Returns: An array of package names.

registerEditor(Class, Class) Method

This method registers an editor for a particular property type.

Syntax: `static void registerEditor(Class targetType, Class editorClass)`

Parameters: editorClass: class object of the editor. If this property is set to null, then any existing definition for this targetType will be removed
targetType: class object of the type of property to be edited

setEditorSearchPath(String[]) Method

A utility method which sets the list of package names which will be used for finding property editors.

Syntax: `static void setEditorSearchPath(String path[])`

Parameters: path: an array of package names

SimpleBeanInfo Class

This class implements BeanInfo and is a basic implementation of the BeanInfo interface which is intended to help programmers provide BeanInfo classes with their Beans. Each method defaults to providing null information, and can be selectively overridden to provide more explicit information on chosen topics. When the Introspector sees the null values, it will apply low level introspection and design patterns to automatically analyze the target bean.

SimpleBeanInfo Constructor

The default constructor for SimpleBeanInfo creates an object that will return null for all methods. For SimpleBeanInfo to be useful, the SimpleBeanInfo class should be extended.

Syntax: `SimpleBeanInfo()`

getAdditionalBeanInfo() Method

A non-operative method which can be overriden to provide explicit information if such information is available. Otherwise, the Introspector will apply low level introspection to analyze the Bean.

Syntax: `BeanInfo[] getAdditionalBeanInfo()`

Returns: Null unless explicitly overridden.

getBeanDescriptor() Method

A non-operative method which can be overriden to provide explicit information if such information is available. Otherwise, the Introspector will apply low level introspection to analyze the Bean.

Syntax: `BeanDescriptor getBeanDescriptor()`

Returns: Null unless explicitly overridden.

getDefaultEventIndex() Method

A non-operative method which can be overriden to provide explicit information if such information is available. Otherwise, the Introspector will apply low level introspection to analyze the Bean.

Syntax: `int getDefaultEventIndex()`

Returns: -1 unless explicitly overridden.

getDefaultPropertyIndex() Method

A non-operative method which can be overriden to provide explicit information if such information is available. Otherwise, the Introspector will apply low level introspection to analyze the Bean.

Syntax: `int getDefaultPropertyIndex()`

Returns: -1 unless explicitly overridden.

getEventSetDescriptors() Method

A non-operative method which can be overriden to provide explicit information if such information is available. Otherwise, the Introspector will apply low level introspection to analyze the Bean.

Syntax: `EventSetDescriptor[] getEventSetDescriptors()`

Returns: Null unless explicitly overridden.

getIcon(int) Method

A non-operative method which can be overriden to provide explicit information if such information is available. Otherwise, the Introspector will apply low level introspection to analyze the Bean.

Syntax: `Image getIcon(int iconKind)`

Returns: Null unless explicitly overridden.

getMethodDescriptors() Method

A non-operative method which can be overriden to provide explicit information if such information is available. Otherwise, the Introspector will apply low level introspection to analyze the Bean.

Syntax: `MethodDescriptor[] getMethodDescriptors()`

Returns: Null unless explicitly overridden.

getPropertyDescriptors() Method

A non-operative method which can be overriden to provide explicit information if such information is available. Otherwise, the Introspector will apply low level introspection to analyze the Bean.

Syntax: `PropertyDescriptor[] getPropertyDescriptors()`

Returns: Null unless explicitly overridden.

loadImage(String) Method

Utility to help load icon images. It takes the given resource name and loads an image object from the file described by the resource name.

Syntax: `Image loadImage(String resourceName)`

Parameters: resourceName: string describing a pathname relative to the directory holding the .class file of the current class

Returns: Image object or null if the load failed.

Class VetoableChangeSupport

A utility class for use by Beans which support constrained properties. The class can either be inherited from or an instance of this class can be used as a member field in a Bean that delegates work to it.

VetoableChangeSupport(Object) Constructor

Creates a VetoableChangeSupport object for the specified object which generated VetoableChangeSupport events.

Syntax: `VetoableChangeSupport(Object sourceBean)`

addVetoableChangeListener(VetoableChangeListener) Method

Adds a VetoableListener to the listener list.

Syntax: `synchronized void addVetoableChangeListener(VetoableChangeListener listener)`

Parameters: listener: the VetoableChangeListener to be added

fireVetoableChange(String, Object, Object) Method

Reports an update in a constrained property to any registered listeners. If any of the listeners vetoes the change, then a new event is fired which reverts back to the old value and the PropertyVetoException is thrown from this method.

Syntax: `void fireVetoableChange(String propertyName, Object oldValue, Object newValue)`

Parameters: newValue: object containing the new value of the property
oldValue: object containing the old value of the property
propertyName: string containing the name of the property which was changed

Throws: PropertyVetoException.

removeVetoableChangeListener(VetoableChangeListener) Method

Removes a VetoableListener from the listener list.

Syntax: `synchronized void removeVetoableChangeListener (VetoableChangeListener listener)`

Parameters: listener: the VetoableChangeListener to be removed

IntrospectionException Exception

This exception extends Exception and is thrown when an exception occurs during Introspection. Some of the causes of this exception could be the failure to map a String class name to a Class object, specifying a method name which has the wrong signature for its intended use, or not being able to resolve a method name specified by a string.

IntrospectionException(String) Constructor

This constructor creates an IntrospectionException object that contains the specified message string.

Syntax: `IntrospectionException(String mess)`

Parameters: mess: a descriptive message

PropertyVetoException Exception

This exception extends Exception and is thrown by a listener where a proposed change to a property is an unacceptable value.

PropertyVetoException(String, PropertyChangeEvent) Constructor

Syntax: `PropertyVetoException(String mess, PropertyChangeEvent evt)`

Parameters: evt: propertyChangeEvent describing the vetoed change
                mess: a descriptive message

getPropertyChangeEvent() Method

Syntax: `PropertyChangeEvent getPropertyChangeEvent()`

Returns: PropertyChangeEvent describing the vetoed change.

AWT API

Component Class

The Component class is the most basic level of component in the Java Abstract Window Toolkit (AWT). It is paramount that Java Beans developers understand this class, as it is the basis of all visual components.

Implements: ImageObserver, MenuContainer, Serializable

Extends: Object class

There have been a couple of changes to the Component API in Java 1.1 to maximize the efficiency and usability of its methods. The table that follows documents these changes. The Java 1.1 methods are referenced appropriately in the sections that follow.

The primary changes have been the renaming of many of the property access methods. For example, *bounds()* was changed to *getBounds()* to meet the method signature required for property access in the Java Beans specification.

Java 1.0 Method	Java 1.1 Replacement Method
bounds()	getBounds()
deliverEvent(Event)	dispatchEvent(AWTEvent event)
disable()	setEnabled(boolean)
enable()	setEnabled(boolean)
enable(boolean)	setEnabled(boolean)
getPeer()	**No longer used**
gotFocus(Event, Object)	processFocusEvent(FocusEvent event)

continues

continued

Java 1.0 Method	Java 1.1 Replacement Method
handleEvent(Event)	processEvent(AWTEvent event)
hide() Method	setVisible(boolean)
inside(int, int)	contains(int, int)
keyDown(Event, int)	processKeyEvent(KeyEvent event)
keyUp(Event, int)	processKeyEvent(KeyEvent event)
layout()	doLayout()
locate(int, int)	getComponentAt(int, int)
location()	getLocation()
lostFocus(Event, Object)	processFocusEvent(FocusEvent event)
minimumSize()	getMinimumSize()
mouseDown(Event, int, int)	processMouseEvent(MouseEvent event)
mouseDrag(Event, int, int)	processMouseMotionEvent(MouseEvent event)
mouseEnter(Event, int, int)	processMouseEvent(MouseEvent event)
mouseExit(Event, int, int)	processMouseEvent(MouseEvent event)
mouseMove(Event, int, int)	processMouseMotionEvent(MouseEvent event)
mouseUp(Event, int, int)	processMouseEvent(MouseEvent event)
move(int, int)	setLocation(int, int)
nextFocus()	transferFocus()
postEvent(Event)	dispatchEvent(AWTEvent event)
preferredSize()	getPreferredSize()
reshape(int, int, int, int)	setBounds(int, int, int, int)
resize(Dimension)	setSize(Dimension)
resize(int, int)	setSize(int, int)

Java 1.0 Method	Java 1.1 Replacement Method
show()	setVisible(boolean)
show(boolean)	setVisible(boolean)
size()	getSize()

add(PopupMenu) Method

This method gives the component the specified popup menu. Popup menus are useful for adding option selections for components in a context-sensitive manner.

Syntax: `public synchronized void add(PopupMenu menu)`

Parameters: menu: the popup menu to add to the component

addComponentListener(ComponentListener) Method

This method adds the specified ComponentListener to listen for component events from this component. Component listeners have up to four of the event target methods implemented. The possible methods are listed in the following table:

Listener Method	Event Reason
componentHidden(ComponentEvent)	component was hidden
componentMoved(ComponentEvent)	component was moved
componentResized(ComponentEvent)	component was resized
componentShown(ComponentEvent)	component was shown

Syntax: `public synchronized void addComponentListener(ComponentListener listener)`

Parameters: listener: the specified listener

addFocusListener(FocusListener) Method

This method adds the specified FocusListener to listen for focus events from this component. Focus listeners have up to two of the event target methods implemented. The possible methods are listed in the following table:

Listener Method	Event Reason
focusGained(FocusEvent)	component has gained keyboard focus
focusLost(FocusEvent)	component has lost keyboard focus

Syntax: `public synchronized void addFocusListener(FocusListener listener)`

Parameters: listener: the specified listener

addKeyListener(KeyListener) Method

This method adds the specified KeyListener to listen for key events from this component. Key listeners have up to three of the event target methods implemented. The possible methods are listed in the following table:

Listener Method	Event Reason
keyPressed(KeyEvent)	key has been pressed
keyReleased(KeyEvent)	key has been released
keyTyped(KeyEvent)	key has been typed (pressed and then released)

Syntax: `public synchronized void addKeyListener(KeyListener listener)`

Parameters: listener: the specified listener

addMouseListener(MouseListener) Method

This method adds the specified MouseListener to listen for mouse events from this component. Mouse listeners have up to five of the event target methods implemented. The possible methods are listed in the following table:

Listener Method	Event Reason
mouseClicked(MouseEvent)	mouse has been clicked over a component
mouseEntered(MouseEvent)	mouse enters a component
mouseExited(MouseEvent)	mouse exits a component
mousePressed(MouseEvent)	mouse button has been pressed over a component
mouseReleased(MouseEvent)	mouse button has been released over a component

Syntax: `public synchronized void addMouseListener(MouseListener listener )`

Parameters: listener: the specified listener

addMouseMotionListener(MouseMotionListener) Method

This method adds the specified MouseMotionListener to listen for mouse motion events from this component. Mouse motion listeners have up to two of the event target methods implemented. The possible methods are listed in the following table:

Listener Method	Event Reason
mouseDragged(MouseEvent)	mouse button is pressed and mouse has moved while over a component
mouseMoved(MouseEvent)	mouse has been moved over a component (no mouse buttons pressed)

Syntax: `public synchronized void addMouseMotionListener(MouseMotionListener listener )`

Parameters: listener: the specified listener

addNotify() Method

This method informs the component that it has been added to a container and the peer should be created. A peer is the platform specific handler of the component.

Syntax: `public void addNotify()`

bounds()Method, *see* getBounds() Method

checkImage(Image, ImageObserver) Method

This method checks the status of the construction of the specified image. Refer to the *prepareImage()* method for other relevant information.

Syntax:
```
public int checkImage(Image image, ImageObserver observer)
```

Parameters: image: the image to check
observer: the image Observer

Returns: the boolean or the flags from the ImageObserver.

checkImage(Image, int, int, ImageObserver) Method

This method checks the status of the construction of the specified image. This is used for checking the status of a scaled representation of an image. The preparation of images occurs in a separate thread from the main execution so this method is used to check the status of the image processing thread. Refer to the *prepareImage()* method for other relevant information.

Syntax:
```
public int checkImage(Image image, int width, int height,
ImageObserver observer)
```

Parameters: image: the image to check
width: the width of the representation to check
height: the height of the representation to check
observer: the image Observer

Returns: the ORed status flags from the ImageObserver:

ABORT	image was aborted before production was complete
ALLBITS	static image is now complete and can be drawn
ERROR	image processing has encountered an error
FRAMEBITS	a complete frame of a multi-frame image is now available to be drawn
HEIGHT	height of the base image is now available and can be taken from the height argument to the imageUpdate callback method
PROPERTIES	properties of the image are now available
SOMEBITS	additional pixels needed for drawing a scaled variation of the image are available
WIDTH	width of the base image is now available and can be taken from the width argument to the imageUpdate callback method

contains(int, int) Method

This method determines whether x and y are coordinates that are contained within the component. This method can be used for drag/drop operations or for implementing context-sensitive help. Refer to the *getComponentAt()* method for locating the components at specified locations.

Syntax: `public boolean contains(int x, int y)`

Parameters: x: the x coordinate
y: the y coordinate

Returns: True if the coordinates are contained in the component; False if not.

contains(Point) Method

This method determines whether the point is contained within the component. This method can be used for drag/drop operations or for implementing context-sensitive help. Refer to the *getComponentAt( )* method for locating the components at specified locations.

Syntax: `public boolean contains(Point point)`

Parameters: point: the point to check

Returns: True if the point is contained in the component; False if not.

createImage(ImageProducer) Method

This method uses the specified image producer to create an image.

Syntax: `public Image createImage(ImageProducer producer)`

Parameters: producer: the ImageProducer to use to create the image

Returns: The image that the producer creates.

createImage(int, int) Method

This method creates an off-screen memory context for drawing an Image. Note, this method will return a null if the peer for this component is not available.

Syntax: `public Image createImage(int width,int height)`

Parameters: width: the width
height: the height

Returns: The off-screen image or null if peer is not set.

deliverEvent(Event) Method, *see* dispatchEvent(AWTEvent event)

disable()Method, *see* setEnabled(boolean)

disableEvents(long) Method

This method disables the specified Boolean ORed events. This method is used to stop events from being accepted by this component. The possible events that can be disabled are in the following table:

Event mask	Type of events
ACTION_EVENT_MASK	Action events
ADJUSTMENT_EVENT_MASK	Adjustment events
COMPONENT_EVENT_MASK	Component events
CONTAINER_EVENT_MASK	Container events
FOCUS_EVENT_MASK	Focus events
ITEM_EVENT_MASK	Item events
KEY_EVENT_MASK	Key events
MOUSE_EVENT_MASK	Mouse events
MOUSE_MOTION_EVENT_MASK	Mouse motion events
TEXT_EVENT_MASK	Text events
WINDOW_EVENT_MASK	Window events

Syntax: `protected final void disableEvents(long eventsToDisable)`

Parameters: eventsToDisable: an event mask to specify which events to disable

doLayout() Method

This method lays the component out, usually during validation of the component. The layout mechinism used is specified by the *setLayout()* method. Refer to the *validate()* and *stLayout()* methods for other relevant information.

Syntax: `public void doLayout()`

enable() Method, *see* setEnabled(boolean) Method

enable(boolean) Method, *see* setEnabled(boolean) Method

enableEvents(long) Method

This method enables the processing of the specified events. You should also realize that events are automatically enabled when the associated listener is added to the component.

The event masks that this method accepts are listed below. These constants are final static and in the Java.awt.AWTEvent class. These events can be 'OR'ed together to enable a component to receive these events. Note if a listener is added to the component; the events corresponding to the event will be automatically enabled.

Event mask	Type of events
ACTION_EVENT_MASK	Action events
ADJUSTMENT_EVENT_MASK	Adjustment events
COMPONENT_EVENT_MASK	Component events
CONTAINER_EVENT_MASK	Container events
FOCUS_EVENT_MASK	Focus events
ITEM_EVENT_MASK	Item events
KEY_EVENT_MASK	Key events
MOUSE_EVENT_MASK	Mouse events
MOUSE_MOTION_EVENT_MASK	Mouse motion events
TEXT_EVENT_MASK	Text events
WINDOW_EVENT_MASK	Window events

Syntax: `protected final void enableEvents(long eventMask)`

Parameters: eventMask: an event mask to specify which events to enable. See the Java.awt.AWTEvent class for information on the masks that can be used.

Component

getAlignmentX() Method

This method gets the component's alignment along the x axis in relation to other components. The default is CENTER_ALIGNMENT, which resolves to 0.5. In order to modify this value a child component must override this method. There is no equivalent *setAlignmentX()* method.

Syntax:　　**public float getAlignmentX()**

Returns:　　The component's alignment along the x axis. 0 is aligned with the axis, 1 is furthest from the axis, 0.5 is in the middle.

getAlignmentY() Method

This method gets the component's alignment along the y axis in relation to other components. The default is CENTER_ALIGNMENT, which resolves to 0.5. In order to modify this value a child component must override this method. There is no equivalent *setAlignmentY()* method.

Syntax:　　**public float getAlignmentY()**

Returns:　　The component's alignment along the y axis. 0 is aligned with the axis, 1 is furthest from the axis, 0.5 is in the middle. This method returns 0.5 for most components.

getBackground() Method

This method gets the background color of the component or the background color of its parent if the component does not have a background color. The *setBackground()* method is used to set the color of the background.

Syntax:　　**public Color getBackground()**

Returns:　　The background color of the component.

getBounds() Method

This method gets the bounding rectangle of the component. This method is used to determine the current size of the component. The method *setBounds()* is used to set the bounding rectangle.

Syntax: `public Rectangle getBounds()`

Returns: The bounds of the component.

getColorModel() Method

This method gets the ColorModel used to display the component. The color model can be used to change the palette used by the component.

Syntax: `public ColorModel getColorModel()`

Returns: The ColorModel used by the component.

getComponentAt(int, int) Method

This method gets the component that contains the specified coordinates. This method can be used for activating components (like animations or highlighting if the mouse is over the component), drag and drop operations, or to implement context-sensitive help. Refer to the *contains()* method for locating a component in a bounding rectangle.

Syntax: `public Component getComponentAt(int x, int y)`

Parameters: x: the x coordinate
                y: the y coordinate

Returns: The component containing the specified coordinates.

getComponentAt(Point) Method

This method gets the component that contains the specified coordinates. This method can be used for activating components (like animations or highlighting if the mouse is over the component), drag and drop operations, or to implement context-sensitive help. Refer to the *contains()* method for locating a component in a bounding rectangle.

Syntax: public Component getComponentAt(Point point)

Parameters: point: the point to check

Returns: The component containing the point.

getCursor() Method

This method gets the cursor set of the component. The cursor returned can be saved so that a new cursor can be set (see *setCursor()*) and then restored after an operation is complete.

Syntax: `public Cursor getCursor()`

Returns: The cursor.

getFont() Method

This method gets the font of the component or the font of its parent if the component does not have a font. Note that this method will return a null if there is no parent or the peer has not been set.

The font object can be used in a *getFontMetrics()* method to obtain text size information. This is most important when determining the minimum size of the component.

Syntax: `public Font getFont()`

Returns: The font of the component.

getFontMetrics(Font) Method

This method gets the font metrics for the specified font. Font metrics are used to get font sizing information and to determine the specific size of text strings. This sizing information is most important when determining the minimum size of the component or to calculate offsets to draw text.

Syntax: `public FontMetrics getFontMetrics(Font font)`

Parameters: font: the font

Returns: The font metrics object for the component.

getForeground() Method

This method gets the foreground color of the component or the foreground color of its parent if the component does not have a foreground color. Refer to the *setForeground()* method for setting the foreground color.

Syntax: `public Color getForeground()`

Returns: The foreground color of the component.

getGraphics() Method

This method gets a Graphics context for this component. The context is used to draw directly onto the component. The origin of the context (coordinate 0,0) is the upper left-hand corner of the component's bounding rectangle. This method is primarily used to get a graphical context outside of the component's *paint()* method's normal execution.

Syntax: `public Graphics getGraphics()`

getLocale() Method

This method gets the locale of the component or the locale of its parent if the component does not have a locale. Locale is the language and location that the component is to be represented for. Use locale to control time, date, and language for the component.

Syntax: `public Locale getLocale()`

Returns: The locale of the component.

Throws: IllegalComponentStateException: thrown if the component does not have a locale and the locale of its parent cannot be determined.

getLocation() Method

This method gets the current location of this component in the parent's component context. This information can be used to aid the layout of the component within a parent. The values returned are in relation to the component's upper left corner, which is at coordinate 0,0.

Syntax: `public Point getLocation()`

Returns: The current location of the component based on the parent container's upper left corner being 0,0.

getLocationOnScreen() Method

This method gets the current location of this component in the screen's context. The values returned are in relation to the screen's upper left corner, which is at coordinate 0,0. This method is primarily used to change the location of windows and frames in relation to the display screen.

Syntax: `public Point getLocationOnScreen()`

Returns: The current location of the component based on the display's upper left corner being 0,0.

getMaximumSize() Method

This method gets the maximum size of this component. Layout managers use the maximum size information when resizing the component. This is especially important when the parent container's layout manager is attempting to resize the current component to fit a specified bounding box. For example the GridLayout manager attempts to resize components to fill each grid cell. By setting values returned by this method, the component will not be resized larger than that specified. The component will then be aligned based on the *getAlignmentX()* and *getAlignmentY()* methods (usually centered).

Syntax: `public Dimension getMaximumSize()`

Returns: The maximum size of the component.

getMinimumSize() Method

This method gets the minimum size of this component. Layout managers use the minimum size information when resizing the component. This is especially important when the parent container's layout manager is attempting to resize the current component to fit a specified bounding box. For example the GridLayout manager attempts to resize components to fill each grid cell. By setting values returned by this method, the grid component will set its minimum size for the cell in that component. The minimum size will also be included in the calculations of the minimum size that the parent component will report (which in turn will be used by its parent to report minimum size).

Syntax: **public Dimension getMinimumSize()**

Returns: The minimum size of the component.

getName() Method

This method gets the name of the component. This can be the localized name of the component used for representation purposes. It can also be used to distinguish several objects of the same type but as different names.

Syntax: **public String getName()**

Returns: The name of the component.

getParent() Method

This method gets the parent of the component. The parent component is a Container object. By having the parent object many operations can be performed on the parent or in relation to the parent like drawing and layout operations.

Syntax: **public Container getParent**

Returns: The parent of the container.

getPeer() Method

This method is no longer used in Java 1.1.

getPreferredSize() Method

This method gets the preferred size of the component. Layout managers use the preferred size information when resizing the component. This is especially important when the parent container's layout manager is attempting to resize the current component to fit a specified bounding box. For example, the GridLayout manager attempts to resize components to fill each grid cell. By setting values returned by this method, the grid component will set its preferred size for the cell in that component. The preferred size will also be included in the calculations of the preferred size that the parent component will report (which in turn will be used by its parent to report preferred size).

Syntax: `public Dimension getPreferredSize()`

Returns: The preferred dimensions of the component.

getSize() Method

This method gets the current size of the component. This information can be used in drawing and layout operations.

Syntax: `public Dimension getSize()`

Returns: The current size of the component.

getToolkit() Method

This method gets the toolkit used by the component. The toolkit is the repository of peers that components use to acquire their respective peer object. Toolkits are platform-dependent, but there are possibly multiple toolkits per platform for various visual representations (like Openlook, NeWS or Motif).

Syntax: `public Toolkit getToolkit()`

Returns: The toolkit used by the component.

getTreeLock() Method

This method gets the locking object for AWT component and all of its child components (if the component is a container). The lock object can be used with a synchronized block to perform operations that depend on the component's stability in a multithreaded environment.

Syntax: `public final Object getTreeLock()`

Returns: The locking object.

gotFocus(Event, Object) Method, *see* processFocusEvent(FocusEvent event) Method

handleEvent(Event) Method, *see* processEvent(AWTEvent event) Method

hide() Method, *see* setVisible(boolean) Method

imageUpdate(Image, int, int, int, int, int) Method

This method is used to paint a specified area of the component. An image processor of the specified image calls this method. If the image has changed (if the flag specified in the flag parameter is FRAMEBITS, ALLBITS, SOMEBITS) or if the component has reached its update rate, the *repaint( )* method is called so that the entire component is redrawn.

Syntax:	`public boolean imageUpdate(Image image,int flags,int x,int y,int width,int height)`
Parameters:	image: the image to update
	flags: the flags(FRAMEBITS, ALLBITS, SOMEBITS, ABORT)
	x: the x coordinate
	y: the y coordinate
	width:the width
	height: the height
Returns:	True if the image has changed; False if not.

inside(int, int) Method, *see* contains(int, int) Method

invalidate() Method

This method makes the component invalid. The parent container uses this information to perform layout operations. After *invalidate()* is called there should be a call to the parent's *validate()* method.

Syntax: `public void invalidate()`

isEnabled() Method

This method determines if the Component is enabled. A component that is enabled should act normally while a disabled component should not accept mouse, keyboard, or other actions that affect the behavior of the component.

Syntax: `public boolean isEnabled()`

Returns: True if the component is enabled; False if it is not.

isFocusTraversable() Method

This method determines if the component can be traversed using Tab and Shift-Tab keys. This method is mainly used to determine the current tab configuration of the component.

Syntax: `public boolean isFocusTraversable()`

Returns: True if the focus is traversable; False if not.

isShowing() Method

This method determines if the Component is showing on screen. If the component and its parent container are both visible then this method returns true. This method can be used to locate components that are not visible.

Syntax: `public boolean isShowing()`

Returns: True if the component is showing; False if it or any of its parent containers is not showing.

isValid() Method

This method determines if the component is valid. Refer to the *validate()* and *invalidate()* methods for other relevant information.

Syntax: `public boolean isValid()`

Returns: True if the component is valid; False if invalid.

isVisible() Method

This method determines if the component is visible.

Syntax: `public boolean isVisible()`

Returns: True if the component is visible; False if invisible.

keyDown(Event, int) Method, *see* processKeyEvent(KeyEvent event) Method

keyUp(Event, int) Method, *see* processKeyEvent(KeyEvent event) Method

layout() Method, *see* doLayout() Method

list() Method

This method prints a string, returned by the object's *toString()* method, at the component's indentation setting to System.out. This method is useful for obtaining the component's text representation or the text representation of a component tree. The default indentation is 0.

Syntax: `public void list()`

list(PrintStream) Method

This method prints a listing to the specified print stream. This method prints a string, returned by the object's *toString()* method, at the component's indentation setting to the specified print stream. This method is useful for obtaining the component's text representation or the text representation of a component tree. The default indentation is 0.

Syntax: `public void list(PrintStream stream)`

Parameters: stream: the stream to output to

list(PrintStream, int) Method

This method prints a listing to the specified print stream at the specified indentation. This method prints a string, returned by the object's *toString()* method. This method is useful for obtaining the component's text representation or the text representation of a component tree.

Syntax: `public void list(PrintStream stream int indent)`

Parameters: stream: the stream to output to
                     indent: the starting position (number of spaces) of the print

list(PrintWriter) Method

This method prints a listing to the specified print writer. The print writer prints formatted representations of objects to a text-output stream. This method prints a string, returned by the object's *toString()* method, at the component's indentation setting to System.out. This method is useful for obtaining the component's text representation or the text representation of a component tree. The default indentation is 0.

Syntax: `public void list(PrintWriter writer)`

Parameters: writer: the print writer to output to

list(PrintWriter, int) Method

This method prints a listing to the specified print writer at the specified indentation. The print writer prints formatted representations of objects to a text-output stream. This method prints a string, returned by the object's *toString()* method, at the component's indentation setting to System.out. This method is useful for obtaining the component's text representation or the text representation of a component tree.

Syntax: `public void list(PrintWriter writer, int indent)`

Parameters: writer: the print writer to output to
                   indent: the starting position of the print

locate(int, int) Method, *see* getComponentAt(int, int) Method

location() Method, *see* getLocation() Method

lostFocus(Event, Object) Method, *see* processFocusEvent(FocusEvent event) Method

minimumSize() Method, *see* getMinimumSize() Method

mouseDown(Event, int, int) Method, *see* processMouseEvent(MouseEvent event) Method

mouseDrag(Event, int, int) Method, *see* processMouseMotionEvent(MouseEvent event) Method

mouseEnter(Event, int, int) Method, *see* processMouseEvent(MouseEvent event) Method

mouseExit(Event, int, int) Method, *see* processMouseEvent(MouseEvent event) Method

mouseMove(Event, int, int) Method, *see* processMouseMotionEvent(MouseEvent event) Method

mouseUp(Event, int, int) Method, *see* processMouseEvent(MouseEvent event) Method

move(int, int) Method, *see* setLocation(int, int) Method

nextFocus() Method, *see* transferFocus() Method

paint(Graphics) Method

This method paints the component in the given graphical context. This method can be called either through *repaint()* or *update()* methods. This method should be the location of the code that will cause the entire area of a component to be rendered.

Syntax: `public void paint(Graphics context)`

Parameters: context: the graphic context to paint onto

paintAll(Graphics) Method

This method causes the *paint()* method to be called for the current component and its subcomponents.

Syntax: `public void paintAll(Graphics context)`

Parameters: context: the graphics

---

paramString() Method

This method returns the component's parameter string. A parameter string lists the value of each property delineated with a period character. The parameter string is made up of all properties that meet the Java Bean's property specification, in other words, the methods that have a set and a get method. This method is used primarily for debugging because the format of the string does not seem to be formally specified for any particular purpose.

Syntax: `protected String paramString()`

Returns: The parameter string.

---

postEvent(Event) Method, *see* dispatchEvent(AWTEvent event) Method

---

preferredSize() Method, *see* getPreferredSize() Method

---

prepareImage(Image, ImageObserver) Method

This method begins the download and conversion of the image to meet the component's current peer requirements for rendering (particularly fitting the number of colors). Note that the processing occurs in a separate thread.

Syntax: `public boolean prepareImage(Image image, ImageObserver imgOb)`

Parameters: image: the image
                imgOb: the image observer

Returns: True if the image is already prepared; False if not.

prepareImage(Image, int, int, ImageObserver) Method

This method prepares an image for rendering on the component with the specified width and height. This method begins the download and conversion of the image to meet the component's current peer requirements for rendering (particularly fitting the number of colors) as well as resizing the component from its original size. Note that the processing occurs in a separate thread.

Syntax: `public boolean prepareImage(Image image,int width,int height,`
`ImageObserver observer)`

Parameters: image: the image
width: the width to represent
height: the height to represent
observer: the image observer

Returns: True if the image is already prepared; False if not.

print(Graphics) Method

This method causes the component to render its representation into the given graphical context. The method is primarily called when printing a component to a graphical device. The default implementation is to call the class's *paint()* method.

Syntax: `public void print(Graphics context)`

Parameters: context: the graphics context

printAll(Graphics) Method

This method prints the component and its subcomponents to render their representations into the given graphical context. The method is primarily called when printing a component tree to a graphical device. The default implementation is to call the class's *paint()* method and sub component's *paintAll()* methods.

Syntax: `public void printAll(Graphics context)`

Parameters: context: the graphics context

processComponentEvent(ComponentEvent) Method

This method processes the component's component events by passing them to an active ComponentListener object.

Syntax: `protected void processComponentEvent(ComponentEvent event)`

Parameters: event: the event

processEvent(AWTEvent) Method

This method processes the component's events. Refer to the *processComponentEvent()*, *processFocusEvent()*, *processKeyEvent()*, *processMouseEvent()*, and *processMouseMotionEvent()* methods for other relevant information.

Syntax: `protected void processEvent(AWTEvent event)`

Parameters: event: the event to process

processFocusEvent(FocusEvent) Method

This method processes the component's focus events by passing them to an active FocusListener object.

Syntax: `protected void processFocusEvent(FocusEvent event)`

Parameters: event: the event

processKeyEvent(KeyEvent) Method

This method processes the component's key events by passing them to an active KeyListener object.

Syntax: `protected void processKeyEvent(KeyEvent event)`

Parameters: event: the event

processMouseEvent(MouseEvent) Method

This method processes the component's mouse events by passing them to an active *MouseListener* object.

Syntax: `protected void processMouseEvent(MouseEvent event)`

Parameters: event: the event

processMouseMotionEvent(MouseEvent) Method

This method processes the component's mouse motion events by passing them to an active MouseMotionListener object.

Syntax: `protected void processMouseMotionEvent(MouseEvent event)`

Parameters: event: the event

remove(MenuComponent) Method

This method removes the specified popup menu from the component. This method prevents the popup menu from activating when future popups are requested.

Syntax: `public synchronized void remove(MenuComponent popup)`

Parameters: popup: the popup to remove

removeComponentListener(ComponentListener) Method

This method removes the specified ComponentListener to listen for component events from this component. This should be done before a component or the listener goes out of the intended scope. If a listener goes out of use before the component, the component retains a copy of the listener, thus preventing the listener from being garbage collected.

Syntax: `public synchronized void removeComponentListener(ComponentListener listener)`

Parameters: listener: the specified listener

removeFocusListener(FocusListener) Method

This method removes the specified FocusListener to listen for focus events from this component. This should be done before a component or the listener goes out of the intended scope. If a listener goes out of use before the component, the component retains a copy of the listener, thus preventing the listener from being garbage collected.

Syntax: `public synchronized void removeFocusListener(FocusListener listener)`

Parameters: listener: the specified listener

removeKeyListener(KeyListener) Method

This method removes the specified KeyListener to listen for key events from this component. This should be done before a component or the listener goes out of the intended scope. If a listener goes out of use before the component, the component retains a copy of the listener, thus preventing the listener from being garbage collected.

Syntax: `public synchronized void removeKeyListener(KeyListener listener)`

Parameters: listener: the specified listener

removeMouseListener(MouseListener) Method

This method removes the specified MouseListener to listen for mouse events from this component. This should be done before a component or the listener goes out of the intended scope. If a listener goes out of use before the component, the component retains a copy of the listener, thus preventing the listener from being garbage collected.

Syntax: `public synchronized void removeMouseListener(MouseListener listener)`

Parameters: listener: the specified listener

removeMouseMotionListener(MouseMotionListener) Method

This method removes the specified MouseMotionListener to listen for mouse motion events from this component. This should be done before a component or the listener goes out of the intended scope. If a listener goes out of use before the component, the component retains a copy of the listener, thus preventing the listener from being garbage collected.

Syntax: `public synchronized voidremoveMouseMotionListener`
`(MouseMotionListener listener)`

Parameters: listener: the specified listener

removeNotify() Method

This method informs the component that it has been removed from a container and the peer should be destroyed. This essentially disconnects all platform-dependent events and platform-dependent processing from the component.

Syntax: `public void removeNotify()`

repaint() Method

This method repaints the component. The default implementation is to call "*repaint(0, x, y, width, height)."* This causes the component to be completely rendered.

Syntax: `public void repaint()`

repaint(int, int, int, int) Method

This method repaints the part of the component specified. This method is used to selectively paint portions of the component.

Syntax: `public void repaint(int x,int y,int width,int height)`

Parameters: x: the new X coordinate
y: the new Y coordinate
width: the new width
height: the new height

repaint(long) Method

This method causes the component's *update()* method to be called after a specified number of milliseconds have expired.

Syntax: `public void repaint(long millis)`

Parameters: millis: milliseconds until *update()* is called

repaint(long, int, int, int, int) Method

This method causes the component's *update()* method to be called to repaint a specific portion of the component after a specified number of milliseconds have expired.

Syntax: `public void repaint(long milis,int x,int y,int width,int height)`

Parameters: millis: milliseconds until *update()* is called
x: the new X coordinate
y: the new Y coordinate
width: the new width
height: the new height

requestFocus() Method

This method requests the input focus. The component must be visible for this method to function correctly. This method is particularly useful for setting the default component or for warping the focus to the particular component.

Syntax: `public void requestFocus()`

reshape(int, int, int, int) Method, *see* setBounds(int, int, int, int)

resize(Dimension) Method, *see* setSize(Dimension) Method

resize(int, int) Method, *see* setSize(int, int) Method

setBackground(Color) Method

This method sets the background color to the color specified. Refer to the *getBackground()* method for other relevant information.

Syntax: `public void setBackground(Color c)`

Parameters: c: the color to use as the background color

setBounds(int, int, int, int) Method

This method sets the new bounds for the component. Refer to the *getBounds()*, *setLocation()*, and *setSize()* methods for other relevant information.

Syntax: `public void setBounds(int x,int y,int width,int height`

Parameters: x: the new X coordinate
                y: the new Y coordinate
                width: the new width
                height: the new height

setBounds(Rectangle) Method

This method sets the new bounds for the component. Refer to the *getBounds()*, *setLocation()*, and *setSize()* methods for other relevant information.

Syntax: `public void setBounds(Rectangle rect)`

Parameters: rect: the new bounds of the component

setCursor(Cursor) Method

This method sets the cursor to the specified cursor. This is useful for setting the cursor of the component to a wait cursor or for setting the cursor to one that makes sense for the context of the component (like a text rectangle).

Syntax: `public synchronized void setCursor(Cursor cursor)`

Parameters: cursor: the predefined cursor type

setEnabled(boolean) Method

This method enables or disables a component. When disabled, the component remains visible but does not accept mouse or keyboard events. Components should be disabled whenever the state of a program does not make use of the particular component. For example, a save button should be disabled until there is something to save.

Syntax: `public void setEnabled(boolean bool)`

Parameters: bool: True to enable the component; False to disable it

setFont(Font) Method

This method sets the component's font to the font specified. Refer to the *getFont()* method for other relevant information.

Syntax: `public synchronized void setFont(Font f)`

Parameters: f: the font to use for the component

setForeground(Color) Method

This method sets the foreground color to the color specified. Refer to the *getForeground()* method for other relevant information.

Syntax: `public void setForeground(Color c)`

Parameters: c: the color to use as the foreground color

setLocale(Locale) Method

This method sets the locale of the component. The locale is the language and location that the component should present itself for. In other words, the font, language, time, and date should match that for users at the particular location. After the new locale is set, the component should be rerendered to match the new locale.

Syntax: `public void setLocale(Locale l)`

Parameters: l: the locale to assign to the component

setLocation(int, int) Method

This method sets the new X, Y coordinates of the component. Refer to the *getLocation()* and *setBounds()* methods for other relevant information.

Syntax: `public void setLocation(int x, int y)`

Parameters: x: the new X coordinate
                 y: the new Y coordinate

setLocation(Point) Method

This method sets the new coordinates of the component. Refer to the *getLocation()* and *setBounds()* methods for other relevant information.

Syntax: `public void setLocation(point p)`

Parameters: p: the point in the parent's space

setName(String) Method

This method sets the name of the component to the specified string.

Syntax: `public void setName(String name)`

Parameters: name: the new name for the component

setSize(Dimension) Method

This method sets the dimensions of the component. Refer to the *getSize()*, *size()*, and *setBounds()* methods for other relevant information. Note that *setsize()* calls the depreciated *resize(Dimension)* method.

Syntax: `public void setSize(Dimension dim)`

Parameters: dim: the new dimensions of the component

setSize(int, int) Method

This method sets the width and height of the component. Refer to the *getSize()*, *size()*, and *setBounds()* methods for other relevant information. Note that this method calls *resize(width, height)*.

Syntax: `public void setSize(int width,int height)`

Returns: width: the new width of the component
           height: the new height of the component

setVisible(boolean) Method

This method makes the component visible or invisible based on the boolean value. Refer to the *isVisible()* method for other relevant information.

Syntax: `public void setVisible(boolean bool)`

Parameters: bool: True to make the component visible; False to make it invisible

show() Method, *see* setVisible(boolean)

show(boolean) Method, *see* setVisible(boolean) Method

size() Method, *see* getSize() Method

toString() Method

This method returns the component's string representation. The default implementation is to return the name of the component and the component's param string.

Syntax: `public String toString()`

Returns: The string containing the values.

Overrides: toString in class Object

transferFocus() Method

This method transfers the focus to the next component. Refer to the *requestFocus()* method for other relevant information.

Syntax: `public void transferFocus()`

update(Graphics) Method

This method uses the graphics to update the component. The default implementation of this method is to first draw a filled rectangle with the component's current background color and then call the component's *paint(Graphics)* method. This method should be overridden to just call the *paint(Graphics)* method if the class's *paint(Graphics)* method controls the painting of the background or uses double buffering techniques to paint. Overriding this function for this reason can prevent the component from flickering between a blank background and the rendered component.

Syntax: `public void update(Graphics g)`

Parameters: g: the graphics to use to update the component

validate() Method

This method ensures that the component has a valid layout. In other words, all child components are resized and positioned in this component according to the current layout policy.

Syntax: `public void validate()`

New Event Model API

By Bill la Forge

Senior Research Engineer
The Open Group
http://www.opengroup.org/~laforge

The java.awt.event package contains the AWT classes and interfaces for the new event model. With the singular exception of PaintEvent, everything in this package conforms to the Java Beans design signatures.

The events are the key organizing factor for this chapter. For each event, there is an event class, one or more listener interfaces, and one or more adapter classes. The events, their classes, listener interfaces, and adapter classes and their corresponding constructors, methods, and variables are covered in the following order:

- ◆ Action
    - ◆ java.awt.event.ActionListener Interface
    - ◆ java.awt.event.ActionEvent Class
    - ◆ Adjustment
    - ◆ java.awt.event.AdjustmentListener Interface
    - ◆ java.awt.event.AdjustmentEvent Class
- ◆ Component
    - ◆ java.awt.event.ComponentListener Interface
    - ◆ java.awt.event.ComponentEvent Class

- ◆ Container
  - ◆ java.awt.event.ContainerListener Interface
  - ◆ java.awt.event.ContainerEvent Class
- ◆ Focus
  - ◆ java.awt.event.FocusListener Interface
  - ◆ java.awt.event.FocusEvent Class
- ◆ Input
  - ◆ java.awt.event.InputEvent Class
- ◆ Item
  - ◆ java.awt.event.ItemListener Interface
  - ◆ java.awt.event.ItemEvent Class
- ◆ Key
  - ◆ java.awt.event.KeyListener Interface
  - ◆ java.awt.event.KeyEvent Class
- ◆ Mouse
  - ◆ java.awt.event.MouseListener Interface
  - ◆ java.awt.event.MouseMotionListener Interface
  - ◆ java.awt.event.MouseEvent Class
- ◆ Paint
  - ◆ java.awt.event.PaintEvent Class
- ◆ Text
  - ◆ java.awt.event.TextListener Interface
  - ◆ java.awt.event.TextEvent Class
- ◆ Window
  - ◆ java.awt.event.WindowListener Interface
  - ◆ java.awt.event.WindowEvent Class

Overview of Events

Each AWT component will either generate the old java.awt.Event(s) or the new java.awt.AWTEvent(s), but not both. The new event objects are produced when an event listener is added to the awt component, or when the *enableEvents()* method is called on the component. The *Component.enableEvents()* method is used when subclassing an AWT component. The AWT event class inheritance tree is shown in figure 14.1.

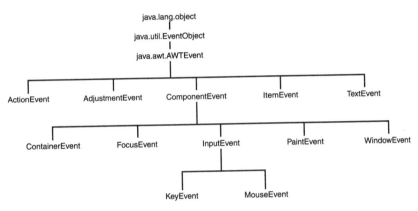

Figure 14.1

AWT Event Class Inheritance Tree.

All events in the new AWT event model are derived from the java.awt.AWTEvent class which extends the java.util.EventObject class. This was necessary for compliance with the Java Beans design signatures. For the same reason, all the listener interfaces extend the java.util.EventListener interface.

AWT components that generate the XXX event have the following two methods:

```
public synchronized void addXXXListener(XXXListener l);
public synchronized void removeXXXListener(XXXListener l);,
```

where XXX could be the following events:

Action	Key
Adjustment	Mouse
Component	MouseMotion

Container	Text
Focus	Window
Item	

The parameter is an instance of a class that implements the corresponding listener interface. It is with the add and remove methods that the source of an event is directly connected with the object that processes the event.

Listener interfaces can contain one or more methods that take the same event as a parameter. Adapters are helper classes that implement a listener interface. The methods of an adapter do nothing. A programmer can subclass an adapter, providing only the methods of interest. No adapter class is provided when the listener interface contains only one method.

Action Events

Action events are defined by an operation being performed upon a component. Action events originate from the following classes:

- java.awt.Button
- java.awt.List
- java.awt.MenuItem
- java.awt.TextField

java.awt.event.ActionListener Interface

This is the action event listener interface that receives action events. This interface does not have an adapter.

actionPerformed() Method

This method is called when an action occurs.

Syntax:
```
public abstract void actionPerformed(ActionEvent e)
```

java.awt.event.ActionEvent Class

This is the class that action events originate from. The constructors, methods, and variables for this class are described in the sections that follow.

ActionEvent Constructor

This constructor creates an ActionEvent with a given source object.

Syntax: `public ActionEvent(Object source, int id, String command)`

Parameters: source: the object creating the event
id: the event type
command: the command string of this event

ActionEvent Constructor

This constructor creates an ActionEvent with modifiers.

Syntax: `public ActionEvent(Object source, int id, String command, int modifiers)`

Parameters: source: the object creating the event
id: the event type
command: the command string of this event
modifiers: identifies the shift, control, alt, or meta keys held down when this event occured

getActionCommand() Method

This method returns the command name associated with the action event.

Syntax: `public String getActionCommand()`

getModifiers() Method

This method returns the modifier keys (shift, control, alt, or meta) that were held down during this action event.

Syntax: `public int getModifiers()`

paramString() Method

This method returns the string equivalent of the event id.

Syntax: `public String paramString()`

ACTION_FIRST Variable

This variable defines the first action event id.

Syntax: `public final static int ACTION_FIRST`

ACTION_LAST Variable

This variable defines the last action event id.

Syntax: `public final static int ACTION_LAST`

ALT_MASK Variable

This variable defines the modifier constant for the alt key.

Syntax: `public final static int ALT_MASK`

ACTION_PERFORMED Variable

This variable defines the event id of the action performed.

Syntax: `public final static int ACTION_PERFORMED`

CTRL_MASK Variable

This variable defines the modifier constant for the control key.

Syntax: `public final static int CTRL_MASK`

META_MASK Variable

This variable defines the modifier constant for the meta key.

Syntax: `public final static int META_MASK`

SHIFT_MASK Variable

This variable defines the modifier constant for the shift key.

Syntax: `public final static int SHIFT_MASK`

Adjustment Events

Adjustment events stem from objects that have adjustable numeric values. Adjustment events originate from the java.awt.ScrollBar class.

java.awt.event.AdjustmentListener

This is the adjustment event listener interface that receives adjustment events. This interface does not have an adapter.

adjustmentValueChanged() Method

This method is called when the value of an adjustment has changed.

Syntax: `public abstract void adjustmentValueChanged(AdjustmentEvent e)`

java.awt.event.AdjustmentEvent Class

This is the class that adjustment events originate from. The constructors, methods, and variables for this class are described in the sections that follow.

AdjustmentEvent() Constructor

This constructor creates an adjustment event.

Syntax: `public AdjustmentEvent(Adjustable source, int id, int type, int value)`

Parameters: source: the component originating the event
id: the type of event
type: the type of adjustment
value: the value of the adjustment

getAdjustable() Method

This method returns the Adjustable object which created the event.

Syntax: `public Adjustable getAdjustable()`

getAdjustmentType() Method

This method returns the type id of the value adjusted.

Syntax: `public int getAdjustmentType()`

getValue() Method

This method returns the adjustment value stored in the event.

Syntax: `public int getValue()`

paramString() Method

This method returns the string equivalent of the event id.

Syntax: `public String paramString()`

ADJUSTMENT_FIRST Variable

This variable defines the first adjustment event id.

Syntax: `public final static int ADJUSTMENT_FIRST`

ADJUSTMENT_LAST Variable

This variable defines the last adjustment event id.

Syntax: `public final static int ADJUSTMENT_LAST`

ADJUSTMENT_VALUE_CHANGED Variable

This variable defines the event id of the adjustment event which occured.

Syntax: `public final static int ADJUSTMENT_VALUE_CHANGED`

BLOCK_DECREMENT Variable

This variable defines the type id for block decrement adjustments.

Syntax: `public final static int BLOCK_DECREMENT`

BLOCK_INCREMENT Variable

This variable defines the type id for block increment adjustments.

Syntax: `public final static int BLOCK_INCREMENT`

TRACK Variable

This variable defines the type id for absolute adjustments.

Syntax: **`public final static int TRACK`**

UNIT_DECREMENT Variable

This variable defines the type id for unit decrement adjustments.

Syntax: **`public final static int UNIT_DECREMENT`**

UNIT_INCREMENT Variable

This variable defines the type id for unit incriment adjustments.

Syntax: **`public final static int UNIT_INCREMENT`**

Component Events

Component events are provided for notification purposes only. The moving and resizing of components is handled automatically and internally by AWT so that the layout of the GUI (graphical user interface) works properly regardless of whether a program is receiving these events. Component events originate from the java.awt. Component class, which is subclassed by ContainerEvent, FocusEvent, InputEvent, PaintEvent, and WindowEvent.

java.awt.event.ComponentListener Interface

This is component event listener interface that receives component events. java.awt.event.ComponentAdapter is the adapter for this interface.

componentHidden() Method

This method is called when a component is hidden.

Syntax: `public abstract void componentHidden(ComponentEvent e)`

componentMoved() Method

This method is called when a component is moved.

Syntax: **`public abstract void componentMoved(ComponentEvent e)`**

componentResized() Method

This method is called when the component is resized.

Syntax: **`public abstract void componentResized(ComponentEvent e)`**

componentShown() Method

This method is called when a component is shown.

Syntax: **`public abstract void componentShown(ComponentEvent e)`**

java.awt.event.ComponentEvent Class

This is the class that component events originate from. The constructors, methods, and variables are described in the sections that follow.

ComponentEvent Constructor

Syntax: **`public ComponentEvent(Component source, int id)`**

This constructor creates a component event.

Parameters: source: originating component
id: event id

java.awt.event.ComponentEvent

---

getComponent() Method

This method returns the originator of the event.

Syntax: `public Component getComponent()`

---

paramString() Method

This method returns the string equivalent of the event id.

Syntax: `public String paramString()`

COMPONENT_FIRST Variable

Syntax: `public final static int COMPONENT_FIRST`

This variable defines the first component event id.

COMPONENT_HIDDEN Variable

Syntax: `public final static int COMPONENT_HIDDEN`

This variable defines the event id for the hidden component.

COMPONENT_LAST Variable

Syntax: `public final static int COMPONENT_LAST`

This variable defines the last component event id.

COMPONENT_MOVED Variable

Syntax: `public final static int COMPONENT_MOVED`

This variable defines the event id for the component moved.

COMPONENT_RESIZED Variable

Syntax: `public final static int COMPONENT_RESIZED`

This variable defines the event id for the component resized.

COMPONENT_SHOWN Variable

Syntax: `public final static int COMPONENT_SHOWN`

This variable defines the event id for the component shown.

Container Events

Container-level events are provided for notification purposes only. The adding and removing of components from a container are handled automatically and internally by AWT. Container events originate from the java.awt.Container class.

java.awt.event.ContainerListener Interface

This is the container event listener interface that receives container-level events. java.awt.event.ContainerAdapter is the adapter for this interface.

componentAdded() Method

This method is called when a component is added to a container.

Syntax: `public abstract void componentAdded(ContainerEvent e)`

componentRemoved() Method

This method is called when a component is removed from a container.

Syntax: `public abstract void componentRemoved(ContainerEvent e)`

java.awt.event.ContainerEvent Class

This is the class that container-level events originate from. The constructors, methods, and variables for this class are described in the sections that follow.

ContainerEvent Constructor

This constructor creates a container event.

Syntax: `public ContainerEvent(Component source, int id, Component child)`

Parameters: source: the container creating the event
id: event id
child: child being added to or removed from the container

getChild() Method

This method returns the child being added or removed.

Syntax: `public Component getChild()`

getContainer() Method

This method returns the originating container.

Syntax: `public Container getContainer()`

paramString() Method

This method returns the string equivalent of the event id.

Syntax: `public String paramString()`

COMPONENT_ADDED Variable

This variable defines the event id of the component added event.

Syntax: `public final static int COMPONENT_ADDED`

CONTAINER_FIRST Variable

This variable defines the event id of the first container event.

Syntax: `public final static int CONTAINER_FIRST`

CONTAINER_LAST Variable

This variable defines the event id of the last container event.

Syntax: `public final static int CONTAINER_LAST`

COMPONENT_REMOVED Variable

This variable defines the event id of the component removed event.

Syntax: `public final static int COMPONENT_REMOVED`

Focus Events

Focus events originate from the java.awt.Component class. When the focus moves from one component to another, the change can be permanent or temporary. Permanent changes in focus occur when the focus is directly moved from one component to another. Temporary changes in focus occur as the indirect result of deactivating a window or dragging a scrollbar. If the change is temporary, then the focus will return. Use the *java.awt.event.FocusEvent.isTemporary()* method to determine if the change in focus is temporary or permament for both FOCUS_GAINED and FOCUS_LOST events.

java.awt.event.FocusListener Interface

This is the focus event listener interface that receives focus events. java.awt.event.FocusAdapter is the adapter for this interface.

focusGained() Method

This method is called when the keyboard focus is gained.

Syntax:　　**public abstract void focusGained(FocusEvent e)**

focusLost() Method

This method is called when the keyboard focus is lost.

Syntax:　　**public abstract void focusLost(FocusEvent e)**

java.awt.event.FocusEvent Class

This is the class that focus events originate from. The constructors, methods, and variables for this class are described in the text that follows.

FocusEvent Constructor

This constructor creates a focus event with a provision for temporary changes in focus.

Syntax:　　**public FocusEvent(Component source, int id, boolean temporary)**

Parameters:　　source: originator of the event
id: event id
temporary: an indication that the change in focus is temporary

FocusEvent Constructor

This constructor creates a focus event. The focus change is permament.

Syntax: `public FocusEvent(Component source, int id)`

Parameters: source: originator of the event
id: event id

isTemporary() Method

This method returns true when the change is temporary.

Syntax: `public boolean isTemporary()`

paramString() Method

This method returns the string equivalent of the event id.

Syntax: `public String paramString()`

FOCUS_FIRST Variable

This variable defines the event id of the first focus event.

Syntax: `public final static int FOCUS_FIRST`

FOCUS_LAST Variable

This variable defines the event id of the last focus event.

Syntax: `public final static int FOCUS_LAST`

FOCUS_GAINED Variable

This variable defines the event id of the focus gained event.

Syntax: `public final static int FOCUS_GAINED`

FOCUS_LOST Variable

This variable defines the event id of the focus lost event.

Syntax: `public final static int FOCUS_LOST`

Input Events

Input events are defined by a keyboard or mouse action for submitting input. Input events are delivered to listener interfaces and subclasses before they are processed, which prevents default processing of input events from their original source. For the most part, this is a workaround to prevent the need for activating the component in question.

java.awt.event.InputEvent Class

This is the class that input events originate from. This class is subclassed by KeyEvent and MouseEvent. The methods and variables for this class are described in the sections that follow.

consume() Method

This method prevents the input from being processed normally by the originating component. This method overrides the java.awt.AWTEvent.consume() method.

Syntax: `public void consume()`

getModifiers() Method

This method indicates which modifiers were present when the input event occured.

Syntax: `public int getModifiers()`

getWhen() Method

This method indicates when the input event occured.

Syntax: `public long getWhen()`

isAltDown() Method

This method indicates the alt key was pressed when the input event occured.

Syntax: `public boolean isAltDown()`

isConsumed() Method

This method indicates that the input event was consumed. This method overrides the java.awt.AWTEvent.isConsumed() method.

Syntax: `public boolean isConsumed()`

isControlDown() Method

This method indicates the control key was pressed when the input event occured.

Syntax: `public boolean isControlDown()`

isMetaDown() Method

This method indicates the meta key was pressed when the input event occured.

Syntax: `public boolean isMetaDown()`

java.awt.event.InputEvent

isShiftDown() Method

This method indicates the shift key was pressed when the input event occured.

Syntax: `public boolean isShiftDown()`

ALT_MASK Variable

This variable defines the modifier constant for the alt key.

Syntax: `public final static int ALT_MASK`

BUTTON1_MASK Variable

This variable defines the modifier constant for mouse button 1.

Syntax: `public final static int BUTTON1_MASK`

BUTTON2_MASK Variable

This variable defines the modifier constant for mouse button 2.

Syntax: `public final static int BUTTON2_MASK`

BUTTON3_MASK Variable

This variable defines the modifier constant for mouse button 3.

Syntax: `public final static int BUTTON3_MASK`

CTRL_MASK Variable

This variable defines the modifier constant for the control key.

Syntax: `public final static int CTRL_MASK`

META_MASK Variable

This variable defines the modifier constant for the meta key.

Syntax: `public final static int META_MASK`

SHIFT_MASK Variable

This variable defines the modifier constant for the shift key.

Syntax: `public final static int SHIFT_MASK`

Item Events

When a component item is selected, deselected, expanded, or contracted, an item event is produced. Item events originate from the following classes (all of which implement the itemSelectable interface):

◆ java.awt.Checkbox

◆ java.awt.CheckboxMenuItem

◆ java.awt.Choice

◆ java.awt.List

java.awt.event.ItemListener Interface

The item event listener interface that receives item events. There is no adapter for this interface.

itemStateChanged() Method

This method is called when an item's state is changed.

Syntax: `public abstract void itemStateChanged(ItemEvent e)`

java.awt.event.ItemEvent Class

This is the class that item events originate from. The constructors, methods, and variables for this class are described in the sections that follow.

ItemEvent Constructor

This constructor creates an item event.

Syntax: `public ItemEvent(ItemSelectable source, int id, Object item, int stateChange)`

Parameters: source: originating ItemSelectable object
id: event id
stateChange: type of change—SELECTED or DESELECTED

getItem() Method

This method returns the selected or deselected item.

Syntax: `public Object getItem()`

getItemSelectable() Method

This method returns the originating awt object.

Syntax: `public ItemSelectable getItemSelectable()`

getStateChange() Method

This method returns the type of change—SELECTED or DESELECTED.

Syntax: `public int getStateChange()`

paramString() Method

This method returns the string equivalent of the event id.

Syntax: `public String paramString()`

DESELECTED Variable

This variable defines the item change type that is deselected.

Syntax: `public final static int DESELECTED`

ITEM_FIRST Variable

This variable defines the event id of the first item event.

Syntax: `public final static int ITEM_FIRST`

ITEM_LAST Variable

This variable defines the event id of the last item event.

Syntax: `public final static int ITEM_LAST`

ITEM_STATE_CHANGED Variable

This variable defines the event id of the state changed item event.

Syntax: `public final static int ITEM_STATE_CHANGED`

SELECTED Variable

This variable defines the item change type that is selected.

Syntax: `public final static int SELECTED`

Key Events

Keyboard events are generating by keyboard actions. Key events originate from the java.awt.Component class.

java.awt.event.KeyListener Interface

This is the key event listener interface that receives keyboard events. java.awt.event.KeyAdapter is the adapter for this interface.

keyPressed() Method

This method is called when a key is pressed.

Syntax: `public abstract void keyPressed(KeyEvent e)`

keyReleased() Method

This method is called when a key is released.

Syntax: `public abstract void keyReleased(KeyEvent e)`

keyTyped() Method

This method is called when a key press has been followed by a key release.

Syntax: `public abstract void keyTyped(KeyEvent e)`

java.awt.event.KeyEvent Class

This is the class that key events originate from.

Variables begining with the prefix "VK" specify a virtual key value. These are the values reported by a KEY_PRESSED or KEY_RELEASED event. Conversly, KEY_TYPED events report the ascii value determined by the key that was released, in combination with the modifier keys SHIFT, CONTROL, ALT, and META.

Note that, except for VK_ENTER, VK_BACK_SPACE, and VK_TAB, the values assigned to virtual keys may change to accomodate additional types (locale-oriented) of keyboards.

VK_0–VK_9 (not shown) have the ascii values '0' thru '9'.

VK_A–VK_Z (not shown) have the ascii values 'A' thru 'Z'.

The constructors, methods, and variables for this class are described in the sections that follow.

KeyEvent() Constructor

This constructor creates a KeyEvent object with the specified source component, type, modifiers, and key.

Syntax: `public KeyEvent(Component source, int id, long when, int modifiers, int keyCode, char keyChar)`

Parameters: source: the object where the event originated

getKeyChar() Method

This method returns the Unicode character specified by the event, or CHAR_UNDEFINED if no such code exists.

Syntax: `public char getKeyChar()`

getKeyCode() Method

This method returns the key code for the event or VK_UNDEFINED if the event is KEY_TYPED.

Syntax: `public int getKeyCode()`

getKeyModifiersText() Method

This method returns an ascii string, as defined by the awt.properties file, which describes the modifiers on the key.

Syntax: `public static String getKeyModifiersText(int modifiers)`

getKeyText() Method

This method returns an ascii string describing the key, as defined by the awt.properties file.

Syntax: `public static String getKeyText(int keyCode)`

isActionKey() Method

This method indicates that the key is an action key.

Syntax: `public boolean isActionKey()`

paramString() Method

This method returns the string equivalent of the event id.

Syntax: `public String paramString()`

setKeyChar() Method

This method sets the character associated with the key in this event. If no valid Unicode character is set for this key event, keyChar defaults to CHAR_UNDEFINED

Syntax: `public void setKeyChar(char keyChar)`

setKeyCode() Method

This method sets the integer key-code associated with the key in this event. For KEY_TYPED events, the default keyCode setting is VK_UNDEFINED.

Syntax: `public void setKeyCode(int keyCode)`

setModifiers() Method

This method sets the ascii string, as defined by the awt.properties file, that describes the modifiers on the key.

Syntax: `public void setModifiers(int modifiers)`

CHAR_UNDEFINED Variable

This variable signifies an undefined key code event.

Syntax: `public final static char CHAR_UNDEFINED`

KEY_FIRST Variable

This variable defines the event id of the first key event.

Syntax: `public final static int KEY_FIRST`

KEY_LAST Variable

This variable defines the event id of the last key event.

Syntax: `public final static int KEY_LAST`

KEY_PRESSED Variable

This variable defines the event id of a key press.

Syntax: `public final static int KEY_PRESSED`

KEY_RELEASED Variable

This variable defines the event id of a key release.

Syntax: `public final static int KEY_RELEASED`

KEY_TYPED Variable

This variable defines the event id of a typed key event, which follows the KEY_RELEASED event.

Syntax: `public final static int KEY_TYPED`

VK_ADD Variable

This variable defines the virtual key code for NUMBER PAD ADDITION (+) key events.

Syntax: `public final static int VK_ADD`

VK_ALT Variable

This variable defines the virtual key code for ALT key events.

Syntax: `public final static int VK_ALT`

VK_BACK_QUOTE Variable

This variable defines the virtual key code for BACK QUOTE key events.

Syntax: `public final static int VK_BACK_QUOTE`

VK_BACK_SPACE Variable

This variable defines the virtual key code for BACKSPACE key events.

Syntax: `public final static int VK_BACK_SPACE`

VK_BACK_SLASH Variable

This variable defines the virtual key code for BACKSLASH (\) key events.

Syntax: `public final static int VK_BACK_SLASH`

VK_CANCEL Variable

This variable defines the virtual key code for CANCEL key events.

Syntax: `public final static int VK_CANCEL`

VK_CAPS_LOCK Variable

This variable defines the virtual key code for CAPS LOCK key events.

Syntax: `public final static int VK_CAPS_LOCK`

VK_CLEAR Variable

This variable defines the virtual key code for CLEAR key events.

Syntax: `public final static int VK_CLEAR`

VK_CLOSE_BRACKET Variable

This variable defines the virtual key code for CLOSE BRACKET(]) key events.

Syntax: `public final static int VK_CLOSE_BRACKET`

VK_COMMA Variable

This variable defines the virtual key code for COMMA key events.

Syntax: `public final static int VK_COMMA`

VK_CONTROL Variable

This variable defines the virtual key code for CONTROL key events.

Syntax: `public final static int VK_CONTROL`

VK_DECIMAL Variable

This variable defines the virtual key code for NUMBER PAD DECIMAL POINT key events.

Syntax: `public final static int VK_DECIMAL`

VK_DELETE Variable

This variable defines the virtual key code for DELETE key events.

Syntax: `public final static int VK_DELETE`

VK_DIVIDE Variable

This variable defines the virtual key code for NUMBER PAD DIVISION (/) key events.

Syntax: `public final static int VK_DIVIDE`

VK_DOWN Variable

This variable defines the virtual key code for DOWN ARROW key events.

Syntax: `public final static int VK_DOWN`

VK_END Variable

This variable defines the virtual key code for END key events.

Syntax: `public final static int VK_END`

VK_ENTER Variable

This variable defines the virtual key code for ENTER key events.

Syntax:　　**public final static int VK_ENTER**

VK_EQUALS Variable

This variable defines the virtual key code for EQUAL (=) key events.

Syntax:　　**public final static int VK_EQUALS**

VK_ESCAPE Variable

This variable defines the virtual key code for ESCAPE key events.

Syntax:　　**public final static int VK_ESCAPE**

VK_F1 Variable

This variable defines the virtual key code for F1 key events.

Syntax:　　**public final static int VK_F1**

VK_F2 Variable

This variable defines the virtual key code for F2 key events.

Syntax:　　**public final static int VK_F2**

VK_F3 Variable

This variable defines the virtual key code for F3 key events.

Syntax:　　**public final static int VK_F3**

java.awt.event.KeyEvent

VK_F4 Variable

This variable defines the virtual key code for F4 key events.

Syntax: `public final static int VK_F4`

VK_F5 Variable

This variable defines the virtual key code for F5 key events.

Syntax: `public final static int VK_F5`

VK_F6 Variable

This variable defines the virtual key code for F6 key events.

Syntax: `public final static int VK_F6`

VK_F7 Variable

This variable defines the virtual key code for F7 key events.

Syntax: `public final static int VK_F7`

VK_F8 Variable

This variable defines the virtual key code for F8 key events.

Syntax: `public final static int VK_F8`

VK_F9 Variable

This variable defines the virtual key code for F9 key events.

Syntax: `public final static int VK_F9`

VK_F10 Variable

This variable defines the virtual key code for F10 key events.

Syntax: `public final static int VK_F10`

VK_F11 Variable

This variable defines the virtual key code for F11 key events.

Syntax: `public final static int VK_F11`

VK_F12 Variable

This variable defines the virtual key code for F12 key events.

Syntax: `public final static int VK_F12`

VK_HELP Variable

This variable defines the virtual key code for HELP key events.

Syntax: `public final static int VK_HELP`

VK_HOME Variable

This variable defines the virtual key code for HOME key events.

Syntax: `public final static int VK_HOME`

VK_INSERT Variable

This variable defines the virtual key code for INSERT key events.

Syntax: `public final static int VK_INSERT`

VK_LEFT Variable

This variable defines the virtual key code for LEFT ARROW key events.

Syntax: `public final static int VK_LEFT`

VK_META Variable

This variable defines the virtual key code for META key events.

Syntax: `public final static int VK_META`

VK_MULTIPLY Variable

This variable defines the virtual key code for NUMBER PAD MULTIPLICATION (*) key events.

Syntax: `public final static int VK_MULTIPLY`

VK_NUM_LOCK Variable

This variable defines the virtual key code for NUM LOCK key events.

Syntax: `public final static int VK_NUM_LOCK`

VK_NUMPAD0 Variable

This variable defines the virtual key code for NUMBER PAD 0 key events.

Syntax: `public final static int VK_NUMPAD0`

VK_NUMPAD1 Variable

This variable defines the virtual key code for NUMBER PAD 1 key events.

Syntax: `public final static int VK_NUMPAD1`

VK_NUMPAD2 Variable

This variable defines the virtual key code for NUMBER PAD 2 key events.

Syntax: `public final static int VK_NUMPAD2`

VK_NUMPAD3 Variable

This variable defines the virtual key code for NUMBER PAD 3 key events.

Syntax: `public final static int VK_NUMPAD3`

VK_NUMPAD4 Variable

This variable defines the virtual key code for NUMBER PAD 4 key events.

Syntax: `public final static int VK_NUMPAD4`

VK_NUMPAD5 Variable

This variable defines the virtual key code for NUMBER PAD 5 key events.

Syntax: `public final static int VK_NUMPAD5`

VK_NUMPAD6 Variable

This variable defines the virtual key code for NUMBER PAD 6 key events.

Syntax: `public final static int VK_NUMPAD6`

VK_NUMPAD7 Variable

This variable defines the virtual key code for NUMBER PAD 7 key events.

Syntax: `Public final static int VK_NUMPAD7`

VK_NUMPAD8 Variable

This variable defines the virtual key code for NUMBER PAD 8 key events.

Syntax:　　**public final static int VK_NUMPAD8**

VK_NUMPAD9 Variable

This variable defines the virtual key code for NUMBER PAD 9 key events.

Syntax:　　**public final static int VK_NUMPAD9**

VK_OPEN_BRACKET Variable

This variable defines the virtual key code for OPEN BRACKET ([) key events.

Syntax:　　**public final static int VK_OPEN_BRACKET**

VK_PAGE_DOWN Variable

This variable defines the virtual key code for PAGE DOWN key events.

Syntax;　　**public final static int VK_PAGE_DOWN**

VK_PAGE_UP Variable

This variable defines the virtual key code for PAGE UP key events.

Syntax:　　**public final static int VK_PAGE_UP**

VK_PAUSE Variable

This variable defines the virtual key code for PAUSE key events.

Syntax:　　**public final static int VK_PAUSE**

VK_PERIOD Variable

This variable defines the virtual key code for PERIOD key events.

Syntax: `public final static int VK_PERIOD`

VK_PRINTSCREEN Variable

This variable defines the virtual key code for PRINT SCREEN key events.

Syntax: `public final static int VK_PRINTSCREEN`

VK_QUOTE Variable

This variable defines the virtual key code for QUOTE key events.

Syntax: `public final static int VK_QUOTE`

VK_RIGHT Variable

This variable defines the virtual key code for RIGHT ARROW key events.

Syntax: `public final static int VK_RIGHT`

VK_SCROLL_LOCK Variable

This variable defines the virtual key code for SCROLL LOCK key events.

Syntax: `public final static int VK_SCROLL_LOCK`

VK_SEMICOLON Variable

This variable defines the virtual key code for SEMICOLON (;) key events.

Syntax: `public final static int VK_SEMICOLON`

VK_SEPARATER Variable

This variable defines the virtual key code for SEPARATER key events.

Syntax: `public final static int VK_SEPARATER`

VK_SHIFT Variable

This variable defines the virtual key code for SHIFT key events.

Syntax: `public final static int VK_SHIFT`

VK_SLASH Variable

This variable defines the virtual key code for SLASH (/) key events.

Syntax: `public final static int VK_SLASH`

VK_SPACE Variable

This variable defines the virtual key code for SPACE key events.

Syntax: `public final static int VK_SPACE`

VK_SUBTRACT Variable

This variable defines the virtual key code for NUMBER PAD SUBTRACTION (-) key events.

Syntax: `public final static int VK_SUBTRACT`

VK_TAB Variable

This variable defines the virtual key code for TAB key events.

Syntax: `public final static int VK_TAB`

VK_UNDEFINED Variable

This variable signifies an undefined key code event.

Syntax: `public final static int VK_UNDEFINED`

VK_UP Variable

This variable defines the virtual key code for UP ARROW key events.

Syntax: `public final static int VK_UP`

Mouse Events

Mouse events originate from the java.awt.Component class. Mouse events are unique among AWT events, in that there are two listener interfaces. This is an important optimization, considering the large number of mouse move events that are generated.

java.awt.event.MouseListener Interface

This is the mouse event listener interface for receiving mouse events on a component. java.awt.event.MouseAdapter is the adapter for this interface.

mouseClicked() Method

This method is called when the mouse is clicked over a component.

Syntax: `public abstract void mouseClicked(MouseEvent e)`

mouseEntered() Method

This method is called when the mouse moves onto a component.

Syntax: `public abstract void mouseEntered(MouseEvent e)`

java.awt.event.MouseListener

mouseExited() Method

This method is called when the mouse moves off a component.

Syntax: `public abstract void mouseExited(MouseEvent e)`

mousePressed() Method

This method is called when the mouse is pressed over a component.

Syntax: `public abstract void mousePressed(MouseEvent e)`

mouseReleased() Method

This method is called when the mouse is released over a component.

Syntax: `public abstract void mouseReleased(MouseEvent e)`

java.awt.event.MouseMotionListener Interface

This is the mouse motion event listener interface for receiving mouse motion events on a component. java.awt.event.MouseMotionAdapter is the adapter for this interface.

mouseDragged() Method

This method is called with each subsequent move of the mouse after the mouse has been pressed over a component. Dragging is ended only when the mouse button is released.

Syntax: `public abstract void mouseDragged(MouseEvent e)`

mouseMoved() Method

This method is called when no buttons are down and the mouse has moved while over the component.

Syntax: `public abstract void mouseMoved(MouseEvent e)`

java.awt.event.MouseEvent Class

This is the class that mouse-generated events originate from. The constructors, methods, and variables for this class are described in the sections that follow.

MouseEvent Constructor

This constructor creates a mouse event object.

Syntax: `public MouseEvent(Component source, int id, long when, int modifiers, int x, int y, int clickCount, boolean popupTrigger)`

Parameters: source: originating component
id: event id
when: timestamp when event was created
modifiers: identifies the modifier keys that were pressed when the event occured
x: x position relative to the originating component
y: y position relative to the originating component
clickCount: count of mouse clicks for this event
popupTrigger: indicates this event is a platform specific, popup trigger event

getClickCount() Method

This method returns the number of mouse clicks associated with this event.

Syntax: `public int getClickCount()`

getPoint() Method

This method returns the position relative to the originating component.

Syntax: `public Point getPoint()`

getX() Method

This method returns the x-position relative to the originating component.

Syntax: `public int getX()`

getY() Method

This method returns the y-position relative to the originating component.

Syntax: `public int getY()`

isPopupTrigger() Method

This method returns whether or not this mouse event is the popup-menu trigger event for the platform.

Syntax: `public boolean isPopupTrigger()`

paramString() Method

This method returns the string equivalent of the event id.

Syntax: `public String paramString()`

translatePoint() Method

This method converts the position based on the position of the originating component.

Syntax: `public synchronized void translatePoint(int x, int y)`

Parameters: x: amount to add to the x coordinate
                 y: amount to add to the y coordinate

MOUSE_CLICKED Variable

This variable defines the event id of mouse clicked.

Syntax: `public final static int MOUSE_CLICKED`

MOUSE_DRAGGED Variable

This variable defines the event id of mouse dragged.

Syntax: `public final static int MOUSE_DRAGGED`

MOUSE_ENTERED Variable

This variable defines the event id of mouse entered.

Syntax: `public final static int MOUSE_ENTERED`

MOUSE_EXITED Variable

This variable defines the event id of mouse exited.

Syntax: `public final static int MOUSE_EXITED`

MOUSE_FIRST Variable

This variable defines the event id of the first mouse event.

Syntax: `public final static int MOUSE_FIRST`

MOUSE_LAST Variable

This variable defines the event id of the last mouse event.

Syntax: `public final static int MOUSE_LAST`

java.awt.event.MouseEvent

MOUSE_MOVED Variable

This variable defines the event id of mouse moved.

Syntax: `public final static int MOUSE_MOVED`

MOUSE_PRESSED Variable

This variable defines the event id of mouse pressed.

Syntax: `public final static int MOUSE_PRESSED`

MOUSE_RELEASED Variable

This variable defines the event id of mouse released.

Syntax: `public final static int MOUSE_RELEASED`

Paint Events

Paint events exist only to see to the serialization of paint requests when the event queue is serialized. The paint and update methods previously overriden should continue to be used.

java.awt.event.PaintEvent Class

This is the class from which paint events originate. Paint events ensure serialization of paint/update method calls in correspondence with other events delivered from the event queue. This event is not designed to be used with the Event Listener model. To ensure proper rendering, programs should continue to override the *paint()* and *update()* methods. The constructors, methods, and variables for this class are described in the sections that follow.

PaintEvent Constructor

This constructor creates a paint event.

Syntax: `public PaintEvent(Component source, int id, Graphics g)`

Parameters: source: event source

id: event id

g: graphical context

getGraphics() Method

This method returns the graphical context with the clip rectangle set to the component to be repainted.

Syntax: `public Graphics getGraphics()`

paramString() Method

This method returns the string equivalent of the event id.

Syntax: `public String paramString()`

PAINT Variable

This variable defines the event id of the paint event.

Syntax: `public final static int PAINT`

PAINT_FIRST Variable

This variable defines the event id of the first paint event.

Syntax: `public final static int PAINT_FIRST`

PAINT_LAST Variable

This variable defines the event id of the last paint event.

Syntax: `public final static int PAINT_LAST`

UPDATE Variable

This variable defines the event id of the update paint event.

Syntax: `public final static int UPDATE`

Text Events

Text events occur when text is edited within a component. Text events originate from the java.awt.TextComponent class.

java.awt.event.TextListener Interface

The text event listener interface for receiving events where text is edited within a component. There is no adapter for this interface.

textValueChanged() Method

This method is called with each change to the text.

Syntax: `public abstract void textValueChanged(TextEvent e)`

java.awt.event.TextEvent Class

This is the class that text events originate from. The constructors and methods for this class are described in the sections that follow.

TextEvent Constructor

This constructor creates a text event.

Syntax: `public TextEvent(Object source, int id)`

Parameters: source: originating text object

id: event id

paramString() Method

This method returns the string equivalent of the event id.

Syntax: `public String paramString()`

TEXT_FIRST Variable

This variable defines the event id of the first text event.

Syntax: `public final static int TEXT_FIRST`

TEXT_LAST Variable

This variable defines the event id of the last text event.

Syntax: `public final static int TEXT_LAST`

TEXT_VALUE_CHANGED Variable

This variable defines the event id of the value changed text event.

Syntax: `public final static int TEXT_VALUE_CHANGED`

Window Events

Window events occur with any changes made to a component window. Window events originate from the java.awt.Dialog class. An application must explicitly hide or destroy a window when a WINDOW CLOSING event occurs, or the window will not be closed.

java.awt.event.WindowListener Interface

This is the window event listener interface for receiving window events. java.awt.event.WindowAdapter is the adapter for this interface. The methods for this interface are described in the sections that follow.

windowActivated() Method

This method is called when a window is activated.

Syntax: `public abstract void windowActivated(WindowEvent e)`

windowClosed() Method

This method is called when the window is closed.

Syntax: `public abstract void windowClosed(WindowEvent e)`

windowClosing() Method

This method is called when a window is being closed. Allows the close process to be overridden.

Syntax: `public abstract void windowClosing(WindowEvent e)`

windowDeactivated() Method

This method is called when a window is de-activated.

Syntax: `public abstract void windowDeactivated(WindowEvent e)`

windowDeiconified() Method

This method is called when a window is expanded from an icon.

Syntax:　　**public abstract void windowDeiconified(WindowEvent e)**

windowIconified() Method

This method is called when a windo is reduced to an icon.

Syntax:　　**public abstract void windowIconified(WindowEvent e)**

windowOpened() Method

This method is called when a window is opened.

Syntax:　　**public abstract void windowOpened(WindowEvent e)**

java.awt.event.WindowEvent Class

This is the class that window events originate from. The constructors, methods, and variables for this class are described in the sections that follow.

WindowEvent Constructor

This constructor creates a window event.

Syntax:　　**public WindowEvent(Window source, int id)**

Parameters:　　source: originating window

id: event id

getWindow() Method

This method returns the originating window.

Syntax:　　**public Window getWindow()**

paramString() Method

This method returns the string equivalent of the event id.

Syntax: `public String paramString()`

WINDOW_ACTIVATED Variable

This variable defines the event id of an activated window event.

Syntax: `public final static int WINDOW_ACTIVATED`

WINDOW_CLOSED Variable

This variable defines the event id of a closed window event. This variable is delivered after a window has been closed by a call to hide or destroy the window.

Syntax: `public final static int WINDOW_CLOSED`

WINDOW_CLOSING Variable

This variable defines the event id of a closing window event. This variable is produced when "Quit" is selected. In addition, the application must explicitly hide or destroy the window.

Syntax: `public final static int WINDOW_CLOSING`

WINDOW_DEACTIVATED Variable

This variable defines the event id of a deactivated window event.

Syntax: `public final static int WINDOW_DEACTIVATED`

WINDOW_DEICONIFIED Variable

This variable defines the event id of a deiconified window event.

Syntax: `public final static int WINDOW_DEICONIFIED`

WINDOW_FIRST Variable

This variable defines the event id of the first window event.

Syntax: `public final static int WINDOW_FIRST`

WINDOW_LAST Variable

This variable defines the event id of the last window event.

Syntax: `public final static int WINDOW_LAST`

WINDOW_OPENED Variable

This variable defines the event id of the opened window event, delivered only once when the window is first made visible.

Syntax: `public final static int WINDOW_OPENED`

WINDOW_ICONIFIED Variable

This variable defines the event id of an iconified window event.

Syntax: `public final static int WINDOW_ICONIFIED`

Serialization API

The following API details the classes, interfaces, and signatures used by Java serialization. Java Beans use serialization to store and retrieve the persistent state of Beans. Serialization stems from several interfaces, classes, and exceptions and their corresponding constructors, methods, and variables in the java.io package. The relevant interfaces, classes, and exceptions are covered in the sections that follow with regards to their role in serialization.

Externalizable Interface

The Exernalizable interface declares a class as a serializable object, which maintains full control of the serialization process. Use this interface instead of the Serializable interface whenever the automated process of serialization is inappropriate. This interface extends the Serializable interface

Syntax: `public interface Externalizable`

---

readExternal(ObjectInput in) Method

This method is implemented to restore the specified object. The ObjectInput serialization stream supplies context for reading the contents of the object.

Syntax: `public abstract void readExternal(ObjectInput in) throws`
              `IOException, ClassNotFoundException;`

Parameters: ObjectInput in: object input stream

Throws: IOException: when an I/O error occurs.
              ClassNotFoundException: when an object is loaded, but the class for the
              object cannot be found in the class path. This exception can be thrown for

invalid class paths, missing class files and for classes that have been renamed since the object was serialized. This exception may also be thrown if a non-Object based class (that is, a primitive built-in data type) is found instead of an Object.

writeExternal(ObjectOutput out) Method

This method is implemented to restore the object. The ObjectOutput serialization stream supplies the context for writing the contents of the object.

Syntax: `public abstract void writeExternal(ObjectOutput out) throws IOException`

Parameters: ObjectOutput out: object output stream

Throws: IOException: when an I/O error occurs.

ObjectInput Interface

The data input interface extends input streams to implement object serialization. Normally, developers do not implement this interface unless special validation or decryption or other processing of input objects is required. Instead of creating a class implementing ObjectInput, use the ObjectInputStream class. This interface extends the DataInput interface. Refer also to the InputStream, ObjectOutputStream, and ObjectInputStream classes.

The documentation refers to the data being read from a stream, but this is not required. This interface can be used in implement an object reader for any file or device type. The only requirement is that the input should follow the same content and position of objects and primitives as they are written. This interface requires that code using an object that implements this interface should call the *close()* method to free up system resources.

Syntax: `public interface ObjectInput extends DataInput;`

available()Method

This method returns the number of bytes available in the input buffer without resorting to blocking I/O. The number returned is usually the amount of data remaining in the input buffer.

Syntax: `public abstract int available() throws IOException`

Throws: IOException: when an I/O error occurs

close() Method

This method closes the object input stream and must be called to free stream resources. This method should be called explicitly to prevent using up system resources such as file handles and hardware devices. Do not depend on garbage collection to free up system resources.

Syntax: `public abstract void close() throws IOException;`

Throws: IOException: when an I/O error occurs.

readObject() Method

This method reads an object from the object-input stream. The object will need to be cast up to the proper type before it can be used.

Syntax: `public abstract Object readObject() throwsClassNotFoundException,`
              `IOException`

Throws: IOException: when an I/O error occurs.
              ClassNotFoundException: when an object is loaded, but the class for the object cannot be found in the class path. This exception can be thrown for invalid class paths, missing class files, and for classes that have been renamed since the object was serialized. This exception may also be thrown if a non-object-based class (that is, a primitive built-in data type) is found instead of an object.

read() Method

This method reads a byte, cast into an int, from the data stream. This method might return −1 if the end of the stream is reached.

Syntax: `public abstract int read() throws IOException`

Throws: IOException: when an I/O error occurs.

read(byte byteBuffer[]) Method

This method reads an array of bytes from the stream. This method might return −1 if the end of the stream is reached.

Syntax: `public abstract int read(byte byteBuffer[]) throws IOException`

Parameters: byte byteBuffer[]: pre allocated array used to store data from the stream

Throws: IOException: when an I/O error occurs.

read(byte, int, int) Method

This method reads bytes into a buffer starting at an index in the buffer and stopping when the end of data is reached or when the specified maximum number of bytes have been read. This method might return −1 if the end of the stream is reached.

Syntax: `public abstract int read(byte byteBuffer[], int startingOffset,`
                `int lengthToRead) throws IOException`

Parameters: byte byteBuffer[]: array of bytes to copy input data into
                int startingOffset: offset in buffer to begin writing data from
                int lengthToRead: number of bytes to be read. Note that this number should be less than or equal to byteBuffer.size–startingOffset or an index out of range exception may be thrown

Throws: IOException: when an I/O error occurs.

skip(long bytesToSkip) Method

This method skips a specified number of bytes in a file and can be used to skip unused data. This method might return less than the specified number of bytes if the end of the stream is reached.

Syntax: `public abstract long skip(long bytesToSkip) throws IOException;`

Parameters: long bytesToSkip: number of bytes to skip

Throws: IOException: thrown when an I/O error occurs.

ObjectInputValidation Interface

This interface is used as a registered callback method interface to be called after an object and its tree have been completely deserialized.

A class object implementing this interface is registered with an ObjectInputStream by calling the *registerValidation()* method. When the ObjectInputStream has completely read the objects tree, the *validateObject()* method is called. If the *validateObject()* determines that the object is invalid, it throws an InvalidObjectException that aborts the object read and causes it to return null. Refer also to the ObjectInputStream class and its *registerValidation()* method.

validateObject() Method

This method determines that the object is invalid.

Syntax: ```public abstract void validateObject() throws```
              ```InvalidObjectExceptionp;```

Throws: InvalidObjectException: if the object cannot be validated. The *validateObject()* method returns normal if the object can be validated.

ObjectOutput Interface

This data output interface extends output streams to implement object serialization. Normally, developers do not implement this interface unless special decryption or other processing of output objects is required. You should use the ObjectOutputStream class instead of creating a class that implements ObjectOutput. This interface extends the DataOutput interface. Refer also to the InputStream, ObjectOutputStream, ObjectInputStream classes.

The documentation refers to the data written to a stream, but this is not required. This interface can be used to implement object output for any file or device type. The only requirement is that the output should follow the same content and position of objects and primitives as they are to be read. This interface requires that code using an object that implements this interface should call the *close()* method to free up system resources.

Syntax: ```public interface ObjectOutput extends DataOutput;```
              ```

close() Method

This method closes the object output stream and must be called to free stream resources. This should be called explicitly to prevent using up system resources like file handles and hardware devices. Do not depend on garbage collection to free up system resources.

Syntax: `public abstract void close() throws IOException;`

Throws: IOException: thrown when an I/O error occurs.

flush() Method

This method flushes any buffered output to the specified file, stream, or device.

Syntax: `public abstract void flush() throws IOException`

Throws: IOException: when an I/O error occurs.

write(byte byteBuffer[]) Method

This method writes an array of bytes to the stream.

Syntax: `public abstract void write(byte b[]) throws IOException`

Parameters: byte byteBuffer[]: array of bytes used to store data to the stream

Throws: IOException: when an I/O error occurs.

write(byte, int, int) Method

This method writes bytes to a stream from a byte buffer starting at an index in the buffer and stopping after the specified maximum number of bytes has been written.

Syntax: `public abstract int write(byte byteBuffer[], int startingOffset,`
                  `int lengthToWrite) throws IOException`

Parameters: byte byteBuffer[]: array of bytes to copy input data into
                  int startingOffset: offset in buffer to begin writing data from
                  int lengthToWrite: number of bytes to write. The number of bytes should

be less than or equal to byteBuffer.size–startingOffset or an index out of range exception may be thrown

Throws: IOException: when an I/O error occurs

write(int writeThisByte) Method

This method writes a byte to the data stream.

Syntax: `public abstract void write(int writeThisByte) throws IOException`

Throws: IOException: thrown when an I/O error occurs.

writeObject() Method

This method writes an object to the object-output stream.

Syntax: `public abstract void writeObject(Object obj) throws IOException`

Throws: IOException: when an I/O error occurs.

Serializable Interface

Any class that implements the Serializable interface is considered serializable. The interface does not implement any methods and contains no final data; however, the interface does turn over the serialization process to the following signature methods. Refer also to the ObjectOutputStream, ObjectInputStream, ObjectOutput, ObjectInput, and Externalizable classes.

Syntax: `Public interface Serializable;`

ReadObject(ObjectInputStream in) Signature Method

This signature method controls the serialization of an object. Note that the *in.defaultReadObject()* method can be called to read the object in the default manner.

Syntax: `private void readObject(java.io.ObjectInputStream in) throws`
             `IOException, ClassNotFoundException;`

Serializable

Parameters:	ObjectInputStream in: object input stream to write contents to
Throws:	IOException: when an I/O error occurs. ClassNotFoundException: when an object is loaded, but the class for the object cannot be found in the class path. This exception can be thrown for invalid class paths, missing class files, and for classes that have been renamed since the object was serialized. This exception may also be thrown if a non-object-based class (that is, a primitive built-in type) is found instead of an object.

WriteObject(ObjectOutputStream out) Signature Method

This signature method controls the serialization of an object. Note that the *out.defaultWriteObject()* can be called to write the object in the default manner.

Syntax:	`private void writeObject(ObjectOutputStream out) throws IOException`
Parameters:	ObjectOutputStream out: object output stream to write contents to
Throws:	IOException: when an I/O error occurs.

ObjectInputStream Class

The ObjectInputStream class implements stream-based object serialization. Objects that can be read by this class must implement the java.io.Serializable or java.io.Externalizable interfaces. This class extends the java.io.InputStream class. Refer also to the DataInput and Serializable interfaces and the ObjectOutputStream class.

This class requires that code using its object should call the *close()* method to free up system resources.

Syntax:	`public class ObjectInputStream extends ObjectInput implements` `ObjectInput;`

ObjectInputStream Constructor

This constructor creates a new ObjectInputStream object, given an open InputStream object. The stream must resolve to an ObjectInputStream object or a StreamCorruptedException will be thrown.

Syntax: `public ObjectInputStream(InputStream in) throws IOException,`
                      `StreamCorruptedException`

Parameters: InputStream in: stream to be read

Throws: IOException: when an I/O error occurs.
            StreamCorruptedException: when the version or magic number is incorrect.

available() Method

This method returns the number of bytes available in the input buffer without resorting to blocking I/O. The number returned is usually the amount of data remaining in the input buffer.

Syntax: `public int available() throws IOException`

Throws: IOException: when an I/O error occurs.

close() Method

This method closes the object input stream and must be called to free stream resources. This method should be called explicitly to prevent using up system resources like file handles and hardware devices. Do not rely on garbage collection to free up system resources.

Syntax: `public void close() throws IOException;`

Throws: IOException: when an I/O error occurs.

ObjectInputStream

defaultReadObject() Method

This method reads all non-static and non-transient fields and their trees. For security reasons, this method can only be called from within the class's *readObject()* method.

Syntax: `public final void defaultReadObject() throws IOException,`
                 `ClassNotFoundException, NotActiveException`

Throws: IOException: when an I/O error occurs.
ClassNotFoundException: when an object is loaded, but the class for the object cannot be found in the class path. This exception can be thrown for invalid class paths, missing class files, and for classes that have been renamed since the object was serialized. This exception might also be thrown if a non-object-based class (that is, a primitive built-in type) is found instead of an object.
NotActiveException: when called outside of the *readObject()*.

enableResolveObject(boolean enable) Method

This method enables objects in the stream to be replaced. This method can only be set to true if the class loader is trusted.

Syntax: `protected final boolean enableResolveObject(boolean enable) throws`
                 `SecurityException;`

Parameters: boolean enable: True to enable; False to disable

Throws: SecurityException: when the classloader of this stream object is non-null (not trusted).

read() Method

This method reads a byte from the data stream and cast it into an int. This method might return −1 if the end of the stream is reached.

Syntax: `public int read() throws IOException`

Throws: IOException: when an I/O error occurs.
EOFException: if the end of file is reached.

read(byte byteBuffer[]) Method

This method reads an array of bytes from the stream. This method might return –1 if the end of the stream is reached.

Syntax: `public int read(byte byteBuffer[]) throws IOException`

Parameters: byte byteBuffer[]: preallocated array used to store data from the stream

Throws: IOException: when an I/O error occurs.
EOFException: if the end of file is reached.

read(byte, int, int) Method

This method reads bytes into a buffer starting at an index in the buffer and stopping when the end of data is reached or when the specified maximum number of bytes have been read. This method continues to read until the specified number of bytes are read or until it reaches the end of file.

Syntax: `public int readFully(byte byteBuffer[], int startingOffset, int`
`lengthToRead) throws IOException`

Parameters: byte byteBuffer[]: array of bytes to copy input data into
int startingOffset: offset in buffer to begin writing data from
int lengthToRead: number of bytes to be read. Note that this number should be less than or equal to byteBuffer.size–startingOffset or an index out of range exception may be thrown

Throws: IOException: when an I/O error occurs.
EOFException: if the end of file is reached.

readBoolean() Method

This method reads a boolean value from the stream.

Syntax: `public boolean readBoolean() throws IOException`

Throws: IOException: when an I/O error occurs.
EOFException : if end of file is reached.

ObjectInputStream

readChar() Method

This method reads a 16 bit Unicode character from the stream.

Syntax: **public char readChar() throws IOException**

Throws: IOException: when an I/O error occurs.
                EOFException: if the end of file is reached.

readDouble() Method

This method reads a double value from the stream.

Syntax: **public double readDouble() throws IOException**

Throws: IOException: when an I/O error occurs.
                EOFException : if the end of file is reached.

readFloat() Method

This method reads a float value from the stream.

Syntax: **public float readFloat() throws IOException**

Throws: IOException: when an I/O error occurs.
                EOFException : if the end of file is reached.

readFully(byte inputBuffer[]) Method

This method reads the number of bytes until end of file.

Syntax: **public void readFully(byte inputBuffer[]) throws IOException**

Parameters: byte inputBuffer[]: preallocated array to store bytes read

Throws: IOException: when an I/O error occurs.
                EOFException: if the end of file is reached.

readInt() Method

This method reads an integer from the stream.

Syntax: `public int  readInt() throws IOException`

Throws: IOException: when an I/O error occurs.
EOFException: if the end of file is reached.

readLine() Method

This method reads a Unicode string line from the input stream. Valid characters for line termination are \n, \r, \r\n, or an EOF. The EOFException is not thrown because EOF is a valid line terminator.

Syntax: `public String readLine() throws IOException`

Throws: IOException: when an I/O error occurs.

readLong() Method

This method reads a long integer from the stream.

Syntax: `public long readLong() throws IOException`

Throws: IOException: when an I/O error occurs.
EOFException: if the end of file is reached.

readObject() Method

This method reads an object from the object-input stream. The object will need to be cast up to the proper type before it can be used.

Syntax: `public Object readObject() throws ClassNotFoundException,`
`IOException`

Throws: IOException: when an I/O error occurs.
EOFException: if the end of file is reached.
ClassNotFoundException: when an object is loaded, but the class for the object cannot be found in the class path. This exception can be thrown for

ObjectInputStream

invalid class paths, missing class files, and for classes that have been renamed since the object was serialized. This exception may also be thrown if a non-object-based class (that is, a primitive built-in type) is found instead of an object.

readShort() Method

This method reads a short integer from the stream.

Syntax: `public short readShort() throws IOException`

Throws: IOException: when an I/O error occurs.
                EOFException: if the end of file is reached.

readUnsignedByte() Method

This method reads an unsigned byte.

Syntax: `public int readUnsignedByte() throws IOException`

Throws: IOException: when an I/O error occurs.
                EOFException : if end of file is reached.

readUnsignedShort() Method

This method reads an unsigned short integer from the stream.

Syntax: `public int readShort() throws IOException`

Throws: IOException: when an I/O error occurs.
                EOFException: if end of file is reached.

readUTF() Method

This method reads and returns an 8-bit UTF string and converts it to Unicode from the stream until the line terminator is reached. Valid characters for line termination are \n, \r, \r\n, or an EOF. The EOFException is not thrown because EOF is a valid line terminator.

Syntax: `public String readUTF() throws IOException`

Throws: IOException: when an I/O error occurs.
EOFException: if the end of file is reached.

skip(long bytesToSkip) Method

This method skips a specified number of bytes in a file and is also used to skip unused data. This method might also return less than the specified number of bytes if the end of the stream is reached.

Syntax: `public long skip(long bytesToSkip) throws IOException;`

Parameters: long bytesToSkip: number of bytes to skip

Throws: IOException: when an I/O error occurs.
EOFException: if the end of file is reached.

ObjectOutputStream Class

The ObjectOutputStream class implements stream-based object serialization. Objects that can be written by this class must implement the java.io.Serializable or java.io.Externalizable interfaces. This class requires that code using its object must call the *close()* method to free up system resources. This class extends the OutputStream class and implements the ObjectOutput and ObjectStreamConstants interfaces. Refer also to the DataOutput and Serializable interfaces and the ObjectOutputStream class.

Syntax: `public class ObjectOutputStream extends ObjectOutput implements`
`ObjectOutput;`

ObjectOutputStream Constructor

This constructor creates a new ObjectOutputStream object, given an open OutputStream object. The stream must resolve to an ObjectOutputStream object or a StreamCorruptedException will be thrown.

Syntax: `public ObjectOutputStream(OutputStream in) throws IOException,`
`StreamCorruptedException`

Parameters: OutputStream in: stream to be written

Throws: IOException: when an I/O error occurs.
StreamCorruptedException: when the version or magic number is incorrect.

DefaultWriteObject() Method

This method writes the non-static and non-transient fields of the current class to a stream. This method can only be called from the *writeObject()* method of the class being serialized. It will throw the NotActiveException if it is called otherwise.

Syntax: `public final void defaultWriteObject() throws IOException`

Throws: IOException: when an I/O error occurs.
ClassNotFoundException: when an object is loaded, but the class for the object cannot be found in the class path. This exception can be thrown for invalid class paths, missing class files, and for classes that have been renamed since the object was serialized. This exception may also be thrown if a non-object-based class (that is, a primitive built-in type) is found instead of an object.
NotActiveException: when called outside of the *writeObject()*.

close() Method

This method closes the object output stream. This method must be called to free stream resources and should be called explicitly to prevent using up system resources like file handles and hardware devices. Do not rely on garbage collection to free up system resources.

Syntax: `public abstract void close() throws IOException;`

Throws: IOException: when an I/O error occurs.

enableReplaceObject(boolean enable) Method

This method enables objects in the stream to be replaced when the method parameter is set to true. The parameter can only be set to true if the class loader is trusted.

Syntax: `protected final boolean enableReplaceObject(boolean enable) throws`
`SecurityException`

Parameters: boolean enable: True to enable; False to disable

Throws: SecurityException: when the classloader of this stream object is non-null (not trusted).

flush() Method

This method flushes any buffered output to the specified file, stream, or device.

Syntax: `public abstract void flush() throws IOException`

Throws: IOException: when an I/O error occurs.

replaceObject(Object obj) Method

This method enables trusted subclasses of ObjectOutputStream to substitute one object for another. The *enableReplaceObject()* method checks that the stream requesting to do replacement can be trusted. Every reference to serializable objects is passed to replaceObject. To ensure that the private state of objects is not exposed, only trusted streams may use the *replaceObject()* method. The capability to replace objects is disabled until the *enableReplaceObject()* method is called.

Syntax: `protected Object replaceObject(Object obj) throws IOException`

Parameters: Object obj: object to be replaced

Throws: IOException: when an I/O error occurs.

write(byte byteBuffer[]) Method

This method writes an array of bytes to the stream.

Syntax: `public abstract void write(byte b[]) throws IOException`

Parameters: byte byteBuffer[]: array of bytes used to store data to the stream

Throws: IOException: when an I/O error occurs.

write(byte, int, int) Method

This method writes bytes into a buffer starting at an index in the buffer and stopping when the end of data is reached or when the specified maximum number of bytes has been written. This method continues to write until the specified number of bytes is written or the end of the file is reached.

Syntax: `public int writeFully(byte byteBuffer[], int startingOffset, int`
                  `lengthToWrite) throws IOException`

Parameters: byte byteBuffer[]: array of bytes to copy output data into
                int startingOffset: offset in buffer to begin writing data from
                int lengthToWrite: number of bytes to be write. Note that this number should be less than or equal to byteBuffer.size—startingOffset or an index out of range exception may be thrown

Throws: IOException: when an I/O error occurs.

write(int writeThisByte) Method

This method writes a byte to the data stream.

Syntax: `public abstract void write(int writeThisByte) throws IOException`

Throws: IOException: when an I/O error occurs.

writeBoolean() Method

This method writes a boolean value from the stream.

Syntax: `public boolean writeBoolean() throws IOException`

Throws: IOException: when an I/O error occurs.
                EOFException : if the end of file is reached.

writeChar() Method

This method writes a 16 bit Unicode character from the stream.

Syntax: `public char writeChar() throws IOException`

Throws: IOException: when an I/O error occurs.

writeDouble() Method

This method writes a 64 bit double value from the stream.

Syntax: `public double writeDouble() throws IOException`

Throws: IOException: when an I/O error occurs.
                 EOFException : if the end of file is reached.

writeFloat() Method

This method writes a float value from the stream.

Syntax: `public float writeFloat() throws IOException`

Throws: IOException: when an I/O error occurs.
                 EOFException: if the end of file is reached.

writeFully(byte outputBuffer[]) Method

This method writes bytes into a buffer until the end of the file is reached.

Syntax: `public void writeFully(byte outputBuffer[]) throws IOException`

Parameters: byte outputBuffer[]: preallocated array to store bytes write

Throws: IOException: when an I/O error occurs.

writeInt() Method

This method writes an integer from the stream.

Syntax: `public int  writeInt() throws IOException`

Throws: IOException: when an I/O error occurs.

writeLine() Method

This method writes a Unicode string line from the output stream. Valid characters for line termination are \n, \r, \r\n, or EOF. EOFException is not thrown because EOF is a valid line terminator.

Syntax: `public String writeLine() throws IOException`

Throws: IOException: when an I/O error occurs.

writeLong() Method

This method writes a long integer from the stream.

Syntax: `public long writeLong() throws IOException`

Throws: IOException: when an I/O error occurs.
                 EOFException: if the end of file is reached.

writeObject() Method

This method writes an object to the object-output stream.

Syntax: `public abstract void writeObject(Object obj) throws IOException`

Throws: IOException: when an I/O error occurs.

writeShort() Method

This method writes a short integer from the stream.

Syntax: `public short writeShort() throws IOException`

Throws: IOException: when an I/O error occurs.

writeUnsignedByte() Method

This method returns an integer containing an unsigned byte.

Syntax: `public int writeUnsignedByte() throws IOException`

Throws: IOException: when an I/O error occurs.
EOFException : if the end of file is reached.

writeUnsignedShort() Method

This method returns an integer containing an unsigned short from the stream.

Syntax: `public int writeShort() throws IOException`

Throws: IOException: when an I/O error occurs.
EOFException: if the end of file is reached.

writeUTF() Method

This method writes an 8 bit UTF string from the stream until a line terminator is reached. The UTF string returns converted into Unicode. Valid characters for line termination are \n, \r, \r\n, or EOF. EOFException is not thrown because EOF is a valid line terminator.

Syntax: `public String writeUTF() throws IOException`

Throws: IOException: when an I/O error occurs.

ObjectStreamClass Class

The ObjectStreamClass class represents the serialized state of a class converted to a stream.

forClass() Method

This method returns the class for the ObjectStreamClass represented by this object.

Syntax: `public Class forClass()`

getName() Method

This method gets the class descriptor of the class retrieved by the *lookup()* method.

Syntax: `public String getName()`

getSerialVersionUID() Method

This method gets the serial version UID for the class. This will be used to validate that object streams and classes match.

Syntax: `public long getSerialVersionUID()`

lookup(Class) Method

This method gets the ObjectStreamClass object for a given class. This is only valid for classes that implement the Serializable or Externalizable interfaces.

Syntax: `public static ObjectStreamClass lookup(Class cl)`

Parameters: Class cl: class to retrieve ObjectStreamClass object for

toString() Method

This method returns a string describing the ObjectStreamClass object.

Syntax: `public String toString()`

InvalidClassException Exception

This exception is raised when the Serialization runtime detects a problem with a class due to the following problems:

◆ the class is not public

◆ the class contains unknown data types

◆ the class does not match the serial version of the class in the stream

◆ the class implements only one of writeObject or readObject methods

◆ the class does not have an accessible no-arg constructor

This exception extends the ObjectStreamException.

InvalidObjectException Exception

This exception is raised by a class when it is explicitly disallowing itself to be serialized.

NotActiveException Exception

This exception is raised when serialization or deserialization is not active.

NotSerializableException Exception

This exception is raised by a class or by the serialization runtime when a class cannot be serialized.

ObjectStreamException Exception

This exception is the superclass of all exceptions that are Object Stream class-specific.

OptionalDataException Exception

This exception is raised if the *readObject()* method has optional data. The eof flag will be true or the length will be the number of bytes available to read.

StreamCorruptedException Exception

This exception is raised when control information read from an object stream violates internal consistency checks.

Java Core Reflection API

The Core Reflection API enables Java code to discover information about the constructors, methods, and fields of loaded classes. Reflected constructors, methods, and fields can be used to operate their underlying counterparts on objects, within security restrictions. The Core Reflection API can be used to accomplish the following:

- access and modify fields of objects and classes

- access and modify elements of arrays

- construct new class instances and new arrays

- invoke methods on objects and classes

java.lang Package

The java.lang package provides the low-level classes used to encapsulate methods for basic program functionality such as compilation handling, security, threading, and the runtime environment. In addition, this package also provides classes representing numbers, strings, and objects. For the purposes of this chapter, the java.lang package is discussed in relation to reflection through documentation of the Class class which implements runtime descriptors for classes and interfaces within a running Java application.

Class Class

Java classes and interfaces are represented at runtime by Class objects. The only entity that creates Class objects is the Java Virtual Machine which automatically constructs a new Class object for each class loaded. Every primitive type is also represented by a unique Class object. Also, every array of the same element type and number of dimensions is represented by a Class object.

Logically, now that reflection is part of the JDK, this class should be located with the rest of the Reflection classes in java.lang.reflect, however, this would have negative implications on compatibility with JDK 1.0x code and so it remains in the java.lang package. This class implements the Serializable interface of the java.io package

forName(String) Method

This method attempts to locate, load, and link a class given its fully qualified name. It is important to note that Class objects representing the primitive data types cannot be obtained with this method. For example, a Class object representing the Container class may be obtained via:

```
Class class = Class.forName("java.awt.Container");
```

Syntax: `public static Class forName(String className)`

Parameters: className: the fully qualified name of the class

Returns: A class object for the named class.

Throws: classNotFoundException: when the class cannot be found.

getClasses() Method

This method creates an array of Class objects that represent all of the public member classes and interfaces of a Class object. Included in this array are the public class and interface members inherited from the superclass chain. This array may have a length of 0 indicating that the class has no public member classes or interfaces. This condition may also indicate that this Class object represents a primitive type.

Syntax: `public Class[] getClasses()`

getClassLoader() Method

This method determines the ClassLoader object that originally loaded the Class object.

Syntax: **public ClassLoader getClassLoader()**

Returns: A ClassLoader object or null if the Class object was not loaded by a ClassLoader.

getComponentType() Method

This method, when called on a Class object that represents an array, determines the component type of the array and returns a Class object of this type. For example, if this method is called on a Class object that represents an array of String objects, it will return a Class object representing java.lang.String.

Syntax: **public Class getComponentType()**

getConstructor(Class[]) Method

This method returns a constructor object that matches the signature of the specified array of Class objects. For example, if the Class object you are working on represents java.lang.Thread and you call this method with an array containing Class objects of type java.lang.ThreadGroup and java.lang.String, a Constructor object representing the java.lang.Thread(ThreadGroup group, String name) constructor will be returned.

Syntax: **public Constructor getConstructor(Class parameterTypes[])**

Parameters: parameterTypes[]: n array of class objects

Throws: NoSuchMethodException: when a matching constructor is not found.
SecurityException: when access to the constructor is denied.

getConstructors() Method

This method determines all of the public constructors of the class represented by the current Class object and returns them in an array format. This array may be of length 0 if this Class has no public constructors, is an interface, or represents a primitive type.

Syntax: `public Constructor[] getConstructors()`

Throws: SecurityException: when access to this information is denied by the SecurityManager.

getDeclaredClasses() Method

This method returns an array of Class objects that represent all of the classes and interfaces declared as members of the Class object. This array will include all public, protected, package, private classes, and interfaces but does not include inherited classes and interfaces. This array may be of length 0 if this class declares no classes or interfaces as members or represents a primitive type.

Syntax: `public Class[] getDeclaredClasses()`

Throws: SecurityException: when access to this information is denied by the SecurityManager.

getDeclaredConstructor(Class[]) Method

This method returns a constructor object that matches the signature of the specified array of class objects. For example, if the Class object you are working on represents java.lang.Thread and you call this method with an array containing Class objects of type java.lang.ThreadGroup and java.lang.String, we will be returned a Constructor object representing the java.lang.Thread(ThreadGroup group, String name) constructor.

This method differs from getConstructor(Class[]) in that it will return a Constructor (if access is allowed) which is protected, private, or of default access.

Syntax: `public Constructor getDeclaredConstructor(Class parameterTypes[])`

Parameters: parameterTypes[]: n array of class objects

Returns: A Constructor object matching the given signature

Throws: NoSuchMethodException: when a constructor matching the defined
                 signature is not found.
                 SecurityException: when access to this information is denied by the
                 SecurityManager.

getDeclaredConstructors() Method

This method returns an array of Constructor objects that represent all public, protected,
package, and private constructors. This array can be of length 0 if this class is an interface
or primitive type.

Syntax: `public Constructor[] getDeclaredConstructors()`

Throws: SecurityException: when access to this information is denied by the
                 SecurityManager.

getDeclaredField(String) Method

This method returns a Field object from the Class object that is specified by the String
name given.

Syntax: `public Field getDeclaredField(String name)`

Parameters: name: String containing the simple name of the field.

Throws: NoSuchFieldException: when a field with this name does not exist.
                 SecurityException: when access to the field is not permitted.

getDeclaredFields() Method

This method returns an array of Field objects which represent all of the fields (public,
protected, default, and private) declared by the specified class or interface. The returned
array does not include any inherited fields. This array may be of length 0 if the class or
interface does not declare any fields or if the Class object represents a primitive type.

Syntax: `public Field[] getDeclaredFields()`

Throws: SecurityException: when access to this information is denied by the
                 SecurityManager.

getDeclaredMethod(String, Class[]) Method

This method creates a Method object representing a method of the Class object that matches the specified name and signature. The array of classes that constitute the signature must be in declared order.

Syntax: `public Method getDeclaredMethod(String name, Class parameterTypes[])`

Parameters: Name: a string containing the name of the method
ParameterTypes: an array of class objects defining the signature of the method

Throws: NoSuchMethodException: when a matching method is not found.
SecurityException: when access to the method is denied.

getDeclaredMethods() Method

This method analyzes the current Class object and returns an array of Method objects representing all of the methods implemented (including all of the public, protected, default, and private methods but excluding inherited methods). This array may be of length 0 if the class or interface does not declare any methods or represents a primitive type.

Syntax: `public Method[] getDeclaredMethods()`

Throws: SecurityException: when access to this information is denied.

getDeclaringClass() Method

If the class or interface that is represented by the Class object is a member of another class, this method will return the Class object that represents it. This method returns null if the specified class or interface is not a member of any other class.

Syntax: `public Class getDeclaringClass()`

getField(String) Method

This method, given a string specifiying the simple name of the desired field, returns a Field object representing the specified publicly accessible field of the class or interface represented by the Class object.

Syntax: `public Field getField(String name)`

Parameters: Name: a string containing the simple name of the field

Throws: NotSuchFieldException: when a matching field does not exist.
SecurityException: when access to the field is denied.

getFields() Method

This method returns an array of Field objects representing all of the publicly accessible fields of the class or interface represented by the Class object, including those declared by its superclasses and superinterfaces. This array may be of length 0 if the class or interface has no publicly accessible fields.

Syntax: `public Field[] getFields()`

Throws: SecurityException: when access to the information is denied by the SecurityManager.

getInterfaces() Method

This method returns an array of Class objects representing the interfaces that the Class object implements. If the specified Class object represents an interface, this method returns an array of Class objects representing the direct superinterfaces of this interface. This may be of length 0 if the specified class implements no interfaces or represents a primitive type.

Syntax: `public Class[] getInterfaces()`

getMethod(String, Class[]) Method

This method returns a Method object that matches the supplied signature. The Method object is located by searching all of the public member methods of the specified class that match the name given and takes exactly the same parameter types as defined in the specified array of classes.

Syntax: `public Method getMethod(String name, Class[] parameterTypes)`

Parameters: name: a string containing the name of a method
parameterTypes: an array of classes containing the arguments of a method

Throws: NoSuchMethodException: when a matching method is not found.
SecurityException: when access is denied by the SecurityManager.

getMethods() Method

This method returns an array of Method objects representing all of the public methods of the class or interface that is represented by the Class object, including those inherited from superclasses and superinterfaces. This array can be of length 0 if the class or interface has no public member methods.

Syntax: `public Method[] getMethods()`

Throws: SecurityException: when access to this information is denied by the SecurityManager.

getModifiers() Method

This method returns an integer that encodes the modifiers for the specified class or interface. This value is the Java Virtual Machine's constant for public, private, protected, static, final, synchronized, volatile, transient, native, interface, and abstract modifiers. These constants should only be decoded using the methods of the java.lang.reflect.Modifier class.

Syntax: `public int getModifiers()`

getName() Method

This method returns a string that contains the fully-qualified name of the class, interface, primitive type, or void that is represented by the Class object.

Syntax: `public String getName()`

getSuperclass() Method

This method returns the superclass of the Class object.

Syntax: `public Class getSuperclass()`

Returns: A Class object or null if the specified class is the Class object, an interface type, or a primitive type.

isArray() Method

This method determines if the Class object is an array type.

Syntax: `public boolean isArray()`

isAssignableFrom(Class) Method

This method determines if the Class object is a superclass or superinterface of the class or interface passed in the parameter.

Syntax: `public boolean isAssignableFrom(Class fromClass)`

Parameters: fromClass: a class object

Returns: True if the Class object is a superclass or superinterface of the given class or interface, False otherwise. True is returned when the specified class is the same as the one passed in the parameter or this Class is a primitive type.

Throws: NullPointerException: when a null Class object is passed to this method.

isInstance(Object) Method

This method determines if the specified object is an instance of the Class object or any of its subclasses. If the Class object is represented by an interface, this method will return true if the class of the specified object implements this interface.

In general, true is returned if the specified object can be cast to the reference type of the Class object with throwing a ClassCastException.

Syntax: `public boolean isInstance(Object obj)`

Parameters: obj: an object

Returns: True if the object is an instance, false otherwise. False is also returned when this Class is a primitive data type or the object passed is null.

isInterface() Method

This method determines if the Class object is represented by an interface.

Syntax: `public boolean isInterface()`

Returns: True if the Class object is represented by an interface, False otherwise.

isPrimitive() Method

Determines whether the Class object is a primitive type. The Java Virtual Machine creates the Class objects that are defined as the Java primitive data types. This method will only return true for objects that are accessed with the following variables:

◆ java.lang.Boolean.TYPE

◆ java.lang.Character.TYPE

◆ java.lang.Byte.TYPE

◆ java.lang.Short.TYPE

◆ java.lang.Integer.TYPE

◆ java.lang.Long.TYPE

- java.lang.Float.TYPE

- java.lang.Double.TYPE

- java.lang.Void.TYPE

Syntax: `public boolean isPrimitive()`

Returns: True if the Class object is a primitive type, False otherwise.

newInstance() Method

This method creates and initializes a new instance of the Class object. The creation and initialization of the new object is performed in the same manner as if an instance creation expression were executed without any arguments.

Syntax: `public Object newInstance()`

Throws: IllegalAccessException: when the class or initializer is not accessible to the calling class.
InstantiationException: when this Class is a primitive type, interface or abstract class.

toString() Method

This method returns the name of the Class object in a string. The format of the string is as follows:

- the word "class," if the Class object represents a class or the word "interface," if the Class object represents an interface

- a blank space

- the name of the Class object

If the Class object represents a primitive type, then the name alone is returned. This method overrides the *toString()* method of the Object class in the java.lang package.

Syntax: `public String toString()`

java.lang.reflect Package

Member Interface

The Member interface reflects identifying information about a class, interface member, or constructor. The methods and variables for this interface are described in the sections that follow.

DECLARED Variable

This variable identifies the declared members of a class or interface. This variable is also used by the SecurityManager class to determine security policy.

Syntax: `public final static int DECLARED`

PUBLIC Variable

This variable identifies the public members of a class or interface. This variable is also used by the SecurityManager class to determine security policy.

Syntax: `public final static int PUBLIC`

getDeclaringClass() Method

This method gets the Class object representing the class or interface that declares the specified member or constructor.

Syntax: `public abstract Class getDeclaringClass()`

getModifiers() Method

This method returns an integer that encodes the modifiers for the specified member or constructor. This value is the Java Virtual Machine's constant for public, private, protected, static, final, synchronized, volatile, transient, native, interface, and abstract modifiers. These constants should only be decoded using the methods of the java.lang.reflect.Modifier class.

Syntax:　　**public abstract int getModifiers()**

getName() Method

This method returns a string that contains the name of the specified member or constructor. The name does not include the name of the declaring class or interface.

Syntax:　　**public abstract String getName()**

Array Class

The Array class exports static methods to create Java arrays with primitive or class component types. This class contains methods to get and set array component values. The Array class cannot be instantiated.

get(Object, int) Method

This method returns the value of the indexed component from the specified array. If the value has a primitive type, it will be wrapped in an object before it is returned.

Each of the primitive types has its own *get()* method, such as *getBoolean()* and *getByte()*. These are more efficient than the *get()* method because the value returned does not have to be wrapped in an object.

Syntax:　　**public static Object get(Object array, int index)**

Parameters:　　array: an array of objects
　　　　　　　　index: an index number of the specific object desired from the array

Throws:　　NullPointerException: when the object passed is null.
　　　　　　IllegalArgumentException: when the object passed is not an array.
　　　　　　ArrayIndexOutOfBoundsException: when the index passed is negative or greater than or equal to the size of the given array.

getBoolean(Object, int) Method

This method returns the Boolean value at the specified index from an array.

Syntax: `public static boolean getBoolean(Object array, int index)`

Parameters: array: an array of objects
                     index: an index number of the specific object desired from the array

Throws: NullPointerException: when the object passed is null.
                     IllegalArgumentException: when the object passed is not an array or the indexed value is not of type Boolean.
                     ArrayIndexOutOfBoundsException: when the index passed is negative or greater than or equal to the size of the given array.

getByte(Object, int) Method

This method returns the byte value at the specified index from an array.

Syntax: `public static byte getByte(Object array, int index)`

Parameters: array: an array of objects
                     index: an index number of the specific object desired from the array

Throws: NullPointerException: when the object passed is null.
                     IllegalArgumentException: when the object passed is not an array or the indexed value is not of type byte.
                     ArrayIndexOutOfBoundsException: when the index passed is negative or greater than or equal to the size of the given array.

getChar(Object, int) Method

This method returns the char value at the specified index from an array.

Syntax: `public static char getChar(Object array, int index)`

Parameters: array: an array of objects
                     index: an index number of the specific object desired from the array

Throws: NullPointerException: when the object passed is null.
IllegalArgumentException: when the object passed is not an array or the indexed value is not of type char.
ArrayIndexOutOfBoundsException: when the index passed is negative or greater than or equal to the size of the given array.

getDouble(Object, int) Method

This method returns the double value at the specified index from an array.

Syntax: `public static double getDouble(Object array, int index)`

Parameters: array: an array of objects
index: an index number of the specific object desired from the array

Throws: NullPointerException: when the object passed is null.
IllegalArgumentException: when the object passed is not an array or the indexed value cannot be converted to a double by an identity conversion or a widening conversion.
ArrayIndexOutOfBoundsException: when the index passed is negative or greater than or equal to the size of the given array.

getFloat(Object, int) Method

This method returns the float value at the specified index from an array.

Syntax: `public static float getFloat(Object array, int index)`

Parameters: array: an array of objects
index: an index number of the specific object desired from the array

Throws: NullPointerException: when the object passed is null.
IllegalArgumentException: when the object passed is not an array or the indexed value cannot be converted to a float by an identity conversion or a widening conversion.
ArrayIndexOutOfBoundsException: when the index passed is negative or greater than or equal to the size of the given array.

Array

getInt(Object, int) Method

This method returns the int value at the specified index from an array.

Syntax: `public static int getInt(Object array, int index)`

Parameters: array: an array of objects
index: an index number of the specific object desired from the array

Throws: NullPointerException: when the object passed is null.
IllegalArgumentException: when the object passed is not an array or the indexed value cannot be converted to an int by an identity conversion or a widening conversion.
ArrayIndexOutOfBoundsException: when the index passed is negative or greater than or equal to the size of the given array.

getLength(Object) Method

This method returns the length of the specified array.

Syntax: `public static int getLength(Object array)`

Parameters: array: an array of objects

Throws: NullPointerException: when the object passed is null.
IllegalArgumentException: when the object passed is not an array.

getLong(Object, int) Method

This method returns the long value at the specified index from an array.

Syntax: `public static long getLong(Object array, int index)`

Parameters: array: an array of objects
index: an index number of the specific object desired from the array

Throws: NullPointerException: when the object passed is null.
IllegalArgumentException: when the object passed is not an array or the indexed value cannot be converted to a long by an identity conversion or a widening conversion.

ArrayIndexOutOfBoundsException: when the index passed is negative or greater than or equal to the size of the given array.

getShort(Object, int) Method

This method returns the short value at the specified index from an array.

Syntax: **`public static short getShort(Object array, int index)`**

Parameters: array: an array of objects
                 index: an index number of the specific object desired from the array

Throws: NullPointerException: when the object passed is null.
                 IllegalArgumentException: when the object passed is not an array or the indexed value cannot be converted to a short by an identity conversion or a widening conversion.
                 ArrayIndexOutOfBoundsException: when the index passed is negative or greater than or equal to the size of the given array.

newInstance(Class, int) Method

This method creates a new array of the given component type and length. Using this method is the same as the following array creation expression:

```
new componentType[length]
```

Syntax: **`public static Object newInstance(Class componentType, int length)`**

Parameters: componentType: a class specifying what type the new array will be
                 length: the integer length of the new array.

Throws: NullPointerException: when componentType is null.
                 NegativeArraySizeException: when length is negative.

newInstance(Class, int[]) Method

This method creates a new array of the given component type and dimensions. Using this method is the same as the following array creation expression:

```
new componentType[dimensions[0]][dimensions[1]]...
```

Syntax: `public static Object newInstance(Class componentType, int[] dimensions)`

Parameters: componentType: a class specifying what type the new array will be
dimensions: an integer array specifying the dimensions of the new array

Throws: NullPointerException: when componentType or dimensions are null
NegativeArraySizeException: when any of the values in the dimensions array are negative.
IllegalArgumentException: when the length of the dimensions array is zero, or if it is greater than the maximum limit supported by the implementation (typically 255).

set(Object, int, Object) Method

This method sets the value of the indexed component in the specified array. If the array has a primitive type, the value will first be unwrapped from the object before it is assigned.

Each of the primitive types has its own *set()* method, such as *setBoolean()* and *setByte()*. These are more efficient than the *set()* method because the value does not have to be unwrapped before it is assigned.

Syntax: `public static void set(Object array, int index, Object value)`

Parameters: array: an array of objects
index: an index number of the object from the array which is to be set
value: the object value to be assigned to the array at the given index

Throws: NullPointerException: when the object passed is null.
IllegalArgumentException: when the object passed is not an array.
ArrayIndexOutOfBoundsException: when the index passed is negative or greater than or equal to the size of the given array.

setBoolean(Object, int, boolean) Method

This method sets the Boolean value at the specified index in an array.

Syntax: `public static void setBoolean(Object array, int index, boolean z)`

Parameters: array: an array of objects
index: an index number of the object from the array which is to be set
z: the Boolean object value to be assigned to the array at the given index

Throws: IllegalArgumentException: when the object passed is not an array.
NullPointerException: when the object passed is null.
ArrayIndexOutOfBoundsException: when the index is negative or greater than or equal to the size of the given array.

setByte(Object, int, byte) Method

This method sets the byte value at the specified index in an array.

Syntax: `public static void setByte(Object array, int index, byte b)`

Parameters: array: an array of objects
index: an index number of the object from the array which is to be set
b: the byte object value to be assigned to the array at the given index

Throws: IllegalArgumentException: when the object passed is not an array.
NullPointerException: when the object passed is null.
ArrayIndexOutOfBoundsException: when the index is negative or greater than or equal to the size of the given array.

setChar(Object, int, char) Method

This method sets the char value at the specified index in an array.

Syntax: `public static void setChar(Object array, int index, char c)`

Parameters: array: an array of objects
index: an index number of the object from the array which is to be set
c: the character object value to be assigned to the array at the given index

Array

Throws: IllegalArgumentException: when the object passed is not an array
NullPointerException: when the object passed is null.
ArrayIndexOutOfBoundsException: when the index is negative or greater
than or equal to the size of the given array.

setDouble(Object, int, double) Method

This method sets the double value at the specified index in an array.

Syntax: `public static void setDouble(Object array, int index, double d)`

Parameters: array: an array of objects
index: an index number of the object from the array which is to be set
d: the double object value to be assigned to the array at the given index

Throws: IllegalArgumentException: when the object passed is not an array or if the
double cannot be converted to a value of the array component type by an
identity conversion or a widening conversion.
NullPointerException: when the object passed is null.
ArrayIndexOutOfBoundsException: when the index is negative or greater
than or equal to the size of the given array.

setFloat(Object, int, float) Method

This method sets the float value at the specified index in an array.

Syntax: `public static void setFloat(Object array, int index, float f)`

Parameters: array: an array of objects
index: an index number of the object from the array which is to be set
f: the float object value to be assigned to the array at the given index

Throws: IllegalArgumentException: when the object passed is not an array or if the
float cannot be converted to a value of the array component type by an
identity conversion or a widening conversion.
NullPointerException: when the object passed is null.
ArrayIndexOutOfBoundsException: when the index is negative or greater
than or equal to the size of the given array.

setInt(Object, int, int) Method

This method sets the int value at the specified index in an array.

Syntax: **public static void setInt(Object array, int index, int i)**

Parameters: array: an array of objects
index: an index number of the object from the array which is to be set
i: the integer object value to be assigned to the array at the given index

Throws: IllegalArgumentException: when the object passed is not an array or if the int cannot be converted to a value of the array component type by an identity conversion or a widening conversion.
NullPointerException: when the object passed is null.
ArrayIndexOutOfBoundsException: when the index is negative or greater than or equal to the size of the given array.

setLong(Object, int, long) Method

This method sets the long value at the specified index in an array.

Syntax: **public static void setLong(Object array, int index, long l)**

Parameters: array: an array of objects
index: an index number of the object from the array which is to be set
l: the long object value to be assigned to the array at the given index

Throws: IllegalArgumentException: when the object passed is not an array or if the long cannot be converted to a value of the array component type by an identity conversion or a widening conversion.
NullPointerException: when the object passed is null.
ArrayIndexOutOfBoundsException: when the index is negative or greater than or equal to the size of the given array.

Array

setShort(Object, int, short) Method

This method sets the short value at the specified index in an array.

Syntax: `public static void setShort(Object array, int index, short s)`

Parameters: array: an array of objects
index: an index number of the object from the array which is to be set
s: the short object value to be assigned to the array at the given index

Throws: IllegalArgumentException: when the object passed is not an array or if the short cannot be converted to a value of the array component type by an identity conversion or a widening conversion.
NullPointerException: when the object passed is null.
ArrayIndexOutOfBoundsException: when the index is negative or greater than or equal to the size of the given array.

Constructor Class

Constructors provide information about, and access to, a single constructor of a declared class. Constructor objects may be used to create and initialize a new instance of the class that declares the reflected constructor, as long as the class can be instantiated.

The only entity that creates Constructor objects is the Java Virtual Machine. To get Constructor references, use the *getConstructor()*, *getConstructors()*, *getDeclaredConstructor()*, and *getDeclaredConstructors()* methods of the Class class.

equals(Object) Method

This method determines if the Constructor object is the same as the specified object. The Constructor and the object are considered equal only if they have the same declaring class and same parameter types. This method overrides the *equals()* method in the Object class.

Syntax: `public boolean equals(Object obj)`

Parameters: obj: the object to be compared

Returns: True if the Constructor and the given object are the same, False otherwise.

getDeclaringClass() Method

This method returns the Class object that declares the Constructor object.

Syntax: `public Class getDeclaringClass()`

getExceptionTypes() Method

This method returns an array of Class objects that match the checked expressions thrown by the Constructor object. The array size is 0 if the Constructor object does not throw any checked expressions.

Syntax: `public Class[] getExceptionTypes()`

getModifiers() Method

This method returns an integer that encodes the modifiers for the Constructor object. This value is the Java Virtual Machine's constant for public, private, protected, static, final, synchronized, volatile, transient, native, interface, and abstract modifiers. These constants should only be decoded using the methods of the java.lang.reflect.Modifier class.

Syntax: `public int getModifiers()`

getName() Method

This method returns a string that contains the name of the Constructor object. This is the same as the fully-qualified name of the Constructor object's declaring class.

Syntax: `public String getName()`

getParameterTypes() Method

This method returns an array of Class objects matching the parameter types of the Constructor object. The array is ordered the same as if the parameter were declared. The array size is 0 if the Constructor object takes no parameters.

Syntax: `public Class[] getParameterTypes()`

Constructor

hashCode() Method

This method returns an integer hash code for the Constructor object. The hash code for the Constructor object will be the same as the hash code for its declaring class. This method overrides the *hashCode()* method in the Object class.

Syntax: `public int hashCode()`

newInstance(Object[]) Method

This method creates and initializes a new instance of the Constructor object's declaring Class object. The new object is then initialized with the specified parameters. If any of the individual parameters are of a primitive type, they are automatically unwrapped. If necessary, widening conversions are performed on the individual parameters.

Syntax: `public Object newInstance(Object initargs[])`

Parameters: initargs[]: an array of objects that will be used to initialize the new instance

Throws: IllegalAccessException: when the Constructor object is not accessible
                 InstantiationException: when this Constructor object's declaring class is an abstract class.
                 NullPointerException: when the formal parameter is of a primitive type, but the corresponding argument in the initargs array is null.
                 IllegalArgumentException: when the number of arguments passed to this method in the initargs array differs from the number of arguments expected by the Constructor object. This exception may also be thrown when the argument in the initargs array cannot be converted to the formal parameter type by an identity conversion or a widening conversion.

toString() Method

This method returns a string describing the Constructor object. The string is formatted as follows:

◆ Java language modifiers for this Constructor (if any)

◆ fully-qualified name of the class declaring this Constructor

◆ comma-separated list of the fully-qualified names of this Constructor's formal parameter types. This list is surrounded by parentheses.

◆ a space

◆ the word "throws"

◆ comma-separated list of the fully-qualified names of the thrown exception types

Syntax: `public String toString()`

Field Class

Fields provide information about, and access to, a single field of a class or interface. The reflected field may be a class variable (static field) or an instance variable (instance field).

The only entity that creates Field objects is the Java Virtual Machine. To get Field references, use the *getField(), getFields(), getDeclaredField(),* and *getDeclaredFields()* methods of the Class class.

equals(Object) Method

This method determines if the Field object is the same as the specified object. The Field object and the specified object are considered equal only if they have the same declaring class and the same name. This method overrides the *equals()* method of the Object class.

Syntax: `public boolean equals(Object obj)`

Parameters: obj: the object to be compared

Returns: True if the Field and the specified object are the same, False otherwise.

get(Object) Method

This method returns the value of the Field object on the specified object. If the value has a primitive type it will be wrapped in an object before it is returned. If the Field is static the argument, which may be null, is ignored.

Each of the primitive types has its own get method, such as *getBoolean()* and *getBtye()*. These are more efficient than the get method because the value returned does not have to be wrapped in an object.

Field

Syntax:	`public Object get(Object obj)`
Parameters:	obj: the object from which this method will get a value
Throws:	NullPointerException: when the Field is an instance field and the object passed is null.
	IllegalArgumentException: when the object passed is not an instance of the class or interface declaring this Field.
	IllegalAccessException: when the Field object is inaccessible and this Field object enforces Java language access control.

getBoolean(Object) Method

This method returns the Boolean value of the Field object on the specified object.

Syntax:	`public boolean getBoolean(Object obj)`
Parameters:	obj: the object from which this method will get a value
Throws:	NullPointerException: when the Field object is an instance field and the object passed is null.
	IllegalArgumentException: when the value is not of type Boolean or the object passed is not an instance of the class or interface declaring the Field object.
	IllegalAccessException: when the Field object is inaccessible and enforces Java language access control.

getByte(Object) Method

This method returns the byte value of the Field object on the specified object.

Syntax:	`public byte getByte(Object obj)`
Parameters:	obj: the object from which this method will get a value
Throws:	NullPointerException: when the Field object is an instance field and the object passed is null.
	IllegalArgumentException: when the value is not of type byte or the object passed is not an instance of the class or interface declaring the Field object.
	IllegalAccessException: when the Field object is inaccessible and the Field object enforces Java language access control.

getChar(Object) Method

This method returns the char value of the Field object on the specified object.

Syntax: `public char getChar(Object obj)`

Parameters: obj: the object from which this method will get a value

Throws: NullPointerException: when the Field object is an instance field and the object passed is null.
IllegalArgumentException: when the value is not of type char or the object passed is not an instance of the class or interface declaring the Field object.
IllegalAccessException: when the Field object is inaccessible and enforces Java language access control.

getDeclaringClass() Method

This method returns the class or interface that declares the Field object.

Syntax: `public Class getDeclaringClass()`

getDouble(Object) Method

This method returns the double value of the Field object for a specified object.

Syntax: `public double getDouble(Object obj)`

Parameters: obj: the object from which this method will get a value

Throws: NullPointerException: when the Field object is an instance field and the object passed is null.
IllegalArgumentException: when the value cannot be converted to a double by an identity or a widening conversion or the object passed is not an instance of the class or interface declaring the Field object.
IllegalAccessException: when the Field object is inaccessible and enforces Java language access control.

Field

getFloat(Object) Method

This method returns the float value of the Field object for a specified object.

Syntax: `public float getFloat(Object obj)`

Parameters: obj: the object from where this method will get a value

Throws: NullPointerException: when the Field object is an instance field and the object passed is null.

IllegalArgumentException: when the value cannot be converted to a float by an identity or a widening conversion or the object passed is not an instance of the class or interface declaring the Field object.

IllegalAccessException: when the Field object is inaccessible and enforces Java language access control.

getInt(Object) Method

This method returns the int value of the Field object for the specified object.

Syntax: `public int getInt(Object obj)`

Parameters: obj: the object from which this method will get a value

Throws: NullPointerException: when the Field object is an instance field and the object passed is null.

IllegalArgumentException: when the value cannot be converted to an int by an identity or a widening conversion or the object passed is not an instance of the class or interface declaring the Field object.

IllegalAccessException: when the Field object is inaccessible and enforces Java language access control.

getLong(Object) Method

This method returns the long value of the Field object for the specified object.

Syntax: `public long getLong(Object obj)`

Parameters: obj: the object from which this method will get a value

Throws: NullPointerException: when the Field object is an instance field and the object passed is null.

IllegalArgumentException: when the value cannot be converted to a long by an identity or a widening conversion or the object passed is not an instance of the class or interface declaring the Field object.

IllegalAccessException: when the Field object is inaccessible and enforces Java language access control.

getModifiers() Method

This method returns an integer that encodes the modifiers for the Field object. This value is the Java Virtual Machine's constant for public, private, protected, static, final, synchronized, volatile, transient, native, interface, and abstract modifiers. These constants should only be decoded using the methods of the java.lang.reflect.Modifier class.

Syntax: `public int getModifiers()`

getName() Method

This method returns a string that contains the simple name of the Field object.

Syntax: `public String getName()`

getShort(Object) Method

This method returns the short value of the Field object for the specified object.

Syntax: `public short getShort(Object obj)`

Parameters: obj: the object from which this method will get a value

Throws: NullPointerException: when the Field object is an instance field and the object passed is null.

IllegalArgumentException: when the value cannot be converted to a short by an identity or a widening conversion or the object passed is not an instance of the class or interface declaring the Field object.

IllegalAccessException: when the Field is inaccessible and enforces Java language access control.

Field

getType() Method

This method determines the declared type of the Field object.

Syntax: `public Class getType()`

hashCode() Method

This method returns an integer hash code for the Field object. The hash code for the Field object is computed as the exclusive-or of the hash codes for the Field object's declaring class name and its simple name. This method overrides the *hashCode( )* method for the Object class.

Syntax: `public int hashCode()`

set(Object, Object) Method

This method sets the value of the Field object for the specified object. If the Field object has a primitive type, the value will first be unwrapped from the object before it is assigned. If the Field object is static, the obj argument is ignored and may be null.

Each of the primitive types has its own set method, such as *setBoolean( )* and *setByte( )*. These methods are more efficient than the *set( )* method because the value does not have to be unwrapped before it is assigned.

Syntax: `public void set(Object obj, Object value)`

Parameters: obj: the object in which the value will be set
                 value: the object value to be assigned

Throws: NullPointerException: when the Field object is an instance field and the object passed is null. This exception may also be thrown when the Field object is a primitive type and the value is null.
                 IllegalArgumentException: when the object passed is not an instance of the class or interface declaring the Field object. This exception may also be thrown when the value cannot be converted to the type of this Field object.
                 IllegalAccessException: when the Field object is inaccessible and enforces Java language access control or the Field object is a final field.

setBoolean(Object, boolean) Method

This method sets the value of the Field object for the specified object to the specified Boolean value.

Syntax: `public void setBoolean(Object obj, boolean z)`

Parameters: obj: the object in which the value will be set
z: the Boolean object value to be assigned

Throws: NullPointerException: when the value is null or when the Field object is an instance field and the object passed is null.
IllegalArgumentException: when the value is not of type Boolean. Also, if the object passed is not an instance of the class or interface declaring the Field object.
IllegalAccessException: when the Field object is inaccessible and this Field enforces Java language access control or the Field object is a final field.

setByte(Object, byte) Method

This method sets the value of the Field object for the specified object to the specified byte value.

Syntax: `public void setByte(Object obj, byte b)`

Parameters: obj: the object in which the value will be set
b: the byte object value to be assigned

Throws: NullPointerException: when the value is null or when the Field object is an instance field and the object passed is null.
IllegalArgumentException: when the value cannot be converted to a byte by an identity or a widening conversion. This exception may also be thrown when the object passed is not an instance of the class or interface declaring the Field object.
IllegalAccessException: when the Field object is inaccessible and enforces Java language access control or the Field object is a final field.

Field

setChar(Object, char) Method

This method sets the value of the Field object for a specified object to the specified char value.

Syntax: `public void setChar(Object obj, char c)`

Parameters: obj: the object in which the value will be set
c: the character object value to be assigned

Throws: NullPointerException: when the value is null or when the Field object is an instance field and the object passed is null.
IllegalArgumentException: when the value is not of type char. This exception is also thrown if the object passed is not an instance of the class or interface declaring the Field object.
IllegalAccessException: when the Field object is inaccessible and enforces Java language access control or the Field object is a final field.

setDouble(Object, double) Method

This method sets the value of the Field object for a specified object to the specified double value.

Syntax: `public void setDouble(Object obj, double d)`

Parameters: obj: the object in which the value will be set
d: the double object value to be assigned

Throws: NullPointerException: when the value is null or when the Field object is an instance field and the object passed is null.
IllegalArgumentException: when the value cannot be converted to a double by an identity or a widening conversion. This exception may also be thrown when the object passed is not an instance of the class or interface declaring the Field object.
IllegalAccessException: when the Field object is inaccessible and enforces Java language access control or the field is a final field.

setFloat(Object, float) Method

This method sets the value of the Field object for the specified object to the specified float value.

Syntax: `public void setFloat(Object obj, float f)`

Parameters: obj: the object in which the value will be set
f: the float object value to be assigned

Throws: NullPointerException: when the value is null or when the Field is an instance field and the object passed is null.
IllegalArgumentException: when the value cannot be converted to a float by an identity or a widening conversion. This exception may also be thrown when the object passed is not an instance of the class or interface declaring this Field.
IllegalAccessException: when the Field is inaccessible and enforced Java language access control or the field is a final field.

setInt(Object, int) Method

This method sets the value of the Field object for the specified object to the specified int value.

Syntax: `public void setInt(Object obj, int i)`

Parameters: obj: the object in which the value will be set
i: the integer object value to be assigned

Throws: NullPointerException: when the value is null or when the Field object is an instance field and the object passed is null.
IllegalArgumentException: when the value cannot be converted to an int by an identity or a widening conversion. This exception may also be thrown when the object passed is not an instance of the class or interface declaring the Field object.
IllegalAccessException: when the Field object is inaccessible and enforces Java language access control or the Field object is a final field.

Field

setLong(Object, long) Method

This method sets the value of the Field object for the specified object to the specified long value.

Syntax: **public void setLong(Object obj, long l)**

Parameters: obj: the object in which the value will be set
              l: the long object value to be assigned

Throws: NullPointerException: when the value is null or when the Field object is an instance field and the object passed is null.
              IllegalArgumentException: when the value cannot be converted to a long by an identity or a widening conversion. This exception may also be thrown when the object passed is not an instance of the class or interface declaring the Field object.
              IllegalAccessException: when the Field object is inaccessible and enforces Java language access control or the Field object is a final field.

setShort(Object, short) Method

This method sets the value of the Field object for the specified object to the specified short value.

Syntax: **public void setShort(Object obj, short s)**

Parameters: obj: the object in which the value will be set
              s: the short object value to be assigned

Throws: NullPointerException: when the value is null or when the Field object is an instance field and the object passed is null.
              IllegalArgumentException: when the value cannot be converted to a short by an identity or a widening conversion. This exception may also be thrown when the object passed is not an instance of the class or interface declaring the Field object.
              IllegalAccessException: when the Field object is inaccessible and enforces Java language access control or the Field object is a final field.

toString() Method

This method returns a string describing the Field object. The string is formatted as follows:

- Java language modifiers for the Field object (if any)
- field type
- a space
- fully-qualified name of the class declaring the Field object
- a period
- name of the field

The modifiers are placed in canonical order as specified in The Java Language Specification. This is public, protected, or private first, and then other modifiers in the following order: static, final, transient, and volatile. This method overrides the *toString()* method from the Object class.

Syntax: **public String toString()**

Returns: String

Method Class

Methods provide information about, and access to, a single Method object of a class or interface. The reflected Method object may be an abstract method, a class (static) method, or an instance method.

The only entity that creates Method objects is the Java Virtual Machine. To get Method references, use the *getMethod(), getMethods(), getDeclaredMethod(),* and *getDeclaredMethods()* methods of the Class class.

equals(Object) Method

This method determines if the Method object is the same as the specified object. The Method object and the specified object are considered equal only if they have the same declaring class, same name and same parameter types. This method overrides the *equals()* method in the Object class.

Syntax: `public boolean equals(Object obj)`

Parameters: obj: the object to be compared

Returns: True if the Method object and the specified object are the same, False otherwise.

getDeclaringClass() Method

This method returns the class or interface that declares the Method object.

Syntax: `public Class getDeclaringClass()`

getExceptionTypes() Method

This method returns an array of Class objects that match the checked expressions that are thrown by the Method object. The array size is 0 if the Method object does not throw any checked expressions.

Syntax: `public Class[] getExceptionTypes()`

getModifiers() Method

This method returns an integer that encodes the modifiers for the Method object. This value is the Java Virtual Machine's constant for public, private, protected, static, final, synchronized, volatile, transient, native, interface, and abstract modifiers. These constants should only be decoded using the methods of the java.lang.reflect.Modifier class.

Syntax: `public int getModifiers()`

getName() Method

This method returns a string that contains the simple name of the Method object.

Syntax: `public String getName()`

getParameterTypes() Method

This method returns an array of Class objects matching the parameter types of the Method object. The array is ordered the same as if the parameter were declared. The array size is 0 if this Method takes no parameters.

Syntax: `public Class[] getParameterTypes()`

getReturnType() Method

This method returns a Class object representing the declared return type of the Method object.

Syntax: `public Class getReturnType()`

hashCode() Method

This method returns an integer hash code for the Method object. The hash code is equal to the exclusive-or of the hash codes of the Method object's declaring class name and its simple name. This method overrides the *hashCode()* method of the Object class.

Syntax: `public int hashCode()`

invoke(Object, Object[]) Method

This method invokes the Method object for the specified object, passing the given arguments. The arguments are automatically unwrapped if their corresponding declared types are primitive. Also, if the return type is primitive, it is wrapped into an object before it is returned. Widening conversions are performed, if necessary, on the arguments and return value.

The object argument is ignored, and may be null if the Method object is a class (static) method.

The arguments array should be null if this Method takes no parameters.

While the method is executing, control is transferred to the underlying Method object. If the Method object is a class (static) method, it is invoked exactly as the underlying method of the declaring class. If it is not a class (static) method, it is invoked using dynamic method lookup and overriding based on the class of the object.

Syntax: `public Object invoke(Object obj, Object[] args)`

Parameters: obj: the object on which the method will be invoked
              args: an array of object arguments to be passed to the method

Returns: The value returned from the invoked Method. The value is wrapped in an object if it is of a primitive type. *Returns:* null if this Method's return type is void.

Throws: NullPointerException: when the obj argument is null and the Method object is an abstract method or an instance method. This exception may also be thrown when an unwrapping conversion is attempted on a null value.

IllegalArgumentException: when the object argument is not an instance of the class or interface declaring the Method object. This exception may also be thrown when the number of arguments supplied differs from the number of arguments accepted by the Method object. Finally, this exception may be thrown when an unwrapped value cannot be successfully converted by an identity conversion or a widening conversion.

IllegalAccessException: when the Method object enforces Java language access control and the method is inaccessible.

InvocationTargetException: when the Method object itself throws an exception. The exception thrown by the Method object is placed in the InvocationTargetException object.

toString() Method

This method returns a string describing the Method object. The string is formatted as follows:

◆ Java language modifiers for this Method (if any)

◆ fully-qualified name of the return type

◆ a space

◆ fully-qualified name of the class declaring this Method

◆ a period

◆ the simple method name

◆ comma-separated list of the fully-qualified names of this Method's formal parameter types. This list is surrounded by parentheses.

◆ a space

◆ the word "throws"

◆ comma-separated list of the fully-qualified names of the thrown exception types.

This method overrides the *toString()* method of the Object class.

Syntax: `public String toString()`

Modifier Class

The Modifier class decodes the Java Virtual Machine's constant for public, private, protected, static, final, synchronized, volatile, transient, native, interface, and abstract modifiers. The modifiers are encoded in an integer value. The Modifier class cannot be instantiated. The constructor, methods, and variables for this class are described in the sections that follow.

Modifier Constructor

This constructor creates a modifier.

Syntax: `public Modifier()`

isAbstract(int) Method

This method determines whether the specified integer includes the abstract modifier.

Syntax: `public static boolean isAbstract(int mod)`

Parameters: mod: an integer to be examined

Returns: True if the integer includes the abstract modifier, False otherwise.

isFinal(int) Method

This method determines whether the specified integer includes the final modifier.

Syntax: `public static boolean isFinal(int mod)`

Parameters: mod: an integer to be examined

Returns: True if the integer includes the final modifier, False otherwise.

isInterface(int) Method

This method determines whether the specified integer includes the interface modifier.

Syntax: `public static boolean isInterface(int mod)`

Parameters: mod: an integer to be examined

Returns: True if the integer includes the interface modifier, False otherwise.

isNative(int) Method

This method determines whether the specified integer includes the native modifier.

Syntax: `public static boolean isNative(int mod)`

Parameters: mod: an integer to be examined

Returns: True if the integer includes the native modifier, False otherwise.

isPrivate(int) Method

This method determines whether the specified integer includes the private modifier.

Syntax: `public static boolean isPrivate(int mod)`

Parameters: mod: an integer to be examined

Returns: True if the integer includes the private modifier, False otherwise.

isProtected(int) Method

This method determines whether the specified integer includes the protected modifier.

Syntax: `public static boolean isProtected(int mod)`

Parameters: mod: an integer to be examined

Returns: True if the integer includes the protected modifier, False otherwise.

isPublic(int) Method

This method determines whether the specified integer includes the public modifier.

Syntax: `public static boolean isPublic(int mod)`

Parameters: mod: an integer to be examined

Returns: True if the integer includes the public modifier, False otherwise.

isStatic(int) Method

This method determines whether the specified integer includes the static modifier.

Syntax: `public static boolean isStatic(int mod)`

Parameters: mod: an integer to be examined

Returns: True if the integer includes the static modifier, False otherwise.

isSynchronized(int) Method

This method determines whether the specified integer includes the synchronized modifier.

Syntax: `public static boolean isSynchronized(int mod)`

Parameters: mod: an integer to be examined

Returns: True if the integer includes the synchronized modifier, False otherwise.

isTransient(int) Method

This method determines whether the specified integer includes the transient modifier.

Syntax: `public static boolean isTransient(int mod)`

Parameters: mod: an integer to be examined

Returns: True if the integer includes the transient modifier, False otherwise.

isVolatile(int) Method

This method determines whether the specified integer includes the volatile modifier.

Syntax: `public static boolean isVolatile(int mod)`

Parameters: mod: an integer to be examined

Returns: True if the integer includes the volatile modifier, False otherwise.

toString(int) Method

This method returns a list that contains the name of each modifier that the specified integer includes. Each modifier in the list is separated by a space.

Syntax: `public static String toString(int mod)`

Parameters: mod: an integer to be examined

ABSTRACT Variable

This variable defines the integer constant for the abstract modifier.

Syntax: `public final static int ABSTRACT`

FINAL Variable

This variable defines the integer constant for the final modifier.

Syntax: `public final static int FINAL`

INTERFACE Variable

This variable defines the integer constant for the interface modifier.

Syntax: `public final static int INTERFACE`

NATIVE Variable

This variable defines the integer constant for the native modifier.

Syntax: `public final static int NATIVE`

PRIVATE Variable

This variable defines the integer constant for the private access modifier.

Syntax: `public final static int PRIVATE`

PROTECTED Variable

This variable defines the integer constant for the protected access modifier.

Syntax: `public final static int PROTECTED`

PUBLIC Variable

This variable defines the integer constant for the public access modifier.

Syntax: `public final static int PUBLIC`

STATIC Variable

This variable defines the integer constant for the static modifier.

Syntax: `public final static int STATIC`

Modifier

SYNCHRONIZED Variable

This variable defines the integer constant for the synchronized modifier.

Syntax: `public final static int SYNCHRONIZED`

TRANSIENT Variable

This variable defines the integer constant for the transient modifier.

Syntax: `public final static int TRANSIENT`

VOLATILE Variable

This variable defines the integer constant for the volatile modifier.

Syntax: `public final static int VOLATILE`

InvocationTargetException Exception

InvocationTargetException is a checked exception that is thrown by an invoked method or constructor. The exception that is thrown by the method or constructor is wrapped into the InvocationTargetException object.

InvocationTargetException Constructor

This constructor creates a protected InvocationTargetException.

Syntax: `protected InvocationTargetException()`

InvocationTargetException(Throwable) Constructor

This constructor creates an InvocationTargetException from the specified exception argument.

Syntax: `public InvocationTargetException(Throwable target)`

Parameters: target: an exception from which to create the InvocationTargetException

InvocationTargetException(Throwable, String) Constructor

This constructor creates an InvocationTargetException from the specified exception argument and the string argument. The string argument is used as a message to describe the exception.

Syntax: `public InvocationTargetException(Throwable target, String detail)`

Parameters: target: an exception from which to create the InvocationTargetException
detail: a string containing a message which describes the exception

getTargetException() Method

This method returns the thrown exception wrapped in this InvocationTargetException.

Syntax: `public Throwable getTargetException()`

Modifier

Internationalization API

The JDK 1.1 provides a robust Internationalization API for developing global applications that have come in high demand with the proliferation of computerized processes across continents. This API is based on the Unicode 2.0 character encoding and includes the capability to format text, numbers, dates, currency, and user-defined objects to fit locale-oriented conventions.

The Internationalization API uses the java.text package for handling locale-sensitive text and the java.util package for handling date and time-specific information. The relevant classes and interfaces of these packages are covered in this chapter. The other part of the Internationalization API, the java.io package, enables the import and export of non-Unicode character data. This package is covered in "Serialization API."

java.text Package

The java.text package contains classes to assist the developer with parsing, converting, sorting, and formatting text, numbers, and dates based on locale. The information to be presented can be localized before display.

CharacterIterator Interface

The CharacterIterator interface parses backward and forward through text. To obtain a beginning index use the *startIndex()* method. The ending index is found using the *getEndIndex()-1* method. To move between characters, you can use *previous()*, *next()*, or *setIndex()* methods to position the cursor anywhere within the bounds. If the cursor moves outside the bounds using one of these methods, they will return as DONE. The current character's index can be obtained using the *getIndex()* method. This interface extends the Cloneable interface from the java.lang package. Refer also to the StringCharacterIterator class.

clone() Method

This method makes a copy of the bounded text. This method overrides the *clone()* method in the Object class.

Syntax: `public abstract Object clone()`

current() Method

This method gets the character at the current position. The current position is obtained using the *getIndex()* method.

Syntax: `public abstract Char current()`

endIndex() Method

This method obtains the end index of the boundary. This is the first position of the text following this boundary.

Syntax: `public abstract Int endIndex()`

first() Method

This method sets the current index to the beginning, as with *startIndex()*, and returns the character at that position.

Syntax: `public abstract Char first()`

getIndex() Method

This method obtains the current index in the text.

Syntax: `public abstract Int getIndex()`

getText() Method

This method returns the text of the boundary.

Syntax: **public abstract String getText()**

last() Method

This method sets the current index to the last index, as with the *endIndex()* method, and returns the character at that position.

Syntax: **public abstract Char last()**

next() Method

This method adds 1 to the current index and returns the character at this position.

Syntax: **public abstract Char next()**

previous() Method

This method subtracts 1 from the current index and returns the character at that position.

Syntax: **public abstract Char previous()**

setIndex(int position) Method

This method specifies a position in the new current index for the boundary and returns the character at that position.

Syntax: **public abstract Char setIndex(int position)**

Throws: IllegalArgumentException: when an invalid position is supplied.

startIndex() Method

This method returns the index at the beginning of the text.

Syntax: **public abstract int startIndex()**

ChoiceFormat Class

This class extends the NumberFormat class for the purpose of adding formatting to a range of numbers. Refer also to the DecimalFormat and MessageFormat classes.

format(double, StringBuffer, FormatStatus) Method

This method specializes a format and overrides the format dictated by the NumberFormat class.

Syntax: **public StringBuffer format(double num, StringBuffer str, FormatStatus status)**

Parameters: num: a number
str: the output buffer
status: formatting status

getFormats() Method

This method gets the list of formats passed in the constructor.

Syntax: **public Object[] getFormats()**

getLimits() Method

This method gets the list of limits passed in the constructor.

Syntax: **public double[] getLimits()**

nextDouble(double) Method

This method finds the least double greater than the supplied double. This method is used to make half-open intervals.

Syntax: `public final static double nextDouble(double d)`

Parameters: d: the supplied double

nextDouble(double, boolean) Method

Finds the least double greater than the supplied double in full intervals.

Syntax: `public final static double nextDouble(double d, boolean bool)`

Parameters: d: the supplied double bool: true means number must be positive; False means it can be either positive or negative

parse(String, ParseStatus) Method

This method returns a long integer if it can. This method overrides the *parse()* method in the NumberFormat class.

Syntax: `public Number parse(String text, ParseStatus status)`

previousDouble(double) Method

This method finds the greatest double less than the supplied double.

Syntax: `public final static double previousDouble(double d)`

setChoices(double[], Object[]) Method

This method sets the choices for formatting.

Syntax: `public void setChoices(double limits[], Object formats[])`

ChoiceFormat

Parameters: limits: the limits to use for formatting starting with the top value and sorted in ascending order

formats: the formats to use with the limits. They can be either objects or strings

CollatedString Class

This class enables the collation of strings of different languages. This class extends the Object class. Refer also to the Collation class.

equals(Object) Method

This method determines if the supplied object is the same as the object for comparison. A value of True is returned if the objects are the same; a value of False is returned if otherwise. This method overrides the *equal()* method from the Object class.

Syntax: `public boolean equals(Object obj)`

Parameters: obj: the object to compare

getCollation() Method

This method gets the current collation object. Refer also to the *setCollation()* method.

Syntax: `public Collation getCollation()`

getString() Method

This method gets the current string being collated. Refer also to the *setString()* method

Syntax: `public Sting getString()`

greater(Object) Method

This method determines if the object for comparison is greater than the supplied object. A value of True is returned if the object for comparison is greater; False is returned if otherwise.

Syntax: `public boolean greater(Object obj)`

Parameters: obj: the object to compare

---

greaterOrEqual(Object) Method

This method determines if the object for comparison is greater than or equal to the supplied object. A value of True is returned if the object for comparison is greater than or equal to the supplied object; False is returned if otherwise.

Syntax: `public boolean greaterOrEqual(Object obj)`

Parameters: obj: the object to compare

---

hashCode() Method

This method gets the hash code for the specified string. This method overrides the *hashCode()* method from the Object class.

Syntax: `public int hashCode()`

---

setCollation(Collation) Method

This method sets the current collation object to the one supplied. Refer also to the *getCollation()* method.

Syntax: `public void setCollation(Collation coll)`

Parameters: coll: the new collation object

---

setString(String) Method

This method sets the current collated string value to the supplied string. Refer also to the *getString()* method.

Syntax: `public void setString(String str)`

Collation Class

This class provides for Unicode string comparisons. This class extends the Object class of the java.lang package and implements the Cloneable and Serializable interfaces of the java.lang and java.io packages, respectively.

clone() Method

This method returns a copy of the specified object. This method overrides the *clone()* method from the Object class in the java.lang package.

Syntax: `public Object clone()`

compare(String, int, int, String, int, int) Method

This method compares two different strings. Values of GREATER/EQUAL/LESS are returned if str1 is greater than/equal to/less than str2, respectively.

Syntax: `public abstract byte compare(String str1, int start1, int end1,`
               `String str2, int start2, int end2)`

Parameters: str1: the first string to compare
                start1: the beginning point for str1, inclusive
                end1: the ending point for str1, exclusive
                str2: the second string to compare
                start2: the beginning point for str2, inclusive
                end2: the ending point for str2, exclusive

Throws: StringIndexOutOfBoundsException: when the starting or ending index is not within the string.

compare(String, String) Method

This method compares two different strings. Values of GREATER or LESS are returned if str1 is greater than or equal to str2, respectively.

Syntax: `public abstract byte compare(String str1, String str2)`

Parameters: str1: the first string to compare
str2: the second string to compare

equals(Object) Method

This method determines if two objects are equal. This method overrides the *equals()* method from the Object class in the java.lang package.

Syntax: `public boolean equals(Object obj)`

Parameters: obj: the target object for comparison

equals(String, String) Method

This method determines if the first string is equal to the second string. Refer also to the *compare()* method.

Syntax: `public boolean equals(String str1,  String str2)`

Parameters: str1: the first string to compare
str2: the second string to compare

getAvailableLocales() Method

This method returns a list of locales for which Collation objects are installed.

Syntax: `public static synchronized Locale[] getAvailableLocales()`

getDecomposition() Method

This method gets the decomposition mode of the Collation object. The decomposition mode determines how Unicode characters are handled with regards to collation. Refer also to the *setDecomposition()* method.

Syntax: `public synchronized byte getDecomposition()`

getDefault() Method

This method gets the Collation object for the current default locale.

Syntax: `public static synchronized Collation getDefault()`

getDefault(Locale) Method

This method gets the Collation object for the specified locale.

Syntax: `public static synchronized Collation getDefault(Locale loc)`

Parameters: loc: the locale

getDisplayName(Locale) Method

This method gets the display name of the object for the specified locale and the default language.

Syntax: `public static synchronized String getDisplayName(Locale objLoc)`

Parameters: objLoc: the desired locale

getDisplayName(Locale, Locale) Method

This method gets the display name of the object for the desired Locale and the desired language.

Syntax: `public static synchronized String getDisplayName(Locale objLoc, Locale displayLoc)`

Parameters: objLoc: the desired locale
               displayLoc: the locale having the desired language

getSortKey(String) Method

This method converts the string into a series of characters that can be compared with the *SortKey.compareTo()* method. Refer also to the *compareTo()* method.

Syntax: `public abstract SortKey getSortKey(String str)`

Parameters: str: the string to get a sort key for

---

getSortKey(String, int, int) Method

This method converts the string into a series of characters that can be compared with the *SortKey.compareTo( )* method.

Syntax: `public abstract SortKey getSortKey(String str, int start, int end)`

Parameters: str: the string to get a sort key for
start: the beginning point in the string, inclusive
end: the ending point in the string, exclusive

Throws: StringIndexOutOfBoundsException: when the starting or ending index is not within the string.

---

getStrength() Method

This method gets the minimum strength (PRIMARY, SECONDARY, and so on) to be used in comparison or transformation. The strength setting determines the minimum level of difference considered significant during comparison. Refer also to the *setStrength( )* method.

Syntax: `public synchronized byte getStrength()`

---

greater(String, String) Method

This method determines whether the first string for comparison is greater than the second string. Refer also to the *compare( )* method.

Syntax: `public boolean greater(String str1, String str2)`

Parameters: str1: the first string to compare
str2: the second string to compare

Collation

greaterOrEqual(String, String) Method

This method determines whether the first string for comparison is greater than or equal to the second string. Refer also to the *compare()* method.

Syntax: `public boolean greaterOrEqual(String str1, String str2)`

Parameters: str1: the first string to compare
                str2: the second string to compare

hashCode() Method

This method gets the hash code for the Collation object. This method overrides the *hashCode()* method from the Object class in the java.lang package.

Syntax: `public synchronized abstract int hashCode()`

setDecomposition(byte) Method

This method sets the decomposition mode of the Collation object. The decomposition mode determines how Unicode characters are handled with regards to collation. Refer also to the *getDecomposition()* method.

Syntax: `public synchronized void setDecomposition(byte mode)`

Throws: IllegalArgumentException: when the new decomposition mode is not valid.

setStrength(byte) Method

This method sets the minimum strength to use in comparison or transformation. The strength setting determines the minimum level of difference considered significant during comparison. Refer also to the *getStrength()* method.

Syntax: `public synchronized void setStrength(byte strength)`

Parameters: strength: the new strength to use

Throws: IllegalArgumentException: when the new strength value is not valid.

CollationElementIterator Class

The CollationElementIterator class parses international strings. Characters in the string are indexed differently according to the language being used. The collation order, or key, of a character is an integer having the first 16 bits representing the primary order, the next 8 bits representing secondary order, and the last 8 bits representing tertiary order. This class extends the Object class in the java.lang package. Refer also to the Collation and TableCollation classes.

next() Method

This method gets the ordering priority of the next character in the string.

Syntax:　　**public int next()**

primaryOrder(int) Method

This method gets the primary collation order.

Syntax:　　**public final static int primaryOrder(int order)**

Parameters:　order: the collation order

reset() Method

This method moves the cursor to the beginning of the string.

Syntax:　　**public void reset()**

secondaryOrder(int) Method

This method gets the secondary collation order.

Syntax:　　**public final static int secondaryOrder(int order)**

Parameters:　order: the collation order

tertiaryOrder(int) Method

This method gets the tertiary collation order.

Syntax: `public final static int tertiaryOrder(int order)`

Parameters: order: the collation order

DateFormat Class

The DateFormat class enables the formatting, parsing, and converting of dates and times in a language-independent manner. This class extends the Format class and implements the Cloneable interface in the java.lang package.

clone() Method

This method creates a new DateFormat object. This method overrides the Cloneable interface.

Syntax: `public Object clone()`

format(Date) Method

This method formats a Date object into a string containing a datetime.

Syntax: `public final StringBuffer format(Date d)`

Parameters: d: a date

format(Date, StringBuffer, FormatStatus) Method

This method formats a Date object into a string containing a datetime. This method overrides the format specified by the Format class.

Syntax: `public final StringBuffer format(Date d, StringBuffer str,`
`FormatStatus status)`

Parameters: date: a date
                str: the result string
                status: formatting status

format(Object, StringBuffer, FormatStatus) Method

This method formats a Date object into a string containing a datetime. This method overrides the format specified by the Format class.

Syntax: `public final StringBuffer format(Object obj, StringBuffer str, FormatStatus status)`

Parameters: obj: a date or a number
                str: the result string
                status: formatting status

getAvailableLocales() Method

This method gets the list of locales having DateFormat objects installed.

Syntax: `public static synchronized Locale[] getAvailableLocales()`

getCalendar() Method

This method gets the calendar system associated with this date-time formatter. Refer also to the *setCalendar()* method.

Syntax: `public Calendar getCalendar()`

getDateFormat() Method

This method gets the date formatter for the default locale having the default formatting style.

Syntax: `public final static synchronized DateFormat getDateFormat()`

DateFormat

getDateFormat(int) Method

This method gets the date formatter for the default locale having the specified formatting style.

Syntax: `public final static synchronized DateFormat getDateFormat(int style)`

Parameters: style: the specified style

getDateFormat(int, Locale) Method

This method gets the date formatter for the specified locale having the specified formatting style.

Syntax: `public final static synchronized DateFormat getDateFormat(int style,`
                 `Locale loc)`

Parameters: style: the specified style
                 loc: the specified locale

getDateTimeFormat() Method

This method gets the datetime formatter for the default locale having the default formatting style.

Syntax: `public final static synchronized DateFormat getDateTimeFormat()`

getDateTimeFormat(int, int) Method

This method gets the datetime formatter for the default locale having the specified formatting style for both date and time.

Syntax: `public final static synchronized DateFormat getDateTimeFormat(int`
                 `dateStyle,  int timeStyle)`

Parameters: datestyle: the specified style
                 timestyle: the specified style

getDateTimeFormat(int, int, Locale) Method

This method gets the datetime formatter for the specified locale having the specified formatting style for both date and time.

Syntax: `public final static synchronized DateFormat getDateTimeFormat(int dateStyle,int timeStyle,Locale aLocale)`

Parameters: datestyle: the specified style
timestyle: the specified style
loc: the specified locale

getDisplayName(Locale) Method

This method gets the display name of the object for the specified locale and default language.

Syntax: `public static synchronized String getDisplayName(Locale objectLoc)`

Parameters: ObjectLoc: the specified Object locale

getDisplayName(Locale, Locale) Method

This method gets the display name of the object for the specifed Locale and language.

Syntax: `public static synchronized String getDisplayName(Locale objectLoc,Locale displayLoc)`

Parameters: ObjectLoc: the specified Object locale
displayLoc: the locale containing the desired language

getNumberFormat() Method

This method gets the number formatter for this datetime formatter. Refer also to the *setNumberFormat()* method.

Syntax: `public NumberFormat getNumberFormat()`

getTimeFormat() Method

This method gets the time formatter for the default locale.

Syntax: `public final static synchronized DateFormat getTimeFormat()`

getTimeFormat(int) Method

This method gets the time formatter for the default locale having the specified formatting style.

Syntax: `public final static synchronized DateFormat getTimeFormat(int style)`

Parameters: style: the specified style

getTimeFormat(int, Locale) Method

This method gets the time formatter for the specified locale having the specified formatting style.

Syntax: `public final static synchronized DateFormat getTimeFormat(int style, Locale loc)`

Parameters: style: the specified style
loc: the specified locale

getTimeZone() Method

This method gets the time zone for the calendar system being used. Refer also to the *setTimeZone()* method.

Syntax: `public TimeZone getTimeZone()`

getValidationMode() Method

This method gets the validation mode. Refer also to the *setValidationMode()* method.

Syntax: `public boolean getValidationMode()`

parse(String) Method

This method parses a datetime string and returns a date, if one is found.

Syntax: `public Date parse(String str)`

Parameters: str: the string to parse

Throws: FormatException: when no date is found.

parse(String, ParseStatus) Method

This method parses a datetime string given the parse status and returns a date, if one is found, or returns null if the parse status is set up to not throw an exception.

Syntax: `public Date parse(String str, ParseStatus status)`

Parameters: str: the string to parse
status: the parse status

Throws: FormatException: when no date is found and the parse status is set up to throw an exception.

parseObject(String, ParseStatus) Method

This method parses the datetime string and returns the date in milliseconds, if a date is found; otherwise null is returned if the parse status is set up to not throw an exception. This method overrides the *parseObject()* method from the Format class.

Syntax: `public Object parse(String str, ParseStatus status)`

Parameters: str: the string to parse
status: the parse status

Throws: FormatException: when no date is found and the parse status is set up to throw an exception.

DateFormat

setCalendar(Calendar) Method

This method sets the calendar system to be used. Refer also to the *getCalendar()* method.

Syntax: `public void setCalendar(Calendar calendar)`

Parameters: calendar: the calendar to use

setNumberFormat(NumberFormat) Method

This method sets the number formatter. Refer also to the *getNumberFormat()* method.

Syntax: `public void setNumberFormat(NumberFormat format)`

Parameters: format: the new number formatter

setTimeZone(TimeZone) Method

This method sets the time zone. Refer also to the *getTimeZone()* method.

Syntax: `public void setTimeZone(TimeZone zone)`

Parameters: zone: the new time zone

setValidationMode(boolean) Method

This method sets the validation mode for the DateFormat object. Refer also to the *getValidationMode()* method.

Syntax: `public void setValidationMode(boolean mode)`

Parameters: mode: if true, exception is thrown for bad dates, if false, it will work with the bad date the best it can

DateFormatData Class

The DateFormatData class enables the localization of formatting styles. This class extends the Object class in the java.lang package and implements the Cloneable and Serializable interfaces in the java.lang and java.io packages, respectively.

clone() Method

This method creates a copy or clone of the DateFormatData object. This method over-rides the Cloneable interface in the java.lang package.

Syntax: `public Object clone()`

equals(Object) Method

This method determines if two objects are equal. This method overrides the *equals()* method from the Object class.

Syntax: `public boolean equals(Object obj)`

Parameters: obj: the object for comparison

getAmpms() Method

This method gets the weekday am/pm names.

Syntax: `public String[] getAmpms()`

getEras() Method

This method gets the era (B.C./A.D.) strings.

Syntax: `public String[] getEras()`

getLocalPatternChars() Method

This method gets the local datetime pattern characters.

Syntax: `public String getLocalPatternChars()`

getMonths() Method

This method gets the names of the months for the calendar system being used.

Syntax: `public String[] getMonths()`

getShortMonths() Method

This method gets the short names of the months for the calendar system being used.

Syntax: `public String[] getShortMonths()`

getShortWeekdays() Method

This method gets short names for the weekdays.

Syntax: `public String[] getShortWeekdays()`

getWeekdays() Method

This method gets the names of the weekdays.

Syntax: `public String[] getWeekdays()`

getZoneStrings() Method

This method gets the names of the timezones for the specified locale.

Syntax: `public String[][] getZoneStrings()`

hashCode() Method

This method gets the hash code for the DateFormatData object. This method overrides the hashCode() method from the Object class in the java.lang package.

Syntax: `public synchronized abstract int hashCode()`

setAmpms(String[]) Method

This method sets the am/pm names for the DateFormatData object.

Syntax: `public void setAmpms(String ampms[])`

Parameters: ampms: the names for am and pm

setEras(String[]) Method

This method sets era (B.C./A.D.) strings.

Syntax: `public void setEras(String eras[])`

Parameters: eras: the new eras to use

setLocalPatternChars(String) Method

This method sets the local datetime pattern characters.

Syntax: `public void setLocalPatternChars(String pattern)`

Parameters: pattern: the local datetime pattern characters to use

setMonths(String[]) Method

This method sets the month strings.

Syntax: `public void setMonths(String months[])`

setPatternLocalized(boolean) Method

This method tells the DateFormatData object whether to use localized datetime pattern characters.

Syntax: `public final void setPatternLocalized(boolean bool)`

Parameters: bool: true means used local pattern characters; False means do not

setShortMonths(String[]) Method

This method sets the short names for the months.

Syntax: `public void setShortMonths(String months[])`

Parameters: months: the list of short names for the months

setShortWeekdays(String[]) Method

This method sets the short names for the weekdays.

Syntax: `public void setShortWeekdays(String weekdays[])`

Parameters: weekdays: the list of short names for the weekdays

setWeekdays(String[]) Method

This method sets the names for the weekdays.

Syntax: `public void setWeekdays(String weekdays[])`

Parameters: weekdays: the list of names for the weekdays

setZoneStrings(String[][]) Method

This method sets the timezone strings.

Syntax: `public void setTimeZoneStrings(String zones[][])`

Parameters: zones: the time zone strings to use

useLocalizedPattern() Method

This method determines if localized datetime pattern characters are used by the DateFormatData object.

Syntax: `public final boolean useLocalizedPattern()`

DecimalFormat Class

This class enables the formatting and localization of decimal numbers. This class extends the NumberFormat class.

clone() Method

This method creates a copy or clone of a DecimalFormat object. This method overrides the Cloneable interface in the java.lang package.

Syntax: `public Object clone()`

equals(Object) Method

This method determines if two objects are equal. This method overrides the *equals()* method from the Object class in the java.lang package.

Syntax: `public boolean equals(Object obj)`

Parameters: obj: the object to compare with this one

format(double, StringBuffer, FormatStatus) Method

This method formats a double into a string. This method overrides the *format()* method from the Format class.

Syntax: `public StringBuffer format(Double number, StringBuffer str,`
`FormatStatus status)`

Parameters: number: a number
str: the buffer for the string
status: formatting status

DecimalFormat

format(long, StringBuffer, FormatStatus) Method

This method formats a long into a string. This method overrides the *format()* method from the Format class.

Syntax: `public StringBuffer format(long number, StringBuffer str,`
                       `FormatStatus status)`

Parameters: number: a number
                 str: the buffer for the string
                 status: formatting status

getFactor() Method

This method gets the factor of the number. For example, percent would have a factor of 100.

Syntax: `public int getFactor()`

getNegativePrefix() Method

This method gets the negative prefix of the number.

Syntax: `public String getNegativePrefix()`

getNegativeSuffix() Method

This method gets the negative suffix of the number.

Syntax: `public String getNegativeSuffix()`

getNumberFormatData() Method

This method gets the NumberFormatData object.

Syntax: `public NumberFormatData getNumberFormatData()`

getPattern(boolean) Method

This method gets the pattern for a number.

Syntax: `public String getPattern(boolean localized)`

getPositivePrefix() Method

This method gets the positive prefix for the number.

Syntax: `public String getPositivePrefix()`

getPositiveSuffix() Method

This method gets the positive suffix for the number.

Syntax: `public String getPositiveSuffix()`

getThousandsInterval() Method

This method gets the thousands interval for a number.

Syntax: `public int getThousandsInterval()`

hashCode() Method

This method gets the hash code for the DecimalFormat object. This method overrides the *hashCode()* method from the Object class in the java.lang package.

Syntax: `public synchronized abstract int hashCode()`

parse(String, ParseStatus) Method

This method parses the string for a Long with consideration for the parse status.

Syntax: `public Number parse(String str, ParseStatus status)`

Parameters: str: the string to parse

status: the parse status; True means to take exception; False means an exception is not taken

setFactor(int) Method

This method sets the factor for a number. For example, percent would use a factor of 100.

Syntax: `public void setFactor(int factor)`

Parameters: factor: the factor to use for the format

setNegativePrefix(String) Method

This method sets the negative prefix for the number.

Syntax: `public void setNegativePrefix(String str)`

Parameters: str: the negative prefix

setNegativeSuffix(String) Method

This method sets the positive suffix for the number.

Syntax: `public void setNegativeSuffix(String str)`

Parameters: str: the negative suffix

setNumberFormatData(NumberFormatData) Method

This method sets the NumberFormatData object.

Syntax: `public void setNumberFormatData(NumberFormatData format)`

Parameters: format: new NumberFormatData object

setPattern(String, boolean) Method

This method sets the pattern for a number. Example: "#,###.00;(#,###.00)" "*", "_", and "0" cannot be used together.

Syntax:	`public void setPattern(String pattern, boolean bool)`
Parameters:	pattern: the pattern to use to format bool: True means it is a local pattern; False means it is not
Throws:	FormatException: when the format is incorrect.

setPositivePrefix(String) Method

This method sets the positive prefix for the number.

Syntax:	`public void setPositivePrefix(String str)`
Parameters:	str: the positive prefix

setPositiveSuffix(String) Method

This method sets the positive suffix for the number.

Syntax:	`public void setPositiveSuffix(String str)`
Parameters:	str: the positive suffix

setThousandsInterval(int) Method

This method sets the thousands interval for a number.

Syntax:	`public void setThousandsInterval(int interval)`
Parameters:	interval: the thousands interval to use

Format Class

The Format class is an abstract base class for formatting locale-sensitive information such as dates, numbers, and time. This class extends the Object class in the java.lang package and implements the Cloneable and Serializable interfaces from the java.lang and java.io packages, respectively.

If formatting does not succeed, ClassCastException is returned. If the format passed to a method is invalid, FormatException is thrown.

format(Object) Method

This method formats an object into a string.

Syntax: `public final String format(Object obj)`

Parameters: obj: the object to format

Throws: ClassCastException: when the object type cannot be formatted.

format(Object, StringBuffer, FormatStatus) Method

This method formats an object into a string.

Syntax: `public abstract StringBuffer format(Object obj, StringBuffer str,`
                 `FormatStatus status)`

Parameters: obj: the object to format
                 str: the result string
                 status: the status of the format

Throws: ClassCastException: when the object type cannot be formatted.

parseObject(String) Method

This method parses a string to get an object.

Syntax: `public abstract Object parseObject(String str)`

Parameters: str: the string to parse

Throws: FormatException: when an object is not found in the string.

parseObject(String, ParseStatus) Method

This method parses a string to get an object with consideration for the parse status.

Syntax: `public abstract Object parseObject(String str, ParseStatus status)`

Parameters: str: the string to parse
                 status: the parse status; True means validate string; False means do not
                 validate

FormatException Class

This class is used to signal exceptions that occur while parsing or formatting.

getErrorOffset() Method

This method gets the offset where the error occurred.

Syntax: `public int getErrorOffset()`

FormatStatus Class

This class is used with the formatting classes for aligning columns of numbers. This class extends the Object class in the java.lang package. Refer also to the Format class.

MessageFormat Class

This class is used to concatenate messages for presentation to the user without concern for the language. This class extends the Format class.

clone() Method

This method creates a copy or clone of a MessageFormat object. This method overrides the Cloneable interface of the java.lang package.

Syntax: `public Object clone()`

equals(Object) Method

This method determines if two objects are equal.

Syntax: `public boolean equals(Object obj)`

Parameters: obj: the object to compare with this one

format(Object, StringBuffer, FormatStatus) Method

This method formats an object into a string.

Syntax: **public final StringBuffer format(Object obj, StringBuffer str, FormatStatus status)**

Parameters: obj: the object to format
str: the sting result
status: the format status

format(Object[], StringBuffer, FormatStatus) Method

This method formats the objects into a pattern where they are substituted for %0–%9.

Syntax: **public final StringBuffer format(Object obj[], StringBuffer str, FormatStatus status)**

Parameters: obj: the list of objects to format
str: the sting result
status: the format status

format(String, Format[], Object[]) Method

This method formats the objects into a specified string pattern.

Syntax: **public static String format(String str, Format formats[], Object obj[])**

Parameters: str: the sting pattern
formats: the formats
obj: the list of objects to format

format(String, Object[]) Method

This method formats the objects into a string pattern.

Syntax: **public static String format(String str, Object obj[])**

Parameters: str: the sting pattern
obj: the list of objects to format

getFormats() Method

This method gets a list of formats that were set with the *setFormats()* method.

Syntax: `public Format[] getFormats()`

getPattern() Method

This method gets the pattern for a string.

Syntax: `public String getPattern()`

hashCode() Method

This method gets the hash code for the MessageFormat object. This method overrides the *hashCode()* method from the Object class in the java.lang package.

Syntax: `public synchronized abstract int hashCode()`

parse(String) Method

This method parses a string to find an object.

Syntax: `public Object parse(String str)`

Parameters: str: the string to parse

Throws: FormatException: when the string cannot be parsed.

parse(String, ParseStatus) Method

This method parses a string for an object, given the parse status.

Syntax: `public Object[] parse(String str, ParseStatus status)`

Parameters: str: the string to parse
status: the parse status

parseObject(String, ParseStatus) Method

This method parses the string for an object. This method overrides the *parseObject()* method from the Format class.

Syntax: `public Object parse(String str, ParseStatus status)`

Parameters: str: the string to parse
                  status: the parse status

setFormats(Format[]) Method

This method sets the formats to use on parameters.

Syntax: `public void setFormats(Format formats[])`

Parameters: formats: the list of formats to use

setPattern(String) Method

This method sets the pattern for a string.

Syntax: `public void setPattern(String str)`

Parameters: str: the pattern to set

NumberFormat Class

This class is the base class for all number formatting. It enables the parsing and formatting of numbers from locales all over the world without the need for concern over local presentation. This class extends the Format class and implements the Cloneable interface in the java.lang package.

clone() Method

This method creates a copy or clone of a NumberFormat object. This method overrides the Cloneable interface in the java.lang package.

Syntax: `public Object clone()`

format(double) Method

This method formats a double as a string.

Syntax: `public final String format(double number)`

Parameters: number: the double to format

format(double, StringBuffer, FormatStatus) Method

This method formats a double as a string.

Syntax: `public final StringBuffer format(Double number, StringBuffer str,`
                  `FormatStatus status)`

Parameters: number: the double to format
            str: the sting result
            status: the format status

format(long) Method

This method formats a long as a string.

Syntax: `public final String format(Long number)`

Parameters: number: the long to format

format(long, StringBuffer, FormatStatus) Method

This method formats a long as a string.

Syntax: `public final StringBuffer format(Long number, StringBuffer str,`
                  `FormatStatus status)`

Parameters: number: the long to format
            str: the sting result
            status: the format status

NumberFormat

format(Object, StringBuffer, FormatStatus) Method

This method formats an object into a string.

Syntax: `public final StringBuffer format(Object obj, StringBuffer str, FormatStatus status)`

Parameters: obj: the object to format
str: the sting result
status: the format status

getAvailableLocales() Method

This method gets the list of locales that have NumberFormat objects installed.

Syntax: `public static synchronized Locale[] getAvailableLocales()`

getCurrencySymbol() Method

This method gets the currency symbol of the default locale.

Syntax: `public final String getCurrencySymbol()`

getCurrencySymbol(Locale) Method

This method gets the currency symbol of the specified locale.

Syntax: `public final String getCurrencySymbol(Locale loc)`

Parameters: loc: the locale

getDefault() Method

This method gets the NumberFormat object for the default locale.

Syntax: `public final static synchronized NumberFormat getDefault()`

getDefault(Locale) Method

This method gets the NumberFormat object for the specified locale.

Syntax: `public final static synchronized NumberFormat getDefault`
              `(Locale loc)`

Parameters: loc: the locale

getDefaultCurrency() Method

This method gets a currency format for the default locale.

Syntax: `public final static synchronized NumberFormat getDefaultCurrency()`

getDefaultCurrency(Locale) Method

This method gets a currency format for the specified locale.

Syntax: `public final static synchronized NumberFormat`
              `getDefaultCurrency(Locale loc)`

Parameters: loc: the locale

getDefaultPercent() Method

This method gets a percentage format for the default locale.

Syntax: `public final static synchronized NumberFormat getDefaultPercent()`

getDefaultPercent(Locale) Method

This method gets a percentage format for the specified locale.

Syntax: `public final static synchronized NumberFormat`
              `getDefaultPercent(Locale loc)`

Parameters: loc: the locale

NumberFormat

getDisplayName(Locale) Method

This method gets the display name for the specified locale and language of the default locale.

Syntax: `public static synchronized String getDisplayName(Locale objectLoc)`

Parameters: objectLoc: the desired locale from the list of available locales

Throws: MissingResourceException: when the objectLoc is not from the list from getAvailableLocales.

getDisplayName(Locale, Locale) Method

This method gets the display name for the specified locale and language.

Syntax: `public static synchronized String getDisplayName(Locale objectLoc,Locale displayLoc)`

Parameters: objectLoc: the desired locale from the list of available locales displayLoc: the locale with the desired language

getIntlCurrencySymbol() Method

This method gets the international currency symbol of the default locale.

Syntax: `public final String getIntlCurrencySymbol()`

getIntlCurrencySymbol(Locale) Method

This method gets the international currency symbol of the default locale.

Syntax: `public final String getIntlCurrencySymbol(Locale loc)`

Parameters: loc: the locale

getMaximumDecimalCount() Method

This method gets the maximum and minimum digit counts for the decimal.

Syntax: `public int getMaximumDecimalCount()`

getMaximumIntegerCount() Method

This method gets the maximum digit count for the integer.

Syntax: `public int getMaximumIntegerCount()`

getMinimumDecimalCount() Method

This method gets the maximum and minimum digit counts for the decimal.

Syntax: `public int getMinimumDecimalCount()`

getMinimumIntegerCount() Method

This method gets the minimum digit count for the integer.

Syntax: `public int getMinimumIntegerCount()`

isDecimalUsedWithInteger() Method

This method determines the behavior of the decimal separator with integers.

Syntax: `public boolean isDecimalUsedWithInteger()`

isIntegerOnly() Method

This method gets the flag to specify whether a number stops at a decimal point.

Syntax: `public boolean isIntegerOnly()`

isThousandsUsed() Method

This method determines the behavior of the thousands separator for a number.

Syntax: `public boolean isThousandsUsed()`

parse(String) Method

This method parses a string for a number and returns it if the number is found.

Syntax: `public abstract Number parse(String str)`

Parameters: str: the string to parse

Throws: FormatException: when the string cannot be parsed.

parse(String, ParseStatus) Method

This method parses a string given the parse status.

Syntax: `public abstract Number parse(String str,ParseStatus status)`

Parameters: str: the string to parse
                 status: the parse status

parseObject(String, ParseStatus) Method

This method parses the string. This method overrides the *parseObject()* method from the Format class.

Syntax: `public Object[] parse(String str, ParseStatus status)`

Parameters: str: the string to parse
                 status: the parse status

Throws: FormatException: when no date is found and the parse status is set up to throw an exception.

setDecimalUsedWithInteger(boolean) Method

This method sets the behavior of the decimal separator with integers.

Syntax:　　　**`public void setDecimalUsedWithInteger(boolean bool)`**

Parameters:　bool: True if decimals should be used with integers; False if not

setIntegerOnly(boolean) Method

This method sets the flag that determines whether a number stops at a decimal point.

Syntax:　　　**`public void setIntegerOnly(boolean bool)`**

Parameters:　bool: True means a number stops at the decimal; False means it does not stop at the decimal

setMaximumDecimalCount(int) Method

This method sets the maximum and minimum digit counts for the decimal.

Syntax:　　　**`public void setMaximumDecimalCount(int count)`**

Parameters:　count: the digit count

setMaximumIntegerCount(int) Method

This method sets the maximum digit count for the integer.

Syntax:　　　**`public void setMaximumIntegerCount(int count)`**

Parameters:　count: the digit count

setMinimumDecimalCount(int) Method

This method sets the maximum and minimum digit counts for the decimal.

Syntax:　　　**`public void setMinimumDecimalCount(int count)`**

Parameters:　count: the digit count

NumberFormat

setMinimumIntegerCount(int) Method

This method sets the minimum digit count for the integer.

Syntax: `public void setMinimumIntegerCount(int count)`

Parameters: count: the digit count

setThousandsUsed(boolean) Method

This method sets the behavior of the thousands separator for a number.

Syntax: `public void setThousandsUsed(boolean bool)`

Parameters: bool: True if thousands separator should be used; False if not

NumberFormatData Class

This class is used for localizing the formatting and parsing of numbers. This class extends the Object class in the java.lang package and implements the Cloneable and Serializable interfaces from the java.lang and java.io packages, respectively.

clone() Method

This method creates a copy or clone of a NumberFormatData object. This method overrides the Cloneable interface in the java.lang package.

Syntax: `public Object clone()`

equals(Object) Method

This method determines if two objects are equal. This method overrides the *equals()* method from the Object class in the java.lang package.

Syntax: `public boolean equals(Object obj)`

Parameters: obj: the object to compare with this one

hashCode() Method

This method gets the hash code for the NumberFormatData object. This method overrides the *hashCode()* method from the Object class in the java.lang package.

Syntax: `public synchronized abstract int hashCode()`

ParseStatus Class

This class is used with the various Format classes to determine the status of any parsing procedures. This class extends the Object class in the java.lang package.

SimpleDateFormat Class

This class enables the formatting, parsing, and normalization of dates and times independent of the language. This class extends the DateFormat class.

clone() Method

This method creates a copy or clone of a SimpleDateFormat object. This method overrides the Cloneable interface in the java.lang package.

Syntax: `public Object clone()`

equals(Object) Method

This method determines if two objects are equal. This method overrides the *equals()* method from the Object class in the java.lang package.

Syntax: `public boolean equals(Object obj)`

Parameters: obj: the object to compare with this one

SimpleDateFormat

format(Date, StringBuffer, FormatStatus) Method

This method formats a Date object into a string containing a datetime, which is in standard millis since 24:00 GMT, Jan 1, 1970. This method overrides the *format()* method from the DateFormat class.

Syntax:
```
public final StringBuffer format(Date d, StringBuffer str,
FormatStatus status)
```

Parameters: date: a date
str: the result string
status: formatting status

getDateFormatData() Method

This method gets the datetime formatting data.

Syntax:
```
public DateFormatData getDateFormatData()
```

getPattern(boolean) Method

This method gets the pattern for datetime formatting.

Syntax:
```
public String getPattern(boolean bool)
```

Parameters: bool: True means the pattern should be localized; False means it should not

hashCode() Method

This method gets the hash code for the SimpleDateFormat object. This method overrides the *hashCode()* method from the Object class in the java.lang package.

Syntax:
```
public synchronized abstract int hashCode()
```

parse(String, ParseStatus) Method

This method parses a datetime string given the parse status and returns a date if one is found; otherwise null is returned. This method overrides the *parse()* method from the DateFormat class.

Syntax: `public Date parse(String str, ParseStatus status)`

Parameters: str: the string to parse
                status: the parse status

setDateFormatData(DateFormatData) Method

This method sets the datetime formatting data.

Syntax: `public void setDateFormatData(DateFormatData format)`

Parameters: format: the DateFormatData to use

setPattern(String, boolean) Method

This method sets the datetime formatting pattern.

Syntax: `public void setPattern(String pattern, boolean bool)`

Parameters: pattern: The pattern to set
                bool: True means the pattern is localized; False it is not

SortKey Class

This class is used for quicker comparisons of strings if they are compared multiple times as in sorting a list of names. The Collation classes create SortKey objects. They hold comparison information about the Collation objects. This class extends the Object class in the java.lang package.

compareTo(SortKey) Method

This convenience method carries out a string (bit-wise) comparison of the two sort keys and returns values of LESS, GREATER, or EQUAL based upon the results of the comparison.

Syntax: `public byte compareTo(SortKey key2)`

Parameters: key2

equals(Object) Method

This method determines if two objects are equal. This method overrides the *equals()* method from the Object class in the java.lang package.

Syntax:　　**public boolean equals(Object obj)**

Parameters:　　obj: the object to compare with this one

hashCode() Method

This method gets the hash code for the SortKey object. This method overrides the *hashCode()* method from the Object class in the java.lang package.

Syntax:　　**public synchronized abstract int hashCode()**

StringCharacterIterator Class

This class implements the CharacterIterator interface to traverse entire strings. This class extends the Object class in the java.lang package.

clone() Method

This method creates a copy or clone of a specified boundary. This method overrides the Cloneable interface in the java.lang package.

Syntax:　　**public Object clone()**

current() Method

This method gets the character at the current position, just as though you were using the *getIndex()* method.

Syntax:　　**public char current()**

endIndex() Method

This method returns the end index of the string.

Syntax: `public int endIndex()`

equals(Object) Method

This method determines if two objects are equal. This method overrides the *equals()* method from the Object class in the java.lang package.

Syntax: `public boolean equals(Object obj)`

Parameters: obj: the object to compare with this one

first() Method

This method sets the position to the beginning of the string, just as though you were using the *startIndex()* method, and returns that character.

Syntax: `public char first()`

getIndex() Method

This method gets the current index of the string.

Syntax: `public int getIndex()`

getText() Method

This method gets the text from a string.

Syntax: `public String getText()`

StringCharacterIterator

hashCode() Method

This method gets the hash code for the enumeration in a string. This method overrides the *hashCode()* method from the Object class in the java.lang package.

Syntax: `public synchronized abstract int hashCode()`

last() Method

This method sets the position to the end of the string, just as though you were using the *endIndex()* method, and returns that character.

Syntax: `public char last()`

next() Method

This method increments the iterator's index by one and returns the character there.

Syntax: `public char next()`

previous() Method

This method subtracts one from the index and returns the character at that position.

Syntax: `public char previous()`

setIndex(int) Method

This method sets the current position in the text to the specified position and returns that character.

Syntax: `public char setIndex(int pos)`

Parameters: pos: the position in the text to set current

Throws: IllegalArgumentException: when pos is outside of the string.

startIndex() Method

This method gets the first position in the string.

Syntax: `public int startIndex()`

TableCollation Class

This is an extension of the Collation class that uses tables to drive the string collation.

clone() Method

This method creates a copy or clone of a TableCollation object. This method overrides the Cloneable interface in the java.lang package.

Syntax: `public Object clone()`

compare(String, int, int, String, int, int) Method

This method compares a range of characters in two different strings. This method returns values of LESS, GREATER, or EQUAL dependent on the results of the comparison between str1 and str2. This method overrides the *compare()* method in the Collation class.

Syntax: `public byte compare(String str2, int start1, int end1, String str2,`
              `int start2, int end2)`

Parameters: str1: the first string to compare
              start1: the begin point for str1
              end1: the end point for str1
              str2: the second string to compare
              start2: the begin point for str2
              end2: the end point for str2

Throws: StringIndexOutOfBoundsException: when the start offset for a string is greater than the end offset.

compare(String, String) Method

This method compares the characters in two different strings. Values of LESS, GREATER, or EQUAL are returned based upon the results of the comparison between str1 and str2.

Syntax: `public byte compare(String str1, String str2)`

Parameters: str1: The first string to compare
                   str2: The second string to compare

equals(Object) Method

This method determines if two objects are equal. This method overrides the *equals()* method from the Object class in the java.lang package.

Syntax: `public boolean equals(Object obj)`

Parameters: obj: the object to compare with this one

getRules() Method

This method gets the rules for the string collation.

Syntax: `public String getRules()`

getSortKey(String) Method

This method constructs a SortKey object for the string. This method overrides the *getSortKey()* method from the Collation class.

Syntax: `public SortKey getSortKey(String str)`

Parameters: str: the string to get a sortkey for

getSortKey(String, int, int) Method

This method constructs a SortKey object for the string from the specified starting index to the specified ending index. This method overrides the *getSortKey()* method from the Collation class.

Syntax: `public SortKey getSortKey(String source, int start, int end)`

Parameters: str: the string to get a sortkey for
start: the begin point for str
end: the end point for str

hashCode() Method

This method gets the hash code for the Collation object. This method overrides the *hashCode()* method from the Collation class.

Syntax: `public int hashCode()`

TextBoundary Class

TextBoundary is a class of methods that find various types of boundaries in text. These boundaries include word, line, sentence, and character boundaries. This class extends the Object class and implements the Cloneable and Serializable interfaces in the java.lang and java.io packages, respectively. Refer also to the CharacterIterator interface.

clone() Method

This method creates a copy or clone of the TextBoundary object. This method overrides the *clone()* method from the Object class in the java.lang package.

Syntax: `public Object clone()`

current() Method

This method gets the index of the current boundary. The current boundary is the last value returned by the *first()*, *last()*, *previous()*, or *next()* methods.

Syntax: `public abstract Int current()`

first() Method

This method sets the current index to the beginning and returns the character at that position.

Syntax: `public abstract Int first()`

getAvailableLocales() Method

This method gets a list of locales that have TextBoundary objects installed.

Syntax: `public static synchronized Locale[] getAvailableLocales()`

getCharacterBreak() Method

This method creates a TextBoundary object for character breaks using the default locale. Refer also to the *getDefault()* method.

Syntax: `public static TextBoundary getCharacterBreak()`

getCharacterBreak(Locale) Method

This method creates a TextBoundary object for character breaks using the specified locale.

Syntax: `public static TextBoundary getCharacterBreak(locale loc)`

Parameters: loc: the locale to use to determine character breaks

getDisplayName(Locale) Method

This method gets the display name for the specified locale and language of the default locale.

Syntax: `public static synchronized String getDisplayName(Locale objectLoc)`

Parameters: objectLoc: the desired locale from the list of available locales

getDisplayName(Locale, Locale) Method

This method gets the display name for the specified locale and language.

Syntax: `public static synchronized String getDisplayName(Locale objectLoc,Locale displayLoc)`

Parameters: objectLoc: the desired locale from the list of available locales
displayLoc: the locale with the desired language

getLineBreak() Method

This method creates a TextBoundary object for line breaks using the default locale. Refer also to the *getDefault()* method.

Syntax: `public static TextBoundary getLineBreak()`

getLineBreak(Locale) Method

This method creates a TextBoundary object for line breaks using the specified locale.

Syntax: `public static TextBoundary getLineBreak(locale loc)`

Parameters: loc: the locale to use to determine line breaks

getSentenceBreak() Method

This method creates a TextBoundary object for sentence breaks using the default locale. Refer also to the *getDefault()* method.

Syntax: `public static TextBoundary getSentenceBreak()`

TextBoundary

getSentenceBreak(Locale) Method

This method creates a TextBoundary objects for sentence breaks using the specified locale.

Syntax: `public static TextBoundary getSentenceBreak(locale loc)`

Parameters: loc: the locale to use to determine sentence breaks

getText() Method

This method gets the text of the boundary. Refer also to the *setText()* method.

Syntax: `public abstract String getText()`

getWordBreak() Method

This method creates a TextBoundary object for word breaks using the default locale. Refer also to the *getDefault()* method.

Syntax: `public static TextBoundary getWordBreak()`

getWordBreak(Locale) Method

This method creates a TextBoundary object for word breaks using the specified locale.

Syntax: `public static TextBoundary getWordBreak(locale loc)`

Parameters: loc: the locale to use to determine word breaks

last() Method

This method gets the index of last character in the text boundary.

Syntax: `public abstract int last()`

next() Method

This method gets the boundary after the current boundary.

Syntax: `public abstract int next()`

nextAfter(int) Method

This method finds the boundary after the specified offset.

Syntax: `public abstract int nextAfter(int offset)`

Parameters: offset: the offset to start searching from

Throws: IllegalArgumentException: Thrown if the offset is invalid. The valid offsets
are determined by the CharacterIterator.

nthFromCurrent(int) Method

This method return the nth (specified) boundary from the current boundary.

Syntax: `public abstract int nthFromCurrent(int n)`

Parameters: n: the number of boundaries to move forward or back from the current
boundary. If the number is negative it gets a previous
boundary

previous() Method

This method gets the boundary prior to the current boundary.

Syntax: `public abstract int previous()`

setText(CharacterIterator) Method

This method sets the text for the boundary. The position is set to the beginning character of the string. Refer also to the *getText()* method.

Syntax: `public abstract void setText(CharacterIterator Text)`

Parameters: text: the new text for the boundary

setText(String) Method

This method sets the text for the boundary. The position is set to the beginning string of the boundary. Refer also to the *getText()* method.

Syntax: `public void setText(String text)`

Parameters: text: the new text for the boundary

Exception FormatException

This exception is raised when an unexpected error occurs while formatting. The single *getErrorOffset()* method for this exception indicates the position where the error was found.

java.util Package

The java.util package contains classes to assist the developer with calendar issues related to internationalization. The developer can obtain information about the locale and the information to be presented can be localized before display.

Calendar Class

The Calendar class is a base class for date manipulation and conversion to and from a set of integer fields representing day, month, year, and so on. This class extends the Object class in the java.lang package and implements the Cloneable and Serializable interfaces in the java.lang and java.io packages, respectively.

Calendar() Constructor

This constructor creates a Calendar object with the default time zone as returned by the *TimeZone.getDefault( )* method, and the default locale.

Syntax: `protected Calendar()`

Calendar(TimeZone, Locale) Constructor

This constructor creates a Calendar object with the specified time zone and locale.

Syntax: `protected Calendar(TimeZone zone, Locale aLocale)`

Parameters: zone: the specified time zone
aLocale: the specified locale

add(byte, int) Method

This method adds the specified date or time amount to the time field.

Syntax: `public abstract void add(byte field, int amount)`

Parameters: field: the time field to add to
int: the amount to add to the time field. The amount is signed.

Throws: IllegalArgumentException: when the field argument is not an acceptable value.

after(Object) Method

This method compares the time field records of this Calendar object and the supplied Calendar object.

Syntax: `public abstract boolean after(Object obj)`

Parameters: obj: the Calendar object for comparison

before(Object) Method

This method compares the time field records of this Calendar object and the supplied Calendar object.

Syntax:　　　`public abstract boolean before(Object obj)`

Parameters:　　obj: the Calendar object for comparison

clear() Method

This method clears the values from all the time fields in the Calendar object.

Syntax:　　　`public final void clear()`

clear(byte) Method

This method clears the value in the specified time field.

Syntax:　　　`public final void clear(byte field)`

Parameters:　　field: the time field to clear

Throws:　　　IllegalArgumentException: when the field argument is not a valid time field.

clone() Method

This method creates a copy or clone of the Calendar object. This method overrides the Cloneable interface in the java.lang package.

Syntax:　　　`public Object Clone()`

complete() Method

This method fills in all the time fields that do not have a value set.

Syntax:　　　`protected void complete()`

computeFields() Method

This method converts UTC as milliseconds to time field values.

Syntax: `protected abstract void computeFields()`

computeTime() Method

This method converts the Calendar object's time field values to UTC as milliseconds.

Syntax: `protected abstract void computeTime()`

equals(Object) Method

This method compares the time field records of separate Calendar objects. This method overrides the *equals()* method from the Object class in the java.lang package.

Syntax: `public abstract boolean equals(Object obj)`

Parameters: obj: the Calendar object for comparison

get(byte) Method

This method gets the value for a given time field.

Syntax: `public final int get(byte field)`

Parameters: field: the time field to get

Throws: IllegalArgumentException: when the field argument is not a valid time field.

getAvailableLocales() Method

This method gets the set of locales that have Calendar objects installed.

Syntax: `public static synchronized Locale[] getAvailableLocales()`

getDefault() Method

This method gets a Calendar object using the default time zone and locale.

Syntax: `public static synchronized Calendar getDefault()`

getDefault(Locale) Method

This method gets a Calendar object using the default time zone and supplied locale.

Syntax: `public static synchronized Calendar getDefault(Locale loc)`

Parameters: loc: the locale to use to get the calendar

getDefault(TimeZone) Method

This method gets a Calendar object using the supplied time zone and default locale.

Syntax: `public static synchronized Calendar getDefault(TimeZone zone)`

Parameters: zone: the TimeZone to use to get the calendar

getDefault(TimeZone, Locale) Method

This method gets a Calendar object using the supplied time zone and supplied locale.

Syntax: `public static synchronized Calendar getDefault(TimeZone zone, Locale loc)`

Parameters: zone: the TimeZone to use to get the calendar
loc: the locale to use to get the calendar

getFirstDayOfWeek() Method

This method gets the day of the week used as the first day of the week. Monday in the U.S., Tuesday in Belgium, for example.

Syntax: `public int getFirstDayOfWeek()`

getGreatestMinimum(byte) Method

This method returns the highest minimum value for the specified time field.

Syntax: `public abstract int getGreatestMinimum(byte field)`

Parameters: byte: the time field to use

getLeastMaximum(byte) Method

This method returns lowest maximum value for the specified time field.

Syntax: `public abstract int getLeastMaximum(byte field)`

Parameters: byte: the time field to use

getMaximum(byte) Method

This method returns the maximum value for the specified time field.

Syntax: `public abstract int getMaximum(byte field)`

Parameters: byte: the time field to use

getMinimalDaysInFirstWeek() Method

This method gets the minimum days required in the first week of the year; three if the first week of the year starts on a Thursday, and so forth. Refer also to the *setMinimalDaysInFirstWeek()* method.

Syntax: `public int getMinimalDaysInFirstWeek()`

getMinimum(byte) Method

This method returns minimum value for the specified time field.

Syntax: `public abstract int getMinimum(byte field)`

Parameters: byte: the time field to use

getTime() Method

This method gets the current time for the Calendar object. Refer also to the *setTime()* method.

Syntax: `public final Date getTime()`

getTimeInMillis() Method

This method gets the Calendar object's current time as a long, which is milliseconds since the epoch. Refer also to the *setTimeInMillis()* method.

Syntax: `protected long getTimeInMillis()`

getTimeZone() Method

This method gets the time zone of the Calendar object. Refer also to the *setTimeZone()* method.

Syntax: `public TimeZone getTimeZone()`

getValidationMode() Method

This method gets the validation mode for the Calendar object. Refer also to the *setValidationMode()* method.

Syntax: `public boolean getValidationMode()`

internalGet(int) Method

This method gets the value for the specified time field.

Syntax: `protected final int internalGet(int field)`

Parameters: field: the time field to get

Throws: IllegalArgumentException: when the field argument is not a valid time field.

isSet(int) Method

This method determines if the specified time field has a value set.

Syntax: `public final boolean isSet(int field)`

Throws: IllegalArgumentException: when the field argument is not a valid time field.

roll(byte, boolean) Method

This method rolls the specified time field up or down one unit of time.

Syntax: `public abstract void roll(byte field, boolean up)`

Parameters: field: the time field to add to
up: if True, roll up; if False, roll down.

Throws: IllegalArgumentException: when the field argument is not an acceptable value.

set(byte, int) Method

This method sets the time field with the given value.

Syntax: `public final void set(byte field, int value)`

Parameters: field: the time field to get
int: the new value for the time field

Throws: IllegalArgumentException: when the field argument is not a valid time field.

set(int, int, int) Method

This method sets the values for the field's year, month, and date.

Syntax: `public final void set(int year, int month, int date)`

Parameters: year: the new value for the YEAR time Field
month: the new value for the MONTH time Field. Note: Jan. = 0
date: the new value for the DATE time Field

set(int, int, int, int, int) Method

This method sets the values for the field's year, month, date, hour, and minute.

Syntax: `public final void set(int year, int month, int date, int hour, int minute)`

Parameters: year: the new value for the YEAR time Field
month: the new value for the MONTH time Field. Note: Jan. = 0
date: the new value for the DATE time Field
hour: the new value for the HOUROFDAY time Field
minute: the new value for the MINUTE time Field

set(int, int, int, int, int, int) Method

This method sets the values for the field's year, month, date, hour, minute, and second.

Syntax: `public final void set(int year, int month, int date, int hour, int minute, int second)`

Parameters: year: the new value for the YEAR time Field
month: the new value for the MONTH time Field. Note: Jan. = 0
date: the new value for the DATE time Field
hour: the new value for the HOUROFDAY time Field
minute: the new value for the MINUTE time Field.
second: the new value for the SECOND time Field

setFirstDayOfWeek(byte) Method

This method sets the day of the week to use as the first day of the week. Refer also to the *getFirstDayOfWeek()* method.

Syntax: `public void setFirstDayOfWeek(byte value)`

Parameters: value: the day to use as the first day of the week

setMinimalDaysInFirstWeek(byte) Method

This method sets what the minimal days required in the first week of the year are: For example, if the first week is defined as one that contains the first day of the first month of a year, call the method with value 1. Refer also to the *getMinimalDaysInFirstWeek()* method.

Syntax: `public void setMinimalDaysInFirstWeek(byte value)`

Parameters: value: the minimum days required for the first week of the year

setTime(Date) Method

This method sets this Calendar object's current time with the specified date. Refer also to the *getTime()* method.

Syntax: `public final void setTime(Date date)`

Parameters: date: the date to set the calendar's current time to

setTimeInMillis(long) Method

This method sets this Calendar object's current time from the specified value, which is milliseconds from the epoch. Refer also to the *getTimeInMillis()* method.

Syntax: `protected void setTimeInMillis(long millis)`

setTimeZone(TimeZone) Method

This method sets the time zone with the supplied TimeZone value. Refer also to the *getTimeZone()* method.

Syntax: `public void setTimeZone(TimeZone zone)`

Parameters: zone: the time zone to use for the calendar

Calendar

setValidationMode(boolean) Method

This method sets the validation mode that controls the behavior of the object that uses the Calendar class.

Syntax: `public void setValidationMode(boolean mode)`

Parameters: mode: True if you want an exception to be thrown for bad dates; False if you want it to try to work with the bad date

GregorianCalendar Class

This class extends the Calendar class and represents the type of calendar that most of the world uses. The Gregorian calendar has two eras, BC and AD. The implementation date of the Gregorian calendar defaults to October 15, 1582, but may be set to a different date.

add(byte, int) Method

This method adds the specified date or time amount to the time field. This method overrides the *add()* method from the Calendar class.

Syntax: `public void add(byte field, int amount)`

Parameters: field: the time field to add to
int: the amount to add to the time field. The amount is signed.

Throws: IllegalArgumentException: when the field argument is not an acceptable value.

after(Object) Method

This method compares time field records. This method overrides the *after()* method from the Calendar class.

Syntax: `public boolean after(Object when)`

Parameters: after: the time field for comparison

before(Object) Method

This method compares time field records. This method overrides the *before()* method from the Calendar class.

Syntax: `public boolean before(Object when)`

Parameters: before: the time field for comparison

clone() Method

This method creates a copy or clone of the GregorianCalendar object. This method overrides the Cloneable interface in the java.lang package.

Syntax: `public Object Clone()`

computeFields() Method

This method converts UTC as milliseconds to time field values. This method overrides the *computeFields()* method from the Calendar class.

Syntax: `protected void computeFields()`

computeTime() Method

This method converts time field values to UTC as milliseconds. This method overrides the *computeTime()* method from the Calendar class.

Syntax: `protected void computeTime()`

equals(Object) Method

This method determines if the time field records are equal. This method overrides the *equals()* method from the Calendar class.

Syntax: `public boolean equals(Object obj)`

Parameters: Obj: the object to compare to this one

GregorianCalendar

getGreatestMinimum(byte) Method

This method returns the highest minimum value for the specified time field. This method overrides the *getGreatestMinimum()* method from the Calendar class.

Syntax: `public int getGreatestMinimum(byte field)`

Parameters: byte: the time field to use

getGregorianChange() Method

This method gets the change date for the GregorianCalendar object. Refer also to the *setGregorianChange()* method.

Syntax: `public final Date getGregorianChange()`

getLeastMaximum(byte) Method

This method returns the lowest maximum value for the specified time field. This method overrides the *getLeastMaximum()* method from the Calendar class.

Syntax: `public int getLeastMaximum(byte field)`

Parameters: byte: the time field to use

getMaximum(byte) Method

This method returns the maximum value for the specified time field. This method over-rides the *getMaximum()* method from the Calendar class.

Syntax: `public int getMaximum(byte field)`

Parameters: byte: the time field to use

getMinimum(byte) Method

This method returns the minimum value for the specified time field. This method over-rides the *getMinimum()* method from the Calendar class.

Syntax: `public int getMinimum(byte field)`

Parameters: byte: the time field to use

hashCode() Method

This method generates a hashCode for the GregorianCalendar object. This method overrides the *hashCode()* method from the Object class in the java.lang package.

Syntax: `public synchronized int hashCode()`

isLeapYear(int) Method

This method determines if the supplied year is a leap year.

Syntax: `public boolean isLeapYear(int year)`

Parameters: year: the year to check

roll(byte, boolean) Method

This method rolls the specified time field up or down one unit of time. This method overrides the *roll()* method from the Calendar class.

Syntax: `public void roll(byte field, boolean up)`

Parameters: field: the time field to add to up: If True, roll up, if False, roll down

Throws: IllegalArgumentException: when the field argument is not an acceptable value.

setGregorianChange(Date) Method

This method sets the GregorianCalendar object cutover date. The cutover default is October 15, 1582 00:00:00. Refer also to the *getGregorianChange()* method.

Syntax: `public void setGregorianChange(Date date)`

Parameters: date: the date to use as the Gregorian cutover date

GregorianCalendar

ListResourceBundle Class

The ListResourceBundle class provides a list of resources for a locale. The *getContents()* method provides the array of case-sensitive keys and associated values. This class extends the ResourceBundle class. Refer also to the PropertyResourceBundle class.

getContents() Method

This method returns a list of case-sensitive keys and associated values for a ResourceBundle object.

Syntax: `protected abstract Object[][] getContents()`

getKeys() Method

This method returns the case-sensitive keys of a ResourceBundle object. This method overrides the *getKeys()* method from the ResourceBundle class.

Syntax: `public Enumeration getKeys()`

handleGetObject(String) Method

This method returns the object associated with a key. This method overrides the *handleGetObject()* method from the ResourceBundle class.

Syntax: `public final Object handleGetObject(String key)`

Parameters: key: the key of the Object in the resource bundle

Locale Class

The Locale class implements objects that represent a specific geographical, political, or cultural region.

clone() Method

This method creates a copy or clone of a Locale object. This method overrides the Cloneable interface in the java.lang package.

Syntax: `public Object Clone()`

equals(Object) Method

This method compares the equality of two Locale objects. This method overrides the *equals()* method from the Object class in the java.lang package.

Syntax: `public boolean equals(Object obj)`

Parameters: obj: the object for comparison

getCountry() Method

This method gets the uppercased two-letter ISO-3166 code for the country. Refer also to the *getDisplayCountry()* method.

Syntax: `public String getCountry()`

getDefault() Method

This method gets the current default Locale. Refer also to the *setDefault()* method.

Syntax: `public static synchronized Locale getDefault()`

getDisplayCountry() Method

This method gets the display country from the default locale. If the localized name is not found, ISO codes are returned.

Syntax: `public final String getDisplayCountry()`

Locale

getDisplayCountry(Locale) Method

This method gets the display country from the specified locale. If the localized name is not found, ISO codes are returned.

Syntax: `public String getDisplayCountry(Locale loc)`

Parameters: loc: the locale to get the display country from

getDisplayLanguage() Method

This method gets the display language from the default locale. If the localized name is not found, ISO codes are returned.

Syntax: `public final String getDisplayLanguage()`

getDisplayLanguage(Locale) Method

This method gets the display language from the specified locale. If the localized name is not found, ISO codes are returned.

Syntax: `public String getDisplayLanguage(Locale inLocale)`

Parameters: inLocale: the locale to get the display language from

getDisplayName() Method

This method gets the display locale. The default locale is used for the language. If the localized name is not found, ISO codes are returned.

Syntax: `public final String getDisplayName()`

getDisplayName(Locale) Method

This method gets the display locale. The specified locale is used for the language. If the localized name is not found, ISO codes are returned.

Syntax: `public final String getDisplayName()`

getDisplayVariant() Method

This method gets the display variant from the default locale. If the localized name is not found, the variant code is returned.

Syntax: `public final String getDisplayVariant()`

getDisplayVariant(Locale) Method

This method gets the display variant from the specified locale. If the localized name is not found, the variant code is returned.

Syntax: `public String getDisplayVariant(Locale inLocale)`

Parameters: inLocale: the locale to get the display variant from

getISO3Country() Method

This method gets the three-letter ISO country abbreviation of the locale.

Syntax: `public String getISO3Country()`

Throws: MissingResourceException: when the three-letter country abbreviation is not available for this locale.

getISO3Language() Method

This method gets the three-letter ISO language abbreviation of the locale.

Syntax: `public String getISO3Language()`

Throws: MissingResourceException: when the three-letter language abbreviation is not available for this locale.

getLanguage() Method

This method gets the uppercased two-letter ISO-639 code for the language. Refer also to the *getDisplayLanguage()* method.

Syntax: `public String getLanguage()`

getVariant() Method

This method gets the programmatic name of field. Refer also to the *getDisplayVariant()* method.

Syntax: `public String getVariant()`

hashCode() Method

This method returns the hash code for the Locale object. This method overrides the *hashCode()* method from the Object class in the java.lang package.

Syntax: `public synchronized int hashCode()`

setDefault(Locale) Method

This method sets the default locale. Refer also to the *getDefault()* method.

Syntax: `public static synchronized void setDefault(Locale loc)`

Parameters: loc: the new default locale

toString() Method

This method gets the entire locale, with the language, country, and variant separated by underscores. This method overrides the *toString()* method from the Object class in the java.lang package. Refer also to the *getDisplayName()* method.

Syntax: `public final String toString()`

SimpleTimeZone Class

This class is an extension of the TimeZone class for use with the Gregorian Calendar. It has limited rules and cannot handle historical changes.

dayOfWeekInMonth refers to the occurrence of a dayOfWeek in the specified month. If dayOfWeekInMonth is negative, it counts backwards from the end of the month, else, it counts forward. Example: The second Tuesday in March would have a 2 for dayOfWeekInMonth, but the last Tuesday in March would have a -1 for dayOfWeekInMonth.

clone() Method

This method creates a copy or clone of a SimpleTimeZone object. This method overrides the Cloneable interface in the java.lang package.

Syntax: `public Object clone()`

equals(Object) Method

This method compares the equality of two SimpleTimeZone objects.

Syntax: `public boolean equals(Object obj)`

Parameters: obj: the SimpleTimeZone object to compare with this one

getOffset(int, int, int, int, int, int) Method

This method gets the timezone offset to add to GMT (Greenwich Mean Time) with consideration for daylight savings to return the locale time. This method overrides the *getOffset()* method from the TimeZone class.

Syntax: `public int getOffset(int era, int year, int month, int day, int dayOfWeek, int milliseconds)`

Parameters: era: the era of the date
year: the year of the date
month: the month of the date where: January = 0, February = 1, and so on
day: the day of the date
dayOfWeek: the day-of-the-week of the date
milliseconds: the millis in day

SimpleTimeZone

getRawOffset() Method

This method gets the timezone offset to add to GMT (Greenwich Mean Time) without consideration for daylight savings time to return the locale time. This method overrides the *getRawOffset()* method from the TimeZone class. Refer also to the *setRawOffset()* method.

Syntax: `public int getRawOffset()`

hashCode() Method

This method generates a hash code for the SimpleDateFormat object. This method overrides the *hashCode()* method from the Object class in the java.lang package.

Syntax: `public synchronized int hashCode()`

inDaylightTime(Date) Method

This method determines if the date is in daylight savings time in this time zone. This method overrides the *InDaylightTime()* method from the TimeZone class.

Syntax: `public boolean inDaylightTime(Date date)`

Parameters: date: the date to check

setEndRule(int, int, int, int) Method

This method sets the ending rule for daylight savings time.

Syntax: `public void setEndRule(int month, int dayOfWeekInMonth, int dayOfWeek, int time)`

Parameters: month: the end month of the rule where: Jan. = 0, Feb. = 1, and so on
dayOfWeekInMonth: the occurrence of the dayOfWeek in the month
dayOfWeek: the day-of-the-week of the date
time: the end time of the rule

setRawOffset(int) Method

This method sets the base timezone offset to GMT (Greenwich Mean Time). This method overrides the *setRawOffset( )* method from the TimeZone class. Refer also to the *getRawOffset( )* method.

Syntax: `public void setRawOffset(int offsetMillis)`

Parameters: offsetMillis: the base offset to GMT

setStartRule(int, int, int, int) Method

This method sets the starting rule for daylight savings time.

Syntax: `public void setStartRule(int month, int dayOfWeekInMonth, int`
                 `dayOfWeek, int time)`

Parameters: month: the start month of the rule where: Jan. = 0, Feb. = 1, and so on
                 dayOfWeekInMonth: the occurrence of the dayOfWeek in the month
                 dayOfWeek: the day-of-the-week of the date
                 ime: the start time of the rule

setStartYear(int) Method

This method sets the daylight savings starting year.

Syntax: `public void setStartYear(int year)`

Parameters: year: the starting year for daylight savings time

useDaylightTime() Method

This method overrides TimeZone Queries if this timezone uses Daylight Savings Time.

Syntax: `public boolean useDaylightTime()`

TimeZone Class

This class contains methods to get timezone offsets with consideration for daylight savings. They can also parse a list of time zone Ids. The user can set a timezone, as well as set daylight savings time. This class extends the Object class in the java.lang package and implements the Cloneable and Serializable interfaces in the java.lang and java.io packages, respectively.

clone() Method

This method creates a copy or clone of a TimeZone object. This method overrides the Cloneable interface in the java.lang package.

Syntax: `public Object clone()`

getAvailableIDs() Method

This method gets all the available time zone IDs.

Syntax: `public static synchronized String[] getAvailableIDs()`

getAvailableIDs(int) Method

This method gets the appropriate time zone IDs for the supplied time zone offset.

Syntax: `public static synchronized String[] getAvailableIDs(int rawOffset)`

Parameters: rawOffset: the raw offset from GMT

getDefault() Method

This method gets the default Time Zone. Refer also to the *setDefault()* method.

Syntax: `public static synchronized TimeZone getDefault()`

getID() Method

This method gets the timezone ID of this timezone. Refer also to the *setID()* method.

Syntax: `public String getID()`

getOffset(int, int, int, int, int, int) Method

This method gets the timezone offset to GWT with consideration for daylight savings.

Syntax: `public abstract int getOffset(int era, int year, int month, int day,`
                   `int dayOfWeek,  int milliseconds)`

Parameters: era: the era of the date
                year: the year of the date
                month: the month of the date where: January = 0, February = 1, and so on
                day: the day of the date
                dayOfWeek: the day-of-the-week of the date
                milliseconds: the millis in day

getRawOffset() Method

This method gets the time zone offset to GMT without consideration for daylight savings time. Refer also to the *setRawOffset()* method.

Syntax: `public abstract int getRawOffset()`

Returns: the offset of the time zone from UTC without consideration for daylight savings time.

getTimeZone(String) Method

This method gets the TimeZone object for the time zone ID.

Syntax: `public static synchronized TimeZone getTimeZone(String ID)`

Parameters: ID: the time zone ID

inDaylightTime(Date) Method

This method determines if the date is in daylight savings time in this time zone.

Syntax: `public abstract boolean inDaylightTime(Date date)`

Parameters: date: the date to check

setDefault(TimeZone) Method

This method sets the default TimeZone object to use. Refer also to the *getDefault()* method.

Syntax: `public static synchronized void setDefault(TimeZone zone)`

Parameters: zone: the new TimeZone default

setID(String) Method

This method sets the time zone ID. Refer also to the *getID()* method.

Syntax: `public void setID(String ID)`

Parameters: ID: The timezone ID to set use for this TimeZone object

setRawOffset(int) Method

This method sets the base timezone offset to GMT. Refer also to the *getRawOffset()* method.

Syntax: `public abstract void setRawOffset(int offsetMillis)`

Parameters: offsetMillis: the base offset to GMT

useDaylightTime() Method

This method determines if the TimeZone object uses Daylight Savings Time.

Syntax: `public abstract boolean useDaylightTime()`

INDEX

H

I

P

This binary code license ("License") contains rights and restrictions associated with use of the accompanying software and documentation ("Software"). Read the License carefully before installing the Software. By installing the Software you agree to the terms and conditions of this License.

1. **Limited License Grant.** Sun grants to you ("Licensee") a non-exclusive, non-transferable limited license to use the Software without fee for evaluation of the Software and for development of Java™ compatible applets and applications. Licensee may make one archival copy of the Software. Licensee may not redistribute the Software in whole or in part, either separately or included with a product. Refer to the Java Runtime Environment Version 1.1 binary code license (`http://www.javasoft.com/products/JDK/1.1/index.html`) for the availability of runtime code which may be distributed with Java compatible applets and applications.

2. **Java Platform Interface.** Licensee may not modify the Java Platform Interface ("JPI", identified as classes contained within the "Java" package or any subpackages of the "Java" package), by creating additional classes within the JPI or otherwise causing the addition to or modification of the classes in the JPI. In the event that Licensee creates any Java-related API and distributes such API to others for applet or application development, Licensee must promptly publish an accurate specification for such API for free use by all developers of Java-based software.

3. **Restrictions.** Software is confidential copyrighted information of Sun and title to all copies is retained by Sun and/or its licensors. Licensee shall not modify, decompile, disassemble, decrypt, extract, or otherwise reverse engineer Software. Software may not be leased, assigned, or sublicensed, in whole or in part. Software is not designed or intended for use in on-line control of aircraft, air traffic, aircraft navigation or aircraft communications; or in the design, construction, operation or maintenance of any nuclear facility. Licensee warrants that it will not use or redistribute the Software for such purposes.

4. **Trademarks and Logos.** This License does not authorize Licensee to use any Sun name, trademark or logo. Licensee acknowledges that Sun owns the Java trademark and all Java-related trademarks, logos and icons including the Coffee Cup and Duke ("Java Marks") and agrees to: (i) comply with the Java Trademark Guidelines at `http://java.com/trademarks.html`; (ii) not do anything harmful to or inconsistent with Sun's rights in the Java Marks; and (iii) assist Sun in protecting those rights, including assigning to Sun any rights acquired by Licensee in any Java Mark.

5. **Disclaimer of Warranty.** Software is provided "AS IS," without a warranty of any kind. ALL EXPRESS OR IMPLIED REPRESENTATIONS AND WARRANTIES, INCLUDING ANY IMPLIED WARRANTY OF MERCHANTABILITY,

FITNESS FOR A PARTICULAR PURPOSE, OR NON-INFRINGEMENT, ARE HEREBY EXCLUDED.

6. **Limitation of Liability.** SUN AND ITS LICENSORS SHALL NOT BE LIABLE FOR ANY DAMAGES SUFFERED BY LICENSEE OR ANY THIRD PARTY AS A RESULT OF USING OR DISTRIBUTING SOFTWARE. IN NO EVENT WILL SUN OR ITS LICENSORS BE LIABLE FOR ANY LOST REVENUE, PROFIT OR DATA, OR FOR DIRECT, INDIRECT, SPECIAL, CONSEQUENTIAL, INCIDENTAL OR PUNITIVE DAMAGES, HOWEVER CAUSED AND RE-GARDLESS OF THE THEORY OF LIABILITY, ARISING OUT OF THE USE OF OR INABILITY TO USE SOFTWARE, EVEN IF SUN HAS BEEN ADVISED OF THE POSSIBILITY OF SUCH DAMAGES.

7. **Termination.** Licensee may terminate this License at any time by destroying all copies of Software. This License will terminate immediately without notice from Sun if Licensee fails to comply with any provision of this License. Upon such termination, Licensee must destroy all copies of Software.

8. **Export Regulations.** Software, including technical data, is subject to U.S. export control laws, including the U.S. Export Administration Act and its associated regulations, and may be subject to export or import regulations in other countries. Licensee agrees to comply strictly with all such regulations and acknowledges that it has the responsibility to obtain licenses to export, re-export, or import Software. Software may not be downloaded, or otherwise exported or re-exported (i) into, or to a national or resident of, Cuba, Iraq, Iran, North Korea, Libya, Sudan, Syria or any country to which the U.S. has embargoed goods; or (ii) to anyone on the U.S. Treasury Department's list of Specially Designated Nations or the U.S. Commerce Department's Table of Denial Orders.

9. **Restricted Rights.** Use, duplication or disclosure by the United States government is subject to the restrictions as set forth in the Rights in Technical Data and Com-puter Software Clauses in d DFARS 252.227-7013(c)(1)(ii) and FAR 52.227-19(c)(2) as applicable.

10. **Governing Law.** Any action related to this License will be governed by California law and controlling U.S. federal law. No choice of law rules of any jurisdiction will apply.

11. **Severability.** If any of the above provisions are held to be in violation of applicable law, void, or unenforceable in any jurisdiction, then such provisions are herewith waived to the extent necessary for the License to be otherwise enforceable in such jurisdiction. However, if in Sun's opinion deletion of any provisions of the License by operation of this paragraph unreasonably compromises the rights or increases the liabilities of Sun or its licensors, Sun reserves the right to terminate the License and refund the fee paid by Licensee, if any, as Licensee's sole and exclusive remedy.

MACMILLAN COMPUTER PUBLISHING USA

A VIACOM COMPANY

Technical ---- Support:

If you need assistance with the information in this book or with a CD/Disk accompanying the book, please access the Knowledge Base on our Web site at **http://www.superlibrary.com/general/support**. Our most Frequently Asked Questions are answered there. If you do not find the answer to your questions on our Web site, you may contact Macmillan Technical Support **(317) 581-3833** or e-mail us at **support@mcp.com**.